Information, Participation, and Choice

Information, Participation, and Choice

An Economic Theory of Democracy in Perspective

Edited by Bernard Grofman

Ann Arbor

THE UNIVERSITY OF MICHIGAN PRESS

First paperback edition 1995
Copyright © by the University of Michigan 1993
All rights reserved
Published in the United States of America by
The University of Michigan Press
Manufactured in the United States of America

1998 1997 1996 1995   4 3 2 1

A CIP catalogue record for this book is available from the British Library.

Library of Congress Cataloging-in-Publication Data

Information, participation, and choice : an economic theory of
  democracy in perspective / edited by Bernard Grofman.
      p.   cm.
  Includes bibliographical references and index.
  ISBN 0-472-10359-8 (alk. paper)
    1. Voting. 2. Political parties. 3. Public administration.
  4. Downs, Anthony. Economic theory of democracy. I. Grofman,
  Bernard.
  JF1001.I54   1993
  320'.6—dc20   93-31958
      ISBN 0-472-1-08343-0 (pbk. : alk. paper)   CIP

Contents

Introduction 1
 Bernard Grofman

Part 1. Information and Choice

Chapter 1. Information Shortcuts and the Reasoning Voter 17
 Samuel L. Popkin

Chapter 2. Downsian Thresholds and the Theory
of Political Advertising 37
 Roger G. Noll

Chapter 3. Information-pooling Models of Electoral Politics 55
 Bernard Grofman and Julie Withers

Part 2. Participation and Choice

Chapter 4. What the Downsian Voter Weighs: A Reassessment of the
Costs and Benefits of Action 67
 Carole Jean Uhlaner

Chapter 5. Political Equilibrium under Group Identification 81
 Amihai Glazer

Chapter 6. Is Turnout the Paradox That Ate Rational
Choice Theory? 93
 Bernard Grofman

Part 3. Spatial Models of Party and Candidate Competition

Chapter 7. The Spatial Model and Elections 107
 John Ferejohn

Chapter 8. A Revised Probabilistic Spatial Model of Elections:
Theory and Evidence 125
 James M. Enelow, James W. Endersby, and Michael C. Munger

Chapter 9. "What This Campaign Is All about Is . . .": A Rational Choice Alternative to the Downsian Spatial Model of Elections   141
Thomas H. Hammond and Brian D. Humes

Chapter 10. Adaptive Parties and Spatial Voting Theory   161
Scott E. Page, Ken Kollman, and John H. Miller

Chapter 11. A Rational Choice Model of the President and Vice-President as a Package Deal   173
Martin P. Wattenberg and Bernard Grofman

Chapter 12. Toward an Institution-Rich Theory of Political Competition with a Supply Side Component   179
Bernard Grofman

Part 4. Reflections on *An Economic Theory of Democracy*

Chapter 13. The Origins of *An Economic Theory of Democracy*   197
Anthony Downs

Chapter 14. The Early Impact of Downs's *An Economic Theory of Democracy* on American Political Science   201
Gabriel A. Almond

Chapter 15. *An Economic Theory of Democracy* as a Theory of Policy   209
M. Stephen Weatherford

Chapter 16. Downsian Logic and the Comparative Study of Party Systems   231
Arend Lijphart

Chapter 17. On the Gentle Art of Rational Choice Bashing   239
Bernard Grofman

References   243
Contributors   269
Index   273

Introduction

Bernard Grofman

Anthony Downs's *An Economic Theory of Democracy,* originally published in 1957, is one of the five founding books of the public choice movement, along with Kenneth J. Arrow's *Social Choice and Individual Values* ([1951] 1962), Duncan Black's *The Theory of Committees and Elections* (1958), James M. Buchanan and Gordon Tullock's *The Calculus of Consent: Logical Foundations of Constitutional Democracy* (1962), and *The Logic of Collective Action* by Mancur Olson, Jr. ([1965] 1971). All were written by economists, and all appeared between the years 1951 and 1965.[1] Each has spawned a vast literature and has had ramifications throughout the social sciences and in allied disciplines such as law and philosophy.[2] Collectively these works and their successors have defined a research approach and a research agenda that has transformed the way political scientists and economists write about politics—the "rational choice" perspective.[3] Of these books, however, it is *An Eco-*

I am indebted to Ziggy Bates for manuscript typing and to Dorothy Gormick for bibliographic assistance. This research was partially funded by the University of California, Irvine, Interdisciplinary Focused Research Program in Public Choice.

1. I would be inclined to add William H. Riker, *The Theory of Political Coalitions* (1962) to this Pentateuch, even though its influence has been largely confined to political science.

2. The example of these works inspired numerous scholars in succeeding decades to apply tools derived from microeconomics and game theory to a wide range of political phenomena, including interest groups, Congress, and the courts.

3. That perspective's success in producing research that fills the pages of the leading political science journals and its perceived normative and empirical shortcomings and claimed ideological bias have led to a recent counterreaction of "rational choice bashing" (see last essay in this volume). This volume is devoted to a study of Downs's influence on the study of voter choice and party competition, and is anchored in empirical debate about competing explanations of specific phenomena and in the development of new models rooted in ideas derived from Downs. With the notable exception of my own brief essay at the end of the volume, all the authors in this book eschew abstract philosophical debate about the merits of rational choice modeling except as the essays happen to deal with specific topics where empirical research can provide at least an indirect test of competing assumptions. As noted in the acknowledgments, many of the chapters in this volume were papers given at the first day of a two-day conference on "*An Economic Theory of Democracy* in Thirty-Year Perspective" held at the University of California, Irvine, in

nomic Theory of Democracy that had both the earlier[4] and the greatest impact on the political science discipline.[5]

Downs's *An Economic Theory of Democracy* is an important work for a number of reasons. First, by positing the desire of politicians to be elected and the corresponding need to construct candidate and party platforms with voter preferences in mind, it introduced a simple model of voter choice and political party competition that has helped make sense of a number of features of American political life that the earlier sociological and social psychological approaches failed to account for satisfactorily. Downs's contribution to modeling party competition, although inspired by ideas from Joseph A. Schumpeter (1950) and Harold Hotelling (1929),[6] models party convergence and the special role of the median voter in a way that makes it virtually impossible to think of these concepts without also thinking of Downs.[7]

Second, *An Economic Theory of Democracy* helped inspire reevaluation of the 1950s (and earlier) civics textbook model of democracy. On the one hand, Downs provides a view of governmental action (harkening back to that in the *Federalist Papers*) that recognizes that government is a human agency

---

1989. Papers given at the second day of that conference dealt with the more philosophical debate about competing theories of politics and human behavior. The latter papers are collected in Monroe 1991, and the reader is referred to that volume and to Mansbridge 1990 for an excellent introduction to the various views in the general debate over the utility of rational choice modeling and about the nature of human nature.

4. Arrow's work began to achieve its present-day prominence after its second edition appeared in 1962, although the ideas of Arrow (and of Duncan Black) were introduced into political science by William H. Riker even earlier (Riker 1958, 1961).

5. As Martin Wattenberg (1991, 17–18) points out: "The six year interval from 1954 to 1960 was a truly formative period in voting behavior research." Three seminal works were published (*Voting* [Berelson, Lazarsfeld, and McPhee 1954], *The American Voter* [Campbell et al., 1960], and *An Economic Theory of Democracy* [Downs 1957b]), each of which "reflected a unique disciplinary perspective" (sociology, social psychology, and economics, respectively) and which, collectively, have "set much of the agenda of voting." Wattenberg (1991) shows that *An Economic Theory of Democracy* is now the most widely cited research work in political science by a living scholar. Shortly after publication its citations began to exceed those to *Voting*, and by the late 1970s its citations exceeded those to the *American Voter*, with the gap continuing to widen. It also far outdistances the best-known successor to the *American Voter*, the *Changing American Voter* (Nie and Verba 1976), with seven times as many citations as that work in 1990.

The areas where *An Economic Theory of Democracy* has probably had its greatest impact are in the study of voter choice (see, e.g., Grofman 1987 for a partial review), party competition (see, e.g., Davis, Hinich, and Ordeshook, 1970, for early work in this area; see especially the excellent summaries of work to date in Enelow and Hinich 1984, 1990b), and voter turnout (see chap. 4 for a partial review).

6. Downs was introduced to the ideas of Schumpeter by Julius Margolis, then a professor at Stanford. Margolis suggested to Downs that he explore Schumpeterian ideas for his dissertation, done under the supervision of Kenneth J. Arrow (see chap. 13).

7. Albeit this way of thinking about politics has become so familiar that citations to its source are now often omitted.

whose (elected) officials must be "privately motivated to carry out their social functions" (Downs 1957b, 290). On the other hand, Downs provides a view of voters that recognizes the almost total absence of incentives for them to gather knowledge about politics or to be politically active. The ideas of rational ignorance and the rationality of abstention developed by Downs have become an indispensable component of any discussion of citizenship, even among those who find these ideas abhorrent to a "strong" concept of participatory democracy (cf. Barber 1984).[8]

Third, there are other contributions of Downs that, although not nearly as well-known as his insights into incentives for party convergence, rational ignorance, and the rationality of abstention in a world where voting is not costless, are, I believe, of the same order of importance as these ideas.[9] These include the notion of ideology as an information heuristic, party labels as signaling devices,[10] and the feasibility of putting together a winning coalition based on single-issue voting blocs.

As a seminal work, *An Economic Theory of Democracy* suffers from the triple dangers of (1) being forever cited but rarely if ever read, with its ideas so simplified as to be almost unrecognizable, (2) being regarded as outmoded or irrelevant, (3) having its central ideas so elaborated by ostensible refinements that what was good and sensible about the original gets lost amidst the subsequent encrustations. Each of these calamities has befallen Downs's 1957 work. On the one hand, the key ideas in it have degenerated into talismanic phrases that are treated as gospel truths, for example, along the general lines of "since Downs showed that parties must converge to the median, then there can't be any real differences between Republicans and Democrats," while, on the other hand, these ideas have been dismissed as irrelevant or nonsensical, for example, along the general lines of "since Downs showed that rational voters don't vote, then Downs (and rational choice modeling in general) must be full of hot air, because people *do* vote; moreover I vote, and you can't tell me that *I'm* not rational." Moreover, Downs's ideas about party competition have inspired a variety of exercises in mathematical modeling, some of which have contributed significantly to our understanding of candidate and voter behavior, but some of which are almost completely divorced from any touch with the politics whose realities Downs was trying to make sense of.[11] As a

---

8. See, e.g., chapter 1 and the various essays in Ferejohn and Kuklinski 1990.

9. My colleague A Wuffle (personal communication, August 1990) has claimed that no book is remembered for more than one or two ideas. It is a mark of the importance of *An Economic Theory of Democracy* that it is remembered for at least three.

10. Built upon by Morris P. Fiorina (1979) in his work on retrospective voting.

11. Some of the social choice literature can best be taken as contributions to pure mathematics and should be judged by those standards. However, most public choice work is intended as a contribution to social science. An unwillingness on the part of some modelers to explain results

consequence of the all too frequent trivializing and/or esotericizing of its message, too few political scientists see *An Economic Theory of Democracy* as the major contribution to political theory that it is, and many of those of who do see Downs as a democratic theorist do so only to reject what he has to say as fundamentally erroneous.[12]

The purpose of this volume is neither to praise Downs nor to bury him. The volume's purpose is threefold. First and quite simply, it is to subject *An Economic Theory of Democracy* to a careful rereading, with the aim of identifying and clarifying its central ideas, including those that have been neglected by succeeding generations of scholars.[13] Like any true classic, *An Economic Theory of Democracy* continues to repay careful reading. A second purpose is to provide a series of essays by scholars summarizing the research findings of the literature in political science and economics that the book has inspired. These essays—on central topics in Downs's classic such as party competition, voter choice, and political participation—are intended to aid political scientists of a less mathematical bent to make sense of the relevant literature subsequent to Downs's work. Third, it is to suggest the potential of what I refer to as "neo-Downsian" modeling, by including chapters (such as one on the implications of vice-presidential selection) that build on *An Economic Theory of Democracy* to develop what I call a more "institution-rich" theory of political competition.

I wish to be quite open about the idiosyncratic features of this volume that so clearly reflect the editor's own prejudices. First, all but one of the contributors to this volume identify with the public choice tradition in which

---

in a fashion that can be understood in intuitive terms by less technically trained scholars makes useful communication between formal modelers and other social scientists unnecessarily difficult. Moreover, a few scholars who see themselves as doing applied modeling have written as if nothing of real importance can be said about a topic such as political party competition unless it is in the form of a theorem about strategic voting over *n*-dimensional issue space, rather than regarding mathematical results as the basis for insights and hypotheses about actual politics.

12. However, even when Downs is wrong he is usually wrong in a useful way, by raising the question of why things are not as the model he proposes suggests they ought to be. For example, confronting the questions "Why don't parties converge?" and "Why do voters vote even in situations where their vote has no discernible likelihood of influencing the outcome?" has forced political scientists to think through important conceptual and empirical issues that had previously either not been thought about or, if thought about, had been given unsatisfactory answers.

13. For example, the only work on threshold models of which I am aware that acknowledges Downs's contributions in this area is chapter 2. In like manner, Downs's discussion of models of political persuasion in a world of uncertainty (Downs 1957b, 83–88), has been almost completely neglected. Chapter 15, however, does develop a notion of persuasion based on appeals to long-run as opposed to short-run interest. Because rational choice modeling is often accused of always taking preferences as fixed, it is particularly unfortunate that few scholars seem aware of Downs's own views of the importance of political persuasion.

An Economic Theory of Democracy is one of the canonical works.[14] Second, my own research contributions to the literature on parties and voter choice and those of my coauthors are very much overrepresented. Third, I have sought to pick chapters for this volume that are true to Downs's view that modeling ought to begin with a desire to understand human behavior and to answer real questions. In the appendix to *An Economic Theory of Democracy,* Downs considers the matchup between his models and real world data, and his modeling efforts were guided by knowledge of the basic features of the data, such as the extent of voter ignorance about politics. I believe very strongly that work that builds on Downs's contribution should follow his lead in that regard.[15]

Information and Choice

The chapters in part one review some of the most important ideas in Downs's work having to do with incentives for political participation and information search. These include information shortcuts such as cost-saving mechanisms, party targeting strategies, and the concept of voting as an instrumentally rational act.

Information (or lack therof) and uncertainty play a critical role in the models of *An Economic Theory of Democracy.* According to Downs many voters rely almost entirely on the free information that comes to them as a by-product of other aspects of their lives. When voters do search for information that will allow them to better choose among candidates or parties, they often make use of information that, while far from perfect, is inexpensive to gather. Chapter 1, by Samuel L. Popkin, describes what we know about how voters

---

14. The exception is Martin Wattenberg, a Michigan-trained scholar whose work has been in the survey research tradition. That he now is a member of the University of California, Irvine, Interdisciplinary Focused Research Program in Public Choice does not affect his fundamental allegiance to his alma mater. Of course, some people might feel after reading my own essays in this volume that cast doubt on some orthodoxies that I am not really a rational choice modeler, despite my being on the editorial board of *Public Choice.* I would not dissent too strongly from this analysis. Like my colleague A Wuffle, I consider myself a "reasonable choice" modeler, and a member in good standing of the California Drive-in Church of the Incorrigibly Eclectic.

15. Of course, some of the classic work in public choice, that of Buchanan and Tullock (1962) or Arrow ([1951] 1962), made its major contribution to the normative theory of democracy, even though it also inspired empirical research on topics such as the prevalence of logrolling or the existence of cycles of preference in legislatures. Indeed, Downs's own work on the role of the median voter, on voter ignorance, and on voter incentives to participate in the political process all have important normative implications for a theory of democracy. I do not in any way wish to slight the importance of the normative aspects of public choice theory. However, I also believe that some theorists have been too quick to assume that the portrait of voters and politicians given in current public choice models of rent seeking, shirking, agenda manipulation, and the like is descriptively accurate (for arguments along similar lines see Farber and Frickey 1991).

make use of information shortcuts such as party labels, ideological positioning, media analysis, and past and present economic conditions as indicators of incumbent and party performance. Popkin sees these shortcuts as providing an electorate able to cast a more-informed vote than might appear from survey data on voter ignorance about candidates and issues. However, he supports Downs's expectations that, as a consequence of voter heterogeneity in interests as well as education, information about any given political issue is likely to be very unevenly distributed. Popkin also devotes considerable attention to a treatment of party identification that is consistent with rational choice modeling.

The second chapter, by Roger G. Noll, takes an idea mentioned in Downs's work, but relatively little developed by that author, the idea of political thresholds, and develops it further in an attempt to account for changes in voter participation. In the process Noll seeks to resolve important ambiguities and inconsistencies in Downs's original formulation of the threshold concept. In Downs's original treatment (1957b, chap. 6) thresholds are used to define the boundaries among five states of support: active support, passive support, neutrality, passive opposition, and active opposition. Information suppliers such as parties and activists will, according to Downs, concentrate their information-dissemination activities on voters who are relatively close to a perception threshold. As the concept is reformulated by Noll, it leads to a theory of electoral and policy inertia that partially resolves the problem of unstable outcomes in majority rule decision making called attention to by authors such as Arrow ([1951] 1962), Richard D. McKelvey (1979) and Linda R. Cohen and Steven A. Mathews (1980).

Noll's observations take him over a wide range of territory, including incentives for new interest groups to form, the role of technological innovations in information delivery, and the uses of negative advertising. An important feature of Noll's chapter is the development of a formal model in the appendix to his chapter that shows when it is sensible for voters to be "rationally" ignorant as a function of factors such as the extent to which parties are similar in their issue positions.

The third chapter is by Julie Withers and myself. This chapter is in many ways a complement to that of Popkin. He deals with empirical evidence on use of information shortcuts by voters. We deal with recent efforts to model the process by which voters can make use of the quite-limited information at their disposal to arrive at choices that are identical to (or at least close to) what they would have achieved had they been perfectly informed. We also review modeling efforts by authors such as McKelvey and Peter C. Ordeshook (1985a, 1985b, 1987) myself and Barbara Norrander (1990), Randall Calvert (1985a), and Nicholas R. Miller (1986), which largely show the positive face of a neo-Downsian analysis of voter ignorance. Instead of the message being that it is rational to be politically ignorant, the central message of these works is that voters who are relatively poorly informed can nonetheless make reasonable choices by making use of a variety of information heuristics, such as following the polls, or paying attention to endorsements provided by reference groups with known political views. Indeed, one of the models we review, that of Miller (1986), shows that even a little learning goes a long way if we look not to the optimality of the choices made by individual voters but rather to the likelihood that the election outcome would have been different had voters been perfectly informed.

Participation and Choice

The three chapters in part two address what is often taken as one of the embarrassingly misguided aspects of "economic" models of voting, the notion of voting as an instrumentally rational act, an act motivated by a concern to affect the outcome of an election in order to elect a candidate whose policies are closer to those the voter most prefers.

The first chapter in this section is by Carole Jean Uhlaner. As Uhlaner notes: "With regard to . . . turnout, . . . Downs's work sets up a paradox. He concludes that most citizens would find it rational to abstain when voting is not costless. . . . However, empirically we do observe substantial numbers of voters." Her chapter reviews the many attempts by political scientists and economists to reconcile the contradiction between what Downs's model predicts and what we actually observe. She observes that the three standard "fixes" are (1) to permit noninstrumental benefits (such as expressive or consumption benefits from voting) to drive voter choice, (2) to assert that costs are a minor factor in voting decisions since the costs of voting are relatively trivial, (3) to allow for misperception of the likelihood that one's vote will be decisive. After commenting on the utility of these ways out of the paradox, she then discusses her own preferred model (see Uhlaner 1989a, 1989b), which involves embedding the voter in a social structure and considering the roles played by intermediaries (such as group leaders) in motivating turnout. She argues that group leaders provide their members with incentives to vote "in order to capture a collective benefit in the form of a favorable shift in candidate position."

The second chapter in this section is by Amihai Glazer. Like Uhlaner, he is concerned with why people vote as well as for whom they vote. Like her, he focuses on the role of group identification in modifying the standard negative conclusions about turnout in the Downsian model, but he does not deal with the entrepreneurial role of group leaders. Rather, Glazer focuses on what he calls "expressive voting." In order to develop nontautological implications, the Glazer model voter posits that choice between parties is not merely a function of the parties' announced issue positions, it is also a function of which groups can be expected to vote for a party given its announced issue positions.

In this model, "a person gets pleasure in voting for a candidate who identifies with the voter's group, and gets pleasure in voting against a candidate who supports a different group." In the last section of his paper Glazer applies the theory of expressive voting to choices among parties and candidates as a function of the extent of their support from black voters. He finds evidence from presidential primaries with Jesse Jackson as a candidate and from congressional elections in the South that support the predictions derived from an expressive model of voting.[16]

The last chapter in this section, of which I am the single author, makes two points: First, it argues that what is often supposed to be the central paradox of rational choice theory, voters choosing to vote even though their vote is unlikely to affect the outcome, is in fact not the problem for rational choice models that it is claimed to be. We need to recognize the use of rational choice models in accounting for *changes* in choices rather than choices per se. Rational choice models cannot explain why, ceteris paribus, the French drink more wine and the Germans drink more beer, either. They can, however, predict that wine consumption and beer consumption in each country will be affected by changes in the relative prices of the two commodities. Moreover, while rational choice models appear to do poorly in predicting who will vote in a given election, so do all other models other than those that posit that people who aren't registered won't vote (Erikson 1981) and those that recognize that the single best predictor of whether or not someone will vote is whether or not they have voted before (Barbara Norrander, personal communication, 1985).

Second, in reviewing a somewhat different aspect of the problem of turnout, the relationship between turnout and electoral closeness, I argue that the models that fail to find such a link are improperly specified largely because of their failure to take into account a long enough time frame and to recognize that turnout variations will often be more a function of long-run than of short-run election-specific factors. Looking at the evidence about the factors that affect voter participation in the aggregate, contrary to most of what has been written on this topic, I find rational choice prediction to do quite well. For example, as the Democratic primary declines in significance in southern elections, turnout levels in the primary (even among Democratic voters) decline relative to turnout in the general election. Similarly, the enfranchisement of blacks in the South in the 1960s triggered a corresponding countermobilization in the turnout rates of white voters *relative to those of blacks* in the areas where whites both were most directly threatened and had a feasible counterresponse (Alt 1994, forthcoming).

---

16. In related, more technical work, Glazer and his coauthors (Glazer, Grofman, and Owen 1991) show how the assumption of group-oriented choice can resolve the problem that, if voters are choosing whether or not and for whom to vote on the basis of how they expect other voters to vote, there may be no equilibrium.

Spatial Models of Party and Candidate Competition

The third section contains papers that build on Downsian ideas of spatial political competition to consider topics such as the incentives for candidates and political parties to honor their commitments, the importance of perceived candidate competence evaluations on voter choice, political campaign tactics that emphasize each party's particular strengths, the role of party uncertainty about voter locations, and the role of the vice-president in models of presidential choice.

A key assumption of *An Economic Theory of Democracy* is that candidates and parties are oriented to electoral success as their primary (if not their only) goal. Hence candidates and/or parties are led to propose positions that they think will gain them votes. But why expect politicians once in office to adhere to their campaign promises? The first chapter in this section, by John Ferejohn, explores the question of the extent to which we can expect campaign platforms to have predictive value to the voter, that is, the conditions under which it makes sense for the voter to act as if candidates will keep their campaign promises and adhere to the positions they espouse in their platform. After first reviewing the basic analytical elements of the spatial model in one and more than one dimension, and then looking at Downs's arguments as to why candidates can be expected to try to implement their platforms (the most plausible of which is based on a concern for reputation—politicians who lie will be much less likely to be reelected), Ferejohn turns to a look at the empirical evidence on promise keeping.

He finds that "whether for Downs's reasons or for others, politicians seem to take positions in an ideological space, and these positions seem quite stable over time." Then Ferejohn reviews recent formal modeling work on the behavior of office-seeking candidates in iterated elections where voters can monitor politicians' behavior directly or indirectly, concluding with a discussion of work on the reputation-bearing nature of political parties, that is, a party label as a cultivated "brand name."[17] Here the insights derived by Ferejohn from formal models and those derived by Popkin from a review of the empirical evidence on party images appear mutually reinforcing.

---

17. My own preferred metaphor is that party label is a franchise. The franchiser seeks to ensure predictability in the product and can screen to a certain extent potential franchisees. Moreover the franchisee has an incentive to conform to expectations and an incentive to tailor the product to the most important audience of local consumers. Thus, just as McDonalds in Tokyo has a product line (including various fishburgers) that is not identical to that in McDonalds in Chicago, so too a Democrat from North Carolina is not the same thing as a Democrat from New York. Nonetheless, in any given state, the Democrat will be to the left (indeed, considerably to the left) of the Republican elected from that same constituency (see, e.g., Grofman, Griffin, and Glazer 1990, which shows consistent 30 to 40-point Americans for Democratic Action (ADA) score differences between U.S. senators of opposite parties from the same state and virtual identity in the ADA scores of senators of the same party elected from the same state).

The second chapter in this section, by James M. Enelow, James W. Endersby, and Michael C. Munger builds on earlier work by Enelow, Melvin J. Hinich, and N. Mendell (1986), Peter J. Coughlin and Schmuel Nitzan (1981), and myself (1987) and looks at the empirical evidence for two competing models of voter choice, one based on the idea that voters choose among candidates on the basis of their announced platforms (issue positions), the other based on the idea that voters attach different credibility weights to each candidate's campaign issue positions based on the candidate's perceived competence to carry out the policies that are being proposed. Under most circumstances the latter model predicts candidates will adopt different positions. An empirical test of the two models based on National Election Survey presidential election data from 1980, 1984, and 1988 does not promote either one, but a hybrid model in which voters discount only challenger issue positions is shown to do the best job of predicting perceived candidate issue positions. This hybrid model helps account for the candidate issue-divergence found in real two-candidate elections.

The third chapter in this section, by Thomas H. Hammond and Brian D. Humes, combines Downsian ideas of multidimensional issue competition with recent work in cognitive psychology on "framing effects," that is, on how the presentation of issues helps shape voter choices. They argue that an important part of political competition is a debate to persuade voters that certain issues (issue dimensions) are important (or more important than others). The outcome of the election will often critically depend upon which issues are salient to the voters (or more generally, how different issue dimensions are weighted).[18] Candidates seek to "activate" those dimensions on which their preferred positions will command majority support.[19] The chapter, although seen by its authors as a preliminary effort, develops a formal spatial model to predict how rational candidates would seek to frame the issues in a political campaign, and is likely to motivate new empirical research on campaign tactics that tests the model's theoretical ideas.

The fourth chapter in this section, by Scott E. Page, Ken Kollman, and John H. Miller, modifies the standard simple Downsian spatial model in a

---

18. A very similar argument is set forth in Popkin 1991: "Because party images vary so widely from issue to issue, party candidates for office try to increase the salience of issues where their party starts out with the largest advantage. Candidates addressing an issue where their party has a strong image have the wind at their back while candidates addressing an issue where their party has a weak image have the wind in their face. Changing issues changes the campaign, if not the outcome."

19. There is an important parallel between this chapter and chapter 8. Enelow and Endersby modify the standard spatial model by weighting issue *positions* by perceived candidate competence; Hammond and Humes modify the standard spatial model by weighting issue *dimensions* by the salience that candidates succeed in attaching to them.

different way than do the other chapters in this section. While accepting that parties seek a vote-maximizing policy location, Page, Kollman, and Miller replace the assumption that parties know voter issue positions with a concept of parties as only "boundedly rational" because of limited knowledge about what voters prefer and limited ability to make optimal use of the knowledge they do possess. This chapter is unique in drawing on the artificial intelligence literature (and even more specifically the use of "genetic algorithms") to develop models of "adaptive" parties. These models are used to trace trajectories of winning party positions. The preliminary conclusion is that parties trace out a dance whose image resembles that of a slowly shrinking dumbbell. In this simulation parties eventually converge, but they need not do so either continuously or rapidly.

The next to last chapter in this section, by Martin Wattenberg and myself, provides a rational choice model of voting for presidential and vice-presidential nominees as a package deal. This model allows for the potential importance of voter preferences among vice-presidential candidates when these differ from the directionality of the voter's preference for the top of the ticket. Wattenberg and I also try to take into account the potential importance of the vice-president in terms of the likelihood that an individual elected to the vice-presidency will become president. The principal purpose of our brief essay is to evaluate how important the choice of vice-president is for a party's vote share, but this essay also serves as an illustration of the claim that it is important to develop more institutionally detailed models of voter choice and party competition, such as by taking into account the fact that, in the United States, the president and vice-president have (since the ratification of the Twelfth Amendment in 1804) been elected as a team.

The last chapter in this section is another of which I am the sole author. It takes its point of departure from the Wattenberg and Grofman chapter and asserts that we need to modify and enrich Downs's basic models so as to more realistically take into account the complex institutional structure of American (and other nations') political competition (e.g., party primaries, campaign-financing rules, competition at different levels of government, multicandidate slates, concurrent and nonconcurrent election cycles, etc.). After reviewing the assumptions of the simplest Downsian model involving voters who choose between political parties based on their announced platforms, and arguing that the usual view of Downs as standing for the proposition that political parties can be expected to converge to Tweedledum, Tweedledee-like identity is false to the remarkably nuanced picture of party competition portrayed in *An Economic Theory of Democracy*, I consider the ways in which modifying each of the "standard" simplifying assumptions can lead us to a more empirically accurate picture of party competition in the United States (and elsewhere). In that realistic picture of U.S. politics there is no reason to expect that parties will converge, since there are centripetal as well as centrifugal incentives to party competition.

Reflections on *An Economic Theory of Democracy*

The lead chapter in this section is a brief autobiographical comment by Anthony Downs. Downs discusses both the personal influences (suggestions by his Stanford professors: Kenneth J. Arrow and Julius Margolis; his experiences as student body president at Carleton College) and the other intellectual influences (especially ideas in Schumpeter's *Capitalism, Socialism, and Democracy* to which Margolis had called his attention) that helped shape *An Economic Theory of Democracy*. Like many another graduate students Downs changed the topic of his dissertation from what he had originally proposed doing—a study of the effects of the Nimitz Freeway on land values in the San Francisco East Bay area. In the process he lost the dissertation fellowship that he had been awarded by the Social Science Research Council, but made social science history.

The second brief chapter in this section is also in the nature of a personal reminiscence. Gabriel A. Almond, who was a fellow at the Center for Advanced Study in the Behavioral Sciences at Stanford a year after Robert Dahl was there, was lent a copy of Downs's dissertation by Kenneth J. Arrow a year prior to its publication. Almond concludes his chapter with a discussion of the initial book reviews of *An Economic Theory of Democracy,* some of which prophetically foresaw its subsequent importance and some of which did not, and with the grounds for his belief that Downs's book is a true classic that will continue to be read for many years to come.

The third chapter in this section, by M. Stephen Weatherford, compares a Downsian view of the process of governance with that of the more traditional normative conception of politics as infused with a pursuit of the public good or the national interest. Weatherford summarizes the Downsian model as one in which choice by voters among competing policy platforms allows the policy goals to be specified by election outcomes. In this model, "governments can be judged by efficiency criteria, leaders are largely fungible, and institutions merely mediate the fundamental relationship between the demand for and supply of policies." After reviewing some of the literature dealing with barriers to consistent policy implementation, in the last section of his chapter Weatherford sketches a model in which the appeal by a president to a common commitment to national economic policy goals can attract sufficient support from reelection-oriented legislators to outweigh competing claims based on more narrowly defined notions of interest.

The fourth brief chapter in this section, by Arend Lijphart, considers the contributions of *An Economic Theory of Democracy* to the comparative study of party systems. Lijphart does not consider formal models of multiparty competition since Downs's but confines himself to an explication in flowchart terms of the model of multiparty competition implicit in Downs's book. Lijphart identifies as one of Downs's greatest insights the early recognition of bidirectional relationships between key variables such as electoral system and the distribution of voter preferences. Lijphart reviews Downs's treatment of the implications of coalition government for a theory of responsible democracy. He argues that two of Downs's assertions about multiparty democracies, the claimed greater difficulty of voters arriving at choices among parties and the claimed difficulty of coalition governments taking effective action to solve basic social problems, are both overstated and do not really follow from the premises stated in *An Economic Theory of Democracy*.

The last chapter in this section, and the concluding one of the volume, is my own. It considers the debate over the utility of rational choice modeling in the context of the topics considered in *An Economic Theory of Democracy*. I argue that it is futile to debate *in the abstract* whether or not (or to what extent) people are rational, self-interested, and making conscious choices rather than responding to operant reinforcement or early socialization. After making the point that there is no such thing as *the* rational choice model of a given institution or behavior, only *a* rational choice model, I then argue that you can't beat something with nothing, and so it is not enough to show that some given rational choice model does not fit the data. It is necessary to show that some other perspective leads to a model with better fit and predictive power. Looking at the empirical track record of rational choice models, I suggest that early rational choice models can best be characterized as having been "insightfully and usefully wrong" by raising important questions about phenomena (such as incentives to vote or to organize for collective ends) that had previously been taken for granted. I also argue that, so far, it has been through its questions, rather than its answers, that the rational choice approach has made its major contribution to empirical democratic theory.

However, I also believe that applications of the rational choice approach to the analysis of political behavior is in its infancy, and that as it moves away from models based on atomic individualism to ones that are institution-rich, historically sensitive, and context-specific, its ability to explain real world phenomena will begin to match its formal sophistication. Moreover, I also believe that there are no other approaches that have its potential for deriving testable predictions about so many important aspects of politics.

Part 1
Information and Choice

CHAPTER 1

Information Shortcuts and the Reasoning Voter

Samuel L. Popkin

Uncertainty is pervasive when voters think about and evaluate parties, candidates, or government policies. As Anthony Downs (1957b) was one of the first to emphasize, in economic terms, the process of procuring, analyzing, and evaluating information carries a cost—the investment of time and energy. Further, as Downs notes, the *expected* return from time invested in reaching political decisions is small compared with the expected return from other uses of the same time—far smaller, certainly, than with decisions about personal consumption. For example, the health of the national economy may in fact have a greater effect on voters than whether their next vacation is fabulous or merely good, but time spent deciding where to travel leads to better vacations, whereas time spent evaluating economic policies leads not to better policies but only to a better-informed vote.

Some persons, of course, find politics so fascinating that they inform themselves even when they have no personal stake in political outcomes. But in general, voters do not devote much time or energy directly to their vote. This does not imply either that voters are uninformed about general conditions or that they have no knowledge of specific government programs. What it means is that much of the information voters use when they vote is acquired—for "free"—as a byproduct of activities they pursue as part of their daily lives (see Popkin 1991, chap. 2).

Political Information as a By-product of Everyday Life

A good deal of economic information is obtained in daily life. One need not be an economist to see which way the economy is going. Politically relevant information is acquired while making individual economic decisions: shoppers learn about inflation of retail prices, home buyers find out the trends in mortgage loan interest rates, and owners of stocks follow the Dow-Jones averages. Generally, half the electorate knows the current unemployment rate

---

This chapter is adapted from chapters 2 and 3 of Popkin, 1991.

within 1 or 2 percentage points, and about the same number has a good idea of what the inflation rate is. These numbers, moreover, understate the extent to which voters are aware when there are dramatic changes taking place, such as the inflation triggered by changes in gas prices in the late 1970s. As inflation rose to 21 percent, half of the populace cut back on the kinds of groceries they bought, two-thirds scaled back on vacations, and four-fifths lowered their thermostats. Not surprisingly, at this time inflation was considered a more important problem than unemployment by five to one. Even less surprisingly, in early 1980 President Carter received the lowest approval ratings of any president since World War II.

The condition of the economy is not the only aspect of the public well-being that is generally visible to citizens. Not only are there innumerable ways in which government actions (or inactions) are visible in the lives of ordinary citizens but also common experiences with crime, schools, roads, and health care delivery systems may shape perceptions of general social conditions and can lead to a desire to use government action to remedy perceived problems and can affect the way in which voters evaluate the capabilities of candidates, especially incumbents.[1]

The collective nature of the vote means that there is low incentive for an individual to collect information solely in order to cast one vote among many millions. But voters may have very detailed knowledge about matters that directly affect their lives. Farmers, for example, gather the information on their own businesses in great detail—not because they are better citizens but because they are independent managers and the information necessary for management is directly related to government policy. What to plant, when to sell, and when to borrow are all decisions that depend on government policies at least as much as they depend on the weather.

Information Shortcuts

However, despite the many kinds of information voters acquire in daily life, there are large gaps in their knowledge about government and politics. To

---

1. For example, one person in four knows a place where drugs are sold, and one in six sees them sold. Half of all Americans know someone hurt by drugs, and three-quarters know someone hurt by alcohol. One in eight Americans has had a crime victim in their family within the past year, and two in five Americans have had a serious crime or felony in their neighborhood within the past year. Within a mile of their home, 57 percent of all women and 28 percent of all men know a place where they are afraid to walk alone at night; one in six persons in America does not feel safe at home during the night. Similarly, in May 1982, 47 percent of the respondents in a national health care survey had a family member who had been in an emergency room during the last year, and 38 percent had a family member who had been hospitalized during the year. One-third of the respondents had sought a second opinion on a medical procedure, and one in five had lost their health insurance for some period.

overcome the limitations of their knowledge, voters use shortcuts. In this chapter I focus on how voters use shortcuts in obtaining information, shortcuts in evaluating information, and shortcuts in storing and recalling information about parties, candidates, and issues. I concentrate on the way in which voters use information to make their choices in U.S. presidential elections.

I make several assumptions about what kinds of information are easiest to obtain and process. (1) It is easier to assess the real world than to make projections about the future. (2) It is easier to track a party by remembering its view of the good society than by trying to examine its past performance. (3) Current data is easier to use and therefore treated as more relevant than past data. (4) Personal morality is easier to understand than institutional morality. (5) It is easier to assess the competence of an individual than to assess his or her legislative performance. (6) Candidates can be understood if their demographic traits are known. And (7) people can be judged by their friends.

These assumptions lead me to focus on the following shortcuts voters may use to assess candidates. (1) Voters may rely on the opinions of others—a point especially emphasized by Downs. Indeed, even when they do have the facts about an issue, voters may turn to others for help with *evaluation* because they are uncertain about the meaning of the information they have.[2] (2) Voters may use running tallies about political parties as shortcuts in storing information and use the party label as a shortcut with which to assess candidates or legislation about which they have little or no information. (3) Voters frequently are able to estimate the candidates' policy stands from the demographic traits of the candidates and their supporters. (4) Voters may assess overall competence and ability to deliver benefits by judging campaign behavior, instead of researching past governmental performance by the candidate. Finally, (5) voters may estimate a candidate's sincerity and adherence to promises not by evaluating past behavior but by extrapolating from private morality to public morality.

Thus, as replacements for harder-to-obtain kinds of data voters incorporate learning from past experiences, daily life, the media, and political campaigns to serve as "second-best" substitutes.

Interpersonal Influence as an Information Shortcut

Citizens do not patrol the government looking for problems, but they do pay attention to people who do. As Russell Neumann, director of the Communications Research Group at MIT's Media Lab notes: "Most citizens don't study

---

2. Downs (1957b, 229) accepted the by-then-received wisdom that persons are not certain what they have learned from the media until they discuss the news with informal opinion leaders. His contribution is to generalize about information shortcuts from findings about interpersonal influence.

the details but look at the bottom line. Are we at war? Is the economy healthy? Most people entrust the rest to experts and specialists. What is important is that there are perhaps five percent who are activists and news junkies who do pay close attention. If they see that something is seriously wrong in the country, they sound the alarm and then ordinary people start paying attention" (1989). When citizens sample information about government, and listen to elites and news junkies who sound alarms, those who are most directly affected by an issue absorb the information first, such as senior citizens who pick up news about changes in social security before others (see especially Iyengar and Kinder 1988, 52, 84–85). If the issue is one that can effectively be connected with government action and benefits desired by voters, it will percolate up through the public.

The communication to voters of the opinions of key opinion leaders can occur through the media as well as through direct contact. But being alerted to potential problems is only the beginning of the story. Uneven levels of political interest and knowledge across voters mean that an essential part of political dynamics takes place between voters. Political campaigns or positions made visible by media attention only send the initial messages; until these messages have been checked with others and validated, their full effects are not felt. When a voter is unsure how to evaluate information, or does not have information, relying on a trusted person for validation is, in essence, a strategy for economizing on information and resolving uncertainty. Because there is a two-step flow of information, a lack of data or "textbook knowledge" understates the political impact that issues can have, and understates the public's ability to make informed decisions.

There are two ways to evaluate the effects of information. One way is to ask voters directly what they know; another way is learn where voters take their cues.[3]

A source where many voters obtain elite interpretations of key events and personalities is television. Television news provides commentary on speeches, proposals, and crises from a variety of well-known political figures from whom voters can triangulate, just as they do with local opinion leaders. The late Claude Pepper ("At my age, I don't even buy green bananas"), for example, was known to senior citizens for his defenses of social security and was always asked to comment on new social security insurance proposals. No

---

[3]. These two methods parallel the two approaches scholars have used to evaluate the influence of members of Congress and their involvement in the affairs of government. Scholars and reporters observing the behavior of a government agency often see no member of Congress observing or interfering in the affairs of the agency. If they don't detect a congressional presence, they often conclude that the legislators are not involved and are not effective. But legislators do not patrol the entire government looking for problems to solve, like police detectives searching out criminals; they wait for constituents to set off alarms so they can race to the scene like firefighters.

coverage of an international crisis is complete without comments from Henry Kissinger and Senator Sam Nunn.

The effect that elite interpretation of political events has on viewers has been studied by Richard A. Brody and C. R. Shapiro (1989). They studied political events where there were large short-term boosts to the president's popularity. Sometimes a large gain in presidential popularity appears to defy explanation. For example, the U.S.-backed invasion of Cuba in 1961 led to an ignominious defeat at the Bay of Pigs, but President Kennedy's popularity soared after the debacle for which he took full responsibility. Brody shows that seemingly incongruous situations like this, when a president's popularity soared after a humiliating fiasco, can be explained by the response of elite figures to the event, as featured in the media. If there is a crisis and the elite figures rally to support the president, then the president's popularity soars, fiasco or not. If the elite is divided and critical, as after the Tet Offensive in Vietnam, the president's popularity can plummet, as it did for Lyndon Johnson.

Two kinds of campaign situations where television coverage after an event can determine the extent of mass reaction are similar to those Brody and Shapiro have analyzed: (1) situations where challengers present their positions on issues; and (2) situations where ambiguous, possibly innocuous, remarks are made. When a challenger, in an attempt to demonstrate credibility and competence, releases details of his or her plans for defense or the budget, for example, public response depends not on an understanding of the details but on elite reaction as reported in the media. For example, in 1972 the Democratic nominee for president, George McGovern, presented his tax and defense plans to the media in an attempt to demonstrate their feasibility. When cabinet member after cabinet member in the Nixon administration attacked the plans and no major figures in the Democratic party, such as well-known senators or former cabinet members, stood up to denounce the attacks as unfair or partisan, McGovern's credibility suffered. Likewise, when Reagan, campaigning for the Republican nomination in 1976, presented plans for cutting the federal budget by 10 percent, and the details were attacked by many during the primaries and defended by none, there was a similar reaction. McGovern and Reagan had not organized enough elite support to counter the many cabinet members who attacked their proposals. They had to defend against the attacks personally, which effectively precluded them from spending their precious airtime on the offensive.[4] Of course, if the elites are

---

4. In 1988, when Vice-President Bush attacked Michael Dukakis for being unpatriotic and not sufficiently defending the flag against "anti-American flag burners," Senator John Glenn, a war hero and former astronaut, and Senator Sam Nunn, the most-respected Democrat on defense issues and a southerner, both offered to make commercials for Governor Dukakis. Glenn, in fact, had already made such commercials to defend—successfully—Senator Howard Metzenbaum against similar attacks. The Dukakis campaign declined the offers.

discredited, it does not matter if the challenger cannot rally prominent members of the establishment to his or her side.

Although some remarks are so revealing when reported in the media that no elite mediation is necessary—such as Jesse Jackson's reference in a personal conversation to New York City as "Hymietown"—many statements do not register as significant to most people unless they are aware of how others evaluate the remarks as well. When a candidate makes careless or poorly worded statements, the public reaction often depends on whether news reports highlight these comments as significant or pass them by. For example, in 1976, in discussing ethnic neighborhoods in a newspaper interview in New York, presidential candidate Carter used the curious phrase "ethnic purity" (Witcover 1977, 302). Until it was featured on television several days later, there was no reaction to the phrase from voters or opposing politicians. After it was widely publicized Carter had to spend several weeks of the campaign rebuilding his links to the black community.[5]

Party Identification

Researchers at Columbia University began their famous 1940 presidential campaign study (Lazarsfeld, Berelson, and Gaudet 1948) with a view of the voter as consumer—a person shopping for products like bars of soap, where price and advertising exert an immediate effect on choices. Their first study was designed to assess the effects of mass media on attitudes and behavior, and they expected that the mass media effects would be sizable and obvious. They found, however, that these effects were much smaller than they had expected, in part because voters had entrenched voting habits, rather like what we now call consumer brand loyalty. In 1940, there was no inkling yet that this notion of entrenched party loyalty was an important concept: in *The People's Choice,* Democrats were simply those persons voting for Roosevelt and persons voting for Wendell Willkie were called Republicans. The 1948 study (Berelson, Lazarsfeld, and McPhee 1954) was the first academic research project to ask a question that separated current vote intention from partisan habits and identifications: "Regardless of how you may vote in the coming election, how have you usually thought of yourself—as a Republican, Democrat, Socialist, or what?"[6]

---

5. He relied on a two-step flow of information. Reverend Martin Luther King, Sr., Andrew Young, and Coretta Scott King all made statements on his behalf.

6. As early as 1937, however, the Gallup Poll asked, "Do you regard yourself as a Republican, a Democrat, a Socialist, or an independent in politics?"; in 1940, the questions was changed to "In politics, do you consider yourself a Democrat, independent, Socialist, or Republican?" Since 1946 the Gallup question has been "In politics, as of today, do you consider yourself a Republican, a Democrat, or an independent?"

If voters have standing decisions about the political parties, then each election does not necessarily present a new choice. "For many people, votes are not perceived as decisions to be made in each specific election. For them, voting traditions are not changed much more often than careers are chosen, religions drifted into or away from, or tastes revised" (Berelson, Lazarsfeld, and McPhee 1954, 17). From this perspective, party loyalties are not easily changed. They reflect past political battles that have shaped the ways in which voters thought about politics and government. Thus:

> In 1948 some people were, in effect, voting on the internationalism issue of 1940, others on the depression issues of 1932, and some, indeed, on the slavery issues of 1860. The vote becomes a kind of "moving average" of reactions to the political past [and the political present]. Voters carry over to each new election remnants of issues raised in previous elections—and so there is always an overlapping of old and new decisions that give a cohesion . . . to the political system. (Berelson, Lazarsfeld, and McPhee 1954, 316)

As noted, party loyalties operate to reduce the effects of the media. In 1940, for example, the media were overwhelmingly Republican, but Democratic voters read and listened to more of their own candidate's stories. The mechanism of *selective exposure* came into play; people chose the material listened to or read, and the more interested and committed they were, the more likely they were to read and listen to the material presented by their own candidate. Availability of information plus a predisposition to consider it, rather than availability alone, determined exposure (Lazarsfeld, Berelson, and Gaudet 1948, 89).

Downs points out that party identification, like reliance on informal opinion leaders,[7] is an information shortcut for voter choice. But this does not mean that voters sacrifice their basic issue orientations or policy goals—for Downs, party attachment depends on the evaluations of past and anticipated future benefits from government. In a simplified Downsian perspective, parties are teams that attempt to gain elective positions through an appeal to the voters that is based on a platform composed of issue positions—but parties also seek to differentiate themselves in terms of political ideology.[8]

---

7. See Katz and Lazarsfeld 1955.

8. As Downs recognizes (1957b, 36–28), it became clear over the course of the two Columbia studies that party identification was more than a voting habit; it was a worldview as well. There were major differences in the social composition of the groups supporting the presidential candidates of each party, and the differences in social philosophies of Democratic and Republican supporters were "even more pronounced than differences in their social composition" (Downs 1957b, 28).

However, if, as Downs seems to suppose, voters care only about the benefits they receive from government, why do political parties devote so much effort to publicizing their ideologies? And why should voters care about party ideologies? The answer is that both parties and voters have found ideology valuable as a shortcut or cost-saving device, where an ideology is, for Downs (1957b, 96), "verbal image of the good society, and of the chief means of constructing such a society."

If voters were not uncertain—if they were fully informed about government and could assess how their own benefits would be affected by a party's platform—they would pay no attention to the party's ideology. They would simply evaluate the party's actual performance and proposals in terms of their personal ideology.[9] In the presence of uncertainty, parties use ideological labels to highlight critical differences between themselves, and to remind voters of their past successes.[10] They do this because voters do not perceive all the differences, cannot remember all the past performances, and cannot relate all future policies to their own benefits. Indeed, Downs emphasizes that uncertainty is a necessary condition for ideological differences between parties.[11] Ideology is thus not a mark of sophistication and education but of uncertainty and lack of ability to connect policies and benefits. Indeed, Downs expects that a party's ideology and past performance would matter only when the voter cannot with certainty predict the party's future behavior from its platform.

The word *ideology* is a loaded one in America, evoking the derogatory sense of ideologues—persons who have belief systems to which they adhere steadfastly.[12] Downs, however, is not equating ideology with intellectual sophistication or moral rigidity but with a loosely integrated set of views in the minds of voters about what parties stand for. Parties try hard to remind voters about their views of the good society and how to achieve it because this helps voters evaluate the implications of the party's approach. We may think of this as a "default value" view of both party identification and party ideologies: when a voter has no information about current performance, or is uncertain of what the effects of a proposal are, he or she reverts to default values.

---

9. As Downs (1957b, 98) puts it: "When voters can expertly judge every detail of every stand taken and relate it directly to their own views of a great society, they are interested only in issues, not philosophies."

10. Ideologies are, in effect, "samples of all the differentiating stands" between parties (Downs 1957b, 98).

11. Of course, when one party convinces voters that its position is demonstrably better on some issue, the other party either adapts or fails to gain votes in the future. "Party ideologies can remain different only insofar as none is demonstrably more effective than the rest" (Downs 1957b, 101).

12. As Clifford Geertz (1964) notes, "I have a social philosophy; you have public opinions; he has an ideology."

But unavailability of data is not the only reason voters revert to default values. They do this when they are so satisfied with their past choices that they see no reason to collect any data. So long as the actions of candidates appear consistent with the generalized notion the voter attaches to a particular label, the voter can avoid the effort of keeping track of all the various activities of government. Sometimes voters do not bother to gather information because they do not expect a fair return on their investment of effort. As Downs (1957b, 85) puts it:

> Finally, some rational men habitually vote for the same party in every election. In several preceding elections, they carefully informed themselves about all the competing parties, and all the issues of the moment; yet they always came to the same decision about how to vote. Therefore they have resolved to repeat this decision without becoming well-informed, unless some catastrophe makes them realize it no longer expresses their best interest. . . . [This habit] keeps voters from investing in information which would not alter their behavior.

Thus, Downs would lead us to expect stability in party identification, but not perfect stability. If party identification reflects a voter's current judgment about the political performance of the two parties, then a voter's evaluations of current policies should affect party identification. Of course, if the only events that affect party identification are catastrophes on the order of the Great Depression, party identification is only a running tally of public reaction to cataclysms, and party voting should be unaffected by the year-to-year turns of politics. If so, then governments are really not being held accountable at the polls for their performance unless it is truly disastrous.

At the national level, the authors of *The American Voter* (Campbell et al. 1960) found a near glacial stability of party identification in America after World War II and the inheritance of partisan identification from one's parents.[13] However, there was one University of Michigan Survey Research Center survey in which the same respondents were interviewed in 1956, 1958, and 1960. When this panel survey (a study in which the same persons are reinterviewed) was carefully reexamined, party identification was far less stable than had been assumed: during these four "normal" years, one of every four persons changed positions on a Democrat-independent-Republican scale.[14]

These short-term changes in party identification (most of which are between independent and one of the two major parties) have been related to

---

13. The authors of *The American Voter* considered the possibility that voters choose a party because of issues but found it "hard to imagine this is common" (Campbell et al. 1960, 185).

14. See especially Brody n.d.; and Fiorina 1979, 86–88.

voters' evaluations of government policy performance and economic management. Morris P. Fiorina's analysis of data from the 1956–58–60 panel survey and from another one covering 1972–74–76 shows that changes in the economy, domestic policy performance, and such highly publicized events as Ford's pardon of former President Nixon all affect party identification (1979, 84–130). Persons move to and from their respective political parties in response to their evaluations of economic and political conditions and in response to their evaluations of the performance of the parties and their candidates.[15] Party identification is neither impervious to change nor devoid of political content. In other words, issues and performance affect partisan identification, and there is a mutual adjustment among political evaluations, party identification, and voting.[16]

Partisanship can best be seen as a *running tally of current party assessment*.[17] Year-to-year changes in party identification reflect voter reaction to recent political events and have a clear and direct effect on voting.[18] Because a Downsian perspective emphasizes using party as an informational shortcut when other information is missing or limited, we need not see party identification and issue or performance voting as incompatible.[19] The question ought

---

15. Unfortunately, there is as yet no satisfactory statement of what kinds of problems and events are most likely to affect political identification.

16. Most contemporary studies based on data from the University of Michigan's Center for Election Studies use a seven-point party scale. Democrats and Republicans are asked if they would call themselves strong or not very strong Republicans or Democrats and are divided into strong and weak Republicans and Democrats. Independents are asked if they consider themselves closer to the Republican or Democratic party and are divided into Democratic-leaning independents, pure independents and Republican-leaning independents. Movement between points on these scales is especially sensitive to short-run changes in political attitudes, and thus use of the seven-point scale erroneously reduces the estimated effect of attitudes and issues as compared to party identification in contemporary polling. See also Markus and Converse 1979.

17. While people often appear to be willing to give their parties the benefit of the doubt, there are limits to this willingness. Republicans and Democrats say that the other party is better overall only when the difference between the two parties is well established or an incumbent of their party has failed badly; it is far more common for partisans, when asked about a perceived party weakness, to say they don't know which party is better. Whether or not people give their party the benefit of the doubt varies from issue to issue and reflects reasoning about past performance. For example, in 1986, less than half of all Republicans believed their party cared more about senior citizens or women, and less than half of all Democrats believed their party cared more about men. Party assessments demonstrate information about government and reasoning about the parties—a running tally of past performance, not simply wishful thinking or expressions of team loyalty.

18. As Jon Krosnick and Matthew K. Berent (1990) put it: "Political scientists should reconsider the widely-held assumption that party identification is more stable over time and has more impact on political cognition than any other political attitude."

19. Indeed, the probable link between voting, party identification, and issue and performance evaluations is almost certainly a complex one. For example, although changes in the party

not to be whether or not issues matter but, rather, to what extent it is new or old issues or new or old performance that matter.

Drawing on a Downsian perspective on information access and economic incentives also allows us to hypothesize about which voters are most apt to use their party identification as a generalized guide to voting and which look to particular issues or current policy performances. Consider the difference in sensitivity to short-run forces between farm managers and urban laborers found in *The American Voter*. For farmers, there were "spectacular links between simple economic pressures and partisan choice" (Campbell et al. 1960, 430). Workers, on the other hand, were found to vote largely along the lines of their party identification. But there was much more current information about economic fluctuations and political performance among farmers than among laborers. Thus, we would expect that farmers would rely less on party identification and would have weaker generalized attachments to party ideologies, since they would always have current information relevant to government performance gathered in the course of their ordinary business activities.[20]

Demographic Attributes of the Candidates and/or Their Supporters

Demographic facts provide a low-cost shortcut to estimating a candidate's policy preferences (though not to evaluating past public performance), and

---

identification of voters are generally slow, often even glacial, changes in voters' comparative assessments of how well parties handle different problems, or what groups the parties stand for, can be rapid. A poor performance on inflation by a Democratic president may give many working-class Democrats weakened faith in the ability of their party to deal with inflation. This may lead them to vote for Republican presidents when inflation looms, but they may not change their views of which party's ultimate views about the good society are most compatible with theirs, and thus they may continue to consider themselves as Democrats. Even the long-standing associations between the Republican party and the depression and between the Democratic party and war were not immutable in the minds of the voters. For example, in their study of the 1956 election, Donald E. Stokes, Angus Campbell, and Warren E. Miller (1958, 373) note: "Four years of Republican prosperity destroyed the major part of a fourteen-to-one margin the Democrats had in the partisanship of these responses. After haunting the Republicans in every election since 1932, memories of the 'Hoover Depression' had receded at least temporarily as a direct force in American politics." Analyzing the changing views of the political parties from 1952 through 1976 on the Survey Research Center surveys and relating changes in party assessments to future changes in party identification, Richard Trilling (1976, 204) writes: "When party images reinforce past identifications, identifications are stable. When party images conflict with past identifications, identifications are likely to be altered."

20. *The American Voter* interprets the "spectacular links" in a reverse fashion, noting that because farmers have weaker partisan identification than do laborers they are "psychologically free to march to the polls and vote the rascals out" (Campbell et al. 1960, 430).

one that may be of considerable value. Characteristics such as a candidate's race, ethnicity, religion, gender, and local ties (hereafter, *localism*) are important cues because the voter observes the relationship between these traits and real-life behavior as part of the voter's daily experience. Where these characteristics are closely aligned with the interests of the voter, they provide a basis for reasonable, accessible, and economical estimates of candidate behavior.[21] It has often been noted that the use of demographic cues in voting probably plays a more important role in campaigns in America than it does in more homogeneous countries.

Further, because voters are necessarily uncertain about what a candidate will do if elected, they take into account the demographic characteristics of the candidate's supporters. Endorsements from feminists, blacks, Christian fundamentalists, Jews, unions, military veterans, and many other demographic groups make a difference. This process of inferring the policy preferences of a candidate from demographic characteristics is the political equivalent of screening job applicants by reading their résumé instead of by evaluating their work, which would take more time and effort.

Television appearances and televised convention proceedings offer quick visual clues to the candidate's support groups and thus make it harder for candidates to pretend to be all things to all people. "If they are supporting him," a voter can ask, "how can he be good for me?" When candidates become aware of such an attitude, they try to change it by offering clues that encourage support. Thus, the black mayor of Los Angeles, Tom Bradley, reminded voters of his experience as a policeman; the rich Bush talked of his down-home love of pork rinds and pitching horseshoes; and Michael Dukakis, the governor of Massachusetts, a state thought to be liberal and therefore soft on defense, went for a ride in an army tank.

The "friends and neighbors" vote that is so often disparaged as irrelevant is another example of using an easy-to-obtain cue to assess a candidate's positions. Particularly on distributive issues—which neighborhood to tear up for a highway, where to put the toxic waste dump, where to build a prison, an airport, or a park, whether or not to allow offshore drilling, where to disburse patronage—localism may be an effective orientation for the voter to use in trying to predict a legislator's preferences.

---

21. In this section I am assuming that voters are interested in the demographics as a way of estimating policy benefits they will derive from government. There are also benefits members of a group—and others—will derive from having a president from a particular group to help legitimate the group. A black or woman president will give many benefits just by being in the office. A president who eats spinach provides immediate benefits to many parents; a president who refuses to eat broccoli gives benefits to many children.

Shortcuts to Inferring Competence

The simple idealized Downsian model posits that voters engage in "proximity voting"—voting for the candidate or party whose position is nearest to theirs. This tacitly assumes that voters consider all candidates and parties equally able to carry out their promises. In reality, voters sometimes care less about the issue positions of candidates than they do about which candidate can deliver the most on these issues, and which candidate can do a better job of simply managing and running the government. In short, they care about competence.

Competence is a relevant dimension of candidate evaluation for three reasons. (1) The candidate's competence directly affects the probability of his or her being able to deliver benefits from the system when elected. (2) Much of what the president (and Congress) does involves the general management of the country. Since voters have only limited information, they may vote for a candidate who seems capable of managing the affairs of the country even if that candidate is not the "closest" to the voters' specific issue preferences. (3) Finally, if the candidate is elected, he or she will have to solve many problems that no one can anticipate on election day. Voters care about the competence of the candidate, not just the candidate's issue positions, because they care about what the candidate is likely to be able to deliver from government. And they worry about the character of the candidate, including his or her sincerity, because they cannot easily read "true" preferences and because strength of character may be important in dealing with the burdens of office. And, as suggested, they care about the policy preferences of the nominee, not just the platform of the party that nominates the nominee, because parties are coalitions that exercise weak controls over presidents.

Competence, then, is a measure of ability to handle a job, an assessment of how effective the candidate will be in office, of whether or not he or she can "get things done." Many aspects of government are noticed only when something goes wrong, and in many other areas, maintaining minimal levels of performance is far more important than policy change. The voter as prudent investor is right to be concerned about the competence of the candidate.[22]

When Boss Curley of Boston was reelected mayor from his prison cell, Jerome Bruner surveyed the voters of Boston to discover the secret of Curley's success. The voters, he found, were aware of Curley's sins, but many—

---

22. What matters to voters when they assess competence can be expected to vary with the concerns of the moment and with how they view the office for which they are voting; thus honesty mattered more after Watergate, and military leadership experience mattered more during the Korean War.

including proper Bostonians who disagreed with his issue positions as well—were voting for Curley because none of the candidates with more desirable issue positions and better reputations appeared capable of controlling government and getting things done (Bruner and Korchin 1946). Similarly, General Eisenhower's victory in 1952 was largely a result of his perceived competence to deal with the issues of the moment. Competence in unfamiliar areas may be inferred from the perceived competence of the candidate in other areas. At the height of cold war tension, with the nation apparently stalemated in a war in Korea against "Red China," a man regarded as one of the most successful military leaders of World War II (and known to be considerate toward enlisted men), a man who had been head of NATO and a university president, was "perceived as a person peculiarly able to cope with the nation's international problems" (Campbell, Gurin, and Miller 1954, 58).

Candidates have more importance in the American system than in most other political systems, and this is especially true for candidates for the presidency.[23] The American system vests power in a single individual with no formal ties to his or her party. The unity of the executive branch, the separation of the executive and legislative branches, and the weakness of the American party system combine to give the American president a degree of power and independence unknown in a parliamentary system. Although American parties have never been teams unified behind a single, centralized source of control like parties in some other countries, voters in the United States customarily focus on the characteristics of a party's presidential candidate because presidents usually have a large impact on the nation's policy agenda.[24]

Moreover, there has been, throughout this century, an antiparty strain of reformism in America that argues for candidate-centered nonpartisan elections. Party labels, it is argued, give to voters the illusion of informed choice while allowing them to ignore important differences between the candidates on the newly emerging issues of the day. Take away party labels, the reformers argue, and voters will pay attention to the "real" differences between candidates on the issues.[25] In fact, however, voters evaluate candidates and form their images of them by using the same types of information shortcuts they use to form their views of parties, and issue positions are by no means their only criteria in the evaluation.

---

23. As congressional campaigns become more extensive, the focus in congressional voting is also moving more toward the candidates, and incumbency has become more important as a voting focal point. Nearly 75 percent of cross-party voting in congressional races is voting for an incumbent (Jacobson 1983; Ferejohn 1977).

24. The American federal system is characterized by widely dispersed patronage centers, local primaries, local fund-raising, and local party organizations. Presidents, therefore, have wide latitude in deciding what course to follow in office.

25. The nonpartisan approach is also tied to concern for good government and opposition to spoils-based politics.

In a world of complete information about the past, even with uncertainty about the future state of the world, voters could assess the competence of the candidate by assessing how well he or she has dealt with past administrative and legislative problems and then extrapolate from that to how the candidate would manage the affairs of office. Where a candidate is an incumbent seeking reelection to the same office, this kind of information may be relatively easy to come by and process.[26] But even for incumbents most voters make use of information shortcuts to avoid a complete evaluation of a candidate's track record, especially as compared to earlier promises.

Rather than seeking out detailed information about what promises a candidate made or how the candidate has managed government and delivered benefits, voters use shortcuts to assess competence, which is itself an information shortcut. They often assess the competence of the candidate on the basis of data that is new and easy to process, particularly information from the party conventions and the political campaign. The party convention allows voters to hear what other, more familiar political leaders have to say on behalf of the nominee. The political campaign exposes voters to the candidate in complex and fast-breaking situations. As they watch the candidate handle crowds, speeches, press conferences, reporters, and squabbles, they can obtain information with which they imagine how he or she would be likely to behave in office.

There is a natural inclination to associate information shortcuts based on campaign behavior with the television era, during which there have been several well-publicized examples of campaign events that affected candidate ratings and votes. The most dramatic example from recent campaigns was in 1972, when Senator George McGovern, the Democratic nominee, lost considerable ground when he appeared weak and indecisive in handling the revelation that Senator Thomas Eagleton, the nominee for vice-president, had received electroshock treatments. When Senator McGovern wavered, many McGovern supporters concluded that he simply was not competent to be president.[27] More recently, Governor Michael Dukakis became the butt of jokes and received much ridicule for looking out of place and foolish in the

---

26. When the voter estimates competence, there is an asymmetry between candidates. An incumbent has dealt with "real" events; the challenger can be judged only by talk and by those events that candidate "manufactures." For candidates who are incumbents or who have spent a long period of time in a prominent position, voters can make judgments about competence based on observation of "actual" behavior. Victorious generals, of which Eisenhower is the only twentieth-century example, are an exception to the rule that challengers are known mainly from campaigns. Having performed notable public service in an arena where their behavior is well publicized and watched closely, they may well be better known, be more carefully evaluated, and feel more familiar to the electorate.

27. Popkin et al. 1976, contains an analysis of the effects of the Eagleton affair and the Democratic convention. See also Kinder and Abelson 1981 and Page 1978.

helmet he wore when he went for a ride in one of the army's new tanks, in an attempt to appear more familiar with defense issues.

Campaign behavior mattered to voters, however, well before television replaced radio and newspapers as the dominant media in American national politics. During the 1948 campaign Governor Thomas Dewey made uncomplimentary remarks about a working man, a railroad engineer who erred in handling Dewey's campaign train. All knowledge of these remarks came from radio and print media and thus did not have the visual immediacy associated with television. Yet, when a national survey asked respondents, "Do you think there was anything special about Dewey that made some people vote against him?" 26 percent of the respondents referred to Dewey's campaign behavior, and among respondents who actually voted, the proportion referring to Dewey's campaign was 31 percent (Campbell and Kahn 1952, 46).

Private Morality as a Cue for Public Action

Because of the problems of learning the true preferences of candidates, voters are concerned with the integrity or sincerity of the candidates. When voters watch a candidate perform on television, making promises and taking hard-line rhetorical positions on issues, it is reasonable to question if avowal and actual feelings are congruent, whether the candidate's support for a cause represents a genuine personal commitment or only a campaign tactic. We care more about sincerity and character when we are uncertain about what someone will do. As Aristotle (1984, 25) notes: "We believe good men more readily and fully than others; this is true generally whatever the question is, and absolutely true where exact certainty is impossible and opinions are divided." This is often the case in daily life, when we must make evaluations with limited information and no theory to guide us.

How do we choose a new baby-sitter for our young children when we must make an emergency trip? How do we choose a nurse for a critically ailing parent who lives at the other end of the continent? We want to hire competent people, but without the time or resources to evaluate their past performance we must make a judgment based largely on clues to personal character, from a telephone conversation, or from what our friends tell us. Will this person do what we would like to have done? Similarly, when voters estimate a candidate's preferences, they take account of perceived sincerity; whether or not the candidate really cares about their concerns. Because it is difficult, for example, to assess whether or not a compromise bill was the best that could be done, or whether or not a politician reneged on commitments, they take shortcuts: they estimate public morality and character from private morality and character—assuming, in the absence of better information, that candidates treat their constituents as they treat their own wives and children.[28]

Information Shortcuts and Incumbency Advantage

Because so much of what government does is not directly observed by voters, an incumbent president—no matter what the president's rating in the polls— can claim credit for such things as keeping the nation out of nuclear war and preserving the basic structure of government. The incumbent is, to a large extent, a known commodity. In contrast, a challenger is often a great unknown. Increasingly, incumbents play on the public's fear of risk.[29] For example, President Ford's 1976 campaign hammered away at how little was known about Carter, and Carter's 1980 campaign in turn did everything it could to raise doubts about what would happen with Reagan's finger on the nuclear button. In 1988, Bush's strategies made essentially the same arguments: as *Newsweek* explained, the vice-president "had to go bareknuckle against Dukakis. . . . It was going to be a lot easier, a senior strategist said, to raise the other guy's negatives than to lower his own; if Bush could not pump himself up, he could at least tear Dukakis down."[30]

Discussion

Despite limited voter knowledge about politics, there are also limits to the prospects for voter manipulation. Candidates cannot use clever campaigns to totally cover their historic performances with smoke and mirrors. The ability of candidates to stake out positions at variance with past party performance on long-standing issues is also limited, since information about past party performance is still an important component of voter evaluations. Information shortcuts based on party identification and party performance on different issues serve as reality tests against which campaign rhetoric is tested. The relative

---

28. In addition, when a candidate is in some sense a neighbor, the voter at least has a better chance of knowing whether he or she is a blatant crook or an obvious fool. Given the problems of expensive, scarce, and unreliable information about the candidates, the voter is more likely to have confidence in a neighbor with a local reputation for competence.

29. See discussion related to this point in Downs 1957b, 40, 46, 107.

30. The asymmetry of incumbents and challengers holds for elections to the Senate and House of Representatives as well. Because incumbents are generally better known, the competitiveness of campaigns is more affected by challenger spending than by incumbent spending. Incumbents may, and generally do, spend more money than their challengers, but the marginal return to money spent by challengers is much higher than the marginal return of money spent by incumbents. Elections are competitive when challengers have sufficient money to convey themselves and their message to voters (Jacobson 1983).

weights of party and candidate will vary both between issues and offices. Candidates matter most where party matters least; the less well developed the party images, the more sensitive voters will be to the candidate (Rahn 1989).[31]

A larger proportion of the electorate has no party loyalty at all, and even the "standing decision" of party members to vote the party line is not as firm as it used to be. In the 1940s, fewer than 25 percent of the persons in the entire country had ever voted for more than one party's candidate for president. Today, over 60 percent of them have voted for both Democratic and Republican candidates for president during their lifetime.[32] The extent of cross-party voting emphasizes just how much more fluid the country has become politically.

As recently as 1948, most voters belonged to politically homogeneous social groups: the social gulf between the parties was so wide that more than 80 percent of all voters had no friends voting differently from them (Berelson, Lazarsfeld, and McPhee 1954, 95). In contrast, the political cleavages that exist today cut more across social groups, which means that voters are typically in less homogeneous family, church, and work settings.[33] A decline in the political homogeneity of primary groups should lead to weaker conviction among voters and therefore allow more latitude for the influence of the mass media and for campaigning. Moreover, all voting studies have found that education is one of the prime indicators of voter ability to process information generated by campaigns and the mass media. In the 1940s, fewer than one in eight voters had been to college; today nearly half of all voters have been to college. In the 1940s, over 40 percent of the electorate had ever reached high school; today this figure is 10 percent.

Whatever their level of education, voters use information shortcuts and cost-saving devices in thinking about parties, candidates, and issues. They use shortcuts to assess ideology, platforms, individual competence, and character. This leads to an asymmetry between the challengers and incumbents and to the likelihood that the election begins centered on the incumbents and their

---

31. The roots of divided government (one party controlling the presidency, the other the Congress) depend upon the use by voters of information about party performance on issues, but with different types of issues relevant to presidential as opposed to congressional elections (Popkin 1991, chap. 3).

32. Martin Wattenberg (1984, 20) gives data for 1952 and 1980.

33. I am basing this claim in part on inference, for there are no directly comparable national surveys from the 1940s and the 1980s. I still make this claim confidently. The generational and gender cleavages and the data that is available on spouses who vote differently are enough in and of themselves to guarantee that more persons today are in politically heterogeneous social groups than in the 1940s. The declining gaps between Protestant and Catholic voters and the breaking up of older ethnic neighborhoods also lend strong support to my claim that fewer persons are in socially homogeneous social settings than in 1948.

present performance. Campaigns can make a difference because voters have limited information about government and uncertainty about the consequences of policies. If voters had full information and no uncertainty, they would not be open to influence from others and hence there would be no campaigns. In reality, voters do not know much about what government is doing or is capable of doing. Thus they are open to influence by campaigners who offer them more information or better explanations of the ways in which government activities affect them. The more educated the electorate, the greater is the electorate's ability to follow news about national and international politics. But the more issues an electorate follows, the more varied the images of the parties will be. Also, the more varied the images of the party, the more it can matter which issues become the most salient in a campaign.

However, the shortcuts that voters use also limit the effects of campaigns. Before public opinion studies of voting, conventional wisdom had it that rational, independent voters gathered and absorbed information, weighed alternatives, and made up their minds just before they voted. Because voters were assumed to gather and assess information, it was expected that voting would be affected primarily by the information to which they were exposed. Therefore, it was assumed that voting was a choice easily manipulated by propaganda. But instead of direct media effects on rational voters without memory, we find a complex pattern in which voters combine historical knowledge about the parties reflected in party images, with information that can be gathered at little cost, information that comes to them as a by-product of other activities, and elite interpretations of the news.

CHAPTER 2

Downsian Thresholds and the Theory of Political Advertising

Roger G. Noll

In *An Economic Theory of Democracy,* Anthony Downs twice mentions the concept of thresholds for political action. Downs's core idea is that differences in candidates for office, or in the circumstances in which their policy proposals are evaluated, must be more than infinitesimal to motivate voters to change their historical pattern of political behavior. In this chapter, I examine Downs's concept of a political threshold. My conclusion is that Downs's insights about thresholds, while technically incorrect as stated in his classic work, are nonetheless interesting and important because they shed light on how parties and candidates mobilize supporters. These ideas are worthy of reemphasis now, for they constitute an aspect of Downs's model of the political system that is generally overlooked but has great practical value. Specifically, Downs's use of the economics of information in analyzing political campaigns is not only the key to understanding thresholds but also reveals how innovations in the process of transmitting information to citizens affect voting behavior.

Downs on Political Thresholds

The concept of political thresholds is explicitly discussed by Downs in two contexts. The first arises in the development of the basic theory of voter behavior under conditions of uncertainty. Downs postulates that voters estimate their expected utility under the regimes that would be formed by the contending candidates for office, and then vote for the one offering the greatest personal utility. In a two-candidate election, this boils down to calculating the expected utility differential of the candidates' platforms. But on page 46 of *An Economic Theory of Democracy,* Downs rejects the notion that a voter

The author gratefully acknowledges the useful comments of Bruce Cain and Gary Cox on an earlier version of this paper and the research support of the John and Mary Markle Foundation.

simply votes for the candidates offering greater expected utility (abstaining only when the expected utilities are identical). Instead he writes: "When the total difference in utility flows is large enough so that he is no longer indifferent about which party is in office, his *party differential threshold* has been crossed. Until then, he remains indifferent about which party is in power, even if one would give him a higher utility income than the other."[1] Thus, according to Downs, abstention will occur not only when a voter is indifferent about the candidates but also when the differences between them are, in some sense, "too small." Moreover, the political threshold is unrelated to voting costs. Whereas voters would be expected to abstain if the differences between candidates were small compared to the costs of voting, this is not what Downs had in mind, for the quoted discussion occurs in a section of the book that assumes that the costs of voting are zero.

The function served by the political threshold is to form a basis for Downs's discussion of persuasion in political campaigns. According to Downs: "The existence of thresholds . . . makes it possible to change a voter's mind by providing him with better information."[2] Downs goes on to say that two kinds of information could alter the evaluation of candidates by voters: information about the policies of the candidates for office and information about the relationships between these policies and a voter's conception of "the good society." Downs then focuses only on the first so that, in the subsequent analysis, all of the uncertainty in his model of voter behavior, and thereby of the connection between voter preferences and policy actions, is *ex ante* random error in estimating the policies that a candidate will pursue if elected.

The second discussion of thresholds appears forty pages later in the explication of the production and use of information during a campaign. This discussion occurs in the extremely important chapter 6, in which Downs links elections to government decisions. The line of argument in this chapter is as follows: new information can cause citizens to change their political alliances and the degree to which they actively participate in campaigns; moreover, various participants in the political process are prepared to supply such information should circumstances change so that a substantial number of voters are likely to be affected by new information; hence, changes in circumstances that would cause an electoral majority to prefer different policies discipline candidates to offer to change policies in the desired way. Here thresholds play a crucial role in the chain of argument, for they govern the supply and demand relationship for political information.

In developing the theory of the production and use of information,

---

1. Downs 1957, 46 (italics in original).
2. Downs 1957b, 46.

Downs defines several categories of voters. The categorization scheme is based upon two factors: the voter's degree of commitment to one or the other party in a race, and the voter's degree of certainty about that commitment. Thus, voters with strong preferences that are held with considerable conviction are called agitators, because they are the ones most likely to work actively for a candidate's election. These people, then, constitute part of the supply mechanism for politically relevant information. At the other extreme are people who perceive no difference between the candidates, and so expect to abstain. If neutrality is held with conviction, these people are unlikely to be swayed much by new information; however, if their neutrality is due to poor information, the agitators may be able to induce their participation by providing information.

Thresholds in this argument are used to define the point at which a voter's perception of the differences between the candidates is at the boundary of two of the five states of support: active support, passive support, neutrality, passive opposition, and active opposition. In general, these boundaries are called *perception thresholds;* the boundary between passive and active states is called the *action threshold,* and the one between neutral and passive states is called the *participation threshold.*

Downs assumes that the act of conveying information to voters is costly, and that information suppliers—parties and agitators, in particular—have limited resources for conveying information. Hence, if they want to maximize the impact that their resources will have on the outcome of the election, they will focus their information-dissemination activities on voters who are relatively close to a perception threshold and who are relatively uncertain about their estimates of the difference between the candidates. Thus, the strategy of campaigning is, first, to convince some supporters that they ought to be agitators, and then to convince people near other perception thresholds to shift favorably. Both are achieved by providing more information about the policies that the candidates will adopt if elected. Of course, each party will provide information favorable to its own cause; however, competition between them works to ensure that all information that is relevant to voters who are near a perception threshold will be forthcoming.[3]

Although Downs does not explicitly identify the cause of political thresholds, the source of the idea is clearly in classical hypothesis testing. According to Downs:

---

3. Downs's argument here is optimistic. He assumes that no one ever lies and that uncertainty about voter preferences among parties does not cause them all to withhold the same information, neither of which can be safely assumed (see Ferejohn and Noll 1978).

> Under conditions of perfect certainty, the slightest iota of difference between parties would be enough to determine a man's vote. But in the real world, and in the world of our uncertainty model, he knows that minute differences he sees are likely to be either illusory or counterbalanced by others he does not see. Therefore, he will wait for a significant degree of difference between parties before relinquishing his neutrality.[4]

Nonetheless, the term "significant" does not have the standard statistical interpretation. Elsewhere, he expresses the same idea as the "level of confidence with which a decision-maker makes each decision" but then, in a footnote, states that he has in mind something similar to the statistical confidence level but "more generalized in nature."[5]

At this point, the student of Downs should be confused. If thresholds arise from something like a significance test based upon subjective probability estimates about the actions of candidates if they are elected, then there is no reason to accept their reality. If voting is costless, a citizen is better off voting for the candidate offering greater expected utility, regardless of the statistical significance of the difference. Abstaining cannot help the voter; "relinquishing . . . neutrality" is an empty concept, because neutrality has no value. Alternatively, if Downs has some other idea in mind besides statistical hypothesis testing, it is certainly obscure and indeed is made more so by shrouding the argument in the framework of expected utility calculations. In either case, there is no theoretical basis for believing that thresholds exist.

The threshold concept faces still another problem. If voters are distributed more or less continuously and uniformly in issue space, parties will not observe a response threshold from the electorate in general even if each voter has response thresholds as defined by Downs. For example, consider the case in which the distribution of voters' estimates of the party differential has an expected value equal to the actual difference, but some finite variance and a single peak at the mean. Suppose one party wishes to convince voters who underestimate the difference that the real difference is larger than they think (or to correct the perception of voters who have an estimated difference that has the wrong sign). This party may then provide a little pertinent information about its positions that alters the calculations of voters only slightly and therefore slides only a few over perception thresholds in a direction favorable to the party.[6] If it provides a little more, a few more voters will cross a

---

4. Downs 1957b, 86–87.
5. Downs 1957b, 78.
6. Of course, the argument requires that information be targeted so that perception thresholds are crossed only in one direction.

threshold, and so on continuously as more information is provided. Likewise, the response of voters to shifts by the party in its true position will be continuous. Holding constant the degree to which voters will be informed, as the party's position drifts in any particular direction, more voters cross the perception threshold.[7] Thus, once again the threshold concept becomes problematic. Each voter may have behavioral thresholds, but from the perspective of a party, the electorate does not exhibit a threshold effect in responding to actions by the party. Only if the party knew precisely how far away each voter was from a perception threshold, and could tailor information for each voter, would the fact of thresholds be useful to a party, and therefore significant in politics. This would require that parties be substantially better informed about voters' estimates of party differentials than is plausible.

The Key to Thresholds

The purpose of this section is to construct a theory of thresholds that copes with both of the arguments against the bare bones theory presented in *An Economic Theory of Democracy*. Moreover, this reconstruction uses concepts found elsewhere in this work, which indicates that Downs's overall view of the political process implies politically significant behavioral thresholds—the combination of actual party differences and information about them has to exceed some minimum combination of values in order to induce *any* voters to change behavior. Thus, the theory of political thresholds that will be developed here is one of electoral and policy inertia. The importance of such a theory is that it works to counterbalance the Kenneth J. Arrow problem of chaotic outcomes in majority rule decision processes.[8] In the main text, the argument will be presented in the style of Downs, by verbal argument and example. In the Appendix, the argument is restated mathematically for those who are skeptical of verbal argument.

To reconstruct threshold theory for individual voters, all that is required is to apply the theory of information acquisition by voters that Downs develops in chapters 11, 12, and 13 of *An Economic Theory of Democracy*. The topic of these chapters is the economics of obtaining and processing political information and then acting upon it. The core assumptions are (1) voters can reduce their uncertainty about the party differential by gathering and evaluating more information, and (2) the costs of becoming more informed are, to an

---

7. Unlike the information argument, it is not plausible that the effect of drift, holding information states fixed, could be targeted; hence a party would drift in a direction that increased its net voter support.

8. Arrow [1951] 1962; McKelvey 1979; Cohen and Matthews 1980.

important extent, nontransferable (i.e., some of the costs must be paid by the voter who seeks to become more informed). These two assumptions imply that voters have response thresholds; that is, the irreducible minimum cost of information processing causes voters to be unresponsive to changes in information flowing to them and to shifts in party positions, even though these changes ought to alter their expected party differentials sufficiently to change their political behavior. For simplicity, we will ignore the threshold between passive support (voting) and active support (agitation) and focus only on distinguishing among supporters, abstainers, and opposers.

The Downs model of political information acquisition is easily explicated by completing (and slightly correcting) an example in Downs. Consider the problem of evaluating the positions of the parties on a cheese tariff. Suppose that the parties are labeled R and D and that voters come in two varieties, cheese makers and cheese eaters. The latter outnumber the former by 100 to 1, and consistent with the welfare economics of tariffs, one dollar in benefit to cheese makers causes two dollars of lost consumers' surplus to cheese eaters (both figures referring to collective, not individual, effects). Assume that party R is the incumbent, and that its policy on cheese tariffs is known with perfect certainty: it supports a modest 10 percent tariff, which it has been implementing during its period in office. No one expects this policy to change if R is reelected. But the policy that the D's would implement is uncertain. Assume that they might eliminate the tariff, leave it unchanged, or double it. The decision problems facing two representative voters, Cheese Maker and Cheese Eater, are shown in table 1, which slightly modifies an example in Downs.[9] Shown in the table is a series of assumptions about the relevant parameters, here values and probabilities of contingent levels of the tariff. The information value that is shown in the table is the value to each representative voter of obtaining certain knowledge about the policy that will be adopted by the D's, given the prior knowledge that is capsulized in the entries for Prob (D). By purchasing this information, each voter can be sure to vote for the party offering the greater value in tariff policy.[10]

The example in table 1 illustrates several important points. First, additional information is far more valuable to the voter who has a substantial amount of wealth riding on the outcome. If nontransferable information costs lie anywhere between sixty cents and ten dollars, Cheese Maker will be responsive to information about the true preference of the D's, but Cheese Eater will not bother to process this information if it is made available.

---

9. Downs 1957b, 242; the cheese story begins on 241.
10. Consistent with the analysis in Downs that motivates the example, this discussion ignores the consequentiality of voting.

TABLE 1. Voter Evaluations of Parties and Information

Voter Type	Variable	Levels of Cheese Tariff			Expected Values	Information Value
		0%	10%	20%		
Cheese Maker	Valuation	−100	0	+100		
	Prob (R)	0	1	0	0	0
	Prob (D)	.1	.4	.5	+40	+10
Cheese Eater	Valuation	+ 2	0	− 2		
	Prob (R)	0	1	0	0	0
	Prob (D)	.3	.4	.3	0	+ .60

Note: Prob (R) and prob (D) are the probabilities that the respective parties will take each of the positions on the cheese tariff.

Second, D has an incentive to advertise itself as the party of cheese tariffs, because only people who will respond favorably to this position—Cheese Maker—will pay attention to the information. If we add Downs's assumption that people do not lie, this means that D has an incentive to adopt the position of favoring the 20 percent tariff. Third, Downs makes an error in analyzing this problem, for he asserts: "The citizens who care most about which party wins a given election have the least need of information; whereas those for whom information is most useful do not care who wins the election."[11] Again, this is Downs the hypothesis tester speaking, not Downs the expected-utility maximizer. As the example illustrates, information is valueless to the indifferent voter (Cheese Eater) because processing costs exceed the value of information. However, Cheese Maker, with a strong preference for party D, nonetheless places a high value on pinning down exactly where D stands on cheese tariffs. The key point is that the value of information to a voter depends on both the diffuseness of the voter's prior beliefs about the policy position of the parties and the degree to which the range of feasible policies matters in the sense that the information produces differences in expected utility that are large enough to justify becoming informed.

With respect to the idea of thresholds, the example actually proves too much. It says that if the value of information to a voter falls short of its minimum irreducible processing cost the voter can never be induced to change behavior. Rather than a threshold, the theory predicts inertia: no matter how much parties actually shift their positions on an issue, and how much information they provide, voters with low information values will remain unmoved. Moreover, the theory tells us who these voters are: people who perceive little or no difference in their valuations of the range of feasible policy outcomes,

---

11. Downs 1957b, 239.

and people who assign largely nonoverlapping probabilities to the parties on issues that they do care about. The latter means that most of the probability is assigned to worse outcomes for one party, while most of the probability is assigned to better outcomes for the other, so that new information has little chance of uncovering an unexpected party difference.

To recover the concept of threshold at this point requires identifying some countervailing factor that will check inertia. The condition to examine is one in which the actual probabilities of policy outcomes by a party differ from the subjective probabilities of the voter sufficiently that, if the actual probabilities were known, the voter would behave differently. To be faithful to Downs, the model will exclude variability in the identity of the feasible range of policies and in the voter's valuations of those states. Thus, the problem is to develop a theory of how a voter might update these probability estimates even though, *ex ante,* the value of doing so is less than the costs.

Thresholds can be resurrected by utilizing the full Downsian model of the production of information. Downs makes two essential observations. The first is that information has several forms: entertainment, production, consumption, and political. The second is that information can reach voters through a variety of channels (and, for a fixed quantity of information, at different costs), which pertains to the magnitude of transferable information costs. Analysis of these concepts demonstrates that the "minimum irreducible cost" of information is dependent on the institutional arrangements of the moment and so is capable of being changed by a form of technological progress.

As Downs notes,[12] the types of information are not mutually exclusive. Information that is primarily related to entertainment, production, and consumption can have secondary political content. For example, pursuing the cheese tariff story, Pizza Maker, consulting recent production information, and Pizza Eater, contemplating the latest consumption information, may, willy nilly, process politically relevant information about cheese tariffs and their effect on cost and price in the pizza market. Mindful of this possibility, parties can lower the effective minimum irreducible processing cost of political information by packaging it with other types. Doing so, however, requires undertaking the costs of developing the new package; hence, parties will do so only if the likely political effect is large enough to return these costs.

Downs also elaborates on the relationship between the kinds of organizations available for providing political information and the extent to which information costs are transferable. Downs separates information costs into seven steps, beginning with data collection and ending with the actual decision to vote (or to abstain), and states that all but the last are transferable.[13]

---

12. Downs 1957b, 215.
13. Downs 1957b, 209–10.

But he further assumes that voters must do some minimum amount of analysis on their own; that is, they do not delegate to someone else the authority to instruct them on how to vote without providing information on which to base the instruction.

At any moment, the extent to which costs have been transferred depends on the kinds of information suppliers that are in operation, which includes professional information suppliers (such as publishers) and interest groups as well as parties.[14] If circumstances have changed so that a group of voters really would value information, but places too low an *ex ante* value on it to pay attention to it, the cause is partly related to the extent to which these information costs are transferable within the existing structure of information-supplying institutions. If a new supplier enters, taking advantage of the possibility for reduced per capita costs of information that is targeted at the affected group, the result is a higher transferable cost (and a lower minimum processing cost) for each member of the group. This, in turn, may be sufficiently large to induce the group to pay attention to the new (cheaper) information. But for this to take place, the costs of constructing the new source of supply (e.g., a new interest group or specialized publication) must be low enough, relative to the costs each group member is willing to pay to become informed, to justify forming the organization. Thus, not all departures of party positions will be large enough to change the information status of voters who, *ex post*, would value the new information; however, at some point the departure of reality from the voters' expectations becomes large enough that entrepreneurial invention of a new information source becomes worthwhile.[15]

The preceding argument resurrects the concept of political thresholds in both respects described earlier, but with some changes in its meaning. First, individuals exhibit thresholdlike responses to shifts in party positions and new political information about these shifts, but not because the relationship between expected party differential and participation response (including "agitation" through volunteering and contributing) is not continuous. The reason is that voters need to have a reason to update their estimates of expected party differentials, given the presence of information costs. Second, the electorate will also exhibit thresholdlike (or discontinuous) responsiveness to changes in party positions and information provision. This is because differences must be "large enough" and transferred costs "large enough" to generate the innovative institutional response that leads voters to recalculate expected party differentials. Of course, for this to happen, either something must have actually

---

14. Downs 1957b, 225–27.
15. Note that this argument corresponds in some respects to the idea of political entrepreneurs (see, for example, Riker 1988, esp. chap. 8).

changed politically, or a new innovation in information provision must have taken place, or both, perhaps because the former induces the latter. In the second and third instances, the observed voting behavior appears retrospective.[16] Under threshold circumstances, voters normally will act complacently and will not pay attention to new information. When the innovation in information provision arrives, however, a seemingly discontinuous shift occurs in voting. Assuming that parties are rational, the challenger, more than the incumbent, is likely to have available profitable changes in position or information packaging (because the incumbent has a better-known and more-fixed position); hence, on balance, the jump in support is more likely to work against incumbents and be interpreted as rejection of their performance in office.[17]

The Policy Significance of Thresholds

Downsian thresholds have important implications concerning the overall policy significance of voting behavior. An especially attractive aspect of Downs's work, beyond its specific conceptual breakthroughs in the application to politics of the theory of decisions under uncertainty, is that his theoretical model is explicitly tied to policy outcomes. Thresholds are no exception. The actual theoretical foundation for thresholds is closely related to two other important aspects of political systems: discretionary behavior by elected officials and politically relevant institutions other than parties.

The presence of thresholds means that incumbent officials can stray from the policy position that won an election without incurring an electoral punishment, as long as they stray along dimensions where voters are not inclined to update their estimates of party differentials. Hence, political competition need not produce the competitive equilibrium (if one exists).[18] The check on straying is primarily through innovative informational institutions, such as new or reorganized interest groups or mass media. This provides an entering wedge for generally salient political issues, such as might affect Cheese Eater; however, the wedge's edge is blunt by comparison to the innovative possibilities available to interest groups. The reason is the higher per capita stakes that

---

16. Fiorina, 1981.

17. For a more comprehensive argument, based on a more elaborate and comprehensive view of voting, that negative voting is behaviorally artifactual but statistically "detectable," see Fiorina and Shepsle, 1989.

18. This conclusion is the same as that reached by Fiorina and Noll 1978; however, the there-uncited Downs deserves a fair share of whatever credit his anticipation of our results is worth.

members of interest groups have in policy issues related to their interests, implying a higher likelihood that, at feasible minimum processing costs, their members will elect to receive new political information. Thus, the import of Downsian thresholds is not just that they impart stability to multidimensional political decision processes but that, for reasons initially developed by Downs, they do so in part because of the role of interest groups in the political process.

The theory of Downsian thresholds also provides a means for examining the implications of technological innovations in the delivery of information. Technological progress has affected two important aspects of the delivery of political information. One is improved technology in delivering an effective unit of information, which reduces both the candidate's and voter's transmission costs and net processing costs. The latter can be reduced by either changing the channels by which information is delivered, such as the substantial displacement of newspapers by broadcasting, or by packaging political information with other information that a voter might value, such as entertainment. The second example of technological progress that has affected information delivery is changes in the ability to target information to subsets of voters, based on increasingly more-sophisticated methods for categorizing voters according to their politically relevant interests, sensitivities, and socioeconomic characteristics.

In some respects these two trends have different effects on political processes. The declining cost of mass delivery of information (and the increasing ability to package it so that it imposes less processing demands on the recipient) may trivialize political campaigns for some, but it is also democratizing. It systematically narrows the range of inertia between the thresholds of inaction. Of course, it does so by focusing on voters who would otherwise be indifferent, and who must be presented relevant information at such a sufficiently low processing cost in such a sufficiently entertaining form that their inertia is overcome. To other voters, this is likely to seem trivial and irrelevant; however, they are not the audience.

By contrast, improved targeting technology enables candidates to better communicate specialized, mobilizing information to citizens with unusual but intensely felt policy preferences. As these methods improve, and as politicians succeed in collecting more funds to deploy these methods, the effect is to reduce the relative importance of the democratizing technologies. In a sense, new targeting technologies represent, in a different form, the reemergence of ward politics, which relied on personalized means of communicating politically relevant information as a means for motivating participation. The modern counterpart to the ward healer is the specialized direct appeal to a small, homogeneous constituency on matters of little or no significance to most voters. The similarity with the first change is that this, too, appears to many voters as a trivialization of politics. But the second change differs from the first in that it accentuates the interest group orientation of politics and serves to create new means of fragmenting constituencies. The consequence is to make policy increasingly distributive in character.

The final aspect of the relation between information technology, thresholds, and public policy is related to the fact that information can be used to create ambivalence as well as to eliminate it. For the most part, analysts tend to think of informational strategies in campaigns as tools for motivating citizens to favor the candidate who is the source of the information. In the context of thresholds, this is interpreted as causing a person to move from the range of opposition or nonparticipation to the range of support. But another possible strategy is to move supporters of an opponent to the range of indifference. One interpretation of "negative campaigns" would be that they seek, among other things, to cause an opponent's supporters to cross the participation threshold into neutrality. If a candidate knows that the opponent's supporters would not respond to truthful knowledge about the candidate's policy positions, the best available informational strategy may then be to expose aspects of the opponent that are unattractive to some of the opponent's supporters and to hope for abstention.

As before, the opponent's supporters may not place much value *ex ante* on new information, so it must be packaged in such a way that its informational effects on evaluations of candidates do not constitute all of the motive for voters to process it. The entertaining sound bite in broadcasting, aimed at passive voters waiting out the interval between other forms of entertainment, appears to be especially well suited to messages designed to convert supporters of the opponent to nonparticipants. One possible explanation for the decline in participation in American national elections during the postwar era is that technological change in the delivery of relevant political information may have favored this strategy over more positive strategies aimed at generating support for a candidate.

Negative advertising in the mass media also works to undermine the relationship of elections to national policy issues. By attacking an opponent, a candidate can avoid staking out a potentially controversial and hence electorally risky position on salient national issues. Instead, mass media information can be oriented toward entertaining broadsides at the opponent. Policy-related information can be confined to the safer domain of targeted material appealing to organized interests or other affinity groups. Of course, if both candidates adopt the same strategy, the outcome will simply be lower participation rates, along with a greater orientation of campaigns and voting decisions to relatively parochial interests. Thus, technology that improves how voters receive and process political information can actually reduce participation, increase indifference, and attenuate the relationship between elections and national policy.

APPENDIX

The argument in the second section of this chapter can be expressed mathematically in a spatial model of electoral competition. Suppose that a group of voters is concerned only about a single policy dimension, and that all feasible policies along that dimension fall in the unit interval. Assume that the incumbent party, Y, has adopted position y^* and is expected to maintain that position with certainty.[1] The challenging party, Z, has a position, z, that is uncertain to voters. Let $U_i(x)$ be the continuous, concave, twice-differentiable utility that person i derives from policy $x \in [0,1]$, $i = 1, n$, and attempts to maximize through political participation. Let x_i^* be the policy that maximizes the utility of person i, $x_i^* \in [0,1]$. Hence, $U_i'(x) < 0$ for $x > x_i^*$, $U_i'(x) > 0$ for $x < x_i^*$, and $U_i'(x_i^*) = 0$. Assume that $x_i^* > y^*$, so that if $z \in (y^*, x_i^*]$ person i will strictly prefer Z as long as i knows the value of z.[2] Define z_i^* as the maximum value of $z > x_i^*$ for which person i prefers Z to Y. That is, $U_i(y_i^*) \leq U(x) \; \forall \; x \in (y_i^*, z_i^*]$, and either $z_i^* = 1$ or $U_i(z_i^*) = U_i(y^*)$. It follows that for $z < y^*$ or $1 \geq z > z_i^*$, person i prefers Y to Z.[3]

Let $p_i(z)$ be person i's subjective probability that Z will adopt position z. If voters are indifferent between Y and Z, the following equality holds:

$$U_i(y^*) = \int_0^1 U_i(z) \, p_i(z) \, dz \quad i = 1, n. \tag{A1}$$

Because these voters are indifferent between Y and Z, they abstain from voting.

Let $q_i(V_i)$ be person i's subjective probability that party Y will win, given person i's voting behavior, $V_i \in \{Y_i, Z_i, A_i\}$ where the elements of V_i are voting for Y, voting for Z, and abstaining, respectively. Finally, let C_i be the cost of voting for person i, which is paid only if $V_i \in (Y_i, Z_i)$. (The cost of abstaining is 0.) Thus, a rational voter solves the following problem.

$$\max_{V_i} \; q_i(V_i) U_i(y^*) + [1 - q_i(V_i)] \int_0^1 U_i(z) \, p_i(z) dz - C_i(V_i).$$

Assume that someone, perhaps a party, launches a campaign to inform members of the group about Z's true position, and that the new information

---

[1]. The assumption that one party's position is known with certainty greatly simplifies the mathematics but is inessential to the main argument.

[2]. Again, this simplification does not change the core results of the model. At this point, voters could be segmented into two groups depending on whether x_i^* was smaller or larger than y_i^*, and the analysis of each would be conceptually identical.

[3]. Again, no generality is lost by this assumption, for parallel arguments apply to groups preferring either party.

will resolve all uncertainties about the value of z. Upon receiving the new information, I, the voter can inspect it at a cost I_i or ignore it at no cost.

By the assumption in (A1), a voter will continue to abstain if the voter does not inspect the new information, and the value of the election, W_i, to voter i will be the following.

$$W_i = q_i(A_i) U_i(y^*) + (1 - q_i(A_i)) \int_0^1 U_i(z) p_i(z) dz = U_i(y^*). \quad (A2)$$

The voter will inspect the information only if doing so is expected to increase the expected value of the election, which will happen only if the information will change person i's voting decision, V_i. With probability $p_i(z)$, Z is expected to deliver $U_i(z)$ to person i, conditional on Z being elected. The voter will actually bear voting costs C_i only if to do so produces a net expected benefit. Hence,

$$V_i = \begin{cases} Y_i \text{ iff } [q_i(Y_i) - q_i(A_i)] [U_i(y^*) - U_i(z)] > C_i \\ Z_i \text{ iff } [q_i(Z_i) - q_i(A_i)] [U_i(z) - U_i(y^*)] > C_i \\ A_i \text{ otherwise.} \end{cases}$$

Let $\underline{Z}_i$ and $\overline{Z}_i$ represent the two ranges of values of z, one around y^* and one around z_i^*, where $V_i = A_i$,[4] and let $\hat{Z}_i$ be the region between $\underline{Z}_i$ and $\overline{Z}_i$ for which $z \in \hat{Z}_i$ implies $V_i = Z_i$. Likewise, $z < z' \in \{\underline{Z}\}$ or $z > z'' \in \{\overline{Z}_i\}$ implies $V_i = Y_i$. Label these regions $\underline{Y}_i$ and $\overline{Y}_i$. Before inspecting I, the voter expects that the information will produce the following new value of the election, W_i^*.

$$W_i^* = \int_{\underline{Y}_i, \overline{Y}_i} [U_i(y^*) q_i(Y_i) + U_i(z)(1 - q_i(Y_i)) - C_i] p_i(z) dz$$

$$+ \int_{\underline{Z}_i, \overline{Z}_i} [U_i(y^*) q_i(A_i) + U_i(z) (1 - q_i(A_i))] p_i(z) dz$$

$$+ \int_{\hat{Z}_i} [U_i(y^*) q_i(Z_i) + U_i(z)(1 - q_i(Z_i)) - C_i] p_i(z) dz$$

$$- I_i. \quad (A3)$$

---

4. If $U_i(y^*) - U_i(x_i^*) < C_i$, the voter will abstain even if $z = x_i^*$, and the two regions overlap. Likewise, if $z^* = 1$ and $U_i(z^*) - U_i(y^*) > C_i$, the second region is empty. Henceforth, assume without loss of generality that neither is the case.

The first term in (A3) represents the expected gain from learning that a vote for Y is worthwhile, while the third term is the expected gain from learning that a vote for Z is worthwhile. The second term represents the expected value if the new information still causes the voter to abstain.

Expression (A3), by rearranging terms and applying (A1), can be rewritten as follows.

$$W_i^* = U_i(y^*) - I_i - C_i \int_{\underline{Y}_i, \bar{Y}_i, Z_i} p_i(z) dz + \int_{\underline{Y}_i, \bar{Y}_i} [U_i(y^*) - U_i(z)][q_i(Y_i) - q_i(A_i)] p_i(z) dz$$

$$+ \int_{Z_i} [U_i(z) - U_i(y^*)][q_i(A_i) - q_i(Z_i)] p_i(z) dz \quad (A4)$$

Note that $q_i(Y_i) \geq q_i(A_i) \geq q_i(Z_i)$ by positive responsiveness. Consequently, $q_i(Y_i) - q_i(A_i) \geq 0$ and $q_i(A_i) - q_i(Z_i) \leq 0$.

A voter will pay the cost of inspecting the information if to do so produces expected net benefits, or if $W_i^* > W_i$. From (A2) and (A4), this requirement can be written as follows.

$$\int_{\underline{Y}_i, \bar{Y}_i} [U_i(y^*) - U_i(z)][q_i(y_i) - q_i(A_i)] p_i(z) dz$$

$$+ \int_{Z_i} [U_i(z) - U_i(y^*)][q_i(A_i) - q_i(Z_i)] p_i(z) dz$$

$$- I_i - C_i \int_{\underline{Y}_i, \bar{Y}_i, \bar{Z}_i} p_i(z) dz \geq 0. \quad (A5)$$

Expression (A5) makes clear the many ways in which voters rationally may decide not to process information (i.e., to remain rationally ignorant).

1. When *voters are nondecisive*, or $q_i(Y_i) = q_i(A_i) = q_i(Z_i)$, the instrumental benefits of voting are 0. Even if voting costs are also 0, voters will prefer to remain uninformed because $W_i^* - W_i = -I_i < 0$. Alternatively, suppose that the $q_i(V_i)$ terms are subjective consumption values of voting that are at most weakly based on decisiveness. Then the weights must be "large enough" to make the expected difference in utilities after the information is received outweigh the information processing and voting costs. The argument given by Downs, and followed in the second section of this chapter, ignores decisiveness and, in essence, sets the weights $q_i(Z_i) = q_i(Y_i) = 1$ and $q_i(A_i) = 0$.

2. When *voters are indifferent*, the utility at stake in a policy is small; that

is, $U_i(y^*) - U_i(z)$ will be small. Again, this makes small the value of knowing which party is preferred. If $U_i(y^*) - U_i(z)$ is always small, the regions of indifference, $\underline{Z}_i$ and $\overline{Z}_i$, will be all (or nearly all) of the feasible policy space, and the voter will not expect the new information to change V_i from A_i. Hence, the information-processing cost, I_i, will dominate (A5), so that $W_i^* - W_i < 0$.

3. When *parties are similar*, voters will assign low probability to values of z that would motivate $V_i = Y_i$ or $Z_i = Z_i$. That is, high probabilities are assigned to the region Z_i, where $/U_i(z) - U_i(y^*)/$ is small, and low probabilities are assigned to other regions, including those where $/U_i(z) - U_i(y^*)/$ is large enough to motivate nonabstention. If the parties are "similar enough" so that $p_i(z)$ in regions $\underline{Y}_i$, $\overline{Y}_i$, and $\hat{Z}_i$ are "small enough," I_i will buy no offsetting benefit, so that $W_i^* - W_i < 0$.

A Downsian threshold can be interpreted as follows. Suppose party Z has shifted its position from the one that, in the past, gave rise to the probability distributions $p_i(z)$. By paying I_i, the voter can gain new information, use it to update the probability distribution, and reconsider the voting decision. (In this case, the assumption has been made that the updated probability distribution assigns a probability of 1 to the true position.) A necessary condition for a Downsian threshold is that a group of voters does not regard the new information as worth acquiring and can be stated as the following proposition.

Proposition on Voter Inertia. If there exists a group of voters who do not expect new information about party positions to be worth its minimum irreducible processing costs (i.e., $W_i^* < W_i, i = 1,n$), then a change in the position of a party, accompanied by its most effective feasible communication to the voter, will have no effect on voting behavior within the group.

Proof: Follows from the argument in the text preceding the statement of the proposition.

The Proposition on Voter Inertia is only part of the story. It explains why a continuous distribution of voter ideal points, X_i^*, will not necessarily produce a continuous relationship between the position taken by a party, holding fixed the opponent's position, and its vote. But, as stated in the second section of this chapter, the proposition proves too much because it predicts that if $W_i^* < W_i$, the voter will *never* process new information and will *never* change voting behavior.

To cause a voter to process information, the voter's processing costs, I_i must be reduced. Let $w_i = W_i^* - W_i < 0$ for voter i, and suppose that processing costs change exogenously by ΔI_i. If $w_i > \Delta I_i$, the voter will decide to process the information. One source of a change in processing costs is technological progress; however, another is that some other voter will subsidize voter i's information processing. For example, the subsidizer may create a political organization that economizes on information costs for all members of the group, or may pay for an entertaining TV advertisement that has a lower processing cost for its viewers than alternatives. In both cases, the subsidizing citizen bears a fixed cost, K, to reduce the processing costs of each group member by ΔI_i. The subsidizing citizen would be willing to bear this cost because of the effect it has on group voting behavior, and hence the value of the election to the subsidizer. Indeed, the maximum amount the subsidizer is willing to pay is the increase in the expected value of the election arising from the subsidy. By assumption, if all members of the group prefer some $z > y^*$, and voters are informed, then, ignoring voting costs, all will vote for Z. But not all will become informed. Instead, only those for whom $w_i > \Delta I_i$ will be informed. Then, as z increases, eventually it will become large enough that, for some voters, it exceeds x_i^* and even exceeds the region $\hat{Z}_i$ in which Z is preferred by Y. Two values of z are of interest: z_m, which is the largest value of z that causes all informed members of the group to vote for Z, and $z_o > z_m$, at which the informed voters split evenly between Y and Z (ignoring those who abstain).

Let ΔI be the vector of ΔI_i if K is spent, and $\Delta q(\Delta I)$ be the resulting change in the probability that Y will win the election. Note that Δq depends on z, being positive and constant for $z \in (y^*, z_m)$, positive and declining for $z \epsilon (z_m, z_o)$, and negative and declining for $z > z_o$.[5]

The *Condition for Information Subsidization* can now be developed. The net gain to the subsidizer, ΔW_s, from paying K is as follows.

$$\Delta W_s = \Delta q\, U(y^*) - \Delta q\, U(z) - K. \qquad (A6)$$

Now consider the behavior of the subsidizer as z is increased from y^*, given the preceding assumptions. Because $U_s(z)$ for the subsidizer is assumed to be continuously differentiable and $U_2'(y^*) > 0$, $U_s(z)$ has the following property. For any $\delta > 0$, there exists an $\epsilon > 0$ such that

$$U_s(y^* + \epsilon) - U_s(y^*) < \delta.$$

In particular, this property holds for

$$\delta = \frac{K}{|\Delta q|}.$$

Thus, in the region $z \epsilon (y^*, z_o)$, where $\Delta q < 0$, there are some values of $z = y^* + \epsilon$ such that

---

5. Alternatively, increasing z may never hit a feasible region in which Z is worse off than if $z = y^*$. The existence of $z_o < 1$ is not essential to the argument.

$$U_s(y^* + \epsilon) - U(y^*) < \frac{K}{|\Delta q|}.$$

If $x_s^* > y^*$ is the subsidizer's ideal value of z, assume that $\Delta q(x_s^*) < 0$ and

$$|\Delta q| \, [U_s(x_s^*) - U_s(y^*)] > K.$$

This assumption requires that more-informed members of the group will vote for Z than for Y at $z = x_s^*$, and that at $z = x_s^*$ the benefits of subsidizing the group's information processing exceeds the cost.[6] By the mean value theorem, it follows that there exists a value of $z = z_s \, \epsilon(y^*, x_s^*)$ such that

$$|\Delta q| \, [U(z_s) - U(y^*)] = K.$$

This value, z_s, is the Downsian political threshold in the following sense. First, for $z < z_s$, the subsidizer (who knows z) will vote for Z but will not subsidize other voters because ΔW_s in (A6) would be negative. Second, for $z = z_s$, K will be paid, and a discrete jump will take place in the number of votes for Z for any value of $z_s \, \epsilon(y^*, z_o)$. (By assumption, $z_s < z_o$.) Third, for $z > z_s$, voter response depends on the relationship between z_s and z_m. If $z_s < z_m$, as z increases from z_s to z_m, no change in voting behavior takes place; however, by hypothesis, for at least part of this range the subsidizer is made better off. For $z_s > z_m$, the net vote for Z declines as z increases. If $x_s^* > z_m$, the optimal value of z to the subsidizer can be in the interval (z_m, x_s^*).

The preceding argument provides sufficient conditions for a political threshold, which are (1) some voters must satisfy the Proposition on Voter Inertia, (2) some voters must be willing to bear the costs of informing themselves if a party changes position, and (3) these informed voters must satisfy the Condition for Information Subsidization for like-minded, rationally ignorant voters. The last group can be members of a party, contributors to a party, or people willing to bear the fixed costs of establishing an independent means of lowering information costs to the rationally ignorant. Finally, it follows that if the costs of targeting like-minded voters declines, the Condition for Information Subsidization becomes easier to satisfy, and the Downsian threshold becomes smaller.

---

6. This assumption is slightly stronger than necessary. All that is required is that at some $z\epsilon(y^*, x_s^*)$ the net benefits of the subsidy are positive.

CHAPTER 3

Information-pooling Models of Electoral Politics

Bernard Grofman and Julie Withers

Much of the work on the role of information in politics has been inspired by the ideas of Anthony Downs. One of the most important contributions of Downs in *An Economic Theory of Democracy* (1957b) is his explicit analysis of the role that information plays in electoral competition. The value of information, along with its costs, methods of evaluation, strategic uses, and means of acquisition and dissemination have been subjects of intensive study and debate over the past thirty years (See Calvert 1986; Ferejohn and Kuklinski 1990; Krehbiel 1990.)

There are five key aspects of Downs's views. First, "in an uncertain world, roads leading toward the good society are hard to distinguish from those leading away from it. Thus, even though voters have fixed goals, their views on how to approach these goals are malleable and can be altered by *persuasion*. Consequently, leadership can be exercised on most policy questions" (Downs 1957b, 87, emphasis added).

Second, *ideological identification* serves as a cognitive shortcut for voters, who then do not need to know the stands of candidates on every issue. Ideology effectively gives voters a sample of the issues that differentiate the parties, thus serving to cut information costs. Downs also points out that ideology is useful to political parties as well as voters; each party fashions an ideology that it believes will attract the greatest number of voters. Uncertainty (combined with social diversity) accounts for why political parties do not offer identical ideological positions (Downs 1957b, 100–101).

Third, because voters are uncertain about what candidates will actually

---

We are indebted to the late Wilma Laws, Susan Pursche, Ziggy Bates, the staff at the Word Processing Center, School of Social Sciences, University of California, Irvine, and Jerry Florence of the Center for Advanced Study in the Behavioral Sciences for typing numerous earlier drafts of this manuscript from hand-scribbled copy. This research was partially supported by NSF Grant SES #85-06376, Program in Decision and Management Sciences, awarded to the first-named author. Research and bibliographic assistance was ably provided by Chris Erblich and Erin McMullen at Washington University and by Dorothy Gormick at the University of California, Irvine.

do in office, if voters are risk-averse, then there will be a *bias toward the status quo* unless the alternative is clearly superior.

Fourth, because voters are uncertain about what candidates will actually do in office, voters use *past performance* and *party labels* as cues. Thus, according to Downs, parties will develop consistent images and seek to keep their promises.

Fifth, because gathering information is not costless, "each citizen decides how much information to acquire by utilizing the basic marginal cost-return principle of economics" (Downs 1957b, 219). According to Downs, for most purposes many voters rely entirely on *free information* that comes to them and use cues provided by the positions and preferences of the media, interest groups, or other more knowledgeable voters in order to ascertain which candidate is most likely to enact policies the voter would prefer.

The first topic area, persuasion, as far as we are aware, has been largely (if not entirely) neglected by subsequent researchers (see, however, chap. 15). The second topic area, ideology as an information cost-reducing cognitive heuristic, also has not generated an extensive literature (see, however, Glazer and Grofman 1989). The third topic area is the subject of chapter 2. The fourth and fifth topics are reviewed in chapter 1. Also, Roger G. Noll (chap. 2) reviews and expands upon Downs's exposition of the concept of "rational ignorance," that is, reasons why voters might choose not to gather additional information about the political choices open to them if the information-gathering process were costly and/or did not provide benefits other than simply the ability to cast a more-informed vote. Our focus is on a few very recent models that look at how voters might process information from *multiple sources* to discern differences between candidates or parties. This chapter can be thought of as a complement to that of Popkin (chap. 1), in which he reviews the empirical literature on voter decision heuristics and information-gathering shortcuts.

As noted, one type of uncertainty[1] that Downs focuses on is the incumbent's and challenger's locations in the issue space.[2] In models of electoral competition, candidates may be characterized by three potentially distinct

---

1. Following Luce and Raiffa 1957, information conditions such as those surrounding a candidate's platform may be classified as certain, risky, or uncertain. A voting decision is said to occur under conditions of *certainty* when the action leads to a known outcome. When the issue space is unidimensional, candidate platforms will be characterized by point locations in a model of electoral competition under complete or certain information. In contrast, a decision under *risk* occurs when the voter faces a known probability distribution over possible outcomes while a decision under *uncertainty* occurs when these probabilities are incompletely known and dependent on some unknown parameter or state of nature.

2. Downs identifies at least five arenas of voter uncertainty, such as the uncertainty arising from the fact that "voters are not always aware of what the government is or could be doing" (Downs, 1957b, 80).

location decisions: the location that they espouse during the campaign, the position they seek to implement once in office, and the policy outcome that actually results. Let the candidates' campaign location be referred to as their *platform*, the location they seek to implement once in office as their *issue effort*, and the location they succeed in implementing after election as their *issue performance* (cf. Enelow and Hinich 1984, 1990b).[3] The platform may be expressed as a set of issue positions or, more loosely, in terms of a general ideology.[4] Voters and other candidates may have some degree of uncertainty about a particular candidate's platform or probable issue effort or eventual issue performance or about all three.[5]

John Ferejohn's essay in this volume reviews the literature on incentives for a candidate's announced positions to accurately reflect the policies the candidate will seek to implement if elected (i.e., on potential divergence between platform and issue effort). Bernard Grofman (1985b) looks at why a candidate may be unable to fulfill promises, leading to those promises being discounted by rational voters (i.e., a potential divergence between issue effort and issue performance). James M. Enelow and James W. Endersby (chap. 8) test for such evidence of voter discounting and find it for voter evaluations of the positions of challengers. However, most of the literature we review in this essay blurs the distinctions between announced platform, issue effort, and probable issue performance. In what follows, for simplicity, the reader may take us to be discussing incomplete information models of candidate platform location.

The degree of uncertainty surrounding a candidate's platform is not the same for all voters. "Uncertainty divides voters into several classes" (Downs 1957b, 82), since "not all citizens receive the same amount of free data, nor are those who do receive the same amount equally able to make use of it" (Downs 1957b, 223). This is true not only of direct information about candi-

---

3. According to Downs, "All rational voters cast ballots in order to influence the *actions* of political parties, not their *statements*" (1957b, 99).

4. Downs points out that ideologies serve to focus attention on the differentiation between parties. Downs asserts that a party's ideology must be consistent with "either (1) its actions in prior election periods, or (2) its statements in the preceding campaign (including its ideology), or (3) both" (1957b, 103). For more on this point see chapter 7.

5. The uncertainty that voters have about postelection outcomes can be attributed to five basic factors: (1) a rational competitor may have incentives to strategically misrepresent postelection intentions, (2) even in the absence of strategic misrepresentation, a rational competitor may have incentives to provide less-than-complete information, (3) other electoral participants (other voters, interest groups, etc.) may have incentives to manipulate the information environment, (4) the mechanism by which information is transmitted to the voters may be imperfect, and (5) postelection events may lead the victor to revise his or her intended policy location. Thus, even if all the parties want the electorate to be fully informed, voter perceptions may still be imperfect due to exogenous policy shocks or the "white noise" associated with information acquisition.

date platforms but also of information on predictive signals of platform location, such as candidate ideology. The presence of these asymmetries within the electorate means that individual voters may be able to decrease their perceived uncertainty about candidate platforms through interaction with or observation of other voters, groups of voters, or the electorate as a whole.

Before we turn to our central topic we briefly review some of the work looking at incentives for candidates to be ambiguous about the policies they espouse or expect to pursue.

The Effect of Policy Ambiguity on Candidate Convergence and Voter Choice

In a model of incomplete information, the exact location of a candidate's platform may not be known. Downs's description of multi-issue politics suggests the notion of candidates as lotteries. Each candidate has an estimated location on the various dimensions of the issue space, but this location need not be a point (Downs 1957b, 132). Voters evaluate a candidate's relative location by weighing "its net position [the mean of its policies] against its spread [their variance]" (133). In effect, the electorate is comparing lotteries in its voting decision. The variance of a lottery gives a measure of the degree of uncertainty surrounding the (expected) location of the candidate's platform.

Research on the effect of the risk environment on candidate location was motivated by Downs's observation that the choice of a lottery with high variance "increases the number of voters to whom a party may appeal" (1957b, 136). Downs anticipates subsequent models by alluding to the fact that this variance may be symmetric or asymmetric across candidates, symmetric or asymmetric with respect to voter perceptions, and either fixed or subject to change as a result of the acquisition of new information or learning within the model.

Kenneth A. Shepsle (1972) develops a model in which candidate platforms are characterized as known probability distributions over the issue space—that is, as lotteries. Voters then must choose between lotteries (candidates) so as to maximize their expected utility. Shepsle restricts the incumbent's choice of electoral strategies to degenerate probability distributions (i.e., certainties) and the challenger to nondegenerate distributions, arguing that an incumbent's platform is inherently less uncertain because of the incumbent's "visibility (which is) enhanced by the media . . . [and the incumbent's ability] to communicate directly with the voters through his control of government activities which alter their utility streams" (560).[6] Shepsle

---

6. This echoes Downs's observation that information about candidate location is distributed asymmetrically across candidates due to, among other reasons, the ability of the incumbent to publish "large amounts of information as an intrinsic part of its governing activities" (Downs 1957b, 222).

shows that, under these assumptions, "strategies of ambiguity" will not occur when the electorate is risk-averse since they can be defeated by degenerate lotteries.

Richard D. McKelvey (1980) shows that when voter preferences are unimodal and there is symmetry in variance across candidates the equilibrium results obtained are the same as those in a complete information model of two-candidate competition. In equilibrium, "parties in a two-party system deliberately change their platforms so that they resemble one another" (Downs 1957b, 115). When candidates already resemble one another in terms of lottery variance, they will then seek to further that resemblance by choosing the same expected value for their platform locations. McKelvey (1980) also found that, in general, "strategies of ambiguity" cannot occur in equilibrium and that, if we interpret ambiguous strategies to be inherently unpalatable to risk-averse voters, then intentional ambiguity will not occur in a Downsian model with risk aversion.

These results seem at odds with Downs's statement that candidates in a two-party system have incentives to be "as equivocal as possible" even when we recognize that this statement is made with the important caveat that candidates' "tendency towards obscurity is limited by their desire to attract voters to the polls since citizens abstain if all parties seem identical or no party makes testable promises" (1957b, 1136). Moreover, casual observation of contemporary politics suggests that candidates for political office (much like candidates for judicial office such as Clarence Thomas) do, with some frequency, engage in a strategy of ambiguity with respect to some important issues. Nixon's "secret plan" for ending the Vietnam War, for example, immediately comes to mind. Thus, it seems clear that the last word has not yet been said with respect to modeling candidate incentives to offer ambiguous policy platforms.[7]

In the remainder of this essay, we review in some detail four models of particular relevance to a Downsian perspective on voter information heuristics and information-pooling tactics: those of McKelvey and Peter C. Ordeshook (1984, 1985a, 1985b, 1986, 1987, 1990), Nicholas R. Miller (1986), Grofman and Barbara Norrander (1987), and Randall Calvert (1985a). The bottom line of these models can be taken to be that, rather than voters being doomed by the incentive structure of collective political choice to "rational ignorance," voters as individuals can become highly knowledgeable about the political choices facing them through a variety of information heuristics and information-pooling devices and can (as a collectivity) often make choices identical to those that would be made by a set of "fully informed" voters.

---

7. Relevant to the development of models designed to match up with reality is the empirical evidence on projection and rationalization phenomena in voter choice that affects how lotteries are actually evaluated by voters.

Recent Information-pooling and Information Heuristic Models

McKelvey and Ordeshook

McKelvey and Ordeshook's model (1984, 1985a, 1985b, 1986, 1987, cf. 1990) demonstrates how voters can use societal performances to determine their own preference. Its basic thrust can be illustrated in one dimension.

Each voter is assumed to know (1) which candidate is further to the left, (2) poll results that characterize the overall preferences of society on the candidates, and (3) where the voter stands on the issue dimension relative to all other voters (i.e., a percentile location).

If the electorate splits, say sixty to forty in favor of the leftmost candidate, A, then a voter, V, whose percentile location on the issue dimension is such that 55 percent of the electorate prefers policies to the right of V and 45 percent prefer policies to the left of V, can calculate that V should also vote for A since he or she must be to the left of the midpoint between A and the other candidate, B. Since the location of that midpoint determines the breakdown of the vote, all voters with ideal points to the right of the midpoint should vote for B, and all with ideal points to the left of it should vote for A.

Generalizing this process, if the voter breakdown is p percent for A and $(100 - p)$ percent for B, and all voters are Downsian and informed as to the location of the candidates, the midpoint of the AB line segment must be at the p percentile. Since our hypothetical voter is below (to the left of) this percentile, if V assumes that the electorate is making an informed choice, V knows his or her preferred choice is identical to that of the society as a whole. For example, if $A = 40$ and $B = 80$, then $A + B/2 = 60$, and the distance between A and V is 5 while the distance between B and V is 35. (Recall that V is at the 55th percentile.) Similarly, suppose $A = 30$ and $B = 90$; then $A + B/2$ is again 60, and A is closer to V than is B. It should be apparent that all that counts is the location of the AB midpoint. Thus, partly informed voters can use societal preferences to determine (by a process of what we might loosely call "triangulation") their own preferred choice.

McKelvey and Ordeshook generalize this model to the multidimensional case and show that, even if some of the electorate is uninformed, a sequential series of polls will allow all voters to make a fully informed choice. They also present experimental evidence that such a convergence in fact takes place, although this convergence is not perfect; only some 14.5 percent of the uninformed voters make erroneous judgments (McKelvey and Ordeshook 1984, 84). These erroneous voters are concentrated in a zone in which choice is difficult because they are close to the true bisecting line; it doesn't matter much to them which choice is made.

Miller

Miller (1986, 175) begins by noting that empirical findings consistently show that U.S. voters are "poorly informed," yet as V. O. Key, Jr., points out (1966, 7), in the large, the electorate behaves about as rationally and responsibly as we should expect, given the clarity of the alternatives presented to it and the character of the information available to it.

Miller then goes on to assert that there is nothing mystical or even surprising about the relative competence of the electorate as a whole, even though it may be composed largely of relatively incompetent voters, and sets forth an account of this phenomenon based on a variant of the Condorcet Jury Theorem (Condorcet 1785; Black 1958; Grofman 1975; Urken 1980; Grofman, Owen, and Feld 1983). The import of the Condorcet Jury Theorem is that, if p, the likelihood that a given voter will make the "correct" choice over some dichotomy is greater than $1/2$—where correctness is defined from the standpoint of some underlying criterion of evaluation—then group competence (i.e., the likelihood that group picks the better of the two alternatives using a majority rule vote) increases as the size of the group increases,[8] and thus "it may be entirely reasonable to entrust an important binary decision for which there is in principle a 'correct' decision (e.g., convicting or acquitting a criminal defendant) to a group of individuals of lesser competence (e.g., a jury) rather than to a single individual of greater competence (e.g., a judge)" (Miller 1986, 179).[9]

Of course, the applicability of the Condorcet Jury Theorem would seem

---

8. *Condorcet Jury Theorem:* Consider a group of n voters (for simplicity, let n be odd), each with a probability p of voting "correctly" on a given measure. The probability that the group majority vote $[m = (n + 1)/2]$ is correct is given by

$$P_n = \sum_{h=m}^{n} \binom{n}{h} p^h (1-p)^{n-h}$$

and

if $p > 1/2$, then $\lim_{n \to \infty} P_n \to 1$

if $p = 1/2$, then $P_n = 1/2$ for all n

if $p < 1/2$, then $\lim_{n \to \infty} P_n \to 0$

9. This result has been generalized by Grofman, Guillermo Owen, and Scott L. Feld (1983), so that it applies to any distribution of competences as long as $\bar{p} > 1/2$ (see also Nitzan and Paroush 1985).

obviously limited to those relatively few domains where there might, in principle, be a single "correct" answer, and it would seem not to be applicable to arenas in which there was conflict of interest (Black 1958, 163; Miller 1986, 179), but Miller shows this commonsense expectation to be erroneous.

Miller's way of generalizing the domain of applicability of the Condorcet Jury Theorem is to recognize that the probability of correctness of a given voter's opinion, p_i, may be taken to be the probability that the voter has "accurately perceived his *own* individual interest—not the public interest or 'true' interests shared by all individuals" (Miller 1986, 180, emphasis ours). In this context, a voter's true interest is simply the preference the voter would have if he or she were perfectly informed. The electoral process "succeeds" (to use Miller's term) when the party that wins is the same as that which would have won had all voters been completely informed.[10]

Miller (1986, 181–83) is able to show that, for two blocs, A and B, those whose true interests would lead them to support positions A and B, respectively, of size n_A and n_B ($n_A + n_B = n$); if p is the probability that a member of each bloc will correctly perceive his or her own self-interest (i.e., vote for candidate A if in bloc A, and for candidate B if in block B), if $p > \frac{1}{2}$, then the probability that the electoral process "succeeds" approaches 1 as n increases. Miller (183–84) then generalizes this result further by showing that it still holds as long as $\bar{p}$, the average competence of the bloc members, is the same for both blocs.

Miller then proceeds to consider the case where the average competence of the voters in the two blocs is different, and where voters sample k bits of information, some of which are reasons for a given voter to favor alternative B and others that are reasons for the voter to favor alternative A. (Note that some given piece of information may provide a reason for one voter to favor candidate A, but that same bit of information may impel another voter with different interests toward candidate B.) Miller proposes a model in which each bit of information is weighted equally and voters choose in accord with the information provided by a majority of their cues.[11] This leads them to a microlevel version of the Condorcet Jury Theorem where n is the number of cues (information bits) sampled, and p is the informativeness of those cues to the individual voter.[12]

---

10. The parallels to the McKelvey and Ordeshook (1987) analyses are straightforward.

11. This model is formally identical to that used in Mackelprang, Grofman, and Thomas 1975 to model individual choice.

12. Miller (1986, 193) also shows that "the same factor—the large size of electorates—that discourages voters from acquiring political information also reduces the need (from the point of view of the chances of 'success' of the electoral process) for individual voters to be well informed."

Grofman and Norrander

Grofman and Norrander (1987, 1990) look at reference groups as sources of cues for voters, permitting cues to differ in their informativeness and also allowing for the possibility of nonequal weighting of information bits. Their 1990 article considers the case of sources located along a single line. They show that, when all reference groups are located on a line, the voter's best choice is to choose in accordance with the recommendation of the *single* reference group to which the voter is closest. In their earlier paper, they consider how to pool information from multiple-independent sources (e.g., each of which provides information about the location of alternatives on exactly one of some set of [orthogonal] axes in the space). For the latter task, they make use of the Shapley-Nitzan-Grofman-Paroush model of information pooling (Nitzan and Paroush 1985; Shapley and Grofman 1984), which is a Bayesian-derived variant of the well-known logit model. If we have n groups with the ith group having probability P_i of giving the voters the correct answer (i.e., picking the alternative whom the voter would choose had the voter full information), then, in the two-party competition, the voter should choose A over B if and only if

$$\sum_{\substack{\text{groups favoring} \\ A}} \log\left(\frac{P_i}{1-P_i}\right) > \sum_{\substack{\text{groups favoring} \\ B}} \log\left(\frac{P_j}{1-P_j}\right).$$

The conclusion of the Grofman and Norrander (1987) paper is that individuals who know very little about the political choices can nonetheless make the choice they would have made with perfect information by combining information from a number of different (reference group) sources whose interests are in part proxies for (or, alternatively, the opposite of) the voters' own interests. Note that in this model the preferences of groups whose interests are seen as opposed to those of the voter can be as highly informative as the preferences of groups with whom the voter identifies. Whether or not this model perfectly fits the information search and utilization pattern of most voters, even if voters fail to make optimal use of the information provided by reference group cues, it is clear from the data looked at in chapter 1 that processes similar to those described in the Grofman and Norrander (1990) model are actually used by voters. Moreover, the work of Arthur Lupia (1990, 1991a, 1991b) on voters' use of information cues derived from referendum endorsements or opposition statements (such as those by Ralph Nader or insurance companies) to determine their referendum voting is consistent with the intuitions suggested by the Grofman and Norrander (1987) approach, although Lupia's research is rooted in more traditional social choice modeling of imperfect information environments. Lupia's work offers further support for the Downsian proposition that voters are able to make relatively "informed" choices about matters about which they lack "hard" information by making use of information decision heuristics.

Calvert

Calvert (1985a) considers the usefulness of biased versus neutral sources of information. In particular, if the individual is choosing between two alternatives, denoted 1 and 0, then the advice of an information source is posited by Calvert to the following simple function of the individual's true interests, for $i \in [0,1]$

$$S = \begin{cases} 1 \text{ with probability} & u_i^{\alpha_i} \\ 0 \text{ with probability } 1 - u_i^{\alpha_i} \end{cases}$$

When $\alpha_i = 1$, the information source is *neutral* toward alternative i; when $\alpha_i > 1$, the information source is *biased against* alternative i; when $\alpha_i < 1$, the source is *biased in favor* of alternative i. Calvert argues, "the value of a source lies in the possibility that its advice may cause the decision maker to change his mind" (539); therefore, when there is a cost to information search, ceteris paribus, a biased source is to be preferred. For an initially undecided decision maker, "a biased observer recommending the alternative that he was biased against is likely thereby to prevent the decision maker from making a relatively large error" (552). Similarly, for a decision maker with a strong predisposition toward one alternative, "in a setting of sequential sampling, the optimal information gathering procedure might use biased advisors first, since this might eliminate the need of any further consulting, again by giving an unexpected recommendation" (552). This classification of information bits according to bias permits the users to increase their efficiency. Of course, the extent to which such a model of optimal information search actually fits the observed patterns is an open question.

Part 2
Participation and Choice

CHAPTER 4

What the Downsian Voter Weighs: A Reassessment of the Costs and Benefits of Action

Carole Jean Uhlaner

In *An Economic Theory of Democracy* (1957b), Anthony Downs derives predictions about citizen political participation by modeling the citizen as assessing the costs and benefits of action and combining these according to the precepts of expected utility maximization. Downs's work has turned the attention of later scholars to systematic and rigorous consideration of the costs and benefits of action. With regard to the specific issue of voter turnout, however, Downs's work sets up a paradox. He concludes that most citizens would find it rational to abstain when voting is not costless: "since the returns from voting are often miniscule, even low voting costs may cause many partisan citizens to abstain" (265). However, empirically we do observe substantial numbers of voters. Many efforts have been made to reconcile the contradiction between prediction and observation. This chapter reviews various efforts of reconciliation and presents a more promising approach.

To set the stage, it is worthwhile to consider first why this paradox has been so troubling. Expected utility maximization provides an appealing model for citizen decision making, but the prediction of general abstention that follows from it not only contradicts observation but also presents a serious challenge to democratic functioning. If no one voted, representative democratic political systems would collapse. Downs himself recognizes the seriousness of the problem raised by his theory's prediction and suggests solving it by introducing into the rational citizen's calculation a benefit that "stems from each citizen's realization that democracy cannot function unless many people vote" (Downs 1957b, 274).[1] The paradox is deepened by the fact that the theory is supported by analyses of aggregate data that *do* show relationships that follow from the model (e.g., positive correlations between turnout and electoral closeness).

---

1. The only authors after Downs who attempted explicitly to model preservation of democracy as a motivation for participation are Norman Frohlich, Joe Oppenheimer, Jeffrey Smith, and Oran Young (1978), who include in their test of Downs the "long-run participation value."

Moreover, extension of the model beyond voting leads to predictions that citizens will rarely undertake any collective action, including most forms of political participation. The demonstration by Mancur Olson, Jr., of the irrationality of individual participation in interest groups parallels Downs's argument. As William H. Riker and Peter C. Ordeshook (1973, 72) summarize the work of Downs and Olson, "thus, the decision to participate is equivalent to the decision to supply or to assist in supplying a collective good." People abstain when action carries costs and they have an essentially equal likelihood of receiving the collective outcome (preservation of democracy and election of a particular candidate or formation of a union) whether or not they act. These situations are n-person Prisoner's Dilemmas. People in these situations have incentives to free ride. Again, predictions contradict observations, since people do undertake collective actions at rates far greater than zero. We could dismiss these choices as "irrational." The greater challenge is to make sense of them.

A long line of scholars has attempted to modify the Downsian rational actor model in ways that produce predictions of turnout (and other political actions) closer to empirically observed levels (i.e., nonzero), while retaining the basic insight that prospective voters weigh costs and benefits. A number of different, not mutually exclusive, approaches have been taken, which are summarized in the next section.

I believe the most fruitful approach involves raising the problem to a different level of analysis and embedding individual decision-making citizens in a social structure. A number of the newer versions of the standard fixes do rely upon the existence of groups for their argument; these are also discussed in the next section. A more far-reaching approach, which I have sketched elsewhere (Uhlaner 1986, 1989a, 1989b), treats groups more dynamically. Group leaders and processes come into play in addition to citizens and candidates. They affect choices of action by affecting costs, benefits, and probabilities. One advantage of this approach is that it can explain the contradictory levels of support for the theory provided by aggregate versus individual-level data. My solution is explained in some detail in the section that follows discussion of the standard fixes. Finally, I present some thoughts on the implications of recent work in the utility theory for resolving the paradox. The conclusion considers some criticisms of this entire line of work.

The Standard Fixes

The three most common sets of solutions to the paradox involve (1) expanding the interpretation of the benefits of voting, especially by adding a benefit term that is not discounted by probabilities, (2) reassessing the cost of voting, or (3) justifying an increased assessment of the probability that the citizen's vote is pivotal or perceived to be pivotal. A few authors have taken a fourth approach and adopted something other than expected utility maximization as a rational decision rule.

Benefits

Most scholars who approach the paradox by reconsidering the nature of benefits expand and formalize Downs's observation that one of the three factors entering into a citizen's return from voting is "the value of voting *per se*" (Downs 1957b, 266). Clearly the most influential of the early articles is that by Riker and Ordeshook (1968). They reformulate the Downsian citizen's voting decision as

$$\text{Vote, if } pB + D > c; \text{ otherwise abstain}$$

where p is the probability that the voter is pivotal, B is the party differential (that is, the difference in the voter's utility if one candidate wins rather than the other) c is the cost of voting, and D measures those positive contributions to the individual's utility where the "magnitude [of the effect] is independent of the individual's contribution to the outcome" (Riker and Ordeshook 1968, 27). This statement of the voter's choice has been widely adopted; the terms are used throughout the following discussion. Riker and Ordeshook define the D term quite generally; Downs's "benefit of preserving democracy" can be subsumed in it. Nonetheless, later readers often interpret their D narrowly as the benefits accruing to the voter from fulfilling a sense of citizen duty. Riker and Ordeshook imply in their discussion that D's value is fixed for any choice period; it is not modeled as an endogenous consequence of political processes. Many later authors, including Morris Silver (1973), Morris P. Fiorina (1976), and Melvin J. Hinich (1981), propose various D term type benefits stemming from the expressive, or consumption, aspects of voting. Since the benefits modeled by the D term are not discounted by the probability that the voter is pivotal, a citizen who perceived D benefits could well find voting more beneficial than abstention.

Other authors focus instead upon expanding benefits by rethinking the party differential, a second factor in Downs's list.[2] In the spatial modeling tradition, there has been careful development of the impact of B upon turnout, in terms of the effects of indifference and alienation upon abstention (e.g., in Hinich and Ordeshook 1969; McKelvey and Ordeshook 1972; Hinich,

---

2. The third factor in Downs's list of voter considerations is the "degree to which he discounts his party differential to allow for the influence of other voters" (Downs 1957b, 266), that is, the probability term.

1978a). While this research is helpful in distinguishing voters from nonvoters, it does not provide a convincing argument for the existence of voters.

A number of authors suggest that voters derive benefits based upon their group affiliations. Thomas Schwartz (1987) takes as given that citizens belong to subelectorates. Within these smaller groups, it is easier to identify the voters and thus to provide them with selective incentives (benefits). Amihai Glazer (1987) suggests that "a person finds it worthwhile to vote because by doing so he signals or informs others about his own preferences, and thereby increases his income or obtains some nonpecuniary benefits" (1987, 257). The benefit of voting then comes to a voter from indicating his or her "type."

In work on another collective action, protest against nuclear power plants, Karl-Dieter Opp (1986) argues that protesters value "soft incentives" (similar to D term benefits). These include not just general duty but also specific obligations to act as a member of some subelectoral reference group. Howard Margolis ([1982] 1984) develops a formal version of a related idea in his proposal that each individual has, in addition to a self-interested utility function, a group-interested function $G-$. A person's utility from this second function increases as a social entity with which he or she identifies receives benefits. For example, contribution to a collective good (e.g., by voting) can increase $G-$.

Perhaps the most acerbic criticism of these various expansions of the benefit terms comes from Brian Barry. He complains that the point of the rational actor approach is lost when the prediction of infinitesimal turnout is solved by saying "that people vote because they derive satisfaction from voting for reasons entirely divorced from the hope that it will bring about desired results. This may well be true but it does not leave any scope for an economic model to come between the premises and the phenomenon to be explained" ([1970] 1978, 16). When all of the action is loaded onto consumption benefit terms, little politics remains in political behavior.

Costs

Costs and benefits are just the negative of each other, as Gordon Tullock (1967, 114) was arguably the first to point out in this context when he noted that the "cost" term in Downs's model could have a negative sign; he gives the example of social pressures to vote. Nonetheless, authors who focus on the cost side of the calculus have tended to raise issues different from those of authors writing in terms of benefits.

One line of research (beginning with Downs) has focused on the effects of information. The better informed might vote more because their costs are lower or less because they understand their low odds of changing the election outcome (Tollison and Willett 1973; Tollison, Crain, and Pautler 1975; Settle and Abrams 1976). Others focus on income effects. Persons who earn more face higher opportunity costs on time (and so should not spend time voting), but they can better afford information and acquire more incidental to their other activities (Frey 1971, 1972; Russell 1972; Tollison and Willett 1973; Crain and Deaton 1977). However, none of these accounts really address the basic problem that the model predicts far less turnout than occurs.

Two arguments about costs that do focus on producing predictions of higher turnout have been advanced: (1) that costs are not really that high anyway (Niemi 1976) and (2) that costs are negatively correlated with pB and D (Riker and Ordeshook 1968; Black 1980).

Perceived Probabilities

The entire cost and benefit calculus changes dramatically if the probability term discounting the party differential (B) has some nontrivial magnitude. Citizens may *perceive* their chances of being pivotal as higher than objectively they are (Riker and Ordeshook 1968; Barzel and Silberberg 1973, 53; Brunk 1980). Schwartz (1987) argues that citizens assess their odds of being pivotal in subelectorates; since these are smaller, the odds are higher.

The equilibrium approach (Ledyard 1981, 1984; Palfrey and Rosenthal 1985) hinges upon the fact that as turnout decreases, any remaining voter has a higher likelihood of being pivotal; at low enough turnout levels, the expected benefit of voting would exceed costs. Some equilibrium level of turnout could thus be expected, although this level would still be very low in most real electorates. Note that Downs's solution discussed earlier under "benefits"—that people vote so that democracy can function—can be read as precursor of the equilibrium approach. The long-run participation value, from preserving democracy, depends upon the number of other voters. The equilibrium then depends upon both the probability of being decisive with regard to who wins the election and with regard to whether or not "enough" people vote.

When group-based approaches touch upon probabilities, they sometimes fall into a levels-of-analysis fallacy. For example, in Charles Tilly's (1969, 1975) discussion of protest, he tends to assume that if a group collectively has interests at stake and a chance of success then individual members will take actions, but he does not explain how a group-level calculus leads an individual to pick up a stone. Opp (1986) more straightforwardly suggests that individuals inflate their probability estimates by using in their action calculus their perception that the *group's* action will be successful. Since each individual calculates as though he or she were identical with the entire group, the odds of affecting an outcome become nontrivial.

Alternative Conceptions of Rationality

One way to generate predictions of substantial turnout is to discard the assumption of expected utility maximization. Under a minimax regret rule, probabilities are ignored. Persons using such a rule select that action that minimizes their maximum regret (where regret is the difference between what they receive using that action under some state of the world and what they could have received had they been able to choose the optimal action). John Ferejohn and M. Fiorina (1974, 1975) demonstrate that minimax regret generates predictions of substantial turnout. Essentially, the "regret" from not voting when you could have broken a tie outweighs the cost of voting. Critics argue that it seems unreasonable that voters would completely ignore the substantial differences in the probabilities of breaking a tie and not doing so. Thus, solutions abandoning expected utility have not caught on.[3]

Amitai Etzioni (1988) takes the more radical approach of arguing that individuals have multiple utility functions because they have multiple goals, and these functions are not tied together into some overarching utility function. While collective action can then be derived without difficulty, little is left of a usable model.

Comments on the Standard Fixes

Some of these solutions, such as the discussion of costs, explain marginal shifts in participation without solving the puzzle of why there is substantial turnout to begin with. Other solutions, such as those relying upon expressive benefits, do account for higher voting rates than the original model, but the solutions provide explanations of turnout variations over time or over individuals that are at best apolitical. None of these solutions convincingly account for secular change in response to changing political conditions. Barry's critique that "the politics" is left out applies fairly generally.

Embedding the Voter in a Group

A better approach to solving the problem presented by the Downsian model embeds the voter in a social structure (see Uhlaner 1989a, 1989b). The actual decision to vote still depends upon the p, B, D, and C terms taking on values such that action is more valuable than abstention. However, unlike the case with the "standard solutions" discussed earlier, the values of these terms can

---

3. However, public service ads encouraging turnout in recent elections play on minimax regret calculations. A typical ad portrays an abstainer watching late returns in which his or her preferred candidate is losing. Someone clearly believes that minimax regret thinking is persuasive.

now be related to politics. Specifically, although in my approach individual citizens still vote primarily because of consumption benefits (in the *D* term), for those citizens who identify with some group(s) with respect to politics (teachers, workers, Latinos, businesspeople, etc.), the value of *D* is deliberately affected by "leaders"—intermediaries between citizens and candidates. The leaders' actions, in turn, depend on instrumental calculations. Politics comes back into the decision to vote.

The standard models typically deal with candidates and isolated individual citizens. However, many individuals belong to groups that orient them in political life; they assess politics in terms of "other people like me." My model starts by assuming that citizens are divided into groups. *Groups* in this usage are a collection of individuals who identify with each other over some extended period of time (so there is some stability) and who have some similarity of preferences, so they may benefit from coordinated action. Such groups could be organized secondary groups with formal membership (e.g., labor unions), but need not be; reference groups with some coherence (African-Americans, born-again Christians) work in the model as well. *Leaders* are at the second level of the model. Leaders of each group are assumed to want to advance the group members' objectives.[4] Leaders of formally defined groups are easy to locate. Otherwise, leaders include respected spokespersons with moral or material resources at their disposal (e.g., the head of the NAACP, various ministers). Finally, *candidates* are the third set of players; they try to win votes in order to win elections.

Citizens are assumed to be utility maximizers who vote when $pB + D > c$ and otherwise abstain, as in the Riker and Ordeshook formulation discussed earlier. For simplicity, I assume that citizens are clear as to who is the preferred candidate. As in the usual story, the odds of the citizen breaking a tie are so low that pB will almost always be essentially zero, so the choice will almost always depend upon a comparison of D and c. Even if the preferred candidate moves to a policy position closer to the citizen's preference, thereby increasing B, discounting by p will produce a vanishingly small instrumental benefit. However, leaders have incentives to increase and decrease D depending upon circumstances.

The strategic picture is quite different for leaders. A leader's utility goes up as the winning candidate's positions approach the policy positions (issues, patronage, or whatever) preferred by members of the group (since the utility of the individual members is then higher). Now, however, a shift in the support of a group of reasonable size *could* alter the outcome of the election, so the size of the probability term comparable to p in the individual calculus may be substantial, producing a significant instrumental benefit.

---

4. This assumption is not as restrictive as it may appear at first glance. A leader who consistently fails to further group interests will eventually be replaced.

Candidates want to increase the probability of winning the election. Since changes in a group's turnout can affect the election, candidates are willing to move closer to a group in policy space in exchange for an increase in the level of support. Candidates' shifts are constrained somewhat by the direct costs of making a shift (e.g., time and staff resources to publicize a new position, perceptions of opportunism) and by votes not received from other groups.

A shift in a candidate position as part of a trade with leaders for turnout produces a surplus. The leaders function as entrepreneurs who provide the structure—and selective incentives—for organization in exchange for capturing a portion of the surplus, similar to the political entrepreneurs discussed by Norman Frohlich, Joe Oppenheimer, and Oran Young (1971). Leaders can use part of the surplus to increase D for group members, thereby creating the increased turnout that is their side of the trade. Sometimes the benefits are economic selective incentives (e.g., dollar bills in envelopes handed to known supporters at the polls or repair of the sidewalk in front of the homes of those who voted). Some of the surplus may be used to decrease the costs of voting (e.g., by providing information or transportation to the polls). Many times the surplus may go into increasing the normative benefits of voting, such as enhancing a sense of fulfilling a group-specific duty to participate. Leaders need only increase D enough to raise the probability of turnout and thus the expected level; there is no need to guarantee any particular individual will vote.

In sum, group leaders provide their members with incentives to vote (by increasing D or decreasing c) in order to capture a collective benefit in the form of a favorable shift in candidate position. The larger the shift, the greater the incentive and the higher the turnout. Candidates are willing to trade position in policy space for increased levels of support. Therefore, while individuals still choose to vote based on consumption benefits (D), the level of D they receive depends upon group trades for candidate policies.

One of the less obviously plausible parts of this model is the claim that leaders often raise D by increasing the normative benefits of voting. Clearly, economic selective incentives provided by leaders for voting are not sufficiently widespread to account for much turnout. The usefulness of this model thus depends upon the other sources of benefits. They therefore deserve a bit more elaboration.

An important component of increased D available to leaders for manipulation is a *group-specific* sense of citizen duty. There is some evidence that it works. In the 1982 congressional elections, the AFL-CIO spent much time and money arguing that Reaganomics was hurting the working men and women of America, and that all good union members should vote in that election to send the message to the Republicans. That message raised the payoffs for voting by augmenting the sense of union members that it was their duty to the group to participate, and an analysis of data from 1978, 1982, and 1986 suggests that the appeal was successful (Uhlaner 1989a, 415–18). Note that leaders need to use real resources—to publish materials, send mail, run telephone banks, and so forth—to heighten a sense of group duty. Note also that a citizen could easily respond to such a sense of duty without being consciously aware of it and even more easily without being aware of its source.[5]

The discussions of group consciousness as a lever to increase participation are consistent with citizens deriving benefits from their actions because of their affiliations. Patricia Gurin and her collaborators (Gurin, Hatchett, and Jackson 1990; Miller et al. 1981) argue that group identity leads to activity when the identity is linked to a political consciousness of the external structures producing the group's circumstances (e.g., a belief that the group's condition is illegitimately inferior to that of others in the society). I would argue that group consciousness increases participation to the extent that it is correlated with increases in benefits (D) as already discussed. Persons who are highly conscious of their group will derive more utility from fulfilling group-based norms and will be more likely to accept political action as the means of fulfillment if there is a political element to their awareness. In particular, if voting is set as a condition of fulfilling group norms, then they will be more likely to vote. B. Fireman and W. A. Gamson (1979) discuss organizers who mobilize action by raising consciousness and increasing solidarity. However, they fail to show what mobilization means in terms of the choices and actions of rational leaders and rational citizens.

The meaning of mobilization and, more generally, explication of the means by which leaders raise the value of the D term, can be illuminated by expanding the model to allow for the valuation of "relational goods" by citizens (Uhlaner 1989b). This expansion can also lead to insights into leaders' opportunities and incentives to alter an individual's perception of the probability of an action being successful. Existing rational choice models of action, including those discussed earlier in this chapter, tacitly assume that the individual's utility depends on privately possessable goods. Relational goods are goods that can only be "possessed" by mutual agreement and after appropriate joint actions by a person and specific other people (or people from a specific set). For example, friendship is a relational good; one (nondelusional) person cannot decide unilaterally to be a friend. Sociability, solidarity, and many instances of norm fulfillment also involve relational goods. Relational goods must be shared to be enjoyed. In contrast, standard public goods could perfectly well be enjoyed in isolation, were the world extravagant enough to

---

5. These two features make direct tests of the model very difficult.

build a dam or a lighthouse for an individual. More importantly, private goods cannot only be enjoyed alone but can also be possessed alone. They may require general and anonymous agreement (like money) but do not depend upon shared possession.

Relational goods may involve either instrumental or consumption benefits. They may arise in situations of direct contact or where the interaction is indirect. If a citizen considering political action includes relational goods in his or her utility function, then a number of situations arise where coordination or negotiation could lead to higher levels of activity. Leaders can mobilize by providing facilities for coordinating and negotiating. The most common circumstances involve indirect consumption goods. In these cases, participation will increase the more the citizen cares about being like others, the less the citizen thinks others care about being like him or her, and the higher the net value the citizen thinks that others place on action. A leader who wished to increase participation can mobilize by fostering the appropriate perceptions of "everyone else." Both in this case and when instrumental relational goods are involved, a person is more likely to choose action when he or she believes that others will act as well. Not only can that belief be enhanced by skillful leaders but the result provides a surprising contrast to what one would expect of free riders.

Recognition that relational goods are part of the citizen's benefits leads us then to an understanding of specific processes by which leaders can mobilize activity. Summarizing roughly, participation will go up to the extent they can foster the desire of citizens to be like others and citizen beliefs that others will act. Whether or not leaders choose to mobilize activity will, however, still depend upon their interactions with candidates.

I promise earlier in the chapter to provide a resolution to the puzzle presented by the contrast between aggregate results showing that closeness affects turnout (Silberman and Durden 1975; Filer and Kenny 1980; Chapman and Palda 1983; Durden and Gaynor 1987) and the lack of relationship in survey data between individuals' assessment of the race's closeness and their propensity to vote.[6] The missing link is that in closer races, group support will be more valuable to candidates. Leaders can therefore extract more surplus when a race is close than otherwise. This surplus will in turn buy more D and lead to higher observed turnout. Thus, the fluctuations in turnout will reflect changes in political circumstances, without, however, need for the individual voter to be aware of responding to changes in probabilities. As a result the aggregate data will show the link while it will be elusive in survey data.

---

6. Frohlich and his coauthors (1978) do find survey data to support the Downsian model of turnout, but it is unclear from their report how much of the weight is carried by which term.

Modification of the Expected Utility Model

Although discarding expected utility maximization altogether seems an unpromising modeling move, experimental results do call into question its descriptiveness. It fits best where makers face high stakes and midrange probabilities; thus, it may serve as a reasonable model for elite choices. If the postulates do not fit the decision making of ordinary citizens, then voting *could* be a rational choice for substantially more people. The paradox may dissolve. The difficulty lies in modeling rational decision making in a way that permits predictions but is more descriptively valid.

The phenomenon of preference reversal suggests one resolution of the paradox (see Luce 1992, 11–13 for a review). Experiments have repeatedly shown people to value gambles where they receive large payoffs with low probability more highly than they value gambles providing low payoffs with high probability. One explanation (Tversky, Slovic, and Kahneman 1990) is that people deal with complexity by evaluating both gambles along the salient dimension of money—the high payoffs in the first case swamp the low probabilities. The comparison of pB and c entailed by the vote calculus fits the conditions for preference reversal. The pB term has the form of a very low probability of winning a large amount; thus, people overestimate the value of the gamble. The cost term actually summarizes a series of moderate probability low-cost chance events, such as that a voter has a long wait at the polls or that he or she missed out on something else while voting. Thus, costs are likely to be underestimated. The net effect would be to produce more voting.

More generally, R. Duncan Luce's (1992) review of the empirical evidence on expected utility leads him to conclude that several of the assumptions on which it is built, including, especially, "universal accounting equivalences," are empirically unsupported.[7] Luce constructs a substitute for expected utility (rank-dependent linear utility) that does not treat gambles as equivalent to their certain equivalents and that allows for the assessment of probabilities to depend upon how outcomes are presented (i.e., with respect to more- or to less-preferred alternatives).

As just noted, c represents a series of chance events reduced to a single supposedly equivalent value. B, the difference in the utility received by the citizen if the preferred candidate wins rather than the less-preferred candidate, is also the reduction of a series of probabilistic events to their equivalent. The utility from the preferred candidate depends upon a whole series of chance events: the candidate follows declared policies, he or she proves to be compe-

---

7. Luce also drops "independence of a common consequence." He keeps transitivity and monotonicity and several of the simplest accounting equivalences.

tent, the citizen actually receives the benefits, and so forth. If the accounting rules do not hold, there is no particular reason to think that these reduce to pB and c in the decision calculus of a citizen.

As far as understanding political processes, possibly the greatest use of the modifications to expected utility theory lies in the insights they give as to how elites can best affect the judgments and choices of citizens. Elites can make different dimensions salient; they can also apparently simplify complex sequences of chance events.

Conclusion

Many approaches have been taken to solving the problem presented by Downs's analysis of voter turnout. Some of the approaches, such as those in the spatial modeling tradition, have made contributions to understanding *which* citizens will vote and what the effects of abstentions upon outcomes will be. With respect to explaining why anyone would vote at all, various scholars have tried modifying our understanding of the benefits, of the costs, of the nature of the probabilities, of the nature of the utility function, and of the nature of rationality. The two main complaints against this literature overall are that (1) it does not succeed in predicting empirically observed levels of activity and (2) it removes politics from political action.

Despite the element of validity in these criticisms, they do nonetheless seem overstated. The theoretical developments discussed here have usually pointed out reasonable aspects of the political world that it makes sense for a model to incorporate, and this discussion has usually (although not always) shown how a model that incorporates them can still yield interesting implications. In particular, that individuals' ends include objectives beyond just effecting the election of one candidate versus another seems descriptively correct. That people misestimate probabilities, and that for some people costs are perceived to be—or are—very low, seem also to be descriptively correct.

The reasonableness of including these insights in a model of citizen participation depends in large part upon the possibilities for modeling them, especially modeling them in terms of politically relevant variables and phenomena. That is, to the extent we can go beyond simply saying "people value other things" to saying "they value these because of early socialization, so we should find variation reflecting differences in socialization," the inclusion makes for a better model. It would be still better if we can expand "people value other things" into a hypothesis about when which kinds of people will value them more in response to what factors. It would be even better if at least some of those factors were themselves related to politics.

The model that places the individual Downsian citizen decision maker within a social context and explicitly includes group leaders provides a promising way of accomplishing these objectives. That model allows for predicting variations in turnout as a function of changing political preferences and contexts. Introduction of "relational goods" in the model, and allowances for the empirical shortcomings of expected utility maximization, permit clearer specification of what elites can do in order to influence levels of mass participation. Not least, this model resolves the paradox posed by Downs's account of rational abstention.

CHAPTER 5

Political Equilibrium under Group Identification

Amihai Glazer

In his classic work Anthony Downs (1957b) explains that because no one person's vote is likely to decide which candidate wins, each person will find the cost of voting to be greater than his expected benefit. Indeed, chapter 14 of *An Economic Theory of Democracy* concentrates on this issue. This point was made over two centuries ago: "As for popular suffrage, it may be further remarked that especially in large states it leads inevitably to electoral indifference, since the casting of a single vote is of no significance where there is a multitude of voters."[1] The present chapter gives one explanation for why people vote and how they vote.

The Free-Rider Problem in Voting

Since a solution to the "paradox of voting" is central to this paper, a brief review of the problem is in order. Note that a vote is decisive only if it breaks or makes a tie. Guillermo Owen and Bernard Grofman (1984) show that if a million voters are about equally split between support for two candidates then the probability that the two candidates get exactly the same number of votes is about 1 in a 1,000. If there are 1,000 voters, and if with probability 60 percent a voter supports candidate A instead of B, then the probability of a tied election is on the order of 1 in 10 billion. John Chamberlain and Michael Rothschild (1981) consider a model where no voter knows the preferences of all other voters. They show that if there are many voters then the probability that any particular voter will cast a decisive ballot is on the order of $1/(2N)$.

Others extend the analysis to consider the equilibrium behavior of rational voters. If no one other than Smith votes, Smith's vote would be decisive—

---

1. Quoted by James M. Buchanan (1974) from Hegel's *Philosophy of Right*, written in 1821.

his benefits from voting would be greater than his costs. Similarly, if, say, only one thousand persons cast ballots, there is a significant probability that any one of the ballots could be decisive; once again Smith and others like him would wish to vote. Nevertheless, Thomas R. Palfrey and Howard Rosenthal (1985) find that in a Nash equilibrium, as the size of the population increases, the proportion of persons who will vote approaches zero. The reasoning is as follows. In equilibrium there exists a cost of voting, say c^*, such that a person (in either group) intends to vote if and only if his cost of voting is less than c^*. Let $F(c)$ be the proportion of potential voters with voting costs less than c. If there are A supporters in the larger group, then in equilibrium $AF(c^*)$ will intend to vote. Similarly, $BF(c^*)$ people in the smaller group will intend to vote. The expected plurality is $AF(c^*) - BF(c^*)$. Numerical results show that any one vote is likely to be decisive only if the expected plurality is very small, say less than one thousand. Thus, if the values of A and B are significantly different, the plurality can be small (and equilibrium conditions for voting hold) only if $F(c^*)$ is very small. For very large populations therefore, the equilibrium level of turnout must be low.

Who Votes?

Downs emphasizes that a theory must explain not only why some people vote but also which people are especially likely to vote. Conventional wisdom has it that the rich are more likely to vote than the poor. In particular, Raymond E. Wolfinger and Steven J. Rosenstone (1980), basing their results on survey data, confirm the effect of income. Aggregate data, however, show much smaller effects; for example, Samuel C. Patterson and Gregory A. Caldeira (1983) find that income does not have a statistically significant effect in a regression that explains turnout in gubernatorial elections in the years 1978 and 1980. Robert S. Erikson (1981) finds that among registered voters income makes no difference at all.

Downs claims a rich person is likely to be better informed about the election and the issues and therefore sees a greater benefit from voting. Other explanations focus on the cost of voting, usually taken to be the earnings lost by going to the voting place, or else the pleasures the citizen could otherwise have derived, for example, by enjoying a more leisurely dinner. Downs claims that because the poor are poor, they can ill afford to spend their time on voting instead of earning money. The counterargument, first mentioned by Bruno S. Frey (1971), claims that the rich have a higher opportunity cost of time than the poor. Unfortunately, these theories do not predict anything other than that the rich are more likely to vote than the poor. They do not predict, for example, which candidate a voter will support.

Explanations for Voting

Downs gives one of the first explanations for voting, with his argument of its long-run participation value: if I don't vote, and others don't either, then in the long run democracy will cease to exist. The problem with this and many other explanations is also given by Downs (1957b, 276) himself: "the difficulty with such arguments is that they rationalize everything. If it is rational to vote for prestige, why is it not rational to vote so as to please one's employer or one's sweetheart? Soon all behavior whatsoever becomes rational because every act is a means to some end the actor values. To avoid this sterile conclusion, we have regarded only actions leading to strictly political or economic ends as rational." Stephen V. Stephens (1975, 914) makes a different criticism: "I am led to the conjecture that a sort of natural selection is involved, that the more lucid papers are so patently silly that many of them fail to achieve publication, leaving the field to papers in which the nonsense is at least obscure."

The richness of the explanations, however, is impressive. Much of this work extends the article by Peter C. Ordeshook and William H. Riker (1968). They suppose the act of voting yields benefits, such as the sense of fulfilling a duty, unrelated to the effects of a vote on outcomes. Some critics complain that these assumptions are arbitrary, though others are willing to accept any assumption if it leads to reasonable conclusions. A different concern is that the assumption does not contribute to an understanding of how people will vote. Does this sense of duty lead voters to prefer candidates who themselves show a sense of duty, or who once in office will reward upright citizens?

Some scholars claim that a person obtains an extra dose of utility if his vote decides the election; this benefit is above and beyond the benefits from seeing one set of policies rather than another enacted (see Strom 1975). Nicolaus T. Tideman (1985) offers the related idea of remorse: voters especially unhappy if the candidate he supported lost, and the voter could have prevented that. Melvin J. Hinich (1981) claims that the voter's utility increases if he votes for a winner, and decreases if he votes for a loser. Thomas Schwartz (1987) claims that an elected official can allocate greater benefits to districts that granted large vote shares to him. Each voter's benefit from voting would then not be the probability that his vote is decisive but instead be the increased benefits obtained by his district if the voter supported the winner.

An approach that has drawn a good deal of attention assumes that voters aim to minimize their maximum possible loss rather than to maximize utility (Ferejohn and Fiorina 1975). That is, a person considering whether or not to vote asks what is the worst possible outcome under the two possibilities. Stephens (1975) points out one logical difficulty with this argument. The worst thing that can happen to a person who votes is not the loss of a dollar or two equivalent to the time spent voting but the possibility that he will die in a traffic accident on the way to the polls. Minimax arguments would therefore argue for staying at home.

If voters are indeed so afraid of possible losses, we should also observe candidates favoring policies that entail no risk of loss to citizens. A candidate who proposed a policy that could bring a billion dollars in benefits, but that entails a small risk of a one dollar loss, could be defeated by a candidate who opposed this policy. If we found that government shows such a high degree of risk aversion, we would have increased confidence in the minimax model of voting; lesser degrees of risk aversion would cast doubt on the theory.

This theory and other theories of rational voting implicitly assume that governmental policy depends in a clear way on who wins the election. That, however, is not at all evident: the literature on Arrow's paradox, on manipulability, and on cycling all show that a voter's choice may not matter because agenda setters can manipulate things to get their own choice. Note finally that a potential voter should realize that he has imperfect information about the candidates and about the effects of the policies candidates propose. A voter should realize that he may make the wrong choice: the candidate he thinks of supporting may not be the candidate whose proposed policies would most favor the voter.

Expressive Voting

Several recent works attempt to solve the paradox of voting by indicating the motive to vote has nothing to do with affecting the outcome of an election. Murray Edelman (1964) gives a key in his view that election campaigns give "people a chance to express discontents and enthusiasms." A related line of thought is pursued by Geoffrey Brennan and Loren F. Lomasky (1985, 1987), myself (1987), Susan Feigenbaum, Lynn Kardy, and David Levy (1988), and Carole Jean Uhlaner (1989b). The former claim that "market and political preferences are different. This difference arises from the fact that the agent is decisive in market contexts . . . , whereas the agent is inherently nondecisive in large-number elections under majority rule. . . . [V]oting involves expressing a preference substantially independent of the consequences of bringing about the outcome with respect to which that preference is expressed." (Brennan and Lomasky 1987, 132). Similarly, Timur Kuran (1990) convincingly argues that social pressures may lead individuals to have private different preferences from public, and that social pressure may lead individuals to vote.

These theories would claim that blacks supported Jesse Jackson in the 1988 presidential primaries in part to express their pride, rather than solely to influence the election. Similarly, in 1968 George Wallace may have gained much of his support from people who found satisfaction in pulling a lever with his name on it; is that not a simple way of expressing their hatreds or angers? How else, except by viewing politics as expressions of emotions, can we explain why one hundred thousand people in San Diego recently signed a petition to change the name of a street from Martin Luther King Way? If people get vicarious pleasure from reading novels or seeing movies, why not from voting? In short, the behavior of people when they vote may resemble their behavior when they go to a movie or cheer for a team at a football game.

Unfortunately, these models do not predict which candidate a voter will support. And in other regards these models have implications similar to those derived from a Downsian model that assumes people have preferences over candidate positions. The critical element in extending such a theory (henceforth called the expressive voting theory) is applying it to explain other features of politics and elections. How, for example, will turnout vary with the types of candidates who run for office? Which candidates are most likely to win? What policies will they pursue?

To make the discussion concrete, suppose the angers and frustrations of potential voters concern relative status. In spirit, therefore, my analysis follows Robert H. Frank's (1985). Each of the two candidates can state with which groups in the population he identifies. Each candidate implicitly also says that groups supported by the other candidate are low status. For example, a candidate like George Wallace can praise the virtues of poor whites; a poor white who voted for Wallace might feel some pride in doing so and also get vicarious pleasure in voting against a candidate who identified with blacks. The 1983 mayoral race in Chicago, in which a black candidate (Harold Washington) was opposed by a white candidate (Bernard Epton), appears to share these characteristics. This emphasis on a candidate's supporters is in part motivated by Richard F. Fenno (1978), who calls attention to the potential divergence between a candidate's geographic constituency, electoral constituency (including primary constituency), and "inner" campaign constituency. John H. Aldrich (1983a, 1983b) revives older ideas of parties as coalitions of interests to posit that each party chooses a platform at the center of gravity of its support coalition (cf. Grofman 1982; Wittman 1983).

Let there be g income groups in the population, ranked in order of increasing income, 1 through g. All individuals within each group are identical. Consider a member of group i with income y_i. In voting for any candidate (and against the other candidate) the individual will have identified with some groups and against others. Thus, let $s_{ij} > 0$ if an individual belonging to group i voted *for* a candidate who identified with group j; $s_{ij} = 0$ otherwise. Similarly $t_{ij} > 0$ if the individual voted *against* a candidate who identified with group j; $t_{ij} = 0$ otherwise. The magnitudes of s_{ij} and t_{ij} can show the strength of a candidate's identification with different groups. The individual's utility is

$U(y_i, s_{ij} \ldots s_{ij}, t_{ij} \ldots t_{ij})$. The individual desires higher income, so $\partial U/\partial y_i > 0$. The voter likes a candidate who identifies with the voter's group, so $\partial U/\partial s_{ii} > 0$ and $\partial U/\partial t_{ii} < 0$. Finally, the voter prefers to support a candidate who does not identify with other groups, so $\partial U/s_{ij} < 0$, and $\partial U/t_{ij} > 0$ for $i \neq j$.

A person gets pleasure in voting for a candidate who identifies with the voter's group, and gets pleasure in voting against a candidate who supports a different group. We can assume either that the voter in question most dislikes groups similar to his, or that he most dislikes groups greatly different from his own. The first assumption means that $|\partial U/\partial s_{ij}|$ and $|\partial U/\partial t_{ij}|$ are greater the smaller the value of $|i - j|$: the person gets greater utility from voting against a candidate who identifies with some other group the closer that group is to the voter's own group. For an analogy, think of college football games. A Yale alumnus gets great pleasure in going to a football game that Yale wins; he enjoys a Yale victory over Harvard, which he envies, more than a victory over Dartmouth or some other lower-ranked college. Fans care about their status relative to those of close competitors, rather than about absolute status. In this chapter I initially make this assumption and then briefly examine an equilibrium in which the dislike is greatest for greatly different groups.

A person who votes will cast his ballot to maximize pleasure from the activity. Each candidate identifies with that set of groups that will bring the most votes. An example with four different income groups illustrates an equilibrium. Let the four equally sized groups be W, X, Y, and Z, with W having the highest income (see table 1). Suppose candidate A identifies with groups W and X, while candidate B identifies with groups Y and Z.

Suppose that for a voter in group i, $|\partial U/\partial s_{ii}| > |\partial U/\partial s_{ij}|$, for all j not equal to i; that is, a person cares more about an increase in his own status than about a decrease in the status of other groups. Under these conditions members of groups W and X will support candidate A; members of groups Y and Z will support candidate B. This set of identifications by the candidate is not, however, in equilibrium. (I define an equilibrium in Nash terms. Given the identifications candidate A adopts, candidate B maximizes his share of the vote by choosing the identifications described by the Nash equilibrium. Analogous statements apply for the best response for candidate A given the identi-

TABLE 1. Identification Not an Equilibrium

W	Identified with Candidate A
X	Identified with Candidate A
Y	Identified with Candidate B
Z	Identified with Candidate B

fications chosen by candidate B. Since in the worst case a candidate can tie the election by duplicating the identifications chosen by the other candidate, a Nash equilibrium must have no candidate winning less than 50 percent of the vote, so that in equilibrium the candidates are tied.)

To see that the assumed set of identifications does not represent an equilibrium, suppose candidate B identifies with groups W and Y rather than with groups Y and Z, as shown in table 2.

Members of group Y will continue to support candidate B; indeed because candidate B no longer identifies with group Z, a close competitor in status, members of group Y will increase their support for candidate B. Similarly, members of group W will prefer candidate B over candidate A: candidate A identifies with group W's close competitors, group X, whereas candidate B does not. Thus, candidate B can increase his vote by identifying with groups W and Y rather than with groups Y and Z.

Another characteristic of equilibrium is that the two candidates will not both appeal to all the same groups. To see this, suppose that initially each candidate identifies with groups W and X. Now consider a change where candidate B identifies with groups X and Z. B would win the support of group Z members and also win the support of group X members: since candidate B does not identify with group W, of whom group X members are envious, but candidate A does, group X members prefer candidate B over candidate A. In summary, candidate A would win the votes only of group W; candidate B would win the votes of groups X and Z.

Similar reasoning suggests that candidates will wish to form minimum winning coalitions. For suppose candidate A identifies with any three groups instead of with only two; to be specific suppose A supports groups W, X, and Y. Groups W and Y will resent A's identification with group X, so that a challenger who identifies with groups W and Y alone can defeat candidate A. This implies that the only equilibrium has one candidate supporting groups W and Y, and the other candidate supporting the other groups, X and Z. Such an equilibrium differs in a fundamental way from that found in the median voter model of Downs: in equilibrium the candidates will not have the same positions, and politics will not have the Tweedledum-Tweedledee characteristic.

TABLE 2. Identifications Candidate B Prefers

W	Identified with both Candidates A and B
X	Identified with Candidate A
Y	Identified with Candidate B
Z	Identified with no candidate

We can turn now to an analysis of the effects of different governmental policies on the reelection chances of an incumbent, and of the policies that an incumbent would wish to support. Recall that, unlike the rational voter model, the expressive voting model supposes that voters do not evaluate incumbents by the success of their policies. The connection between policies and electoral support is indirect: policies can change the incomes or sizes of different groups and thereby change the popularity of appeals to different groups. For example, suppose the incumbent, candidate A, can better appeal than most potential challengers to groups W and Y. One way the incumbent can increase his chances of winning reelection is to reduce the size of competing groups. Legislation extending suffrage to new immigrants, eighteen year olds, and women can have these effects.

The incumbent can further increase chances of reelection by changing the relative incomes of different groups. Suppose that candidate A identifies with groups W and Y; let candidate B identify with groups X and Z (see table 3). Consider the effects of a reduction in the incomes of group X members. The gap between groups X and Y will decline, and the gap between groups W and X will increase. My assumptions imply that members of group X will become even more concerned with expressing their dislike for group Y and vice versa. This effect would lead more group Y members to turn out to vote for candidate A, and more group X members to turn out to vote for candidate B. The decline in group X's income causes groups W and X to be more distant from each other, and therefore less concerned with expressing their dislike of the other group; this effect will cause a decline in turnout among members of these two groups. The total effect of a decrease in the incomes of group X members can therefore be to increase the total share of the vote that candidate A receives. Policies can affect the incumbent's electoral chances even though, by assumption, no voters judge candidates by their policies or by their performance in office.

Reasonable assumptions also lead to the conclusion that under expressive voting close elections will see high turnout. In terms of the model presented here, an election will not be close if one of the candidates identifies with only a few groups, or with a set of groups that does not appeal to many voters. For

TABLE 3. Candidates Appeal to Different Groups

W	Identified with Candidate A
X	Identified with Candidate B
Y	Identified with Candidate A
Z	Identified with Candidate B

example, if candidate A identifies with groups W and Y, while candidate B identifies only with group Z, then candidate A will win overwhelmingly with the votes of two groups against the votes of only one group for candidate B. In addition, turnout will be low because members of groups W and Y cannot vent their anger at group X by voting against candidate B (B does not identify with that group). Members of group X can vent their anger at groups W and Y by voting against candidate A (who identifies with groups W and Y), but they would have even greater reason to vote if candidate B had identified with their group. Thus, if candidate B identifies with group X in addition to group Z, turnout among members of groups W, X, and Y will all increase, and candidate B will get a larger share of the vote (the election will be closer). Similar analyses for other combinations of groups that the candidates support yield similar conclusions: high turnout will be associated with close elections.

Let's consider the alternative assumption next: voters care most about a candidate supporting groups that differ widely from theirs (versus supporting groups similar to theirs). For simplicity, let's suppose that voter turnout does not vary with different identifications adopted by the candidates. Who the voters prefer, however, will vary. Consider again the example of the four groups: W, X, Y, and Z. Suppose that initially we have the situation depicted in table 1.

Suppose that instead candidate A identifies with group Y and drops identification with group W. Since B identifies with Z, members of W will continue to vote for candidate A, as will members of group X. That is, candidate A can increase his vote share by dropping support for W and identifying with Y; table 1 thus does not depict an equilibrium. A possible equilibrium is shown in table 4. In this table, though candidate A does not identify with group W, its members support A because candidate B identifies with group Y, which is greatly disliked by group W.

Here, then, candidate A would obtain the support of groups W and X, and candidate B the support of groups Y and Z. If, instead, candidate A also identifies with group W, A would lose some support from members of group X. And if A identifies with group Y, A would lose the support of group W. Note that this equilibrium has some of the characteristics associated with the me-

TABLE 4. Equilibrium when Voters Care about Distant Groups

W	Identified with no candidate
X	Identified with Candidate A
Y	Identified with Candidate B
Z	Identified with no candidate

dian voter result in the Downsian model: the candidates appeal to voters in the middle of the population and eschew appeals to the extremes. The reasons for the result, however, differ.

Note several other implications of the theory of expressive voting, implications that are consistent with the facts. A person motivated by psychological gratifications, rather than by the desire to affect electoral outcomes, will vote even if there is only one candidate, and even if he expects the election to be a landslide. For similar reasons, turnout will not decrease after the result of an election is known. Indeed, contrary to predictions of the rational voter model, West Coast turnout did not decline when television networks in 1980 clearly predicted the national winner in a presidential election several hours before the polls closed there (see Epstein and Strom 1981; Carter 1984).

Racial Voting

Expressive voting can be applied to racism. A good deal of evidence suggests that white voters in the United States consider race when deciding how to vote. Edward G. Carmines and James A. Stimson (1989) show that voter images of the national political parties track changes in the racial issue positions of party activists. Robert Huckfeldt and Carol Kohfeld (1989) show that as black support for the Democratic national party increased, white support for that party's presidential candidate declined. Milton Lodge and others (1985, 1986) show that party images have changed so that the terms *Democrat* and *liberal* in part connote "problack." Other authors argue that even though white support for overt segregation has declined dramatically, white behavior still reflects what David O. Sears and Donald R. Kinder call "symbolic racism" (McConahay 1982; Sears and Kinder 1971; Sears, Hensler, and Speer 1979).

Another test of expressive voting consists of asking whether an increase in the number of blacks in a congressional district leads whites to oppose a liberal candidate supported by blacks. Examining congressional elections in southern states in 1982 shows that Republicans were more likely to win election from districts with a 30 percent to 40 percent black population than from districts with a 20 percent to 30 percent black population (41 percent versus 26 percent of congressmen were Republican). Moreover, in 1982, for both Democratic and Republican congressmen in the South, mean Americans for Democratic Action (ADA) scores showed congressmen to be more liberal in districts with 20–30 percent black population than in districts with a 30–40 percent black population. (The ADA scores were fifty-two and forty-four respectively for southern Democrats; fifteen and four for southern Republicans.) Of course, districts with more than a 40 percent black population overwhelmingly elected liberal Democrats (by southern standards).

Similar effects appeared in the 1988 Democratic presidential primary. In that year Jesse Jackson, a black, obtained about 90 percent of the black vote. The data show that the fraction of whites who supported Jackson was greater the smaller the fraction of blacks in that state. The CBS/*New York Times* poll had 1988 exit poll data on whites who voted in primary elections in twenty-two states. I used these to estimate a linear regression in which the dependent variable is the percentage of whites who voted for Jackson in a particular state, and the explanatory variable is the percentage of blacks in that state. I find

Percentage for Jackson = 16.65 − 0.41 percent black

The t-statistic on the percentage black variable is a highly significant 3.64; the correlation coefficient for the regression is 0.62. This regression says that, on average, a 1 percentage point increase in the proportion of blacks in a state's population is associated with a drop of about a 0.5 percentage point in the support of white voters for Jesse Jackson. The same relationship holds for southern states alone.

The CBS/*New York Times* poll also had election poll data on white voters in twenty-three states for the 1988 general election. Using these data I again estimated a linear regression in which the dependent variable is the percentage of whites who voted for the Democratic candidate, Michael Dukakis, in a particular state, and the explanatory variable is the percentage of blacks in that state. The results are

Percentage for Dukakis = 48.7 − 0.78 percent black

The correlation coefficient is 0.59, the t-statistic is a highly significant 3.3; a dummy variable for the South is not statistically significant. Throughout the country, a 1 percent increase in black population is associated with a drop of over a 0.75 percentage point in white support for Dukakis in 1988.

The effects are not much different from those in the 1968 presidential election between Hubert Humphrey, George Wallace, and Richard Nixon. Using a large sample survey, Gerald C. Wright (1977) finds that the probability a white in a southern state would have voted for Wallace is an increasing function of the proportion of blacks in the voter's country and state. This follows on the demonstration by V. O. Key, Jr., that racial concerns are overwhelmingly important in explaining southern politics, that black population concentrations explain some of the differences in the intensity of Jim Crow laws among deep South and border South states, and that black concentrations predict which countries were prosecession at the time of the Civil War. The link between the vote for Wallace and the percentage of blacks appears for the South as a whole and for counties in North Carolina if an ecological regression is used (Grofman, Glazer, and Handley 1988). Huckfeldt and Kohfeld (1989) give confirming evidence.

Racial voting, or similar ethnic and linguistic divisions, also appear outside the United States. Witness the English-French split in Canada, the popularity of Le Pen's anti-Arab stands in France, or the anti-Turk demonstrations in Bulgaria following the popular revolution of 1989.

Conclusion

The expressive voting model is not complete, it has not been subjected to empirical test, and it cannot explain some important phenomena (for example, why survey data show that the rich are especially likely to vote, while cross-section data show that turnout in states with poor residents does not differ much from turnout in states with wealthy residents). But other theories are spectacularly unsuccessful in explaining voting. Theories that at first appear unreasonable are worthy of some study when other theories fail.

CHAPTER 6

Is Turnout the Paradox That Ate Rational Choice Theory?

Bernard Grofman

Morris P. Fiorina (1989) has recently suggested that a very good argument can be made for the claim that "turnout is the paradox that ate rational choice theory." The motivation for this claim is the belief that the two most commonly derived predictions from models of instrumental rationality—(1) that few if any voters will vote and (2) that turnout will be higher the closer the election—are contradicted, in the first case, and either contradicted or at least not strongly supported, in the second case, when one looks at the empirical evidence. While many authors have sought to modify the standard Downsian analysis of turnout to avoid the embarrassment of its repudiation by the facts (e.g., by asserting that voters minimax regret, or by introducing consumption benefits or expressive benefits to voting, or by modeling turnout as a group-centered process where entrepreneurial group leaders bargain with politicians using turnout as their currency: see reviews in Grofman 1987; chap. 5, this volume; chap. 4, this volume), virtually everyone who has written on this topic has accepted the view that the Downsian model of turnout is fundamentally at variance with the facts. Moreover, numerous critics of rational choice (beginning with Barry 1964) have asserted that the rational choice approach to turnout can only be rescued by heroic measures (such as the introduction of citizen duty) that do not fit easily within a rational choice framework.

In this chapter I advance the heretical views (1) that Downs and the authors who have followed him (including myself, in earlier work) have been fundamentally wrong in what they thought a rational choice model of turnout was capable of predicting, (2) that most attempts to test rational choice–based predictions of aggregate voting behavior have been fundamentally flawed, and (3) that, when we limit the predictions of a rational choice approach to turnout

---

I am indebted to Ziggy Bates for manuscript typing and to Dorothy Gormick for bibliographic assistance. This research was partially funded by the University of California, Irvine, Interdisciplinary Focused Research Program in Public Choice. This paper draws on earlier work done jointly with Amihai Glazer, especially Glazer and Grofman 1992.

to ones that reasonably follow from its fundamental premises, a rational choice model does quite well.

What Can We Expect of a Rational Choice Model of Turnout?

If rational choice models are taken to require us to assume that the only motivation governing individual behavior is self-interest, narrowly conceived, then it is not surprising that rational choice models often yield results that are ludicrously at variance with the facts (people do salute the flag when no one is looking). The view that a rational choice model requires that the *only* element to be allowed in a voter's utility function is the expected short-run *instrumental* benefit from voting is like saying that the only way we could use rational choice models to predict eating behavior is to limit people's motivations for their food choices to a *single* parameter—for example, an instrumentally rational choice of a consumption bundle that maximizes expected longevity. If so, there would be no accounting for chocolate![1]

Even more important, it is appropriate to think about rational choice models in the context of accounting for changes in choices, rather than choices, per se. Rational choice models cannot explain why, ceteris paribus, the French drink more wine than the Germans and the Germans drink more beer than do the French, either. They can, however, predict that wine consumption and beer consumption in both countries will be affected by changes in the relative prices of the two commodities. Moreover, while rational choice models appear to do poorly in predicting who will vote in a given election, so do all other models other than those that posit that people who aren't registered won't vote (Erickson 1981; Wolfinger, 1993) and those that recognize that the single best predictor of whether or not someone will vote is whether or not they have voted before (Barbara Norrander, personal communication, 1985).

What is the Expected Relationship between Turnout and Political Competition?

The extensive empirical literature on the relation between turnout and political competition universally assumes that the Downsian (rational actor) model of voting implies that turnout should be higher the smaller the expected plurality of the winning candidate (See, e.g., Downs 1957b; Ferejohn and Fiorina 1975; Foster 1984; Gray 1976; Grofman 1983; Patterson and Caldeira 1983;

---

[1]. I am indebted to my colleague, A Wuffle (personal communication, December 2, 1991) for this example. Wuffle also insists, more generally, that one should never do anything for only one reason. The more reasons one has, the less likely one is to be disappointed.

Settle and Abrams 1976; Tollison, Crain, and Paulter 1975). This conclusion appears to follow from the assumption of the Downsian model that a person's expected benefit from voting is

$$PU + (B - C), \tag{1}$$

where P is the probability that a shift of a single vote will change the election outcome, U is the utility attached by the voter to electing the candidate of his or her choice, C is the noninstrumental cost of voting (e.g., time spent at the polls), and B is the noninstrumental benefit of voting (e.g., "psychic" satisfaction for expressing solidarity with a candidate or position). A rational person would vote if this expected benefit is positive. It would appear that a person who expects the election to be close will assign P a high value and, thus, ceteris paribus, will be more likely to vote. Thus, for the electorate as a whole, an election expected to be close should induce a high level of turnout. The additional assumption that the actual results of an election correlate with people's prior expectations about the results yields the prediction that turnout will be higher the closer the election results.

There are four key problems with this analysis. First, more-sophisticated equilibrium analyses of rational voting behavior (e.g., Palfrey and Rosenthal 1984, 1985; Owen and Grofman 1984; Ledyard 1984), in which voters are seen as involved in a game where mutual expectations matter rather than simply solving a problem in expected utility maximizing, give rise to a more complex picture of the link between turnout and closeness. The models in Ledyard 1984 and Palfrey and Rosenthal 1984, 1985, give rise to the result that, in equilibrium, all elections will be close, regardless of the distribution of preferences within the population. The usual interpretation of the Downsian model assumes that P is exogenously given, whereas these authors' expectational model leads to the conclusion that the value of P depends on the strategic behavior of potential voters and will always be close to one-half. Gordon Tullock (1967, 110) may have been the first person to realize that the Downsian model does not actually predict zero turnout even when costs are high.[2]

Second, as Amihai Glazer and I have shown elsewhere (Glazer and Grofman 1992), a simple relation between turnout and closeness may not hold once we consider the reasons why some elections are closer than others. Consider an election in which most constituents see little difference between

---

2. These models do say that turnout will be higher the more evenly split the preferences are of the citizens; indeed, Thomas R. Palfrey and Howard Rosenthal show that in equilibrium the level of turnout is about double the number of potential voters who prefer the less popular candidate. Thus, turnout should be higher if only 51 percent of the constituents prefer the Democratic candidate than if 70 percent prefer the Democratic candidate.

the candidates: the value of $U_a - U_b$ will be small, and the probability that any one person prefers the Democratic candidate is about one-half. For any given level of total turnout the probability, P, that any one vote is decisive is larger the more evenly divided is the electorate in its preferences. Thus, in terms of equation (1) a race between similar candidates makes P a large number and U a small one. In contrast, suppose that all, or almost all, voters agree that one of the candidates is better than the other; the better one may be viewed as more effective or as more in tune with the voters' views. The election is therefore likely to give the winner (almost certainly the better candidate) a large plurality. For a given level of turnout this means that the probability, P, that any one vote is decisive, is low. To say that voters see one candidate as better than the other is to say that they think the value of U is large. Combining these two effects implies that the value of PU used in equation (1) can be either larger or smaller when voters see little difference between the candidates.

Thus, turnout in close elections (which under our assumptions usually occur when most constituents are indifferent about the candidates) may be either higher or lower than turnout in landslide elections (which will occur when most constituents agree that one candidate is far better than the other). Similarly, Glazer and Grofman (1992), consider what happens when voters with different preferences have different costs of voting. Imagine a snowstorm that increases the cost of voting. Suppose that, other things equal, rich people can drive to the polling booth and need not take public transportation, so that bad weather increases their voting costs by less than it increases the costs for the poor. Suppose also that the rich and the poor prefer different candidates. Inclement weather would then depress turnout in total and depress the turnout of the rich by less than that of the poor. How turnout varies with the margin of victory thus depends on the relative numbers of rich and poor people. We make the point that, in general, we simply cannot predict what the relationship between turnout and election closeness will be at the aggregate level.

Third, in most states, it is impossible to vote without being registered, and the decision to register is usually made far in advance of any given election (Wolfinger 1993, forthcoming). In instrumental terms the decision to register must therefore be viewed in the context of the *potential* to influence *many* future elections and, like the chip in a poker game sometimes required for "openers," represents a decision that one still wishes to leave open the option of staying in the game.[3] Moreover, insofar as registration indicates some degree of interest in the electoral process, and insofar as the costs involved in

---

3. Alternatively, as Julie Withers (personal communication, 1990) put it: "If you don't vote, then you're not allowed to bitch at the outcome."

registering are usually greater than the costs in voting, a rational choice approach suggests that a high proportion of those who are registered (a self-selected set who has already surmounted the major hurdle to voting) ought to vote—as, of course, they do.

Fourth, the models that fail to find a link between turnout and electoral closeness are, in my view, improperly specified largely because of their failure to take into account a long enough time frame and to recognize that turnout variations will often be more a function of long-run than of short-run election-specific factors. Moreover, the models suffer from a variety of methodological problems, some quite severe.

Four approaches have been commonly used to test what is taken to be the Downsian prediction of the relation between turnout and political competition.

1. Cross-sectional analysis of the link between observed election closeness (as a post hoc measure of expected election closeness) and voter turnout across different political units (such as states) for a given type of election.
2. Correlation between a game-theoretic measure of power to affect outcomes (such as the Banzhaf Index, based on the posterior likelihood of casting a decisive vote derived from observed election closeness) and actual turnout.
3. Longitudinal analysis of the relation between observed election closeness (again used as a surrogate for perceived election closeness) and voter turnout in the same political unit (such as a state) for a given type of election.
4. Analysis of survey data to see whether or not potential voters who believe a given election will be close are, ceteris paribus, more likely to vote.

Analyses of the types described commonly run regressions in which the dependent variable is the rate of turnout among voters, and the critical explanatory variable (or at least one of the critical variables) is a measure of the likelihood that any one vote will decide the election. The Downsian model is considered to be supported if the coefficient on this explanatory variable is significantly positive. The null hypothesis is that closeness and turnout are not related. The empirical evidence is mixed (see Foster 1984 for a useful survey).

I claim that each of these approaches suffers from methodological flaws, and none represents a proper test of the Downsian model. A general problem with the first three types of aggregate-level analyses is that the claim that actual election closeness is a good surrogate for perceived election closeness is not well supported by survey data (see Uhlaner and Grofman 1986; Wolfinger 1993, forthcoming). However, each of the methods has other, even more severe, drawbacks.

Cross-sectional studies

Carroll B. Foster (1984) uses a cross-sectional approach to examine turnout in the fifty states for the presidential elections in the years 1968, 1972, 1976, and 1980. Foster finds that the critical explanatory variable—the fraction of the vote received by the winning candidate in a particular year in a particular state—has a significantly positive effect on turnout in 1968, a significantly negative effect in 1972, and an insignificant effect in 1976 and 1980. Gubernatorial elections appear to show stronger results. Samuel C. Patterson and Gregory A. Caldeira (1983) examine turnout for gubernatorial elections in 1978 and 1980; they find that the closer the election the higher the turnout. Robert D. Tollison, W. Mark Crain, and Paul Paulter (1975) find that for the 1970 gubernatorial elections turnout is greater if the election is close.

The cross-sectional approach, however, suffers from two major difficulties. First, and most importantly, it can give rise to an ecological fallacy when the search for the relation between turnout and closeness uses states as units of observation. In particular, in comparing states, we find that turnout is far lower in the old one-party South, but that the link between closeness and turnout in cross-sectional studies has diminished as the South has become more competitive and as barriers to voting by southern blacks fell in the mid 1960s. Similarly, the partisan composition of a state's constituency may affect turnout. Thus, because, in general, Republicans are more likely to vote than are Democrats, a state with many Republicans will usually see a higher turnout than a state with few Republicans. A researcher who compares turnout in states in which Republicans are a small minority to turnout in states in which Republicans are almost a majority will therefore find a positive correlation between turnout and closeness. Jonathan Silberman and Gary C. Durden (1975) introduce controls for demographic differences in congressional districts in the two election years they look at, 1962 and in 1970, that, in principle, vitiate this criticism, but their study (and similar studies using multivariate methods with cross-sectional data) potentially suffers from an even more-damaging flow.

Cross-sectional studies that look at a single type of election (indeed *any* studies of turnout that look only at a single election) commit what A Wuffle (1984) calls the "two front teeth" fallacy—the failure to recognize that, in any given election, voters choose candidates for a variety of offices (and often vote on referenda as well). Because different races in a given jurisdiction may differ in how close they are expected to be, a study that focuses on an election for a single office will lead to a misreading of the effects of close races on turnout. Indeed, even Foster's (1984) otherwise excellent reanalysis of alternative models fails to fully recognize this fact. Moreover, it is troubling when a study of *gubernatorial* races finds closeness related to turnout in 1980 (Patterson and Caldeira 1983), but a study of *presidential* elections (Foster 1984) finds no such effect in 1980. Obviously, in many states voter turnout could have been affected by the closeness in either type of contest—as well as in other types of contests.

Game-Theoretic Power Scores

Studies of the relation between the electoral power of a jurisdiction and its level of turnout in presidential elections (e.g., Kau and Rubin 1976, 1977; Collins 1981) suffer from the same difficulties identified here, but they also have other problems. Game-theoretic considerations argue that differences in the size of each state's electoral vote mean that in some states the probability that a particular voter will decide the national (and not just the state) election will differ from that probability in other states. This has two implications: voters in some states will have a greater benefit from voting, and candidates will have a greater incentive to attempt to influence votes in some states than in others. Empirical studies of turnout in presidential elections have focused on the first effect and ignored the second.

Thus, consider one of the fifty states in the United States that has a large electoral vote in presidential elections. This state is especially important for a candidate to win, and therefore the candidate will spend more time in it. But it may well be that a citizen is more likely to vote the more this individual has heard about the race, and therefore that turnout will be higher in that state. Turnout and closeness will therefore be correlated because of the candidate's strategies; the correlation need have nothing to do with a potential voter's calculation of the probability that his or her vote will be decisive. The electoral college analysis of Richard J. Cebula and Dennis R. Murphy (1980) takes a somewhat different tack—but one that creates problems of its own. They find that turnout votes are lower in states with a high proportion of Democratic control and attribute it to free-rider behavior. Unfortunately, there are other demographic factors at work that suggest a plausible alternative model. In particular, turnout is much lower in the South.

Survey Data

An alternative approach to studying the relation between turnout and closeness uses survey data: ask people whether or not they expect the election to be close and also ask them whether or not they intend to vote. Support for the

Downsian hypothesis would then appear to consist of a positive correlation between individuals' intention of voting and their expectations about the closeness of the election. Unfortunately, survey data can yield misleading results about the behavior of voters. The difficulty appears when people's expectations about the election results are correlated with their electoral preferences.

Two methods can be used in survey research. One way to use survey data is to test whether, on average, turnout is higher when voters expect the election to be close (e.g., Ordeshook and Riker 1968). Another way is to correlate the beliefs of each respondent about the closeness of a forthcoming election with the respondent's intentions of voting. The problem with these approaches is that turnout and expected closeness can be correlated for reasons that may have nothing to do with the incentives to vote.[4]

Let us posit that three types of persons vote in any given election—those who usually vote, those who often abstain but who this time prefer the Democratic candidate, and those who often abstain but who this time prefer the Republican candidate. Consider a jurisdiction in which Republicans are usually a minority, but let the Republican candidate in the given election be uncommonly effective or attractive, so that those people who usually abstain but who now vote disproportionately favor the Republican candidate. Persons who are asked whether or not they believe the election will be close must form some estimate of the behavior of others. Many people probably attribute to others feelings similar to their own. Persons who find the Republican candidate uncommonly attractive may well think that others find that candidate uncommonly attractive as well and that other citizens who, like them, often abstain will turn out this time to vote for the Republican. Given these beliefs the respondent would expect the election to have a high turnout and the winner to have a small plurality (since the respondent thinks that Republicans are usually a minority, but that in this election others will also find the Republican uncommonly attractive). Persons who usually abstain but who this time prefer the Democratic candidate will show the opposite opinion—they think that others will also prefer the Democratic candidate, and that therefore the Democratic candidate will win an unusually large proportion of the vote. Since, however, by assumption, turnout among Republicans in the given election is unusually high, the usual Democratic majority will be atypically small, the election results will be unusually close, and the data will show that, on average, persons who turn out in this election believe that it will be closer than

---

4. Glazer and I (1992) specify models in which high turnout will be associated with close elections because the variance in the proportion of persons who vote for a particular candidate is smaller the larger the sample size. We refer the reader to the discussion of this relatively esoteric point.

usual. Finally, persons who are not motivated to vote may think that, as usual, the Democratic candidate will easily win. We would therefore find that on average those persons who do not intend to vote expect the election to be won by a large (Democratic) majority.

Combining these effects we conclude that the data will show that turnout is higher among persons who expect the election to be close. The reason, however, for this correlation lies in the ways voters form their expectations and has nothing to do with a Downsian calculus that considers the possible decisiveness of a vote.

The opposite relation between turnout and closeness can also hold. Suppose, as before, that in the particular election the Republican candidate is unusually attractive. But, in contrast to the previous story, let Republicans normally be a majority in the district. A Republican who votes will likely believe that other Republicans will vote as well, and therefore that the election will be a landslide. In contrast, a Republican who does not vote is likely to believe that other Republicans will not and therefore believes that the election will be close. Republican respondents would thus exhibit a negative correlation between turnout and beliefs about the closeness of the election. Democratic respondents would show the opposite effect: a Democrat who intends to vote believes other Democrats will turn out as well and therefore that the election will be closer than usual. Since by assumption there are more Republicans than Democrats in the jurisdiction, the data will show that, on average, those people who intend to vote also think that the election results will show a large plurality for the (Republican) winner.

The fertile mind can imagine other possibilities that lead to different correlations between turnout and closeness when survey data are analyzed. The point of our discussion is not to argue in favor of any particular correlation. Rather, it shows that assumptions about the ways voters form *expectations* can affect the correlation between turnout and closeness. Both positive and negative correlations can appear even if no voter considers the likelihood that his or her vote will be decisive when deciding whether or not to vote.

Longitudinal Studies

In a longitudinal study Virginia Gray (1976) concludes that if one examines the same state over time, rather than different states at the same time, the relation between turnout and closeness disappears. In contrast, Russell F. Settle and Buron A. Abrams (1976) find in their time-series study of all presidential elections over the period 1868–1972 that turnout is higher the closer the election. Reanalyzing the data of Wolfram and Foster (1981), Foster (1984, 685) also finds a link between an *ex ante* measure of expected closeness and turnout but argues that the statistical link may be dominated by the southern effect (that is, legislative imbalance has historically been higher, and turnout lower, in southern states).

In our view the key problem with existing longitudinal studies (with the exception of Settle and Abrams 1976) is that they do not study a sufficiently long time period. A link between competition and turnout is most likely to be found by comparing turnout in states before and after they experienced a shift in the degree of partisan competition that is both long lasting and substantial. Thus, as the South became less Democratic and more competitive, we would expect an increase in turnout relative to previous levels of turnout, at least once we control for the secular downtrend in the national average. Indeed, this has occurred (see Stanley 1987, 14–15, figs. 5 and 6; cf. Alt 1994, forthcoming).

Other Predictions of a Neo-Downsian Approach to Turnout

Looking at the evidence about the factors that affect voter participation in the aggregate, and taking a longitudinal rather than a cross-sectional perspective, I believe rational choice predictions do quite well. For example, as the Democratic primary declined in significance in southern elections as *the* decisive election, turnout levels in the primary (even among Democratic voters) declined relative to turnout in the general election. Similarly, the enfranchisement of blacks in the South in the 1960s triggered a corresponding countermobilization in the turnout rates of white voters relative to those of blacks in those jurisdictions where there was a black threat and realistic potential for a white counterresponse (see Alt 1994, forthcoming). Moreover, it is worth restating the obvious points that, ceteris paribus, turnout is lower when the weather is bad, when the barriers to registration are steep, and in elections whose outcomes few care about.[5] Furthermore, if we compare turnout in presidential election years to that in nonpresidential years, we see a marked and consistent sawtooth pattern. Indeed, even within a ballot there are significant variations in which posts people bother to vote for—with turnout dropping off significantly as we go toward offices at the bottom of the ballot (a phenomenon known as roll-off). Also, extremely high-intensity contests where there is a realistic potential for a change in control that would dramatically shift power relationships can mobilize voters—for example, the election in which Harold Washington was elected Chicago's first black mayor (Kleppner 1985). Similarly, in Louisiana in 1991, more than sixty-four thousand persons registered to vote in the final two days before the close of

---

5. Raymond E. Wolfinger (1993, forthcoming) makes these points, and reminds us that most *registered* voters do vote.

registration for the November gubernatorial primary in that state, "most apparently for or against the candidacy of [former Ku Klux Klan member] David Duke" ("Lousiana Gubernatorial Primary Result" 1991). Conversely, when the potential for major change disappears (or when politics is routinized), turnout is reduced. For example, after Jesse Jackson was not nominated by the Democratic party in 1988, the majority of black voters newly registered during the primary campaign did not bother to vote in the general election (Martin P. Wattenberg, personal communication, 1991).

All of these phenomena can be accounted for as straightforward predictions of a rational choice approach to turnout that seeks to explain variations across elections.[6] To neglect the accuracy of such commonsense predictions is to mischaracterize the empirical evidence about the utility of a rational choice perspective! As is apparent, the approach to turnout I advocate is one that makes no grandiose claims to explain everything but does what microeconomic models customarily do best—namely, account for change at the margin.

---

6. Regarding the importance of sensitivity to variations across elections, I might also note that recent work (Niemi, Whitten, and Franklin 1991) shows that, in multicandidate contests in the 1987 British general election, when we confine ourselves only to those electoral situations where there are strong incentives to vote tactically and to those voters who have such incentives, a significantly large proportion of the British electorate votes tactically, that is, against the party or candidate who would otherwise be their first choice in favor of a candidate who might be seen as having a better chance of being elected or in favor of a party that is seen as likely nationally to go underrepresented. Similarly, the recent concern with divided party rule in the United States at the congressional and presidential levels has uncovered evidence that a very substantial portion of the electorate prefers that Congress and the presidency be in the hands of different parties (Jacobson 1990).

Part 3
Spatial Models of Party and Candidate Competition

CHAPTER 7

The Spatial Model and Elections

John Ferejohn

If it had made no other contribution to our thinking about politics, Anthony Downs's *An Economic Theory of Democracy* would be widely and justly acclaimed for introducing and expositing the spatial theory of electoral competition. This theory not only provided the basis for the development of formal models of electoral politics—specifically for a unification of a theory of voting behavior and a theory of electoral competition within the same model—but it also transformed the way that empirical researchers and even casual observers think and talk about electoral politics. It became common to try to account for the fortunes of candidates by referring to their "locations" in an issue space relative to the distribution of voter preferences. Indeed—and this is the acid test of the acceptance of a theory—as it became clear that various of the "predictions" of the spatial theory were not actualized in data from real elections, researchers responded by trying to improve measurement and observation technology, or by refining the theory, rather than by jettisoning the spatial theory as a whole.

The spatial metaphor has by now become such a common and powerful way of portraying electoral competition that students and journalists unselfconsciously depict electoral phenomena in its terms, without recognizing either its limitations or its foundational assumptions. But in his original introduction of the spatial model Downs is actually quite cautious with regard to the applicability of the spatial theory to actual elections. He spends a good deal of effort and space in his book examining the conditions under which electoral competition could be understood in the terms of the spatial model. Specifically, he tries to develop a theory in which parties compete for office by making promises and voters base their votes on a comparison of these promises.

This chapter was originally a paper presented at the conference on "An Economic Theory of Democracy in Thirty-Year Perspective," University of California, Irvine, October 28–29, 1989. While holding all blameless, I wish to thank Geoffrey Garrett, Judy Goldstein, Jim Morrow, and Barry Weingast for their comments on the paper.

In this chapter I explore an issue that is crucial to the applicability of the spatial model of elections: the question of whether or not, within the spatial model, campaign platforms can actually have predictive or informational value for the voter. Obviously, unless platforms contain information as to what candidates would do in office, it would not be rational for voters to base their behavior on them. In this sense, the spatial model rests on the assumption that campaign platforms are useful guides to the future behavior of politicians. I show that it is by no means obvious that platforms can serve this function required of them by the spatial approach.

The Spatial Theory of Elections

In the spatial theory of elections, candidates, who care only about enjoying office, announce policies that they promise to implement upon taking office. These policies correspond to points in an issue space. Voters are assumed to be "policy oriented" in the sense of caring only about the policy that is implemented following the election, and to have well-behaved preferences.[1] Moreover, we assume that there are exactly two candidates for office and therefore no possibility of entry by third candidates. In effect, then, the "pure" theory of spatial competition conceives of candidate competition as a two-person, zero-sum, symmetric game.[2]

For symmetric games, if x is an equilibrium strategy for one player, it must also be an equilibrium strategy for the other player. Thus, if there are any equilibria in a spatial competition game, there must be "convergent" equilibria where both candidates play the same strategy. If there is a mixed strategy equilibrium, then there must be a convergent equilibrium at which both candidates announce the same *platforms*. Moreover, again by symmetry, at any equilibrium, both candidates must have an expected payoff of zero.

In a one-dimensional space with voters distributed according to a density function, following the seminal arguments of Harold Hotelling and Duncan

---

1. The usual assumptions are that voters have preferences that are representable by quasi-concave, differentiable utility functions.

2. Since the candidates care only about obtaining, without loss of generality, we may scale the payoffs so that the candidate that wins gets a payoff of 1, while the loser gets -1. We denote the payoff to candidate one of announcing platform x, while candidate two announces platform y, as $P(x,y)$.

$$P(x,y) = -P(y,x)$$

Spatial competition games also have infinitely many strategies, and on the space of pure strategy pairs, the payoff function is discontinuous. In such games it is hard to guarantee the existence of equilibria. Gerald H. Kramer proves an existence theorem for games that are similar to these in Kramer 1978.

Black, Downs shows that there will always be a position—the position of the median voter—that cannot be defeated by any other in a majority vote and that both parties will, therefore, "converge" on it. Thus, in this case there is a pure strategy equilibrium in the spatial competition game. This equilibrium has the property that each voter is indifferent about the two candidates and that the election is a tie. Most importantly, in this case, electoral competition produces an outcome that is functionally connected to the distribution of voter preferences. This is the familiar Downsian analysis of two-party competition.[3]

A few years after the appearance of Downs's book, analysts began wondering if theory of two-party competition could be extended to multidimensional issue spaces. In effect, this amounts to asking whether or not spatial competition games on multidimensional spaces could be expected to have pure strategy equilibria. Beginning with the work of Otto A. Davis and Melvin J. Hinich, an impressive literature grew up that centered on this question. Over the ensuing two decades, a number of powerful and important results were found that indicated how this question can be answered. Without giving details, I briefly sketch these developments here. First, the convergence result—that both parties adopt the same issue position—will obtain only if the distribution of voter preferences is symmetric in a certain sense. The results of Charles R. Plott and others characterize these conditions and, essentially, suggest that they are very difficult to satisfy.[4] Whereas the convergence property always holds in one-dimensional spaces, it holds in two-dimensional spaces only for very unusual distributions of preference. Thus, in multidimensional spatial competition, if there are any equilibria, they will almost always be in mixed strategies.

Second, using a somewhat more restrictive set of assumptions on preferences, Richard D. McKelvey found that,[5] when the convergence result fails—when there is no policy proposal that both candidates urge in equilibrium—every platform in the space may be contained in the smallest "top cycle" on the space.[6] This implies that any platform, x, can be reached from any other in

---

3. In order to ensure uniqueness of equilibria wherever possible, we assume throughout that there is an odd number of voters or that the number of voters corresponds to a continuous density on an interval.
4. Plott 1967.
5. McKelvey 1976.
6. Let M stand for the strict majority rule relation. We write xMy in case x beats y by a majority vote. We write that xNy in a set A, if there is a sequence of alternatives, $z_1, z_2, \ldots z_k$ contained in A, such that $x = z_1$, $y = z_k$, and $z_i M z_{i+1}$ for each i. Then, a set A is a cycle if, for each pair of alternatives, x,y, contained in it, xNy in A. A is a top cycle if there is no alternative, x, such that xMy for all y in A.

finitely many steps. From this point of view, it might appear, therefore, that virtually any platform might be announced in some mixed strategy equilibrium. This turns out to be false.

Let $P(x,y)$ stand for the proposition of the electorate that prefers platform x to platform y. Then, we say that x (weakly) dominates y if $P(x,z)$ is at least as great as $P(y,z)$ for all z, with strict inequality holding for at least one z. McKelvey and Peter C. Ordeshook show that the set of platforms that could be announced with positive probability in some mixed strategy equilibrium is confined to the set of weakly undominated platforms.[7] This set is contained in the set of Pareto–optimal outcomes and is usually significantly smaller than this set. Indeed, an argument of the sort reported by myself, McKelvey, and Edward Packel establishes that the set of strategies that can be played with positive probability can be shown to be small whenever the distribution of preferences "nearly" has a pure strategy equilibrium.[8] Thus, in this sense, spatial competition can be expected to produce relatively restricted outcomes.

These results depend, of course, on the hypothesis that voters are policy oriented—that they care only about which policy is implemented after the election—and that candidate platforms credibly promise postelection policy. The remainder of this chapter investigates the plausibility of these assumptions.

The Paradox of Spatial Models of Electoral Competition

At the heart of the spatial theory of elections is a paradox:[9] in general, if voters behave according to the assumptions of the spatial model and make their choice among candidates for office based on a comparison of their platforms, successful candidates will not rationally implement these platforms once they are in office, so that voters would have been irrational to have based their decisions on a comparison of platforms. Thus, it seems irrational to behave according to the assumptions of the model.

Downs presents this paradox in chapter 4 of his book. In that chapter, he develops the justly famous "coalition of minorities" argument, which establishes that in almost all cases in a multidimensional setting any platform can be defeated in a majority vote by some other platform. Thus, incumbents, who must defend their policies, will always lose and therefore will not have an

---

7. McKelvey and Ordeshook 1976.
8. Ferejohn, McKelvey, and Packel 1984.
9. This is not, of course, the only paradox in Downs's voting theory.

incentive to keep campaign promises.[10] Downs puts the matter as follows: "if no government can possibly be reelected then party motivation for action cannot long remain the desire to be reelected. Experience will soon convince each party that this desire is futile" (62). Thus, the incumbents might just as well do what they prefer to do (either shirk or follow their own policy preferences) rather than honor their campaign pledges.

The heart of the problem is this: campaigning and governing take place in a multidimensional setting and in real time. Thus the problem of "time consistency" is inherent in the electoral relationship: since there is generally no majority winner, elected officeholders will not find it in their interest actually to carry out promises made during the campaign since they cannot succeed in being reelected anyway. Voters will, in turn, anticipate that candidates would not rationally keep their promises, and so they have no reason to base their votes on campaign promises.

Ordinary citizens seem intuitively aware of this problem. When asked about whether or not they expect politicians to be truthful, they typically display a healthy (or unhealthy) level of skepticism. They know that political candidates are trying to win election and that they will promise many different things to achieve this end. They know too that when the time comes for delivering on campaign promises, the shadow of the past election will have faded and the prospect of a future one will be remote. Besides, there will be many ways to excuse or even to hide the failure to live up to a campaign promise by pointing to the occurrence of unforeseen circumstances or to the ambiguity of the promise itself. Perhaps then it is not too surprising that, powerful as the spatial metaphor is, there is a good deal of evidence that it explains only a fraction of voting decisions and that voters ordinarily rely on other information about candidates in making their voting decisions.

For many years after the appearance of *An Economic Theory of Democracy,* researchers ignored this problem. They assumed that candidates were somehow able to commit to implementing campaign pledges whether or not they wished to carry out these promises when the time came to do so. Instead, theorists concentrated their efforts on the classical, static, complete information formulation of the spatial theory in multidimensional choice spaces. It's fair to say that enormous advances were made in understanding both the logical structure of electoral politics as well as some aspects of real electoral politics. But it seems appropriate now to begin to ask about the nature of electoral competition when candidates cannot commit to carrying out their promises.

---

10. Downs assumes in that chapter that the incumbent will follow the "majority principle" on an issue-by-issue basis. Such an assumption is not relevant to the present argument, and so I have dispensed with it.

Downs's Proposed Solutions to the Paradox

In chapters 4 and 7, Downs suggests two forces that, he argues, have the effect of inducing candidates to honor their platform promises and thereby provide a foundation for spatial theory: one, which is by now quite familiar in game-theoretic literature, is essentially "reputational" and suggests that if incumbents fail to keep their promises in the current period the voters may choose not to reelect them,[11] or not to believe their promises when the incumbents are next the challengers. The second argument is that uncertainty as to the preferences of the voters and the actions of the candidates will alter the dimensionality of the space of electoral competition in an essential manner.

We begin with a brief statement of Downs's ideology argument. Downs argues that, because of candidate uncertainty as to the preferences of voters and because voters themselves do not have the incentive to pay much attention to what the candidates are doing or saying, candidates are moved to compete for office not in the (highly multidimensional) issue space but, instead, in a lower dimensional space of ideologies. "In a world beclouded by uncertainty, ideologies will be useful to parties as well as voter" (100).

But, in light of recent theoretical developments, we know that the substitution of an ideological space of lower dimensionality than the original issue space is not sufficient to alleviate the effects of Downs's paradox, unless the dimensionality of that space is less than two. On this issue Downs is irritatingly vague. His discussion of ideology in chapter 7 makes no explicit claims as to its dimensionality. Rather, he begins chapter 8 with a one-dimensional example and thereafter, whenever he discusses the relationship of the left-right continuum to the original issues, he writes as though voters base their choice on some sort of weighted average. "Let us assume . . . that each party takes stands on many issues, and that each stand can be assigned a position on our left-right scale. Then each party's net position on this scale is a weighted average of the positions of all the particular policies it upholds" (132). In any case, it is clear that Downs must argue that the ideological space in which parties and candidates position themselves is one-dimensional.

Various justifications may be presented for this claim. Candidates may restrict themselves to a one-dimensional space of platforms because (they know that) (1) voters are psychically unable to process multidimensional information (cognitive limitations of voters), (2) voters do not find it worthwhile to process more-complicated information (cognitive costs), or (3) candidates must economize on calculation or information transmission (advertising) costs. Whatever the actual mechanism he proposes (and he writes most

---

11. Of course, it is not clear that voters can credibly threaten not to reelect an incumbent who has failed to honor a promise. The incumbent may make some voters better off than he or she promised while worsening the lot of others.

often about 2 and 3), Downs argues that the normal sources of uncertainty surrounding campaigns implicate one or more of these processes.

In this setting, if we assume (as Downs does) that the incumbent candidate's issue position is identified with the policies the incumbent executed while in office, the time consistency problem dissolves. In this case, as long as the office is sufficiently valuable and the candidates do not discount the future "too much," the incumbent will be motivated to implement the median position since if the incumbent fails to do so the challenger can announce that position and will prevail in the next election.

Downs's argument here is that party ideologies will be *reliable* (or informative) predictors of their actions in office and they will be *stable* in the sense that they don't change much from one period to the next (Downs calls this property "responsibility").

Obviously, everything in this argument turns on the claim that electoral competition will be reduced to a one-dimensional phenomenon (which he then analyzes in chap. 8), a claim for which Downs provides little support. But, in any event, if party ideologies are confined to a single dimension, they will be good predictors of what the parties will do in office (since officials can do no better than to implement the platform they promised during the election). Voters are well-advised to employ them to make their voting decisions (and will do so in equilibrium), so that the paradox disappears. The incumbent and the challenger will each take the same position in the ideological space, and the incumbent will have an incentive to behave in a fashion consistent with his or her platform promises.

Thus, Downs's argument has two key components: one, a reputational argument that relies on a repeated games story, claims that parties will keep their promises (even though they cannot commit themselves to do so) because they wish to continue to be elected in future elections. The second component appears to rest on some sort of cognitive limitation or information-economizing story and claims that voters and parties will end up relying on one-dimensional predictors of party behavior in office rather than paying attention to the full space of issues. I think most analysts nowadays find his second argument ad hoc in the sense that no theory is presented that would justify a one-dimensional ideological space. In any event recent research largely ignores this line of argument.

Instead theorists have tended to extend more credulity to the reputational element of Downs's argument and have attempted to develop a theory of electoral competition for cases in which candidates cannot commit themselves to keeping their campaign promises. In one of the following sections we review a few such efforts. In the end I argue that the reputational argument is not sufficient to support the spatial theory and that some sort of reduction of the issue space to a single dimension seems necessary in a world in which candidates cannot commit to implementing their promises. First, however, I briefly survey a few strands of empirical research that seem to bear on the problem.

Empirical Research

Depending on how the question is asked, there is either very little research on the topic of whether or not candidates keep campaign promises or there is a great deal. There is relatively little literature that directly addresses the question of whether or not candidates honor campaign pledges. On the other hand there is a great deal of writing that argues (and produces evidence) for the proposition that American political parties differ sharply and systematically from each other and that ordinary citizens can and do rely on these differences in behavior in making their voting choices. Thus, parties are stable or responsible (in Downs's sense).

Among the most prominent of these studies are the writings of Douglas A. Hibbs, Jr., which suggest that the parties attempt to implement distinct monetary and fiscal policies.[12] More evidence of this nature is provided by the writings associated with the Manifesto Project.[13] Evidence for the proposition that, in the aggregate, citizens perceive policy differences among the candidates is found in a well-known paper by Richard A. Brody and Benjamin I. Page and in many other places as well.[14]

The literature that would appear to bear most directly on the question of promise keeping is that which measures candidate promises or platforms and then investigates the degree to which these platforms are implemented by the candidate who was elected. I found several such attempts, all of which suffer from characteristic methodological weaknesses that seem endemic to this genre of research.

A good example of this sort of study is Jeff Fishel's book, *Platforms and Promises*.[15] Fishel develops codings of campaign platform promises, presidential efforts from Kennedy to Reagan, and success in implementing platform promises. He finds, for example, that Presidents Carter and Reagan were both reasonably faithful in attempting to implement their campaign promises

---

12. Hibbs 1977, 1987.
13. Budge, Robertson, and Hearl 1987.
14. Brody and Page 1972.
15. Washington, DC: Congressional Quarterly Press, 1985.

with legislative proposals but that Carter was not very successful in getting promised policies through Congress (though he scored a bit better than Nixon). The percentages reported here seem reasonably high (as they are in other studies), but they are sufficiently dependent on subjective codings to constitute a fairly weak form of evidence. At best studies of this sort might convince the skeptic that there is some information in platform promises.

Moreover, leaving aside issues of coding, it's not clear what should be considered a large percentage. As many recent presidencies illustrate, events can intrude and force presidents to alter their agendas in ways that prevent them from pursuing promises in a manner that is perfectly excusable by most voters.

In the end, because of the inherent ambiguities of measurement and interpretation that plague this approach, this kind of study seems not to be very useful in answering the most-interesting questions in this area. Specifically, do elected officials systematically depart from keeping their campaign promises? We would expect that if candidates fail to keep promises, they would instead do what they want. That is they would "shirk" by pursuing office perquisites, avoiding onerous tasks, or implementing their own ideological preferences.

There are a number of other studies that address promise keeping in a more indirect way once some assumptions are made as to what kinds of objectives politicians might have. For example, a number of recent discussions of congressional roll call voting behavior focus on a phenomenon that Joseph Kalt has labeled ideological shirking (see the exchange between Kalt and Mark Zupan and Samuel Peltzman).[16] Kalt and Zupan demonstrate that roll call voting cannot be fully accounted for by constituency characteristics and that the residuals in their regressions amount to the ideological tastes of members of Congress. They argue that members run for office in part because they have strongly held policy preferences that they want to implement, and that this implies that congressional behavior cannot be wholly accounted for by constituency characteristics. In the context of a one-dimensional spatial model, one might expect ideological shirking to take on a characteristic form: having promised to be centrist or moderate in the election campaign, a politician returns to his or her ideological preferences when in office (Reagan becomes Reagan), at least early in his or her term. For a direct argument for this sort accounting for "honeymoons" and mandates see Alt 1985.[17]

---

16. Kalt and Zupan 1984; Peltzman 1984.
17. Alt 1985.

One might argue that insofar as unanticipated ideological shirking is observed there is indirect evidence of a failure to keep campaign promises. Either the incumbent has misled supporters into believing that partisan policies will be implemented or the incumbent has misled centrists by implying that moderate policies will be adopted. On the other hand, such behavior, while perhaps not fully faithful to campaign promises taken literally, might still be predictable and so voters would be expected to anticipate that Democrats are more liberal than Republicans irrespective of campaign statements (at least right after the election), and to base their choices on those anticipations. It's not clear of course how precisely the voters will be able to place the candidates if they are known to be announcing platforms that they do not intend to carry out. As shown in the following, it may be that candidates with very different intentions will announce the same platform so that, even though voters have rational expectations, voters will be unable to tell the difference among candidates whose behavior in office will in fact diverge.

A related line of work concerns the existence of electoral cycle effects. The classical works in this genre have to do with macroeconomic effects on voting behavior. This work suggests that citizens are myopic in their voting decisions, paying more attention to recent events than more distant ones, and therefore that officials will respond by behaving differently as elections approach. In this case, candidates would shirk early in their terms, returning to more attractive electoral positions as the election approaches. See the work of William Nordhaus and Edward Tufte in this regard.[18] Once again, candidate platforms would offer little guidance as to how elected officials will act early in their terms. Of course, electoral cycles may be anticipated: voters may know that early in their terms Democrats will implement policies further to the left and Republicans policies further to the right than were promised. Thus voters may employ information other than campaign pledges in deciding how to vote.

While the original papers in this area focus on macroeconomics and either presidential elections or aggregate congressional votes, more recent investigations show cyclical effects in a number of other domains. D. Roderick Kiewiet and Mathew D. McCubbins suggest that such effects exist in the budgetary process and Robert A. Bernstein and Gerald C. Wright, while disagreeing with each other to some degree, present evidence of such cycles in roll call voting in the Senate.[19] Specifically, Bernstein and Wright

---

18. Nordhaus 1975; Tufte 1978.
19. Kiewiet and McCubbins 1989; Bernstein 1988; Wright 1988.

both report election cycle effects: senators who are more extreme than their constituencies tend to shift in a moderate direction during election years.

There is some related evidence on roll call voting over the course of a congressional career. One would expect that if members of Congress intend to retire after their current term, they would be free to pursue the sorts of policies they prefer. This "last period" effect resembles the motivation for electoral cycles and ideological shirking and suggests that political actors will behave differently over the course of their careers. Somewhat surprisingly, John Lott shows that in their roll call behavior members of Congress do not seem to shift their ideological positions in the "last period" but that they do tend to vote less often.[20] In other words, the ideological shirking that may be expected to occur seems not to be observed, but ordinary shirking is found instead. Lott and W. Robert Reed suggest that there are mechanisms at work that sort out those politicians who are unrepresentative of their constituents, and so the longer incumbents are in office the more likely it is that their preferences resemble those of their constituents.[21]

While this survey is admittedly cursory, I think it is possible to draw some preliminary conclusions. First, there is substantial evidence in the United States (and the evidence is much stronger in other nations) that the parties and their candidates differ systematically and consistently on important issues. Moreover, the evidence for shirking seems to suggest that such behavior is regular and can be anticipated by voters and, as far as I can tell, the magnitudes of these effects are not large. Thus, I conclude that the empirical evidence suggests that politicians are surprisingly predictable over time. And, though the evidence on campaign promises is weak, it seems to suggest that candidates attempt to keep many of their promises once they take office. I take it, therefore, that there is a fact out there that needs to be explained: politicians don't seem to shirk or lie as much as the classical multidimensional spatial model seems to imply. Why not? What mechanisms induce them to behave stably and reliably rather than doing as they please once in office?

Indeed, other evidence suggests that Downs's ideas about ideology might deserve renewed attention. Recent work by Keith Poole and Howard Rosenthal suggests that ideology may be low-dimensional or even (in their bolder claims) a one-dimensional phenomenon.[22] Whether for Downs's reasons or for others, politicians seem to take positions in an ideological space, and these

---

20. Lott 1987.
21. Lott and Reed 1987.
22. Poole and Rosenthal 1985.

positions seem quite stable over time. While this work remains controversial and while it lacks a theory to explain the dimensionality of ideology, it and related work seem worthy of greater attention in this context.

Campaigns without Precommitment

If candidates cannot precommit to keeping campaign promises, they may find it rational to behave differently in office than they promised. Thus, voters will not rationally rely on platforms as predictors of the behavior of politicians in office. And, if voters can better anticipate how candidates will behave in office by observing their characteristics and past behavior rather than by observing their promises, they would rationally base their votes on these data rather than on announced platforms. Thus, the following question arises: under what conditions would campaign promises be informative as to subsequent policy-making activity?

There are two sorts of models in which this question has been addressed. In the first—the *moral hazard* model—the voters are assumed to know what the candidates' preferences are, but they cannot observe incumbent policy choices directly[23] Thus, citizens choose voting rules that depend on observable information about candidates, including the performance of the government under the current incumbents as well as campaign promises. In equilibrium, citizens cast ballots in such a way as to limit the amount of shirking that candidates will engage in while in office. Not surprisingly, in such models the amount of shirking will depend on the ability of voters to monitor the actions of incumbent officials. If citizens could observe policy choices directly, they would be able to eliminate shirking altogether.

Because candidate objectives are identical and commonly known, moral hazard models allow little scope for reputational effects. If the candidates are known to have the same characteristics, they would find the same actions optimal in each situation, and so what information would reputation convey? All voters can do in such models is to provide incentives for candidates to pursue the interests of citizens when in office.

The way that voters can provide these incentives to candidates is to punish them if governmental performance is poor during their incumbency—retrospective or performance-oriented voting. Thus, such models are essentially based on repeated play so that the focus of the analysis is on what has been called "supergame equilibria."

---

23. Barro 1973; Becker and Stigler 1974; Ferejohn 1986.

Campaign promises do not play much of a role in most models of this sort since the voters know candidate preferences and can calculate candidate policy choices when in office. Promises in such models convey no additional information and so would simply be ignored. In these models if elections are sufficiently frequent and politicians (or parties) are infinitely lived, voters can choose a voting policy that limits shirking in office. As shown in the following, this conclusion seems to hold only in the case in which the set of alternative platforms is one-dimensional.[24]

With finitely lived politicians, the last period problem causes unraveling. If the last period could be anticipated, voters would know that the incumbent would surely shirk, and so they would certainly choose the challenger. But if voters were to follow this policy, incumbents would shirk in the penultimate period, and so on. Thus, as a way to alleviate this problem it is sometimes suggested that, although politicians have finite lifetimes, parties are infinitely lived and find a way (such as enabling retiring politicians to become consultants and lobbyists after their official careers have ended) to reward politicians for not shirking in their final period.

Alberto Alesina has presented a series of papers in which the preferences of the candidates or parties are common knowledge in a finite period model.[25] Because of the finite horizon, campaign promises that are different from the candidates' true preferences are not credible, and candidates pursue their preferred policies when in office, and voters correctly anticipate this. In an infinite horizon model, supergame equilibria exist that allow the candidates to pursue "electoralist" policies that are distinct from the ones they actually prefer.

In an original departure that allows campaign promises to be credible, David Austen-Smith and Jeffrey Banks have shown in a two-period moral hazard model that voters can credibly commit to punishing incumbents who deviate from their platform promises in the first period.[26] The second-period incumbent would shirk in any case so the voters incur no cost by punishing incumbents who fail to keep first-period promises. Thus, voters are free to condition their vote on the relationship between first-period campaign promises and performance. This argument appears to extend to arbitrary numbers

---

24. Ferejohn, "Incumbent Performance," shows that in a multidimensional setting candidate shirking is essentially uncontrollable.
25. Alesina 1987; 1988.
26. Banks and Austen-Smith 1989.

of periods. One problem with this approach is that it relies crucially on the existence of a known final period that does not depend on the career aspirations of the candidates, and this seems a rather artificial assumption. If, instead, each candidate is known to be willing to serve at most two periods, the usual unraveling argument will prevent the enforcement of campaign pledges.

In the second class of models—*adverse selection* or signaling models—candidate preferences cannot be directly observed by the electorate; voters must infer these preferences in order to anticipate how these politicians would behave in office. Here most of the work is in a two-period model with a single election and in a single dimensional ideological space. In this context, following the election, the candidates would simply do what they wished no matter what they promised during the campaign. Banks shows that if candidate preferences contain a penalty for executing policies much different from those promised there are equilibria in which preelection promises are (sometimes) informative.[27] Specifically, candidates whose preferences are far from the median will truthfully reveal their preferences, while those nearer to the median voter will "pool." Banks's assumption about candidate preferences may be justified as embodying "reputational" effects that would emerge in a multiperiod model.

Joseph Harrington shows that, if voter preferences are unknown and if candidates are not penalized for carrying out policies divergent from their promises, informative equilibria may not exist.[28] That is, in all equilibria, candidates with different preferences will pool so that campaign promises are uninformative. When he assumes that candidates are less likely to be able to implement policies the more distant they are from the median voter, he finds that fully informative equilibria exist. The idea here is that candidates are motivated to reveal their true preferences knowing that if they happen to be elected then they will be relatively likely to be able to implement their preferred policy.

Note the resemblance of the equilibrium strategies in these models to the "strategy of ambiguity" discussed by Downs. In equilibrium, a candidate who announces that he or she is at the median position is actually telling the voters that his or her preferred position is distributed in an interval around that point. Thus, while it is often thought that as long as voters are risk-averse, candidates would not announce ambiguous strategies, when there is private information, they will generally choose to do so.

Alesina and Alex Cukierman provide a model in which candidate prefer-

---

27. Banks 1990.
28. Harrington 1988.

ences are not observed and demonstrate that candidates systematically "converge" toward the median voter in the first period and shirk in the second period.[29] Thus, in a finite horizon model, voters can induce the incumbent to implement policies they prefer early in the incumbent's career by (credibly) threatening to replace him or her.

These papers suggest that in a multiperiod model with a one-dimensional issue space, candidates, independent of their characteristics, will take moderate positions early in their careers, and these platforms will be good predictors of their actions in office. But as times goes on, candidates should shirk in the direction of their most-preferred positions. If there are reputation-bearing mechanisms such as political parties, we might expect promises to be fully informative as to future actions (but not informative at all as to candidate preferences) at all times. In this case the static spatial model would be a good heuristic for the analysis of real elections.

While this survey of recent theoretical papers is too brief to have considered all of the relevant work in the area or to have presented in any detail the work of the various authors, I think that the general outlines are pretty clear. In one-dimensional moral hazard models, candidates can be induced to perform predictably if elections are repeated indefinitely and to the extent that voters are able to monitor the behavior of officials. If politicians have (known) finite horizons, things are more subtle. Either infinitely lived "reputation bearers" (parties) can be invented or, as supported by Austen-Smith and Banks, voters can credibly threaten to punish candidates who don't deliver on promises until the last period. If the last period is not common knowledge but is private information held by one of the candidates, the situation is, once again, one of adverse selection.

In one-dimensional signaling models voters seem to be able to induce politicians to make truthful promises (i.e., promises that will be kept) in early periods. Thus, either candidates will tell the truth about what they would do in office (if they have sufficiently extreme preferences) or candidates whose preferences are close to the median voter will pool at the median in order to get reelected (and they would implement this promise). In either case, in many of these models, behaving predictably (so that past actions are a good guide to future actions) or keeping campaign promises seems consistent with equilibrium behavior.

All of these "positive" results seem to rely essentially on the assumption that the issue space is one-dimensional. In a multidimensional setting—the setting of Downs's paradox—things are much less hopeful and much less understood. We turn to this subject in the next section.

---

29. Alesina and Cukierman 1989.

Ideology

Downs's original statement of the paradox of truthful candidates relies essentially on the existence of majority rule cycles. But most of the theoretical discussions of campaigns without precommitment take place in one-dimensional settings in which there is an electoral equilibrium. The only exception I know of is my multidimensional moral hazard model, which shows that, in a model where policies correspond to alternative distributions of wealth, candidates are entirely undisciplined by the electorate. Incumbents will shirk completely, and the electorate will nevertheless have no reason to remove them from office; the voters could rationally expect no better of the challengers. Of course, the electors will anticipate this shirking, and so they will not be surprised. Campaign promises would not be believed anyway. In a sense then, this is a model in which candidates are truthful but depressingly truthful.

There is, however, another way to interpret this result, a way that provides a connection with Downs's story about ideology. I argue earlier that Downs's claim that parties compete not in the full space of alternative policies but, instead, in a one-dimensional space of ideologies seems (in the book) to rest either on a disputable empirical claim about psychology or else on an allegation that a reduction of an issue space to one dimension is a (unique) solution of a voter's optimization problem: either candidates and voters rely on one-dimensional messages because they are incapable of transmitting or calculating with richer information or they employ one-dimensional messages as a way to "economize" on psychic costs. Either theoretical foundation for such a notion of ideology seems to me at best ad hoc and is certainly undefended by Downs. Without much further argument there is no reason to think that the dimensionality of the space would reduce to one, independently of the dimensionality of the original issue space and independently of any other parameters having to do with voters or candidates.

My result suggests another possibility: a strategic basis for the choice of a one-dimensional ideological space. Unless voters (implicitly agree to) base their assessments of candidates on a one-dimensional space, incumbents would be completely uncontrollable. Thus, there is simply no purpose to using ideology at all unless it is essentially a single dimensional concept. If ideology is multidimensional, it is useless as a method of disciplining politicians and so, one might conjecture, does not play much of a role in politics. We would expect ideological argument, communication, and calculation to survive only in cases in which the ideological space is one-dimensional.

Of course, I provide no theory as to how such a single dimensional concept could arise or be agreed upon, and it may be that such a theory would fall outside of game-theoretical models of the sort discussed here. Perhaps an appropriate way to think of ideology is as a "focal point" type of phenomenon in which alternative concepts of ideology allow various electoral equilibria to be sustained. Related work along this line has been done by David Kreps (1988), but here what is "focal" is not the proposed equilibrium outcome but the dimension along which competition will occur. All this is, of course, conjecture, and much more work needs to be done before we can hope to understand this phenomenon more fully.

Moreover, if it turns out that a satisfactory theory of the structure of ideology can be generated, it would also help to integrate a number of intriguing empirical results. For one thing, campaign promises do seem more informative than one would expect in multidimensional settings. Candidates of different parties tend to take predictably distinct positions and attempt to implement distinct types of policy. Secondly, politicians do seem to locate themselves in more or less generally understood left-right terms, and their locations seem, at least on the evidence that Poole and Rosenthal have assembled, to be pretty stable over time and to predict their behavior well in higher dimensional policy space. Thirdly, such a theory might help us to understand the phenomenon that Kalt and Zupan have termed "ideological shirking." They claim that politicians simply hold (unobserved) ideological positions that explain their behavior in Congress and that are not predictable from constituency characteristics. Perhaps, instead, politicians are choosing ideological positions (and perhaps even announcing them) as a way to develop what might be called a "brand name" that voters could use to calculate their anticipated behavior in office.

Discussion

We return now to the question of the foundations of spatial models. Why should voters base their electoral choices on a comparison of the platforms of candidates? It would make sense to do so only if candidate behavior in office is reasonably consistent with these platforms. The empirical literature, while only partially addressing the issue, suggests that there is a fair connection between promises and performance, and (while we did not review evidence on voting behavior) there is some evidence that voters pay some attention to campaign statements in deciding how to vote.

But if promises are informative, why do incumbents keep getting reelected? One answer proposed by Downs and largely ignored in the literature is the emergence of a single dimensional ideology for the purpose of evaluating politicians and parties. In any case it seems clear that we cannot hope for campaign pledges to be fully informative in multidimensional models since, if they were, Downs's paradox would reemerge. But it may be true that promises are partially informative in this setting and that some degree of promise keeping would emerge. My intuition at least doesn't give much guidance on what to expect in a model of this sort.

The foundations of spatial modeling remain to be constructed. In multi-period models with one-dimensional ideology, it seems likely that the spatial model could provide an appoximation to equilibria of richer intertemporal electoral games without commitment. In that setting, the results of such models might be useful guides to thinking about more realistic interactions. But where the issue space is intrinsically multidimensional, Downs's paradox should still induce skepticism as to the utility of the spatial model of real elections.

CHAPTER 8

A Revised Probabilistic Spatial Model of Elections: Theory and Evidence

James M. Enelow, James W. Endersby, and Michael C. Munger

Probabilistic spatial models of elections have proved to be quite fruitful, both theoretically and empirically. The distinguishing feature of these models is the presence of a random element either in the voter's decision calculus or in the candidate's ability to predict the vote. In either case, probabilistic models allow all candidates in an election campaign a nonzero chance of winning and assume that each candidate's vote share varies continuously with a change in strategy. In contrast, deterministic models assume that for any given choice of candidate strategies one candidate wins with probability one and all other candidates with probability zero. Furthermore, candidate vote shares are typically discontinuous in each candidate's strategy variable.

The assumption of probabilistic voting has been given several empirical justifications. Melvin J. Hinich, John O. Ledyard, and Peter C. Ordeshook (1972) base their probabilistic model on the possibility of voter abstention. As the voters' utility for their favorite candidate declines, the probability of voting for this candidate also declines. This assumption models the effect of alienation, which influences both the individual's probability of voting and the candidate for whom he or she votes. In addition, the voter's probability of voting for the better-liked candidate in a two-candidate race decreases as the utility difference between the candidates decreases. This second assumption models the effect of indifference, which also affects both the probability of voting and the candidate for whom the individual votes.

Another justification for probabilistic voting is offered by James M. Enelow and Hinich (1982a, 1984). Some aspects of the candidate that influence voter evaluations are not subject to candidate control. Age, experience, ethnic and marital background, and, of course, name are just some of the

---

This chapter was originally a paper presented at the 1990 annual meeting of the American Political Science Association, San Francisco, August 30–September 2, 1990.

features of a candidate that he or she can do little if anything about and that are independent of the candidate's issue positions. If voter perceptions of these nonspatial candidate characteristics vary, the nonspatial utility difference between two candidates can be modeled as a continuous random variable, and the candidate vote shares will vary continuously as a function of changes in their issue positions.

A similar approach to justifying probabilistic voting is to assume randomness at the individual level. After evaluating the candidate along both spatial and nonspatial dimensions, a residue of uncertainty may still remain in the voter's mind regarding the voter's overall utility for the candidate. Omitted variables, measurement error, and prospective uncertainty may all justify the voter being less than sure about how to cast his or her vote. Alternatively, a candidate may view each individual vote as containing a certain element of chance, even if each voter knows how he or she is going to vote.

Including nonspatial candidate characteristics in the voter's utility function admits that factors specific to the candidate are relevant to the voter's decision making. Along the spatial dimensions of the campaign, however, it is always assumed that the only information relevant to the voter are the issue positions of the candidate. Thus, what distinguishes Carter from Reagan on the issues of the 1980 American presidential campaign is the issue positions adopted by each candidate and nothing else. Thus, if Carter had adopted the same issue positions as Reagan, the voters would have seen no difference between the issue positions of the two candidates and given them the same evaluation on these dimensions.

Leaving aside the matter of honesty, it seems reasonable to argue that the issue evaluation of candidates depends on who they are and not just what issue positions they take. Carter was widely viewed as less competent than Reagan, and it therefore follows that any issue position adopted by Carter should be "discounted" more heavily by voters than Reagan's position on the same issue. Defining competence in terms of the candidate's ability to fulfill a campaign promise, it makes sense for the voter to weight the candidate's issue statements by the candidate's competence if the candidate is interested in actual results. This competency factor is candidate-specific like the additive nonspatial term used by Enelow and Hinich but has a multiplicative effect on the voter's issue evaluation of the candidate.

In the following section, we derive some theoretical results for a probabilistic spatial model that incorporates the competency factor described. It is straightforward to show that this candidate-specific factor leads to a major difference in theoretical expectations about candidate issue positions. In the probabilistic voting models described here, as well as those of Peter J. Coughlin and Schmuel Nitzan (1981), Coughlin, Dennis Mueller, and P. Murrell (1988), Robert S. Erikson and D. Romero (1990), and others, the equilibrium issue positions of two candidates in a simple plurality election are the same. In the model developed in the next section, the equilibrium positions of the candidates are typically distinct. Thus, our model accounts for what is widely observed in real elections: candidate divergence on the issues.

In a succeeding section, we analyze empirical results designed to test our new probabilistic model against the older model of Enelow and Hinich, which assumes that candidate-specific effects influence voter evaluations only as an additive term. Using National Election Survey (NES) data from the 1980, 1984, and 1988 presidential elections, we find that the new model predicts individual votes almost exactly as well as the older model. We also compare the two models with respect to their ability to predict candidate issue positions and find that the new model predicts the average perceived issue positions of challengers much better than the older model. At the same time, the older model does a much better job of predicting the issue positions of incumbents. These findings suggest a third model in which voters discount challenger issue positions but not those of incumbents. This third model is shown to predict candidate issue positions better than either of the other two models.

In conclusion, while we are unable to reject the simple additive model of Enelow and Hinich, some modification of probabilistic spatial models appears necessary both to explain the distinction voters make between challenger and incumbent issue positions as well as to account for the candidate issue divergence found in real two-candidate elections. This chapter takes the first step in this direction.

The Model

We assume two candidates, R and D, compete in a simple plurality election, where everyone votes, or else a fixed, known, constant proportion of the electorate votes. The total utility of voter i ($i = 1, \ldots, n$) for candidate R is

$$v_{iR} = k_{iR} + u_i(\ell_{iR} t_R) \tag{1}$$

where k_{iR} is i's nonpolicy (i.e., nonspatial) utility for R, u_i is i's policy utility function, ℓ_{iR} is i's perception of R's competence, and t_R is R's position on a compact one-dimensional policy scale T. Defining the status quo policy as the origin of the issue space, we can conceive of t_R as a proposal of where to move the status quo. The competency weight ℓ_{iR} is i's prediction of how successful R will be in carrying out this proposal, where $0 \leq \ell_{iR} \leq 1$. This definition of competence is the same as that used by Bernard Grofman (1985b). The assumption of a one-dimensional policy space is made merely for simplicity. Unlike deterministic voting models, there is no generic difference between one-dimensional and multidimensional probabilistic spatial models (Coughlin 1990a).

The total utility of voter i for candidate D can be defined similarly as v_{iD}. Our basic assumption, then, is that voter i votes for R over D if and only if

$$d_i = v_{iR} - v_{iD} > \epsilon_i \qquad (2)$$

where ϵ_i captures the unobservable factors that add randomness to i's vote decision. We model ϵ_i as a continuous random variable that is twice differentiable. If F_i is the distinction function of ϵ_i, then $F_i(d_i)$ is the probability that i votes for candidate R. The probability that i votes for D is $1 - F_i(d_i)$.

Each candidate is assumed to choose his position in T in order to maximize his or her expected vote (as n approaches infinity, this objective is equivalent to maximizing the probability of winning). R's objective, then, is to pick t_R to maximize

$$EV_R = \sum_i F_i(d_i) \qquad (3)$$

and D's objective is to pick t_D to maximize $EV_D = \sum_i [1 - F_i(d_i)]$. The necessary first-order conditions for expected vote-maximizing positions t_R^* and t_D^* are

$$\partial EV_R / \partial t_R = \sum_i f_i(d_i) \ell_{iR} \partial u_i / \partial \ell_{iR} t_R = 0 \qquad (4a)$$

$$\partial EV_D / \partial t_D = \sum_i f_i(d_i) \ell_{iD} \partial u_i / \partial \ell_{iD} t_D = 0 \qquad (4b)$$

The second-order sufficient conditions for the existence of t_R^* and t_D^* are straightforward to derive and are similar to those found in Enelow and Hinich 1989.

Examination of (4a) and (4b) shows that unless $\ell_{iR} = \ell_{iD}$ for all voters, the two first-order conditions of the candidates are not the same. This means that the equilibrium issue positions of R and D will also not be the same. To illustrate this point, let $f_i(d_i) = 1$ for all i. Thus, ϵ_i is distributed uniformly on some unit interval. The location of this interval and the values of k_{iR} and k_{iD} determine R and D's expected vote but are irrelevant to the location of t_R^* and t_D^*.

For purposes of this example, let $i = 1,2$, and assume $u_1 = -(\ell_{1j} t_j)^2$ and $u_2 = -(\ell_{2j} t_j - 1)^2$ where $j = R, D$. In words, both voters have quadratic policy utility functions with 1's ideal issue position at $t = 0$ and 2's at $t = 1$. Substituting these functions and $f_i(d_i) = 1$ into (4a) and (4b) yields

$$t_R^* = \ell_{2R}/(\ell_{1R}^2 + \ell_{2R}^2)$$

$$t_D^* = \ell_{2D}/(\ell_{1D}^2 + \ell_{2D}^2)$$

Clearly, if $\ell_{1R} = \ell_{1D}$ and $\ell_{2R} = \ell_{2D}$, $t_R^* = t_D^*$. If each voter sees R and D as equally competent, the two candidates will adopt the same position in equilibrium; $t = \frac{1}{2}$. However, if voters see R and D as having different levels of competence, the candidates will adopt different positions in equilibrium. For example, if both voters see R's competence as twice D's, $t_R^* = \frac{1}{4}\ell_{iD}$ and $t_D^* = \frac{1}{2}\ell_{iD}$. Thus, agreement among voters on candidate competence is not sufficient to cause candidate convergence.

The effect of ℓ_{iR} and ℓ_{iD} on candidate equilibrium locations is to cause R and D to adjust for the discount that will be applied to their positions when they calculate their optimal locations. In the simple case, where voters agree about the candidate's competence, the candidate chooses the position that, multiplied by his or her competence, equals $\frac{1}{2}$. When voters disagree about a candidate's competence, the adjustment is not as simple. In the preceding example, if $\ell_{1R} = \frac{3}{4}$ and $\ell_{2R} = \frac{5}{6}$, $t_R^* = .66$, while if $\ell_{1R} = \frac{5}{6}$ and $\ell_{2R} = \frac{3}{4}$, $t_R^* = .60$. It matters to the candidate's position both how the candidate is perceived and who perceives him or her in different ways.

To provide some intuition behind the model, we might imagine a gubernatorial candidate who recognizes that she is seen by voters as being soft on crime. To be perceived as sufficiently tough on crime, she may have to overshoot the mark, advocating stronger penalties for a long list of criminal offenses, since voters will discount any position she takes (perhaps due to past offenses of her own).

In the simple additive model of Enelow and Hinich (1982a, 1984) $\ell_{ij} = 1$ for each voter i and candidate j. Otherwise, the model is the same as that expressed in equations (1), (2), and (3). Substituting for ℓ_{ij} in equations (4a) and (4b), it follows that the candidates will adopt the same issue position in equilibrium. In our two-voter example this position is $\frac{1}{2}$.

Whether or not voters compensate for perceived candidate competence is an empirical question. In the following section, we seek to answer the question of whether or not a probabilistic spatial model that sees voters as adjusting candidate issue positions by perceived competence performs better than the simple additive model that accepts these positions at face value. We compare the competence-adjusted issue model with the unadjusted issue model two ways. First, we see which does a better job of predicting individual votes, and second, we see which more accurately predicts average perceived candidate issue positions. Our data are the NES data of the 1980, 1984, 1988 American presidential elections.[1]

There is almost no difference between the two models in their ability to predict individual votes. However, the two models perform quite differently in predicting candidate issue positions, with the adjusted model predicting challenger issue positions much better than the unadjusted model, and the unadjusted model doing a much better job of predicting incumbent issue positions. These findings suggest a third model in which voters adjust the issue positions of challengers but not those of incumbents. This hybrid model is shown to predict candidate issue positions better than either of the other two models. Our conclusion is that while we are unable to reject the simple additive model of Enelow and Hinich, some modification of standard probabilistic spatial models appears necessary to better predict candidate issue differences.

Empirical Analysis

The NES asks a number of questions that are helpful for operationalizing the new probabilistic model described in the preceding section. Since we are interested in prediction, we confine ourselves to the preelection wave of each study. In table 1 four-point scales are listed that respondents were asked about; these represent the personal characteristics of the major candidates in the presidential elections of 1980, 1984, and 1988. In addition, respondents were presented with a set of issue scales, usually comprising seven points, and asked to locate themselves, the major candidates, and the federal government on each of these scales. The issue scales used in our analysis are also listed in table 1.

To arrive at a measure for k_{ij}, i's utility for candidate j's nonpolicy characteristics, we began by selecting the questions that asked about unambiguously positive candidate attributes (e.g., "intelligent") and discarding those that asked about attributes that may appeal to some respondents but not to others (e.g., "religious"). In table 1 the traits we selected are listed.

We then performed a principal-components analysis on the difference in candidate attribute scores for the Republican and Democratic candidate in each of the three election years to see how many factors underlie each of the three question sets. The purpose of this analysis was to determine whether a

---

1. The data utilized in this study were made available by the Inter-university Consortium for Political and Social Research. The data for the American National Election Studies were originally collected by Warren E. Miller and the National Election Studies (1982, 1986, 1989). Neither the collector of the original data nor the consortium bears any responsibility for the analyses or interpretations presented here.

TABLE 1. Traits and Issues Used in Construction of Nonpolicy and Policy Variables

Candidate Traits	1980	1984	1988
Able to solve our economic problems	X		
Commands respect		X	
Compassionate		X	X
Decent		X	X
Develops good relations with other countries	X		
Dishonest[a]	X		
Fair		X	
Hardworking		X	
Honest			X
In touch with ordinary people		X	
Inspiring	X	X	X
Intelligent		X	X
Kind		X	
Knowledgeable	X	X	X
Moral	X	X	X
Power hungry[a]	X		
Provides strong leadership	X	X	X
Sets a good example		X	
Weak[a]	X		
Issues			
Abortion[b]	X		
Central America		X	
Cooperation with Russia		X	X
Defense spending	X	X	X
Employment and inflation	X		
Government services and spending	X	X	X
Jobs and standard of living		X	X
Minority aid/no aid		X	
Status of women		X	
Taxes and tax cuts[b]	X		

[a]Scale inverted.
[b]Transformed to length of a seven-point scale.

single or multiple set of evaluative dimensions was represented by each set of questions.

Our results indicate that in all three election years, a single factor explains most of the variance in the data. For the 1980 analysis, a single factor explains 61.2 percent of the variance with a sharp drop from the first to second eigenvalue (5.51 to 0.73). Similar results occurred for the 1984 and 1988 analyses. Thus, we decided not to try to distinguish empirically between k_{ij} and ℓ_{ij}. This is unfortunate, since, ideally, we would prefer to be able to distinguish between competence and nonpolicy utility, but the data leave us no choice.

Reversing the scale on three traits (power hungry, weak, and dishonest) so that all scales run in the same direction, we created a simple measure of $k_{ij} = \ell_{ij}$ varying between 0 and 1, with higher values representing greater nonpolicy utility (and competence). The issue scales were all transformed to the length of a 7-point scale, and an independent variable was created for each issue scale in each election using the locations given by each respondent on self, the Democratic candidate, the Republican candidate, and the federal government (which we assume to be the status quo). Each respondent was assumed to possess a quadratic policy utility function, separable over issues $k = 1, \ldots, m$, so

$$u_{iR} = -\sum_k a_{ik}(A_{Rik} - x_{ik})^2 \tag{5}$$

where a_{ik} is the salience of issue k to respondent i, x_{ik} is i's ideal position on issue k, and $A_{Rik} = SQ_{ik} + \ell_{iR}(t_{iRk} - SQ_{ik})$ is a generalization of $\ell_{iR}t_R$ when individual perceptions of R's issue position vary as well as perceptions of the status quo.

Since $F_i(d_i)$ is the probability that i votes for R, we performed a logistic regression for each election, with the dichotomous two-candidate vote as the dependent variable and $d_i = v_{iR} - v_{iD} = k_{iR} - k_{iD} + u_{iR} - u_{iD}$ as $m + 1$ independent variables $(k_{iR} - k_{iD}), I_1, \ldots, I_m$, where

$$I_k = [(A_{Dik} - x_{ik})^2 - (A_{Rik} - x_{ik})^2] \tag{6}$$

The logistic regression estimates a common salience weight a_k for each issue $k = 1, \ldots, m$, as well as a weight for $(k_{iR} - k_{iD})$, and a constant term. If $\ell_{ij} = 1$ for each voter i and candidate j, then $A_{Rik} = t_{iRk}$, and the model reduces to the simple additive model of Enelow and Hinich. We can therefore run another regression for each election year with $\ell_{ij} = i$ and compare the results of the two regressions by election year to see which performs better.

Since the two models (one with ℓ_{ij} allowed to vary, which we label $\ell_{ij} \neq 1$, and one with $\ell_{ij} = 1$) are not nested, there are no simple statistics to allow a direct comparison between the two regressions for each year. We therefore use two indirect tests. First, we compare the two models in terms of their ability to predict individual votes, and second, we compare them in terms of their ability to predict average perceived candidate issue positions.

In tables 2, 3, and 4 statistics from the six logistic regressions are listed, two each for 1980, 1984, and 1988, while in table 5 the predictive comparisons are reported for each of these three years. The results shown in the third

TABLE 2. Results of Logistic Regressions, 1980

Variable	$\ell i \neq 1$	$\ell i = 1$	$\ell i_D = 1, \ell i_R \neq 1$
Constant	−0.625	−0.842	−0.688
	(0.410)	(0.346)	(0.402)
Nonpolicy	27.459**	26.563**	27.660**
	(6.237)	(5.865)	(5.967)
Abortion	0.063	0.021	0.052
	(0.060)	(0.028)	(0.038)
Defense spending	0.022	0.040	0.060
	(0.072)	(0.047)	(0.058)
Employment and inflation	0.337*	0.178*	0.244*
	(0.150)	(0.081)	(0.097)
Government services and spending	0.249**	0.113*	0.177**
	(0.081)	(0.044)	(0.064)
Taxes and tax cuts	0.089	0.030	0.046
	(0.065)	(0.037)	(0.054)
−2 log likelihood	64.23**	70.35**	69.79**
	(6 df)	(6 df)	(6 df)

Note: Standard error in parentheses.
*Significant at the .05 level.
**Significant at the .01 level.

column of tables 2, 3, and 4 and the third, sixth, and ninth rows of table 5 are discussed later in the chapter. As shown in table 3, the vote prediction rates of the two models are almost identical. For 1980, both the adjusted and unadjusted issue models correctly predict 156 cases out of 169 (92.3 percent). The distribution of false predictions is slightly less symmetric for the adjusted issue model with a bias toward Carter.

For 1984, the results follow the same pattern, with the adjusted issue model correctly predicting 726 cases out of 774 (93.8 percent) and the unadjusted model correctly predicting 725 cases (93.7 percent). The distribution of false predictions is nearly the same for both models, almost equally distributed between Reagan and Walter Mondale. Finally, for 1988, the adjusted model correctly predicts 506 cases out of 547 (92.5 percent) while the unadjusted issue model correctly predicts 508 cases (92.9 percent). As for 1980, the erroneous predictions of the unadjusted model are more evenly distributed between the two candidates than those of the adjusted issue model, which is biased toward Bush.

Obviously, the differences in prediction rates between the two regressions are statistically nonsignificant at any reasonable probability level for each of the three elections, leaving us with the tentative conclusion that the two models perform equally well at predicting individual votes. This finding supports earlier work by Enelow, Hinich, and N. Mendell (1986), which

TABLE 3. Results of Logistic Regressions, 1984

Variable	$\ell_i \neq 1$	$\ell_i = 1$	$\ell_{i_R} = 1, \ell_{i_D} \neq 1$
Constant	1.266**	1.165**	1.393**
	(0.200)	(0.191)	(0.204)
Nonpolicy	14.048**	13.380**	13.826**
	(1.483)	(1.522)	(1.511)
Central America	0.029	0.024	0.037
	(0.028)	(0.019)	(0.024)
Cooperation with Russia	0.036	0.026	0.016
	(0.032)	(0.022)	(0.026)
Defense spending	0.041	0.029	0.038
	(0.029)	(0.020)	(0.026)
Government services and spending	0.135**	0.093**	0.129**
	(0.041)	(0.027)	(0.035)
Jobs and standard of living	0.102*	0.066*	0.048
	(0.051)	(0.031)	(0.034)
Minority aid	0.042	0.017	0.030
	(0.045)	(0.031)	(0.032)
Status of women	−0.032	−0.015	−0.041
	(0.034)	(0.024)	(0.029)
−2 log likelihood	272.63**	272.23**	276.88**
	(8 df)	(8 df)	(8 df)

Note: Standard error in parentheses.
*Significant at the .05 level.
**Significant at the .01 level.

TABLE 4. Results of Logistic Regressions, 1988

Variable	$\ell_i \neq 1$	$\ell_i = 1$	$\ell_{i_R} = 1, \ell_{i_D} \neq 1$
Constant	1.060**	0.851**	1.048**
	(0.209)	(0.211)	(0.202)
Nonpolicy	13.747**	13.188**	14.223**
	(1.753)	(1.829)	(1.720)
Cooperation with Russia	0.179*	0.134*	0.122*
	(0.071)	(0.050)	(0.049)
Defense spending	0.092*	0.079**	0.088*
	(0.042)	(0.030)	(0.039)
Government services and spending	0.091*	0.065*	0.059
	(0.042)	(0.028)	(0.034)
Jobs and standard of living	0.184**	0.143**	0.140**
	(0.054)	(0.042)	(0.046)
−2 log likelihood	214.98**	200.13**	223.71**
	(5 df)	(5 df)	(5 df)

*Significant at the .05 level.
**Significant at the .01 level.

TABLE 5. Classification Results

Model	Predicted R, Observed R	Predicted R, Observed D	Predicted D, Observed D	Predicted D, Observed R	Percentage Correct
1980 ($N = 169$)					
$l_i \neq 1$	93	5	63	8	92.3
$l_i = 1$	94	6	62	7	92.3
$l_{iD} = 1, l_{iR} \neq 1$	93	5	63	8	92.3
1984 ($N = 774$)					
$l_i \neq 1$	440	24	286	24	93.8
$l_i = 1$	439	24	286	25	93.7
$l_{iR} = 1, l_{iD} \neq 1$	440	27	283	24	93.4
1988 ($N = 547$)					
$l_i \neq 1$	282	25	224	16	92.5
$l_i = 1$	279	20	229	19	92.9
$l_{iR} = 1, l_{iD} \neq 1$	276	27	222	22	91.0

Note: R denotes the Republican candidate; D denotes the Democratic candidate.

compares the simple additive model with a model that includes a standard set of interactive variables.

As a second test, we compared the two probabilistic spatial models in terms of their ability to predict average perceived candidate issue positions. An advantage of spatial voting models over behavioral models of the vote is that spatial models are explicitly designed to answer the question of what issue positions the candidates will adopt. Thus, we can compute the equilibrium issue positions for the candidates for each of the two probabilistic spatial models and then see which predicts actual (i.e., average perceived) issue positions more accurately in each of the three elections.

For the multi-issue probabilistic model with the separable, quadratic policy utility function given by equation (5), the equilibrium candidate position on each issue is a straightforward generalization of that for the one-issue model. Using equation (5) as the voter's policy utility function, but dropping the voter subscript from the candidate's issue position, we can calculate R's equilibrium position on issue k as

$$t_{Rk}^* = \frac{\sum_i f_i(d_i)\ell_{iR}a_{ik}(x_{ik} - SQ_{ik} + \ell_{iR}SQ_{ik})}{\sum_i f_i(d_i)\ell_{iR}^2 a_{ik}} \tag{7}$$

while t_{Dk}^* can be obtained by substituting ℓ_{iD} for ℓ_{iR} in equation (7).

Examination of (7) shows that, if $\ell_{iR} = 1$, t_{Rk}^* reduces to the weighted mean equilibrium of Enelow and Hinich (1984),

$$t_{Rk}^* = \frac{\sum_i f_i(d_i)a_{ik}x_{ik}}{\sum_i f_i(d_i)a_{ik}} \tag{8}$$

and $t_{Dk}^* = t_{Rk}^*$.

In computing t_{Rk}^* and t_{Dk}^* from the NES data, we are faced with several constraints. First, the logistic regression assumes a single distribution function for the underlying dependent variable, so we must drop the voter subscript i from the density function f_i and use a common voter density. Second, logit estimates a common voter salience weight on each issue, so we must drop the voter subscript i from a_{ik} and use a common voter salience weight. Otherwise, the data are sufficient to estimate equation (7) for the Republican candidate and the companion equation for the Democrat.

In tables 6 and 7 we present the results of paired comparisons between the equilibrium predictions of equations (7) and (8) for the Republican and Democratic candidates on the five issues of 1980, the seven issues of 1984, and the four issues of 1988, giving us thirty-two comparisons in all. The results reported in the column labeled $\ell_{i\text{INC}} = 1$, $\ell_{i\text{CHAL}} \neq 1$ are discussed later in the

TABLE 6. Candidate Equilibrium Positions

	Mean		$\ell_{i_j} \neq 1$		$\ell_{i_j} = 1$	$\ell_{i\text{INC}} = 1$, $\ell_{i\text{CHAL}} \neq 1$	
	R_k	D_k	t^*_{Rk}	t^*_{Dk}	t^*_{jk}	t^*_{Rk}	t^*_{Dk}
1980							
Abortion	3.33	4.66	4.74	4.70	5.18	4.67	5.22
Defense spending	5.60	3.50	6.42	6.50	5.12	6.37	5.30
Employment and inflation	3.56	4.47	4.04	3.99	4.27	3.98	4.06
Government services and spending	3.23	5.15	3.54	3.43	4.60	3.46	4.10
Taxes and tax cuts	4.36	2.21	5.05	5.20	3.62	5.13	3.80
1984							
Central America	2.69	4.53	5.67	5.54	4.71	4.67	5.49
Cooperation with Russia	5.18	3.13	3.31	3.37	3.68	3.82	3.37
Defense spending	5.78	3.19	2.88	2.95	3.59	3.75	3.02
Government services and spending	2.75	5.10	4.65	4.57	4.36	4.16	4.53
Jobs and standard of living	5.16	3.17	3.80	3.88	3.92	4.15	3.90
Minority aid	4.68	3.06	4.02	3.98	3.87	4.04	4.03
Status of women	4.65	3.03	3.53	3.53	3.63	3.79	3.58
1988							
Cooperation with Russia	4.22	3.28	3.29	3.38	3.64	3.56	3.36
Defense spending	5.39	3.09	3.08	3.21	3.96	3.90	3.29
Government services and spending	3.38	5.26	4.32	4.32	4.23	4.12	4.31
Jobs and standard of living	5.27	3.12	4.00	4.13	4.33	4.40	4.15

TABLE 7. Distance between Mean and Predicted Candidate Issue Positions

	$\ell_{i_j} \neq 1$		$\ell_{i_j} = 1$		$\ell_{i_{INC}} = 1, \ell_{i_{CHAL}} \neq 1$	
	$\lvert t^*_{Rk} - R_k \rvert$	$\lvert t^*_{Dk} - D_k \rvert$	$\lvert t^*_{jk} - R_k \rvert$	$\lvert t^*_{jk} - D_k \rvert$	$\lvert t^*_{Rk} - R_k \rvert$	$\lvert t^*_{Dk} - D_k \rvert$
1980						
Abortion	1.41a	0.04ab	1.85	0.52	1.34b	0.56
Defense Spending	0.82	3.00	0.48ab	1.62ab	0.77	1.80
Employment and inflation	0.48a	0.48	0.71	0.20ab	0.42b	0.41
Government services and spending	0.31a	1.73	1.37	0.55ab	0.23b	1.05
Taxes and tax cuts	0.69ab	2.99	0.74	1.41ab	0.77	1.59
1984						
Central America	2.98	1.01	2.02a	0.18ab	1.98b	0.96
Cooperation with Russia	1.87	0.24ac	1.50a	0.55	1.37b	0.24c
Defense spending	2.90	0.24a	2.19a	0.40	2.03b	0.17b
Government services and spending	1.90	0.53ab	1.61a	0.74	1.41b	0.57
Jobs and standard of living	1.36	0.71a	1.24a	0.75	1.01b	0.73b
Minority aid	0.66a	0.92	0.81	0.81ab	0.64b	0.97
Status of women	1.12	0.50ab	1.02a	0.60	0.86b	0.55
1988						
Cooperation with Russia	0.93	0.10a	0.58ab	0.36	0.66	0.08b
Defense spending	2.31	0.12ab	1.43ab	0.87	1.49	0.20
Government services and spending	0.94	0.94ab	0.85a	1.03	0.74b	0.95
Jobs and standard of living	1.27	1.01ab	0.94a	1.21	0.87b	1.03

a denotes closer predictor of the first two models.
b denotes closest prediction of all three models.
c denotes a tie for closest prediction between two models.

chapter. It can be argued that since we predict a single position for each candidate on each issue, we should view the status quo position on each issue as a single value. For this reason, we computed equation (7) two ways; one with SQ_{ik} taken from the data and one setting SQ_{ik} equal to its mean perceived value $\Sigma_i SQ_{ik}/n$. The two sets of predictions are quite similar. In tables 6 and 7 the results used are based on setting SQ_{ik} equal to its mean value.

Our goodness-of-fit measure is the absolute distance between the predicted value of $t_{jk}*$ and the average perceived value of candidate j on issue k, R_k for candidate R, and D_k for candidate D. In table 7, the more accurate of the two predictions of absolute difference is identified. Inspection of the table shows that the models of equations (7) and (8) perform about equally well from this standpoint. Out of thirty-two cases, the adjusted issue model of equation (7) predicts more accurately than the unadjusted issue model of (8) fifteen times (47 percent). This is certainly a small difference.

If we adopt the convention that a prediction closer than 0.5 is "correct" and is otherwise "incorrect," the competence-adjusted issue model predicts correctly eight times out of thirty-two (25 percent), while the unadjusted issue model predicts correctly five times (16 percent). Neither rate is good. If we assume that a prediction closer than 1 is correct, the adjusted model predicts correctly eighteen times (56 percent), while the unadjusted model predicts correctly nineteen times (59 percent). Again, a disappointment.

Examination of table 7 does reveal one interesting result. If we view Bush as the incumbent in 1988, the adjusted model does a much better job than the unadjusted model of predicting the issue positions of challengers. In thirteen out of sixteen cases (81 percent), the adjusted model predicts challenger issue positions better than the unadjusted model. At the same time, the unadjusted model predicts incumbent issue positions better than the adjusted model in fourteen out of sixteen cases (88 percent). This finding is highly suggestive, indicating that voters view challenger issue positions differently than they do those of incumbents. A possible explanation is that voters take incumbent positions at face value, having had time to apply an appropriate discount before the survey is conducted, while not having sufficient time or information to do the same for the challenger.

What is suggested in table 7 is that a hybrid model may be appropriate with $\ell_{ij} = 1$ for the incumbent and $\ell_{ij} \neq 1$ for the challenger. We therefore constructed a third probabilistic model with precisely this feature. Empirically, this means that the m independent issue variables described in equation (6) are replaced by m variables I_k ($k = 1, \ldots, m$), where

$$I_k = [(A_{Dik} - x_{ik})^2 - (t_{Rik} - x_{ik})^2] \quad \text{if } R = \text{incumbent} \qquad (9)$$

$$I_k = [(t_{Dik} - x_{ik})^2 - (A_{Rik} - x_{ik})^2] \quad \text{if } D = \text{incumbent} \qquad (10)$$

with the candidate of the incumbent's party considered the incumbent if the incumbent does not seek reelection. The independent variable ($k_{iR} - k_{iD}$) and, of course, the dependent variable remain the same.

The equilibrium issue positions of the two candidates for this hybrid model are equation (7) for the challenger and equation (8) for the incumbent. However, d_i differs because the voter policy utility function is described by (5) if R is the challenger, while if R is the incumbent A_{Rik} is replaced by t_{iRk}. This change also applies to u_{iD}. In computing equilibrium issue positions for this hybrid model, d_i is estimated by the third logit described here, with different regression coefficients and a different constant term.

In the third columns of tables 2, 3, and 4 statistics are reported from three logistic regressions based on this hybrid model. The third, sixth, and ninth rows of table 5 represent the classification results of the hybrid model for each election year. As shown in table 5, the hybrid model predicts individual votes about as well as the other two probabilistic models, but certainly no better.

The real difference between the hybrid model and its competitors is found in table 6 and 7: the hybrid model predicts candidate issue positions much more accurately than does either the simple or adjusted issue models. In table 7 the closest prediction of absolute difference is identified for the three models. In sixteen out of thirty-two cases (50 percent), the hybrid model predicts issue positions as well as or better than *either* of the other two models. The simple model does best nine times (28 percent), and the adjusted model does as well or better than the other two models eight times (25 percent). The hybrid model beats or equals the simple additive model twenty-one times (66 percent) and the adjusted issue model twenty-four times (75 percent).

Also of note is the improved ability of the hybrid model to predict candidate issue differences. All predicted issue differences are in the same direction as the difference in average issue perceptions. In addition, the predicted issue differences correspond much more closely to those found in the data. In 1980 the average $|R_k - D_k|$ across k is 1.68, while the average $|t_{Rk}^* - t_{Dk}^*|$ for the hybrid model is 0.73. For 1984, the average $|R_k - D_k|$ is 2.01, while the average $|t_{Rk}^* - t_{Dk}^*|$ is 0.40. For 1988, the average $|R_k - D_k|$ is 1.82, while the average $|t_{Rk}^* - t_{Dk}^*|$ is 0.31. The hybrid model does not go far enough in predicting candidate issue differences, but it does a much better job than either the competence-adjusted model or the unadjusted issue model, which predicts no differences at all.

In conclusion, some modification of the standard probabilistic spatial model is appropriate if we are to better explain voter perceptions of candidate issue positions. While the hybrid probabilistic model does a better job than either the standard probabilistic model or the competence-adjusted model, there is still a lot of room for improvement. Given the limitations of our data, we are unable to conclude whether the fault lies with our models, the data, or both. We can only say that probabilistic spatial models need to incorporate features that explain the persistent issue differences we find in the data.

Conclusions

In this chapter, we offer a revised probabilistic spatial model of two-candidate simple plurality elections that assumes that voters discount candidate issue positions by the perceived competence of the candidate. We show that, theoretically, this modification is sufficient to explain candidate divergence on the issues of the campaign, unlike the standard probabilistic spatial model that predicts candidate convergence.

We performed two tests to compare the revised probabilistic model against the standard model. Using NES data from the 1980, 1984, and 1988 American presidential elections, we compared the ability of the two models to predict individual votes, finding that both models performed equally well. We also compared the ability of the two models to predict average perceived candidate issue positions, finding that the revised model did a better job than the standard model of predicting challenger issue positions, while the reverse is true for incumbents.

These two findings suggested a third model in which voters discount the issue positions of challengers but not those of incumbents. We found that this hybrid model predicts individual votes no better than the other two models, but it does a much better job of predicting candidate issue positions.

This is not to say that this third model should be embraced. The ability of the hybrid model to predict candidate issue positions exceeds that of the other two models, but it is still far from perfect. Although the data are admittedly unsatisfactory for testing these models, more work clearly needs to be done on developing probabilistic spatial models that predict different candidate issue positions.

CHAPTER 9

"What This Campaign Is All about Is . . . ": A Rational Choice Alternative to the Downsian Spatial Model of Elections

Thomas H. Hammond and Brian D. Humes

It has long been commonplace to hear political campaigns described in terms of how each candidate attempts to "frame the issue" or "shape the political debate." For example, a prominent feature of presidential elections in the United States has been that each candidate tends to stress a particular kind of issue as being *the* paramount issue in the campaign, as with the "community values" campaign of Bush in 1988, symbolized by his concern with flag burning and Willie Horton. Each candidate's intent, of course, is to portray that he or she has views that are compatible with those of a majority of voters, and to portray the opponent as having views that are incompatible with those of the voters.

As uncontroversial as this view of political campaigns is, it is not, we believe, captured in the rational choice models of political campaigns that stem from Anthony Downs's *Economic Theory of Democracy* (1957b). In its simplest form, the spatial model of political campaigns advanced by Downs treats elections as occurring on a single ideological dimension. The central result is that candidates, in an effort to win a majority of the votes, adopt issue positions that converge on the location of the median voter in the electorate.

It has long been accepted, of course, that Downs's original model, itself based on the model of spatial competition developed by Harold Hotelling (1929), suffers from a variety of inadequacies. Since its initial presentation Downs's spatial model has been modified in a wide variety of ways, incorporating such matters as multiple issue dimensions (Black and Newing 1951; Black 1958; Davis, Hinich, and Ordeshook 1970), abstention and alienation (Hinich and Ordeshook 1969), voter attitudes toward risk (Shepsle 1972), probabilistic voting by voters (Coughlin 1982), candidate uncertainty as to where voter ideal points lie (Enelow and Hinich 1984), primary nominations

---

The original version of this chapter was presented at the annual meeting of the American Political Science Association, San Francisco, August 30, 1990.

(Aldrich 1983a, 1983b), and the subtleties of just what it is that candidates are maximizing (Hinich and Ordeshook 1970; Wittman 1973, 1977). James M. Enelow and Melvin J. Hinich (1984) provide a comprehensive review and synthesis. Despite these and other modifications, the basic model originally posited by Downs remains relatively unchanged: campaigns are contests about position taking on a preexisting and broadly accepted set of issue dimensions.

In this chapter we argue that the essential vision of electoral competition posited by Downs is empirically inaccurate. At least two reasons might be noted. First, a candidate publicly shifting an issue position to suit the voters' tastes engenders suspicion, distrust, and uncertainty among voters: as a voter might reason, "If the candidate is shifting his views for me today, he may shift his views for someone else tomorrow." Second, while campaigns are indeed multidimensional affairs, as suggested, this does not mean that each voter takes all, or even many, of these dimensions into account when voting. Due to *imperfect information* voters, for example, may be unable to make the multidimensional calculations of "distance" that are required. Alternatively, due to the fact that voters find it *costly* to make the required multidimensional calculations of distance, they may be *unwilling* to make the required calculations. However one conceives of the capabilities of voters, the consequence is that voters generally consider only a handful of the dimensions, perhaps just one or two, when deciding how to vote.

These circumstances create a very different kind of political problem for a candidate. A rational strategy—and one that we think is more characteristic of actual candidate behavior than the traditional Downsian model—is for the candidate to portray issues in such a way that, on the dimension emphasized by the candidate, the candidate appears spatially "close" to a majority of voters, or the other candidate as spatially "further away" from the voters. Thus when we see a candidate proclaiming, "What this campaign is all about is . . . ," it should be seen as a means of framing voters' perceptions of the candidate's spatial location, given their spatial locations and that of the other candidate. In effect, the campaign takes place not by candidates moving their actual positions to optimal spatial locations, which is the essence of the traditional Downsian model, but by using campaign rhetoric and emphasizing issues in such a way that each candidate's spatial location is perceived by the voters to be closer to theirs than the other candidate's. Instead of candidates trying to figure out what positions to take, then, political campaigns are turned into contests about what the issue dimensions of the campaign will be. In the Downsian model, the voters move the candidates around; in our alternative model, the candidates can be said to move the voters around.

Some of this approach has already appeared, in bits and pieces, in the political science literature. Three decades ago Elmer E. Schattschneider (1960) sketched out a view of political conflict that stresses how a political actor, when appearing likely to lose on the current dimension of interest, will raise a second, crosscutting issue to reduce the opponent's support and increase his or her own. In criticizing the Kenneth A. Shepsle (1972) model of spatial elections, Benjamin I. Page (1976) proposes an "issue emphasis" model of campaigns in which candidates emphasize some issue dimensions and say nothing about others. Nicholas R. Miller (1983) notes connections between arguments like Schattschneider's, derived in part from the traditional literature on pluralism in American politics, and more recent rational choice models. In Miller's view, the introduction of new crosscutting issues, à la Schattschneider, is similar to the way rational choice theorists might discuss campaigning and policy-making in multidimensional issue spaces. Indeed, at roughly the same time that Miller was advancing these views, William H. Riker began publishing a series of studies of how rational political actors could take advantage of the fundamental instabilities in the electorate's collective preferences by raising issues that cut across the current coalition lineup, (see Riker 1982a, chaps. 8–9, 1983, 1984, 1986; and also Fink (1987). In these studies of what he calls *heresthetic,* Riker describes a number of instances in which issue framing has dramatically affected political outcomes.

None of these scholars, however, has adequately incorporated these original insights into a clearly specified model of how rational candidates ought to proceed in their issue-framing enterprise. Indeed, in *The Art of Political Manipulation* (1986) Riker observes that "heresthetic is an art, not a science. There is no set of scientific laws that can be more or less mechanically applied to generate successful strategies" (ix). Riker does suggest (xi) that heresthetic was recognized by academics as a field of theoretical inquiry before they recognized it as a practical art. Yet the available theoretical studies mostly serve to point out the *possibilities* of manipulation; they do little to provide a way of calculating what might be optimal strategies for the actors engaging in such maneuvers.

The purpose of this chapter is to make the art of heresthetics somewhat more of a science. In a more recent paper Riker (1990) calls for the development of a spatial model of heresthetical manipulation and offers a number of suggestions as to how this might be developed. A slightly earlier paper by Scott L. Feld and Bernard Grofman (1988a) can be seen as a contribution to what Riker calls for, since the authors describe how the "structure of debate" could affect majority rule outcomes in one-issue-at-a-time decision making. Their model, however, is undeveloped in a number of important ways. See also Paine 1989 and Humes (1993).[1]

---

1. The James M. Enelow and Melvin J. Hinich (1984, chap. 4) spatial model involving a "predictive dimension" appears to have some similarities to ours. However, their predictive dimension is not something that is selected or imposed by the candidates; instead it is more a function of the voters' original means of evaluating the candidates. In addition, the two candidates in the Enelow-Hinich model will *share* a predictive dimension, while in our model the two candidates will normally select different dimensions as strategies.

In our chapter we present a two-dimensional spatial model of issue framing by two candidates for elective office. We have five goals here. First, we want to develop a set of techniques by which the optimal issue-framing strategies of candidates can be described. Second, we want to use these techniques to calculate what the optimal strategy is when there is just one candidate. Third, when there are two candidates, we want to determine whether candidate strategies are independent from each other or interdependent. Fourth, we want to calculate what the optimal strategies are when there are two candidates; in particular, we want to determine whether or not the candidate strategies *converge* (i.e., do they both choose the same dimension as a strategy?). Fifth, we want to discuss possible applications of our ideas to political arenas other than electoral politics. Our ultimate purpose is to develop a multidimensional spatial model that can be used as a framework for studying the phenomenon of issue framing in a wide variety of political institutions.

Assumptions and Notation

Our model is based on a set of assumptions commonly used in spatial modeling. There is a multidimensional issue space, and each actor has an ideal point in this issue space. To ease the development and presentation of the model for this particular chapter, we make two simplifying assumptions: there are just two issue dimensions, and each actor has circular indifference curves over points in this two-dimensional space. There are two candidates and an odd number of voters. (The candidates themselves are assumed not to vote.) The candidates know the location of each voter's ideal point in the issue space as well as their own ideal point and that of the other candidate.

We assume that no voter can determine the Euclidean distance from his or her own ideal point to either candidate's ideal point; we can assume, for example, that the information-processing costs are too great.[2] But when a dimension is supplied by a candidate, the voter can determine how far away the candidate is *on that particular dimension*. In effect, the voters can measure and count, but they cannot do geometry. Moreover, we assume that a voter can evaluate the candidates only in terms of one issue dimension presented by each candidate, for a total of only two issue dimensions. This means that candidate 1 will state, in effect, that he wants the voters to evaluate him in terms of some issue dimension i, on which he makes his own position known. Similarly, candidate 2 wants the voters to evaluate her in terms of

---

2. Our ultimate goal is a multidimensional model not restricted to two dimensions. In this larger issue space the (assumed) incapacity of voters to calculate multidimensional distances is more convincing than when there are just two issue dimensions.

some issue dimension j, on which she makes her own position known. (Dimension i may or may not be the same as dimension j.) We assume that candidate 2 will not make her position known on candidate 1's dimension i, nor will candidate 1 make his position known on candidate 2's dimension j. Only if dimension i is identical to dimension j will a voter have a common means of evaluating both candidates.

Finally, we assume that a voter will cast a ballot for the candidate who is closer to him or her on either of these two dimensions: for example, if the voter is closer to candidate 1 on dimension i, which was presented by candidate 1, than the voter is to candidate 2 on dimension j, which was presented by candidate 2, then the voter will vote for candidate 1. The candidate who wins the election is the candidate who is able to find an issue dimension that places his or her ideal point closer to those of a majority of voters than is the ideal point of the opponent of this opponent's dimension.

Examples and Observations

We now examine the implications of these assumptions for the choices and strategies of the candidates. We proceed primarily with a series of examples. (In a subsequent paper we hope to develop a more rigorous specification and proof of our arguments.)

We begin by examining the optimal strategy of a single candidate considered in isolation from the other candidate. In Fig. 1 there is just one candidate, labeled C_1, and one voter, labeled V_1. The candidate's set of strategies is composed, in effect, of all possible rotations $\Theta = \{0°$ to $360°\}$ of a straight line through the candidate's ideal point. We label a strategy in terms of its counterclockwise rotation from a horizontal line. Thus one possible strategy for $\Theta = 0°$, and for V_1 this strategy induces a preference of $v_1(0°)$ on the $\Theta = 0°$ line. Note in figure 1 that this strategy $\Theta = 0°$ induces a preference for V_1 that is not identical to the candidate's ideal point. However, if the candidate selects a strategy of $\Theta = 160°$, V_1's induced ideal point on the $\Theta = 160°$ line, $v_1(160°)$, is *identical* to that of the candidate. For the candidate to gain the support of this voter, then the candidate's optimal strategy is to present a dimension that is perpendicular to the line drawn through his or her ideal point and that of the voter. If we define the angle between the candidate and voter as $\alpha°$ (measured from the horizontal baseline), the optimal strategy, $\Theta°$, for the candidate is $(\alpha + 90)°$. We can summarize this point in the following manner:

> *Observation 1.* If the angle between the candidate and any single voter is $\alpha°$, the candidate can best attract the voter's support by adopting a strategy of $\Theta^* = (\alpha \pm 90)°$ such that $\Theta^* \epsilon [0°, 180°]$.

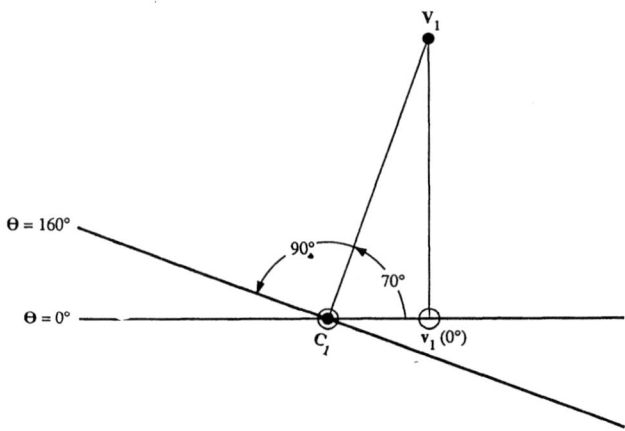

Fig. 1. An optimal strategy with a single voter

It is obvious that this $\Theta^* = (\alpha + 90)°$ strategy will always exist, and the only qualification on the observation is that the other candidate has available a similar strategy that will bring that candidate's own ideal point and that of the voter into alignment. If there is just one voter and each candidate adopts his or her optimal strategy, the voter's induced ideal point on each dimension will be located at the ideal point of *each* candidate. In this case, we could assume that the voter either does not vote or votes randomly, but this matter will not play any role in our analysis here.

As this observation suggests, a candidate's strategies range, for all practical purposes, from $\Theta = 0°$ to $\Theta = 180°$. For rotations of $\Theta = 180°$ and beyond, the strategies become equivalent (at least when there are two underlying issue dimensions) to the strategies for the range of $\Theta = 0°$ to $\Theta = 180°$. Thus $\Theta = 0°$ is equivalent to $\Theta = 180°$, $\Theta = 1°$ is equivalent to $\Theta = 181°$, $\Theta = 2°$ is equivalent to $\Theta = 182°$, and so forth. Hence we can state

Observation 2. A candidate's strategies are equivalent (in two dimensions) for $\Theta + k(180°)$ for any real k.

If there are several voters and one candidate, what is the optimal strategy for the candidate? To address this question, consider the three voters, V_1, V_2, and V_3, in figure 2. From the viewpoint of the candidate, V_2 is the "median" voter in the sense that a line from C_1 to V_2 bisects the voters into two groups; on or to the left of the C_1-V_2 line lie half the voters (V_1 and V_2), and on or to

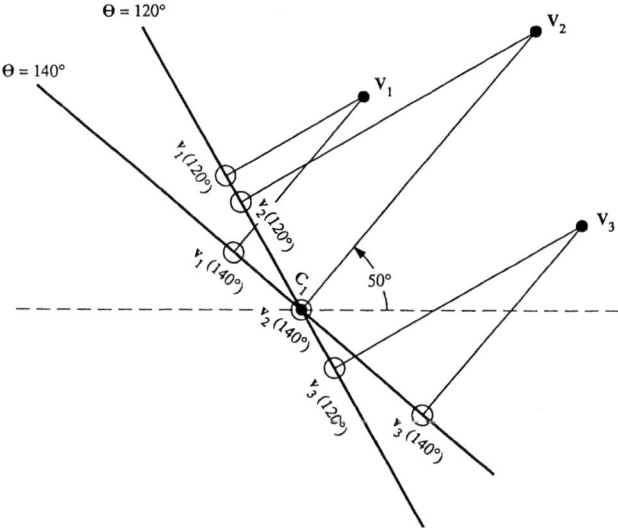

Fig. 2. An optimal strategy with three voters

the right of the C_1-V_2 line lie half the voters (V_2 and V_3).[3] Now assume that the candidate adopts a strategy that ensures the support of V_2. Since V_2 lies at an angle of 50° from the horizontal, $\Theta = 50° + 90° = 140°$. In this way, voter V_2's induced ideal point comes to be located at C_1's ideal point, while V_1's induced ideal point is $v_1(140°)$ and V_3's induced ideal point is $v_3(140°)$, as indicated in the diagram.

Can the candidate adopt some other strategy that would increase the support given to the candidate by the three voters? For example, consider $\Theta = 120°$, as indicated in figure 2. This change in strategy from 140° changes the induced ideal points of all three voters. Voter V_2's induced ideal point is no longer located at C_1's ideal point but at $v_2(120°)$, while V_1's induced ideal point is now $v_1(120°)$ and V_3's is $v_3(120°)$, as indicated. Note that the induced ideal points of two of the voters—V_1 and V_2—are now farther away from C_1 and only one induced ideal point—that of V_3—is closer. The candidate thus increases the support from only one voter but decreases the support from two voters. A rotation in the other direction, such as a change to $\Theta = 160°$, has much the same effect; in this case (not shown in fig. 2), the support of V_2 and V_3 decreases, while the support of only V_1 increases. We can conclude that if

---

3. The C_1-V_2 line can be considered a kind of "electorate bisector," in the sense developed in Hammond and Miller 1987.

the angle between the candidate and the "median" voter is $\alpha°$, the optimal strategy, Θ^*, for the candidate is $(\alpha + 90)°$. This point can be summarized in the following manner:

> *Observation 3.* If the angle between the candidate and the "median" voter is $\alpha°$, the candidate can maximize support from the voters by adopting a strategy of $\Theta^* = (\alpha + 90)°$.

It is only rarely the case, of course, that elections in the United States have just one candidate, and so Observation 3 might seem to have a relatively limited scope of applicability. There are political contexts, however, in which there is just one major actor that nonetheless does require public support (as with a one-party state or a bureaucracy that has no jurisdictional competitors), so this observation is of some interest. We discuss these other applications later in the chapter.

In figure 2 note that the candidate's ideal point lies *outside* the Pareto set of the voters (i.e., outside the triangle formed by V_1, V_2, and V_3). This ensures that there is only one best strategy for the candidate since there will be only one "median" voter. If the candidate's ideal point lies *inside* the voters' Pareto set, however, there is no longer necessarily just one optimal strategy for the candidate. For example, consider the diagram in figure 3, in which C_1 lies inside the V_1-V_2-V_3 triangle. In this case there are *three* possible median voters, depending on which Θ the candidate chooses. If the candidate chooses $\Theta = 9°$, V_3 becomes the median voter whose ideal point is induced to coincide with that of C_1. If the candidate chooses $\Theta = 50°$, V_1 becomes the median voter whose ideal point is induced to coincide with that of C_1. And if the candidate chooses $\Theta = 153°$, V_2 becomes the median voter whose ideal point is induced to coincide with that of C_1. Thus there are three strategies from which C_1 may choose. We can summarize this point as follows:

> *Observation 4.* A candidate has a larger set of potentially optimal strategies when the candidate's ideal point lies inside the voters' Pareto set than when the ideal point lies outside the voters' Pareto set.

In figure 3, one of these strategies, $\Theta = 50°$, is clearly dominated by the $\Theta = 9°$ strategy: since $v_2(50°)$ is farther from C_1 than $v_2(9°)$, and $v_3(50°)$ is farther from C_1 than $v_1(9°)$, it would seem that we can eliminate $\Theta = 50°$ as a viable strategy. It is not so easy, however, to choose between $\Theta = 9°$ and $\Theta = 153°$ since $v_1(153°)$ is farther from C_1 than $v_1(9°)$, but $v_3(153°)$ is closer to C_1 than $v_2(9°)$, there is not a clear dominance relation between the $\Theta = 9°$ and $\Theta = 153°$ strategies. If the candidate is trying to minimize the sum of the distances from the candidate's ideal point to the induced ideal points of the

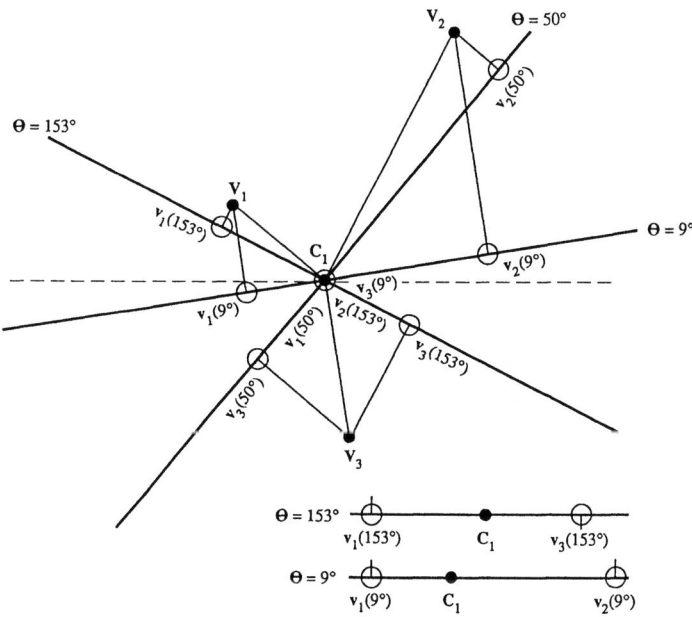

Fig. 3. Strategies when the candidate lies inside the voters' Pareto set

nonmedian voters, then $\Theta = 153°$ is the better strategy: the sum $\{|v_1(153°) - C_1| + |v_3(153°) - C_1|\}$ is less than the sum $\{|v_1(9°) - C_1| + |v_2(9°) - C_1|\}$.[4]

As a candidate varies his or her strategy from $\Theta = 0°$ to $\Theta = 180°$, the distance from the candidate's ideal point to the voter's induced ideal point follows a regular and predictable pattern. In figure 4 consider the line from the candidate's ideal point, C_1, to the voter's ideal point, V_1, as the diameter of a circle. Draw the circle for which this line is a diameter; a circle can be inscribed with its center at the point r halfway along this line. With $\Theta = 0°$, the resulting $v_1(0°)$ is identical to the candidate's ideal point at C_1 With $\Theta = 30°$, the resulting induced ideal point falls at $v_1(30°)$, the point at which the $\Theta = 30°$ line intersects the circle just constructed. With $\Theta = 60°$, the induced ideal point falls at $v_1(60°)$, the point at which the $\Theta = 60°$ line intersects the circle. The induced ideal points for the $\Theta = 90°, \Theta = 120°, \Theta = 150°$, and $\Theta = 180°$ strategies likewise fall at $v_1(90°), v_1(120°), v_1(150°)$, and $v_1(180°)$ on the circle. Thus it is relatively easy to determine for each candidate and each

---

4. Later in the chapter it appears that this possible candidate objective—minimize the sum of the distances of the voters' induced ideal points from the candidate's ideal point—may be irrelevant, given interdependence in candidate strategies.

150   Information, Participation, and Choice

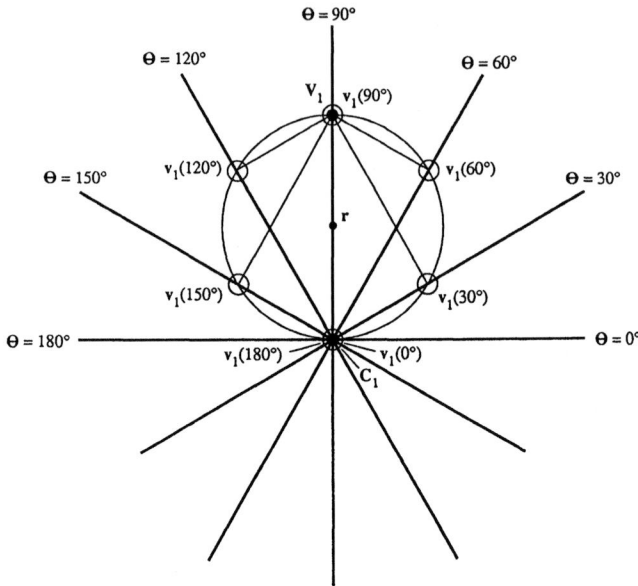

Fig. 4. A voter's induced ideal point, given various candidate strategies

candidate strategy precisely where each voter's induced ideal point will lie. If we define the chord resulting from a particular Θ strategy as the Θ-chord for a voter, we can conclude the following:

> *Observation 5.* Given a strategy Θ by a candidate, the distance from a voter's induced ideal point to the candidate's ideal point is the length of the Θ-chord of the circle for that voter.

This will be a useful technique for conducting our analysis.

Let us now bring a second candidate into the fray but require that the two candidates must choose the *same* strategy, that is, $\Theta_1 = \Theta_2$. We abandon this (rather artificial) requirement in the following, but it does lead to an observation that provides some intuition and insight for when we later address the question of which candidate can be expected to win an election.

Assume there is an electorate consisting of just one voter whose support is being sought by two candidates. Note in figure 5 that candidate 1's ideal point is considerably closer to that of the voter, in Euclidean distance, than is candidate 2's ideal point. This appears to have important implications for the outcome of an election. Given the ideal point locations in figure 5, candidate C_1 of course has a $\Theta° = 0°$ (see A in fig. 5), while candidate C_2 has a $\Theta^* =$

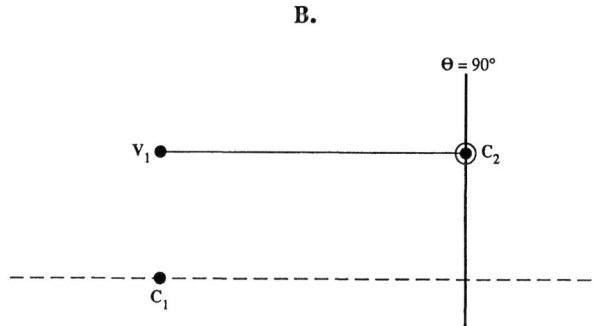

Fig. 5. Two candidates with the same strategy

90° (see B in fig. 5). Thus C_1 wins if $\Theta = 0°$ is adopted, while C_2 wins if $\Theta = 90°$ is adopted.

But now consider what happens if strategies of $\Theta = 45°$ or $\Theta = 135°$ are adopted. These strategies are, in a sense, "halfway" in between the $\Theta = 0°$ strategy, which would be advantageous to candidate 1 (the voter's induced ideal point would coincide with that of candidate 1), and the $\Theta = 90°$ strategy, which would be advantageous to candidate 2 (the voter's induced idea point would coincide with that of candidate 2). If the Euclidean distance from a candidate to the voter were irrelevant, one might expect that the $\Theta = 45°$ and $\Theta = 135°$ strategies would not favor either candidate. In fact, however, *both* strategies favor candidate 1. In figure 6, A, we show the consequences of a $\Theta = 45°$ strategy adopted by the candidates. If we label the Θ-chord involving candidate 1 as length x and the Θ-chord involving candidate 2 as length y, it is obvious that x is shorter than y, and so V_1 would vote for candidate 1.

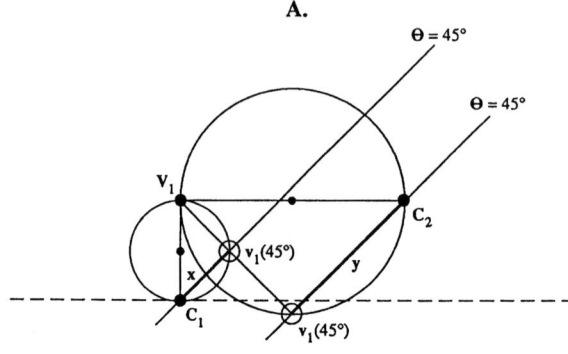

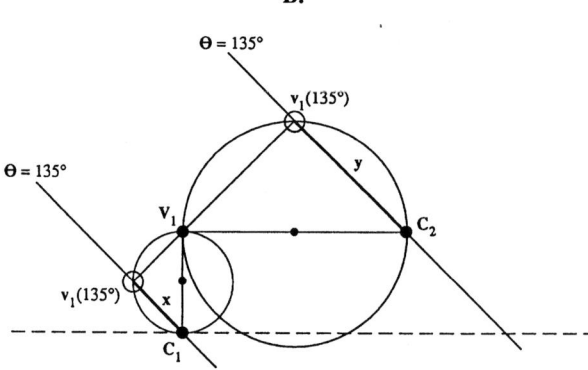

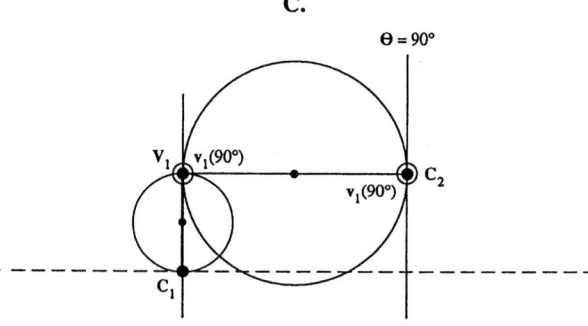

Fig. 6. The closer candidate does better, given identical candidate strategies

Similarly, in figure 6, B, we show the consequences of a $\Theta = 135°$ strategy adopted by both candidates. The Θ-chord lengths are the same as in figure 6, A, and again, the chord x involving candidate 1 is shorter than the chord y involving candidate 2, so V_1 would again vote for candidate 1.

The reason for this consistent behavior favoring candidate 1 stems from the simple fact that, for a given angle, the chord of a smaller circle is shorter than the chord of a larger circle. It is only strategies in the vicinity of $\Theta = 90°$—candidate 2's optimal strategy—that candidate 2 is favored; see figure 6, C. All other strategies favor candidate 1. While this matter requires considerably more thought, it may not be extrapolating too much from this simple example to draw the following conclusion:

> *Observation 6.* If two candidates adopt the same strategy, the candidate who is "closer to" a majority of the voters will be favored by a large number of Θ strategies than will the candidate who is "farther away."

What needs more thought is to define precisely what it means to describe one candidate as being "closer to" a majority of the voters than the other candidate.

We now abandon the assumption that the two candidates must adopt identical strategies. That is, it will no longer necessarily be the case that $\Theta_1 = \Theta_2$. Our initial observation here is that two candidates will not, in general, adopt identical strategies: with the two candidates in figure 6, C, for example, $\Theta^* = 0°$ for candidate 1 while $\Theta^* = 90°$ for candidate 2. With one voter, the only case in which two candidates would adopt identical strategies would be the unlikely case in which the ideal points of the voter and the two candidates all lie on a straight line. In this case, each candidate would be able to induce a voter ideal point that is identical to his or hers on their mutually agreed on dimension. Whenever the two candidates' ideal points do not fall on a straight line, their optimal strategies will necessarily differ. Hence we have

> *Observation 7.* Except under rare circumstances, the optimal strategy of candidate 1 will differ from the optimal strategy of candidate 2.

This nonconvergence of candidate strategies might seem to be compatible with the frequently made complaints about political campaigns that "the candidates are talking past each other" and that "the candidates are not joining in a genuine debate with each other."

Our final and most important question is this: does a candidate necessarily have a stable, optimal strategy when the other candidate is free to adopt his or her own strategy? It seems clear that when there is just one candidate who faces any number of voters, there is a stable optimal strategy, as argued in Observation 3. But when there is a second candidate who can adopt his or her own strategy, does this stable optimal strategy even exist for the first candidate?

If one could demonstrate that the optimal strategies of the two candidates are *independent* from each other, then one might conclude that each candidate has a *dominant strategy:* this means that candidate 1 would adopt the same Θ no matter what Θ candidate 2 adopts. A dominant strategy is necessarily in equilibrium, and so we could make a prediction as to what strategies the two candidates would adopt. However, we provide an example in which the candidates' strategies are *not* independent: the strategy candidate 1 adopts affects the strategy candidate 2 adopts, and vice versa.

In figure 7 there are three voters, V_1, V_2 and V_3, whose support is being sought by two candidates, C_1 and C_2. Given the locations of the voters' ideal points, C_1 would choose $\Theta = 0°$ if C_1 could ignore C_2's choice, and C_2 would choose $\Theta = 102°$ if C_2 could ignore C_1's choice. With this pair of strategies, it is straightforward to determine that C_2 would win. To see this, note first that V_2 would vote for C_1 because V_2's induced ideal point, $v_2(0°)$, is identical to C_1's ideal point, while V_1 would vote for C_2 because V_1's induced ideal point, $v_1(102°)$, is identical to C_2's ideal point. V_3 thus becomes the critical voter. On the $\Theta = 0°$ line, we label the distance from C_1 to $v_3(0°)$ as y, and on the $\Theta = 102°$ line we label the distance from C_2 to $v_3(102°)$ as w. Since w is shorter than y, as indicated in the diagram, V_3 casts a ballot for C_2, who thus wins the election.

But C_1 has a strategy that counters the $\Theta = 102°$ strategy of C_2: it is to choose a strategy in the vicinity of $\Theta = 165°$. With a strategy of $\Theta = 165°$, the voters' induced ideal points are now $v_1(165°)$, $v_2(165°)$, and $v_3(165°)$. With this strategy, the induced ideal point of V_3 is now closer to C_1 on the $\Theta = 165°$ line than it is to C_2 on the $\Theta = 102°$ line. Hence V_3 now votes for C_1 instead of C_2. This shift in C_1 strategy does run the risk of shifting V_2's induced ideal point so far that V_2 would vote for C_2, thereby negating the purpose of C_1's new strategy. But with the $\Theta = 165°$ strategy, the induced ideal point of V_2 does remain closer to C_1 (the distance is x) than it is to C_2 on the $\Theta = 102°$ line (the distance is z), so V_2 continues to vote for C_1. Hence this strategy shift by C_1 achieves its purpose: V_2 and V_3 now vote for C_1, and only V_1 votes for C_2. C_1 thus wins the election, given C_2's strategy of $\Theta = 102°$.

This does not end the story, however, because C_2 has a strategy that counters the $\Theta = 165°$ strategy of C_1: it is to choose a strategy of $\Theta = 112°$, a modest shift from the original $\Theta = 102°$ strategy. With a strategy of $\Theta = 112°$, the voters' induced ideal points for C_2 are now $v_1(112°)$, $v_2(112°)$, and $v_3(112°)$. With this strategy, the induced ideal point of V_3 is now closer to C_2 on the $\Theta = 112°$ line than it is to C_1 on the $\Theta = 165°$ line. Hence V_3 now

"What This Campaign Is All about Is . . ."

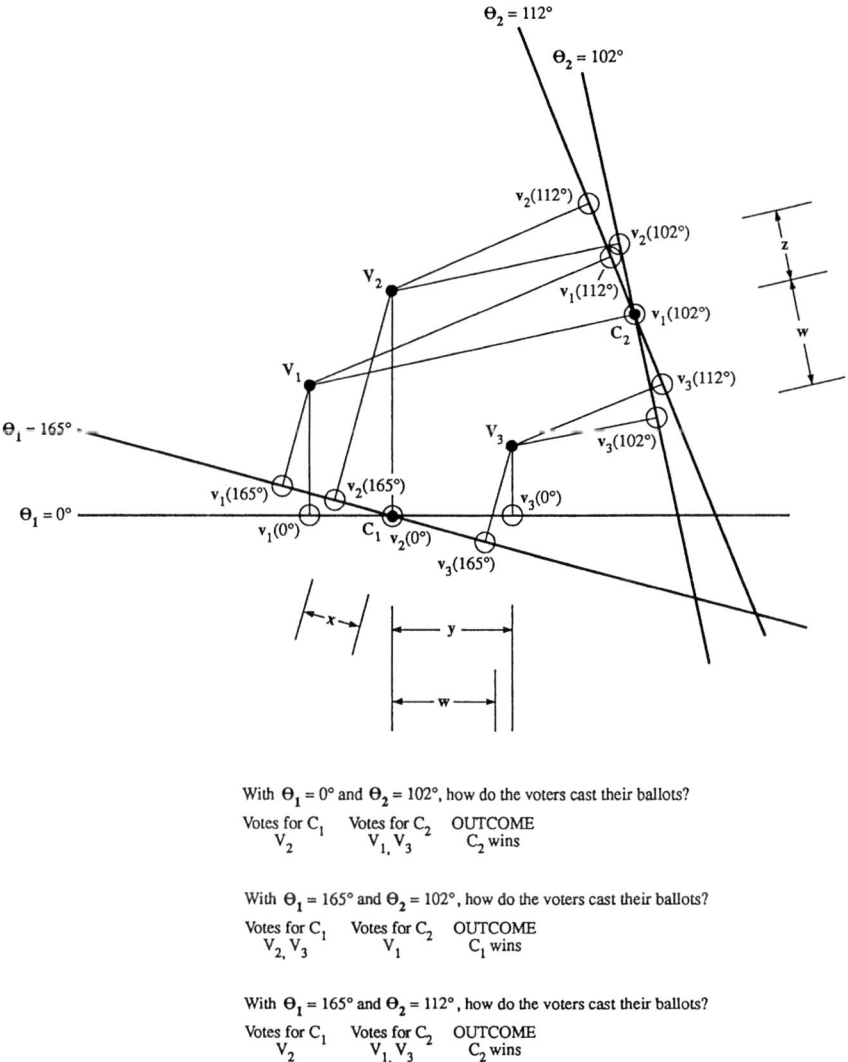

With $\Theta_1 = 0°$ and $\Theta_2 = 102°$, how do the voters cast their ballots?

Votes for C_1	Votes for C_2	OUTCOME
V_2	V_1, V_3	C_2 wins

With $\Theta_1 = 165°$ and $\Theta_2 = 102°$, how do the voters cast their ballots?

Votes for C_1	Votes for C_2	OUTCOME
V_2, V_3	V_1	C_1 wins

With $\Theta_1 = 165°$ and $\Theta_2 = 112°$, how do the voters cast their ballots?

Votes for C_1	Votes for C_2	OUTCOME
V_2	V_1, V_3	C_2 wins

Fig. 7. The candidates' strategies may be interdependent

votes for C_2 instead of C_1. This change in C_1's strategy does run the risk of shifting V_1's induced ideal point so far that V_1 would vote for C_1, thus negating the purpose of C_2's strategy shift. But with the $\Theta = 112°$ strategy, the induced ideal point of V_1 does remain closer to C_2 than it is to C_1, so V_2 continues to vote for C_2. Hence this strategy shift by C_2 achieves its purpose:

V_1 and V_3 now vote for C_2, and only V_2 votes for C_1. C_2 now wins the election, given C_1's strategy of $\Theta = 165°$.

From this example we can draw the following two observations:

Observation 8. The strategy a candidate adopts with no opponent is not necessarily identical to the strategy the candidate adopts with an opponent.

Observation 9. The coalitions supporting each candidate can be expected to change as candidate strategies change (indeed, this is the point of changing a strategy).

The figure 7 example demonstrates that candidates do not necessarily have a dominant strategy: it appears instead that candidate strategies can be interdependent. Given this apparent interdependence, the key question that must now be addressed is whether or not there are *equilibrium strategies* of any sort for the candidates. For example, is there a Nash equilibrium such that if candidate 1 does not change strategy, candidate 2 will not change strategy, and such that if candidate 2 does not change strategy, candidate 1 will not change strategy? While we do not yet have an answer to this central question, we are inclined to think that since there is no equilibrium in the underlying Euclidean majority rule game among voters, there is no equilibrium in the electoral game we have imposed on top of it. Nonetheless, even if our surmise is correct, our figure 7 example does show how carefully calibrated the candidate strategies must be: as we note in the discussion of that example, when attempting to gain the vote of voter 3, candidate 1 had to be careful not to lose the support of voter 2. Candidate 2 had a similar concern in attempting to counteract candidate 1's strategy. Hence it might be that each candidate's strategies are limited to a relatively small set and do not wander all over the available $\Theta = 0°$ to $\Theta = 180°$ range.

Four Modifications

The model developed here is not the only possible model that might be developed for exploring issue framing as a campaign tactic.

First, it would of course be desirable to extend our analysis to contexts in which there are more than just two underlying dimensions.

Second, an obvious alternative involves what is usually referred to as "negative campaigning": the candidate chooses a dimension such that the *other* candidate has (or seems to have) a location on this dimension that is *far* from the voters'. This version of the issue-framing model could utilize without much change the approach and techniques developed here.

Third, another modification involves simply adding more candidates. As far as we can see, most of our techniques could be used here as well. Given a larger number of candidates, in fact, it might be that candidate strategies are more constrained than they appear to be in the two-candidate case.

A fourth version of the issue-framing model diverges somewhat more from what we present here. In our model, each voter is presented with two issue dimensions by which candidates might be evaluated, and the voter just votes for whichever candidate appears "closer." But it might be that a voter would treat each presented dimension as being of some importance, and consequently base the choice of candidate on some "weighted" value that incorporates *both* the distance from the candidate's ideal point *and* the importance to the voter of the dimension involving that distance. In this way the voter's cultural norms and values might be incorporated in an issue-framing model.

Other Applications of the Issue-framing Model

Our models have been developed in the context of electoral competition. But by no means are all of the politics involving elective officials such as the president, representative, or senator multicandidate politics. Much of the officials' time in office, after all, is spent without knowing who their next opponent will be. So these officials may choose ways of representing themselves that maximize the support that the public is likely to give them in the absence of an identifiable candidate. Thus our single candidate model, developed primarily as a way station on the road to a multicandidate model, may have some utility of its own.

Moreover, the single candidate model may have a much broader scope of application than this. For example, it has long been customary for one-party regimes to hold elections. Since even dictatorships generally have finite (and sometimes rather short) lifetimes if there is little or no public support, dictators have an incentive to develop policies for the public, and to present themselves in a favorable light, in such a way that public support (or at least nonopposition) is maximized.

Many other political institutions must also concern themselves with the maintenance of support from the public. Indeed, in their own ways, David Easton (1965) and Murray Edelman (1964) each stress this issue—Easton in a systems framework based on political "demands" and "supports" and Edelman from the viewpoint of a regime that is manipulating symbols to gain public support.

And consider the situation that government agencies face in a separation-of-powers system of government: it has long been understood that they are substantially on their own—that is, they are responsible for creating and maintaining their own public support—to a considerably greater degree than their counterparts in, say, parliamentary regimes. As Francis E. Rourke (1969) and others point out, these agencies use a wide variety of techniques to generate support for themselves. These techniques range from providing benefits to a broad and well-connected segment of the electorate to providing individualized services to particular members of Congress and their constituents. The agencies of course also maintain offices devoted to publicizing the agencies' good works.

One understudied aspect of the ways in which agencies maintain support for themselves involves precisely the kind of "framing" and "representation" that we have analyzed in terms of electoral candidates.[5] Students of bureaucracy have remarked that government agencies frequently develop "doctrines," "ideologies," or "philosophies" that summarize their purpose and meaning. For example, in *TVA and the Grass Roots* (1949) Philip Selznick refers to the "functions of official doctrine" and remarks that

> among the many and pressing responsibilities of leadership, there arises the need to develop a *Weltan-schauung,* a general view of the organization's position and role among its contemporaries. For organizations are not unlike personalities: the search for stability and meaning, for security, is unremitting. It is a search which seems to find a natural conclusion in the achievement of a set of morally sustaining ideas, ideas which lend support to decisions which must rest on compromise and restraint. (47)

Herbert A. Simon, Donald W. Smithburg, and Victor A. Thompson (1950, 543) discuss what they call "bureau philosophies," Downs (1967, 238) refers to "bureaucratic ideologies" in similar terms, and Morton H. Halperin (1974, 28) discusses the "essence" of an organization in a fashion similar to that of Selznick. Carl H. Builder (1989) provides a far-ranging study of these bureaucratic ideologies in the U.S. armed forces.

Yet these studies (except for Selznick's) do not generally engage in a sustained attempt to account for why these bureaus adopt their *particular* doctrines. Other authors, however, have suggested that there is a particular *target audience* for these doctrines. In a study of the bureaucratic ideology of "citizen participation," for example, Elliott Krause (1968) argues that

> ideologies are texts, theories, doctrines, phrases, or concepts which are proposed by an interest group [proponent] with a target group or groups

---

5. Indeed, Thomas H. Hammond first began thinking about these kinds of strategic issues in the context of bureaucratic politics and not in the context of electoral politics; see Hammond (1979, chap 8, "'Wildlife Management' and the Functions of Official Doctrine").

in mind, for the intended purpose of directing, politically organizing and energizing the target group toward behaving in a manner which is stated in the specific text of the message. This behavior is explicitly or implicitly stated as valuable and desirable as an activity or goal for the target group. Whether it is in fact valuable for the target group is an open question for research. (132)

Given these observations, we would argue that bureaucratic ideologies are chosen, at least in part, with an eye toward presenting the bureau and its activities in a way that interprets the bureau's activities to its critical audience, which rationalizes and makes sense of the bureau's activities to this audience, and which maximizes the support this audience is willing to provide. Our model of a single actor selecting a dimension—that is, a way of representing itself—within a multidimensional space thus may provide a very apt and useful way of thinking about this peculiar activity of bureaucracies.[6]

Conclusion

In this chapter we pursue the Riker (1990) call for the development of a spatial model of "heresthetic" processes in politics. We use an electoral metaphor to explore ideas on how a candidate might choose an optimal heresthetic strategy for defeating an opponent. We develop a set of simple spatial techniques for representing the candidate's heresthetic strategies, and we present a series of observations about what kinds of results might be expected from such a model. Clearly, our approach is underdeveloped, and we lack in particular an adequate understanding as to whether or not there is any kind of equilibrium set of strategies in our multicandidate issue-framing contests. We hope our brief study will stimulate others to explore this approach in more detail and with greater sophistication and rigor.

---

6. Though completely outside the realm of politics, we also find a rich tradition in sociology, exemplified in the works of Erving Goffman, for example, on how individuals and organizations present themselves to others and on the strategies they use to do this. In studies such as *The Presentation of Self in Everyday Life* (1959) and *Frame Analysis* (1974) Goffman describes the individual as behaving in a strategic manner, attempting to manipulate others' views and interpretations of him or her in a way that this person finds beneficial. As with the study of bureaucratic doctrines, the approach and techniques developed in this chapter may provide a useful formal framework for analyzing these actor-audience interactions.

CHAPTER 10

Adaptive Parties and Spatial Voting Theory

Scott E. Page, Ken Kollman, and John H. Miller

Practitioners of spatial voting models use the intuitive notion of ideological distance to develop plausible explanations for observable electoral trends. The most famous of these trends is the Downsian idea that in a two-party system, given certain strict assumptions, the parties will converge toward a median position on the continuum of possible voter positions. Further research in spatial modeling, however, has led to a very different conclusion. Following the voting paradox and the results of Plott (1967) and McKelvey (1976), some scholars have speculated that chaotic results are possible and, in some cases, likely. In two or more dimensions, given strict assumptions, parties can move all over the space to defeat their opponent(s). Whereas some scholars lament the predicted instability in multidimensional voting models (Riker 1982a), others see the Downsian convergence of parties on issues as a more accurate description of reality, not to mention more stable and (perhaps) more normatively desirable. There is a search, therefore, for reasonable modifications of multidimensional models that produce more stable results (see Coughlin 1990b).

Electoral outcomes in fact *are* more stable empirically than the chaotic results predict, so scholars are on the right track in seeking alternative assumptions to get more realistic outcomes. Nevertheless, both the original spatial models and contemporary revisions rely on unrealistic assumptions to produce equilibria. They require parties to have complete knowledge and to perform very complex calculations in locating good regions of the issue space. Even probabilistic voting models require parties to *know* the probabilities of voters' actions. Is it possible to generate realistic results without

---

The authors wish to thank Michael Kirschenheiter, Roger Myerson, and Benjamin I. Page for helpful comments on earlier drafts. A technical version of this chapter appears in *American Political Science Review* 86(4): 929–37. This research is partially supported by the Center for Mathematical Studies in Economics and Management Science, Northwestern University, the Santa Fe Institute, and Sun Microsystems. Copies of the computer programs are available from the authors.

relying on unrealistic assumptions about the information and computational abilities of parties?

We use an artificial adaptive agent (AAA) model to study the dynamics of spatial elections. Underlying our approach is the idea that there exist important classes of generic behavior that can be captured in models too complex for traditional mathematical analysis. Absence of equilibria in a model (or equilibria that require hyperrational agents to locate) does not necessarily imply a lack of predictability. Using AAA allows us to search previously inaccessible models for patterns of generic behavior. The model we describe here does not stretch the boundaries of our technique and may even be amenable to equilibrium analysis. We envision future research that presents more-complicated and descriptively accurate models. Our present purposes, however, showing the strength of our approach and relaxing informational assumptions, are best served by a simple model.

Our model incorporates most of the assumptions of spatial voting models, with some important exceptions. First, modeling parties as strictly office seeking has troubled many political scientists. We considered two kinds of parties, ideological and purely office seeking. Some, most notably Barry Goldwater, have formulated the difference as being between a "choice and an echo."

Second, we relaxed the assumption of identical voter preference intensities. Empirical evidence does indicate that preferences often correlated with how much voters care about issues (Jackson 1973, 234; Dalton 1988, 193–200), but many spatial models assume all voters have circular indifference curves, or that any deviations from symmetry will average out (Davis, Hinich, and Ordeshook 1970, 434). We included what we call issue "strengths" in our model. Strength is just the degree that voters care about a particular issue in relation to other issues.

Third, most theoretical results rely on perfectly informed and optimizing voters and candidates. Even probabilistic models assume that the candidates know perfectly the expected outcome and that they can position themselves optimally. Our parties are not perfectly informed. They do not explicitly know the individual voter utility functions. Rather, they obtain vote totals in an election against the incumbent for a finite number of tested platforms. Because parties have a finite amount of time to move, they are often not able to find an optimal location.

The unique feature of our approach is the use of boundedly rational agents. Spatial models assume that parties act as if they perfectly make all relevant calculations. In reality, of course, large numbers of voters, as well as the idiosyncracies of individual elections, may complicate the problem to such an extent that the positioning strategies of parties cannot possibly be optimal. In this chapter, we consider three procedures for candidate positioning and show that our results are invariant to the procedure chosen. Our results tend to agree with the small body of literature on experimental research involving spatial voting models (McKelvey and Ordeshook 1990). For the most part, experiments confirm the analytical result that parties move toward the center of voters' preferences. Our complex systems approach allows for the inclusion of relevant internal and external forces on the behavior of voters and candidates.

Artificially Adaptive Agents in the Social Sciences

Why use computers? Why create boundedly rational AAA? John Holland and John Miller (1990) argue that AAA models offer tools to link mathematical rigor with the contingencies of the real world, while at the same time allowing us to observe emergent phenomena not predicted a priori. "AAA models, specified in a computer language, retain much of the flexibility of pure linguistic models, while having precision and consistency enforced by the language" (366).

There are precedents for the use of AAA in the social and behavioral sciences. Robert Axelrod stimulates punishment strategies in his paper on the evolution of norms (Axelrod 1986). He has also used genetic algorithms (which we used as well) to develop strategies against a representative field from his famous repeated Prisoner's Dilemma tournament (Axelrod 1984, 1987). Miller (1987) has explored the coevolution of strategies using genetic algorithms as learning rules in the repeated Prisoner's Dilemma game with both perfect and imperfect information. And economists have begun to apply AAA to traditional economic problems (see Holland et al. 1986).

The use of AAA has important consequences for selection from among equilibria and from among equilibrium concepts. One goal of this line of research is to determine whether or not AAA will find the equilibria predicted by rational expectations. Our approach differs from previous AAA models in one important respect: rather than rely on one search technique, we compared three techniques with different known strengths and weaknesses and show that conclusions are strikingly similar for all three. Our parties faced a sequence of decisions against fixed environments, and we analyzed the trajectory of those decisions. Note that our dynamic interaction was not a game in the formal sense. Were we to cast the interaction as a game where both parties move simultaneously, we would generically have no equilibria. In many ways our model was in the spirit of Gerald H. Kramer (1977), who, in the absence of an available model of pure strategy equilibria, sought to explain trajectories of party platforms in a sequence of elections, and to define the set to which these trajectories converge (the minmax set). Of particular interest was whether we would find a pattern of convergence to good regions of the issue space or a trajectory of random platforms. In other words, would our parties converge, or would they move aimlessly about the space constantly in search of the "best" position?

The Basic Model

We began with a skeletal model. Our model does not escape the criticism of unrealistic assumptions, nor does it deal with the many contingencies we hope eventually to incorporate. Our voters and parties had simple preferences and uncomplicated actions.

There were two parties competing for votes in an n-dimensional issue space. Each voter was represented by a vector of integers, which are the voter's ideal points and strengths on the n issues. The inclusion of strengths means that the indifference curves were ellipses, a departure from the standard spatial model. A strength is the amount of importance that a voter attaches to each issue. The utility to a voter from a party's platform is the negative of the squared weighted Euclidean distance, where the weight on each issue is the strength associated with that issue by the voter.

The robustness of computer simulation results often hinges upon sensitivity to parameter values. The results we present appear invariant to reasonable parameter alterations. An increase in the number of voter types to 1,000 or positions to 25 does not qualitatively affect the results. In particular, the number of issue strengths appears to have little effect, provided the number of strengths is small relative to the number of voter types. The parameter values that we used

Voter types (V)	251
Number of issues (n)	15
Positions per issue (k)	7
Strengths (s_{ji})	3
Elections	12

fall safely within the ranges for which we observed no significant changes in the conclusions.

Both strengths and ideal points were independently and uniformly distributed. This assumption does not necessarily imply regularity. A relatively small number of voters were generated in a large space. A spray of points is a more appropriate way to think of the distribution than a continuous uniform distribution. Central limit theorems and the like are not appropriate given the relatively small number of voters and the size of the space.

Each voter cast a ballot for the party giving him or her the higher utility. To evaluate the trajectory of democratic outcomes, we used *centrality*, a measure of the goodness of each outcome (or the aggregate utility). Without such a measure we could not compare our model analytically to any other model, nor could we compare outcomes across elections. Centrality is calculated as follows: first, sum the utilities of the individual voters if the winning party were located at the median on all issues; second, sum the utilities resulting from the winning party in the election; third, divide the first number by the second.

$$c(y) = \left[\sum_j u_j(\text{median}) \right] / \left[\sum_j u_j(y) \right]$$

It follows that $c(\text{median}) = 1$. This normalization has the following interpretation: the higher the centrality, the closer the winning candidate is to the weighted center of voter preferences, and therefore the better the democratic outcome. The median need not give the highest utility; there may exist points with centralities greater than one. Moreover, the use of centrality ascribes no normative significance to the median as an outcome. It merely exploits the fact that the median will generally be of very low average distance. Ideally the point of minimal average distance's utility would be used as the numerator, but the costs in computer time outweigh any advantages. Regardless of the numerator, we have a measure of aggregate utility, or the average weighted distance to a voter.

Our electoral model began with an incumbent party (arbitrarily chosen) sitting at its ideal point, which was randomly generated from the same distribution as the voters. The party issue strengths were equal to one on all issues. Thereafter, through twelve elections, the incumbent party was fixed, and the challenger party attempted to locate a platform in the issue space that defeated the incumbent. The winner in each election then became the fixed incumbent. The challenger party attempted to defeat the incumbent by choosing a candidate to represent it. How a party chose its candidate was a crucial component of our model, for unlike most spatial models, we assumed that candidates do not have any information about voters' preferences other than vote totals. This implies that our parties did not have explicit knowledge of the mean or median position of voters on an issue. Our parties, though, had some information. The challenger party, during a finite campaign, tested platform on the voters and received feedback in the form of vote totals. Voters were assumed to have perfect information about candidate positions, so these tests were like opinion polls about candidate popularity. While standard spatial models attempt to show where and why parties locate where they do, our model helps to answer the following questions: How quickly (if at all) do boundedly rational parties converge toward a central location? How do different motivations and search techniques on the part of parties alter this convergence?

Choices and Echoes

We considered two types of parties: *ambitious parties* and *ideological parties*. Ambitious parties cared only about winning elections, and their party ideal points served only as starting points for the initial campaign. Ideological parties also wanted to win the elections, but they wanted to win with a platform that was close to their party ideal point. Ambitious parties attempted to maximize their vote total in the hopes that a larger margin of victory would make them more difficult to defeat in subsequent elections. Ideological parties had lexicographic preferences. Their primary goal was to win the elections. Once this was accomplished, they attempted to get as close to their ideal point as possible. This construction allowed the possibility that an ideological party would choose a candidate on a platform that was less preferred by the party than the incumbent's platform. However, such an event would only happen if the distance between party ideal points was improbably small.

Both ambitious and ideological parties were constrained in how they searched the issue space for good platforms. First, the campaigns were of finite length, so parties were limited in the number of polls that they could take. For example, a party may only be able to take forty polls before the election. Second, our parties were limited by the number of issues they could change during any position adaptation. And third, our parties were constrained in the degree of position change on an issue during each platform adaptation. These constraints imply that our parties would fail to fulfill their goals optimally. On the one hand, ideological challengers rarely lost but were forced to accept platforms further from their party ideal points then necessary to win. On the other hand, ambitious challengers' limitations were manifested in losses. One reason for ambitious party losses (besides well-positioned opponents) was the lack of information about the median, a position that, if known, would easily defeat incumbents in the first few elections.

How Parties Find Platforms

Once the assumptions of perfect information and perfect rationality are relaxed, behavior can be modeled in a myriad of ways. There are many ways to be imperfectly rational. We chose parties with three policy location procedures: random adaptive parties (RAP), climbing adaptive parties (CAP), and genetic adaptive parties (GAP). For the most part, we considered these to be crude approximations of actual procedures. They should be viewed as types of boundedly rational parties. Most important, they provide reasonable upper and lower bounds on the ability of parties to locate positions. The procedures themselves are mechanisms for a party to choose a platform. All procedures are discussed here within the context of ambitious parties. The extension to ideological parties is straightforward.

RAP were the least adaptive of our parties. RAP randomly generated forty platforms in a neighborhood of their previous platform and chose the point (candidate) that received the most votes against the incumbent. The analogy would be a party who chooses a candidate from among volunteers. The member who fared best against the incumbent carried the mantle of the party into the election. Neither the party nor the candidate altered positions on issues to improve the vote total. RAP were intended as lower bounds on the ability of parties to position themselves.

In contrast to RAP, CAP and GAP refined their platforms to improve vote totals. Challenger CAP began with their current party platform and experimented, slightly changing positions on a few issues. If the new platform fared better against the incumbent than did the previous one, the party switched to the new position. The number of hill-climbing iterations that a party performed before the election is called the campaign length, and we experimented with campaigns of length forty and sixty. Beyond forty variations in campaign length made little difference. CAP entered the elections with their final and, therefore, best-to-date position. CAP represent parties who select a candidate and then adapt the candidate's positions to the electorate's view by testing alterations in positions with focus groups and speeches. The challenger made a finite number of adaptations before facing the incumbent.

GAP, the third type of parties we considered, employed a genetic algorithm to guide their searches. Our genetic algorithm began with a population of positions, in our case twelve. A new population of positions was generated using three genetic operators: reproduction, crossover, and mutation. The reproduction operator created a new population based upon the relative fitness of the positions in the previous population. After reproduction, the crossover operator was applied. Crossover began by randomly pairing each candidate with another. For each issue, with positive probability they would trade positions (i.e., candidate 1 would assume candidate 2's position, and candidate 2 would assume candidate 1's position). The final genetic operator, mutation, introduced a small probability of a random change on each issue for a candidate who modifies his or her position using crossover. After twenty generations of the genetic algorithm (which we considered a campaign of length forty), the best-to-date platform was chosen by the party.

GAP represent parties whose members learn from each other and teach one another which combinations of positions on issues help garner votes against the incumbent. A successful party member is one whose platform is well received with respect to the incumbent's platform. This process corresponds to a party evolving candidates during the campaign and then choosing the best, survival of the fittest as it were.

Results

Our research suggests that, despite the absence of equilibria, and the lack of perfect information and computational abilities, two-party democratic elections may lead to normatively appealing outcomes. Parties converge as spatial models predicted all along. More specifically, the results from our simulations support three primary conclusions. First, democratic elections lead to good outcomes, where goodness is measured by centrality. Second, ambitious parties reach higher centrality than ideological parties; echoes may be better than choices given the assumptions of our model. And third, the type of adaptive party does not qualitatively change the trajectory of election outcomes.

Election outcomes must be viewed with respect to their relative aggregate utility. Approximate distribution and density functions for centrality of platforms are shown in figure 1. Note that a platform having centrality of .55 lies in the upper 17 percent of the distribution, and a centrality of .60 lies in the upper 6 percent of the distribution.

Ambitious Parties

For ambitious parties, three features deserve attention. First, of all search algorithms, centrality increased over time (see fig. 2). By the sixth election, CAP and GAP had expected centralities above .9 and RAP above .8, which places all three types of parties in the top .01 percent of all platforms. Convergence to high centrality and the increase in centrality over time appear invariant to the particular type of adaptive party.

Second, CAP and GAP had higher centrality than RAP. Yet when these centralities are viewed with respect to the distribution, the differences are not very great (fig. 1). Third, for all three types of parties the probability of winning decreased from almost 1 to below 0.4 by the twelfth election (results not shown). Our findings suggest that incumbents' advantages may be partly attributable to challengers' lack of information. Typically, spatial models resort to an exogenous incumbency advantage to explain winning incumbents. In our elections, a strong incumbent wins because the opposing party cannot locate a winning platform.

Ideological Parties

We expected the centrality of outcomes to be lower and the probability of winning to be higher in ideological contests. Our findings confirmed these expectations. The probability of winning was higher in the ideological case,

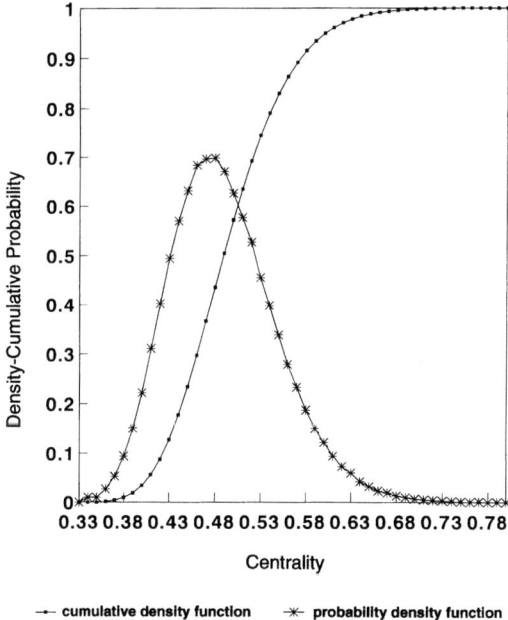

Fig. 1. Centrality distribution/density, 10,000 Monte Carlo trials

while centrality was lower (see fig. 3). Note that centrality increased over time for all three AAP. There was surprisingly little difference between RAP and GAP, while CAP performed better than the others. Because they were less able to fine-tune positions toward their ideal points, ideological RAP and GAP obtained higher centrality than ideological CAP, although the magnitude of this centrality difference was small.

For ambitious parties the satisfaction of party objectives can be measured by the winning percentage. For ideological parties, the distance of winning platforms from the party ideal also measures the ability of parties to meet their objectives. For all ideological parties we observed that the distance of party ideal increased by small amounts, while the distance to the median decreased (see fig. 4 for GAP example). We refer to this positioning behavior as the dumbbell waltz. The challenging party danced in the neighborhood of its ideal point until it found a winning platform. A chart of the winning platforms would consist of two disjoint neighborhoods, one near each of the party ideal points, and resemble a dumbbell. The ends of the dumbbell slowly converge as the number of elections increases (see fig. 5 for illustration).

In conclusion, the main result that democratic elections lead to normatively appealing outcomes appears invariant to both party motivation and method of position search. All six types of parties yielded similar results.

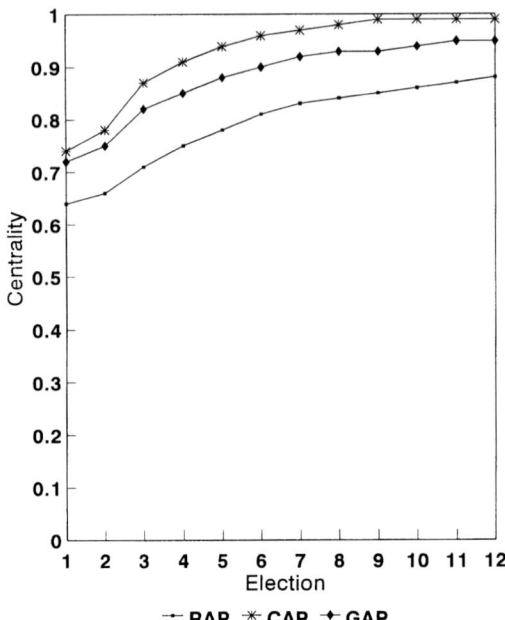

Fig. 2. Centrality of ambitious parties, 200 trials

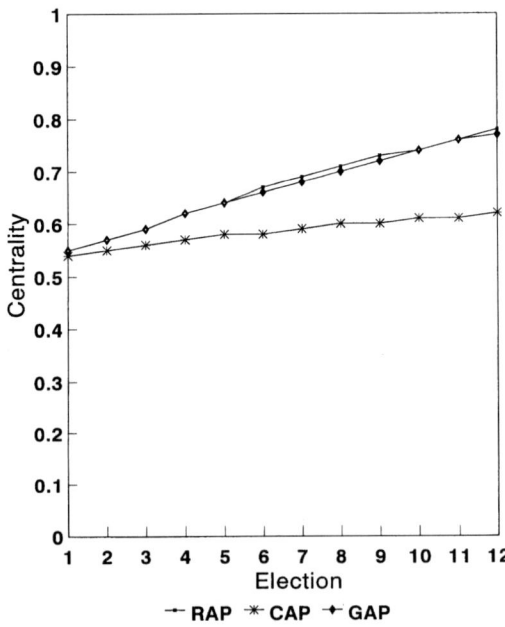

Fig.3. Centrality of ideological parties, 200 trials

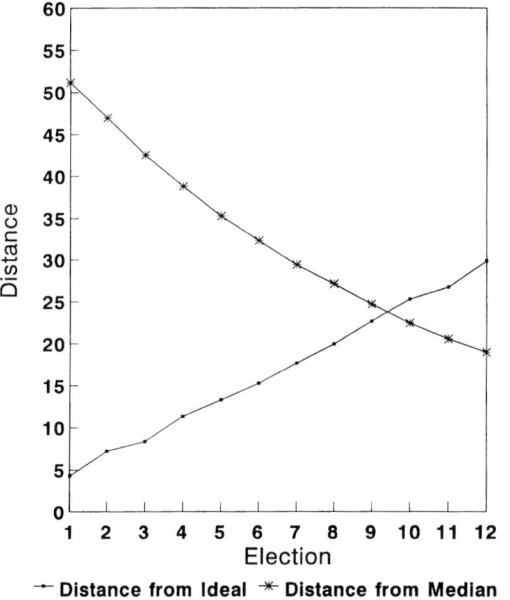

Fig. 4. Distance from ideal and median for ideological GAP, 200 trials

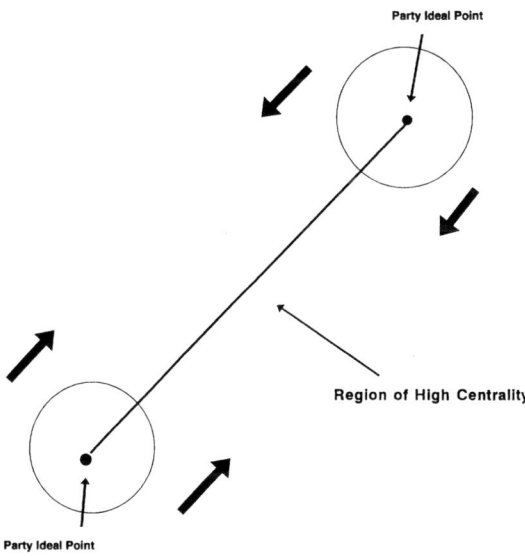

Fig. 5. Dumbbell waltz for ideological parties

While these results do not prove that democratic elections lead to good outcomes, they do substantiate the intuition that two-party elections ensure leaders who reflect voters' preferences.

Discussion

This chapter addresses several important topics in political science. We explore the dynamic behavior of adaptive political parties in democratic elections. In doing so, we extend traditional spatial voting theory by incorporating complex adaptive systems techniques. We envision political theory expanding in this direction.

Our research tends to support convergence results in spatial voting models. Two-party democratic elections yield good outcomes with respect to our centrality measure. Even ideological parties will move toward the center in efforts to win. These conclusions are even more convincing given that they appear invariant to parameter choice, within reasonable bounds, and to type of boundedly rational party.

Our results mimic the results of previous spatial models, but our methods do not. We promote the role of computers, generally, and AAA models, specifically, to the study of parties and voters in electoral models. Our techniques were designed to analyze the behavior of a complex adaptive system, a system that exhibits dynamic aggregate behavior emerging from the knowledge-based behavior of individual agents. We claim that our model can be extended in many directions, incorporating a variety of components known to exist in the real world. We hope to include variations in the way voters and parties behave in the real world. These possibilities may not only let us revise our judgments about the role of technology in constructing spatial voting theory they may lead us to important insights about what occurs in democratic elections.

CHAPTER 11

A Rational Choice Model of the President and Vice-President as a Package Deal

Martin P. Wattenberg and Bernard Grofman

Beginning with Anthony Downs's seminal work (1957b), economists (and political scientists following their lead) have modeled voter choice in two-party political competition in terms of the relative utility of having one's preferred candidate elected as compared to the candidate of the other party. There have been scores of articles following up on Downs's insights (see, e.g., Enelow and Hinich 1984; Grofman 1987 for useful reviews). Remarkably, however, in looking at voter preferences in U.S. presidential contests, we find voter preferences for vice-president have been completely neglected in both theoretical work and empirical work even though (since the Twelfth Amendment) voters must choose a president and a vice-president as a package deal (cf. Wuffle 1984).

The aim of this chapter is to provide a rational choice model of voting for president that recognizes the potential importance of voter preferences among vice-presidential candidates when these differ from the directionality of their preference for the top of the ticket.

Given that the influence of the vice-president on national or world affairs is effectively nonexistent as long as the president is alive and well, why ought any voter to care who is vice-president? A simple answer is that the vice-president may become president. There are two ways this may occur: (1) through resignation, death, or permanent disability of a sitting president or (2) by succession.

Over the course of U.S. history, vice-presidents have replaced presidents who have died or resigned a total of nine times. In 25 (one-eighth) of the first 200 years of U.S. history, a vice-president served out the term of the president with whom he was elected.

We are indebted to members of the Interdisciplinary Focused Research Program in Public Choice, University of California, Irvine, for helpful comments on an earlier draft of this paper, to the Word Processing Center, School of Social Sciences, University of California, Irvine, for manuscript typing, and to Dorothy Gormick for bibliographic assistance.

Even if a vice-president does not replace a president during that president's term of office, in recent years a vice-president is highly advantaged in obtaining his party's nomination for president in the future. Democratic vice-presidents Hubert Humphrey and Walter Mondale and Republican vice-presidents Richard Nixon and George Bush have all been nominated for the presidency over the last three decades.

A rational choice model of voter decision making would hold that preferences for the vice-presidency could only be relevant when (1) the voter prefers one party's presidential candidate to the other's, but the preference ordering is reversed for the two parties' vice-presidential candidates, or (2) the voter is indifferent about the presidential candidates but has a preference for one of the vice-presidential candidates.

In the first of these two cases, we posit that a voter will treat this preference for vice-president as a relevant factor (i.e., one with a nonzero weight). In the second case, where a voter is indifferent about the presidential candidates, it seems reasonable to believe that at least some voters will use their preference for a vice-presidential candidate to decide which ticket to vote for. However, we recognize that, even if the voter is indifferent about the presidential nominees, factors other than vice-presidential preferences may be decisive (e.g., a "standing commitment" to one or the other political party).

The conditions under which vice-presidential preferences could even in principle be decisive are rarely met. Most voter preferences for president and vice-president will be consistent as to party. Indeed, from 1968 to 1988 condition 1 was satisfied by an average of only 11.5 percent of the electorate, and condition 2 was satisfied by an average of only 5.5 percent of the electorate. See table 1.

Most of the cross-pressured voters in condition 1 preferred a Republican

TABLE 1. Percentage of Major Party Voters Who Evaluate the Candidates Such That Vice-Presidential Ratings Are Potentially Consequential

	1968	1972	1976	1980	1984	1988
Prefer Republican president and Democratic vice-president	12.0	8.7	4.2	5.0	8.5	12.3
Prefer Democratic president and Republican vice-president	1.1	2.0	3.5	6.0	2.6	3.3
No presidential preference; Prefer Democratic vice-president	4.2	3.5	3.1	2.6	3.9	6.1
No presidential preference; Prefer Republican vice-president	0.2	2.3	2.1	2.6	1.5	1.0
Total percentage	17.5	16.5	12.9	16.2	16.5	22.7

Source: Center for Political Studies/Survey Research Center National Election Studies.

candidate for president but a Democratic candidate for vice-president. Among those who preferred a vice-president of a different party than their preferred candidate for president, the inconsistency sometimes considerably reduced their support for the party of their presidential choice. For example in 1976, those who preferred a Republican president but a Democratic vice-president were more than 20 percentage points less likely to vote Republican than those who preferred both Republican candidates to their Democratic counterparts. On average, from 1968 to 1988, the difference in support for the Republican slate between consistent Republican leaners and those who preferred a Democratic vice-president was 11.6 percentage points. (See table 2.)

Similar results obtain when we compare those with consistent Demo-

TABLE 2. Percentage Voting Republican by Selected Presidential/Vice-Presidential Preference Pairings

	1968	1972	1976	1980	1984	1988
Republican president/						
Democratic vice-president	94.8	79.4	76.3	91.9	86.4	90.9
Republican president/Republican						
vice-president	99.4	95.8	97.2	98.7	98.6	98.2
Vice-president impact	−4.6	−16.4	−20.9	−6.8	−12.2	−7.3
Vice-president weighted impact[a]	−.55	−1.43	−.88	−.34	−1.04	−9.0
Democratic president/						
Republican vice-president	11.1	34.5	16.3	27.3	24.2	3.5
Democratic president/						
Democratic vice-president	1.4	4.6	2.3	8.8	4.9	3.5
	+9.7	+29.9	+14.0	+18.5	+19.3	0
Vice-president weighted impact[a]	+.11	+.60	+.49	+1.11	+.50	0.0
Neutral president/Democratic						
vice-president	41.2	34.0	43.2	73.7	34.0	31.5
Total sample	53.8	64.3	48.5	56.3	58.2	59.0
Neutral president/Republican						
vice-president	—	66.7	56.7	68.4	63.2	55.6
Vice-president weighted impact[b]	−.53	−1.01	+.01	—[c]	−.87	—
Net weighted vice-president						
impact	−.97	−1.84	−.38	+.77	−1.41	−2.26

Source: Center for Political Studies/Survey Research Center National Election Studies.

Note: + is pro-Republican.

[a]Impact on the vote is simply the difference in support between those with consistent and inconsistent preferences. Weighted impact on the vote is calculated by multiplying the difference in the Republican vote between those with consistent versus those with inconsistent preferences times the percentage of voters in the latter category (as shown in table 1).

[b]Impact on the vote is calculated by taking the deviation of each neutral category from the national vote and then multiplying this times the percentage of voters. The pro-Democratic impact is then subtracted from the pro-Republican impact.

[c]Because in this case both presidential neutral categories voted more Republican than average, there is no reason to suspect that the vice-presidential candidates had any impact.

176   Information, Participation, and Choice

cratic preferences with those who preferred a Republican to a Democratic vice-president. In 1972, for example, the former were 29.9 percentage points more likely to support the Democratic slate than the latter. On average, from 1968 to 1988, the difference in support for the Republican slate between voters who preferred both presidential and vice-presidential candidates of the Democrat versus those who preferred the Democrat for president but the Republican for vice-president was 15.2 percentage points.

A Rational Choice Model of "Two Front Teeth" Voting

Let $u_{DP}^{(i)}$ be the value attached by the ith voter to the election of the Democratic presidential nominee; $u_{DV}^{(i)}$ be the value attached by the ith voter to the election of the Democratic vice-presidental nominee. Similarly, we obtain values for the two Republican nominees as $u_{RP}^{(i)}$ and $u_{RV}^{(i)}$. Now a voter should vote for the Democratic ticket if and only if

$$(u_{DP}^{(i)} - u_{RP}^{(i)}) + (u_{DV}^{(i)} - u_{RV}^{(i)})(w_{VP}^{(i)}) > 1 + \lambda^{(i)} \qquad (1)$$

where $W_{VP}^{(i)}$ is the relative weight the voter attaches to the vice-presidency (the weight attached to the presidency is normalized at a value of one), and where $\lambda^{(i)}$ reflects whatever other factors may enter the voter's decision calculus. If $\lambda^{(i)}$ is positive, the voter has a noncandidate-based bias toward the Republicans. If $\lambda^{(i)}$ is negative, the voter has a noncandidate-based bias toward the Democrats.

We can reexpress equation (1) in ratio terms as the following rule: Vote for the Democratic ticket if an only if

$$(u_{DP}^{(i)} - u_{RP}^{(i)})/(u_{DV}^{(i)} - u_{RV}^{(i)}) > (1 + \lambda^{(i)})/W_{VP}^{(i)} \qquad (2)$$

In order to specify how a given voter should vote, we would need to know the $\lambda^{(i)}$ values and the $u^{(i)}$ values, as well as $W_{VP}^{(i)}$. The $u^{(i)}$ can be proxied by voter scores for presidential and vice-presidential candidates based on what is called a "feeling thermometer." As for the relative weight to be attached to the vice-presidency, we might expect that $W_{VP}^{(i)}$ should be a proxy for the (subjective) probability that a vice-president will serve as president, because when not stepping in as president the vice-president is of trivial policy importance.

We may treat $\lambda^{(i)}$ as stochastic error. If it is small, we may safely disregard it. If a voter's subjective probability of vice-presidential replacement of the president during office corresponds to the historical reality of 12.5 percent, then $W_{VP}^{(i)}$ should be one-seventh; if voters also take into account the likelihood that a vice-president will be elected as president in his own right,

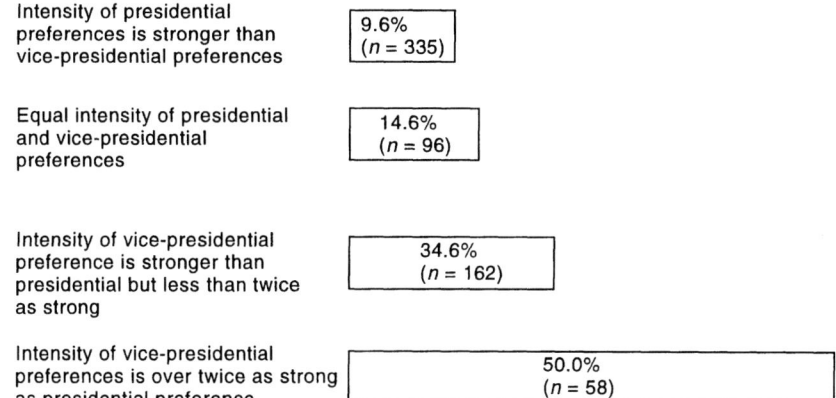

Fig. 1. Percentage of voters with split presidential–vice-presidential voting in line with their vice-presidential preference (combined data from 1968–88 U.S. National Election Survey)

then $W_{VP}^{(i)}$ will be much higher. But in any case, we would not expect most voters who prefer the vice-presidential nominee of the opposite party to their presidential preference to use the vice-presidential preference to guide their vote unless they are much more intense in their feelings about the vice-presidential nominee than about the presidential nominee. As shown in figure 1, this is exactly what we find.

The probability of voters voting for the party whose *vice*-presidential candidate they prefer does not go above 0.5 unless the ratio in figure 1 is above 2. Thus, for most voters it would appear that the weight (value) attached to the vice-presidency is less than one-third.

CHAPTER 12

Toward an Institution-Rich Theory of Political Competition with a Supply Side Component

Bernard Grofman

The Downsian model of two-party competition is based on victory-oriented political parties and candidates. Anthony Downs adopts the self-interest axiom as a "cornerstone of analysis" (1957b, 28). A voter is assumed to be "rational" in the sense of having well-defined preferences over the issue space that lead the voter to choose among the electoral alternatives "that which ranks highest in his preference ordering" (1957a, 6). Candidates' actions are similarly motivated by self-interest in that they formulate policies in order to "attain the income, prestige, and power which come from being in office" (1957a, 28) (i.e., "parties formulate policies to win elections, rather than win elections in order to formulate policies" [28]). Candidates thus locate so as to maximize their probability of election, based on their perception of voter preferences.[1]

In its very simplest incarnation, competition over a single ideological policy dimension, the Downsian model gives rise to a prediction of the convergence of candidates to the preference of the median voter. *An Economic Theory of Democracy* has led a generation of public choice scholars on a long quest to identify the necessary and sufficient conditions for party convergence. In the process, more attention has been paid to technical issues (see, e.g., the review in Riker and Ordeshook 1972, 342–43, tables 12.1 and 12.2), and less to what actually happens in real world elections, than at first blush might seem desirable. But the often rococo theoretical explorations of the formal literature on spatial models have helped us understand how robust the

---

I am indebted to Sue Pursche, Ziggy Bates, and the staff of the Word Processing Center, School of Social Sciences, University of California, Irvine, for typing several drafts of this manuscript, to Dorothy Gormick for bibliographic assistance, and to Robert Griffin, Manfred Holler, and Donald Wittman for helpful suggestions. Any errors remaining are solely the responsibility of the author.

1. What we refer to as the "Downsian model" is a spatial model in the tradition of Hotelling (1929) and Smithies (1941). Two parties (one of whom is the incumbent government) compete for the votes of a large electorate on the basis of their spatial locations. There is an inherent danger in trying to characterize *the* Downsian approach (see Grofman 1987 and this volume).

convergence result is, and how modifications to Downs's initial set of assumptions affect the predicted outcomes. There is, however, one basic problem. On many of the most important issues that divide the nation, parties and candidates in the United States simply do not look like Tweedledum and Tweedledee. Nor does party competition look like the random walks over issue space that are predicted by the next generation of models of political competition over a set of multidimensional issues (see, e.g., Riker 1982a). Similarly, in multidimensional issue competition, when the incumbent is constrained by reputation or other factors to a subset of the policy space, under the usual simple Downsian assumptions the challenger can be expected to be able to find a position that can defeat the incumbent, yet incumbents, in fact, rarely lose.

Stylized Facts That Any Model of Party Competition in the United States Must Seek to Explain

1a. By and large there is a considerable divergence in the policy positions of candidates of opposite parties who run against each other in U.S. congressional elections (Sullivan and Uslaner 1978).

1b. Almost without exception, there is a divergence in policy preferences (as measured by Americans for Democratic Action (ADA) or American Constitutional Union (ACU) scores) between members of Congress of the opposite parties, even after statistically controlling for the characteristics of the constituencies each represents (Bullock and Brady 1983; Poole and Rosenthal 1985).

1c. There is a striking divergence in the ADA scores of senators of *opposite parties* elected from the *same state*—roughly 40 points (on a 100-point scale) over the period 1962–84 (Grofman, Griffin, and Glazer 1990). However, there is also a striking similarity in the ADA scores of senators from the *same state* elected from the *same party,* or when a seat changes hands to a member of the same party (Grofman, Griffin, and Glazer 1990).

1d. When a House seat changes party affiliation, there is a considerable difference in the voting patterns (ADA scores) of the old and the new incumbent (Fiorina 1974). However, there is little change in voting behavior when the seat changes hands but remains under the control of the same party.

2a. Many states have exhibited noncompetitive policies for state office for long periods of time, with one party clearly dominant over the course of two or more decades. There are important regional aspects to the geographic pattern of party control.

2b. U.S. politics at the national level has exhibited decades-long periods of oscillation, with one party "the sun" (the majority party) and the other "the moon" (the minority party), to use Samuel Lubell's (1952) apt phrasing.

2c. Many incumbents are reelected time and time again, often by large margins.

The failure of the simple Downsian model to match up with empirical observations such as those identified here might make it appear that all the effort devoted to elaborating Downsian models of party competition has been much ado about nothing. But this conclusion is premature. Downs provides the basis for modeling party competition, but *An Economic Theory of Democracy* should certainly not be regarded as the last word. Rather, we can return to Downs's original postulates to see how they must be modified in order to fashion a more realistic and empirically descriptive model of political competition. Moreover, in rereading Downs's work we can be attentive to subtleties in Downs's own analysis of political competition that are missed in most of the subsequent efforts to formally model Downsian ideas. In so doing, we are led to what I refer to as an "institution-rich" theory of politics, with a substantial "supply side" component.

Let us now turn to an inventory of the assumptions underlying the simplest Downsian model.

In addition to the basic assumption of a context of democratic politics (see especially Downs 1957b, 23–24, 30) there are nine key assumptions of the basic Downsian model.

1. There are only two political parties.
2. Elections take place within a single constituency.
3a. There is a single election.
3b. The election chooses a single candidate.
3c. The election is decided by a plurality vote.
4. Policies can be located along a single (left-right) dimension.
5. Candidate policy positions are well-defined.
6a. Candidate policy positions are estimated by each voter.
6b. Voters care only about the next election.
6c. Voters care only about which candidate/party will enact policies closest to the preferences of the voter.
7. Parties/candidates care only about winning.
8. Candidates are part of a unified party team.
9. Eligible voters go to the polls if the expected benefits of their vote's contribution to the election of their candidate exceeds the "costs" of voting.

Assumption 9 is discussed in the chapters on voter turnout in this volume, and I say nothing further about it here. Assumptions 1 through 8, on which I focus, give rise to the implication of Tweedledum-Tweedledee politics, with both candidates choosing policy positions of the median voter, that is customarily seen as the defining aspect of a Downsian approach to two-party political competition. Also, in this ultrasimplified model, elections would be expected to be decided by relatively narrow margins (since candidates are expected to be identical in their only *relevant* attributes, i.e., their policy preferences or anticipated policy choices).

However, there are plausible modifications of *each* of these assumptions that can give rise to predictions of nonconvergence or noncompetitive politics. Indeed, while assumptions 1–9 are often thought of as *the* Downsian model, Downs (1957b) is actually far more sophisticated and sensitive to the nuances of U.S. (and non-U.S.) electoral politics and to the reality of an imperfect information universe. However, like most seminal works, *An Economic Theory of Democracy* is no longer read. Rather, the classic comic book simplification of Downs is now part of the common memory of the political science discipline.

In focusing on the first eight of the assumptions I review theoretical developments since Downs's that help us better understand how electoral politics in the United States actually works. I focus on party competition (especially the conditions for party convergence) and only have a few things to say about the vast literature on voter choice (see Grofman 1987; Enelow and Hinich 1984). Also, I do not attempt to deal with the implications of Downs's work for multiparty nonplurality elections except in passing, nor do I deal with the policy aspects of Downs's work (see chap. 15).

Modifying the Assumptions of the Basic Downsian Model

Two-Candidate Competition

If we permit more than two candidates/parties, then the convergence argument does not go through in any straightforward fashion, even for plurality competition in a single dimension, and certainly not for electoral competition under any form of proportional representation. However, Maurice Duverger (1951) argues that, over the course of several elections, for plurality-based elections, there will be pressure to reduce the field of competition down to two parties—effectively, a center-right party and a center-left party. Downs considers this question and reaches similar conclusions (see especially Downs 1957b, 139–41), but he is apparently unfamiliar with the work of Duverger.

According to Duverger there will be a psychological effect, voter unwillingness to vote for parties with no chance of victory (known in the public choice literature as "sophisticated voting"), and a mechanical effect, the convergence of left-wing and right-wing parties toward locations nearer to the center, thus squeezing out centrist parties. Downs (1957b, chap. 3, see also

298, proposition 9) similarly argues that, in multicandidate/multiparty elections, voters may have an incentive to vote for a party/candidate other than the one the voters most prefer.

The scope and empirical validity of what William H. Riker (1982a) refers to as "Duverger's hypothesis" remains in dispute (Riker 1982a; Sartori 1986; Duverger 1984; Taagepera and Grofman 1987; Cox 1987). Rein Taagepera and I (1987), for example, claim that the mechanisms generating empirical support for Duverger's hypothesis hold only in polities characterized by unidimensional politics. Our views on the interaction of electoral structure and ideological distribution are similar in spirit to those of Downs, although the only extensive discussion on this point in *An Economic Theory of Democracy* (Downs 1957b, 123–25) focuses on the unidimensional case.

Steven J. Brams (1980) and Brams and Philip Straffin (1982) have looked at the "entry" problem: "Where must two political parties locate so as to be able to discourage the likelihood of a third party preempting their vote support?" The result of those modeling efforts suggests that concern to deter entry will usually imply that, in plurality-based elections over a single dimension, parties will *not* converge to the median. Other relevant work, much of it dealing with elections under rules other than simple plurality, includes Cox 1987; Eaton and Lipsey 1975; Greenberg and Shepsle 1987; and Rapoport, Felsenthal, and Maoz 1988. Shepsle and Cohen 1990 and Cox 1990, taken in conjunction, provide an excellent review of the formal modeling literature relevant to entry and multicandidate or multiparty competition.

Single Constituency

David Austen-Smith (1984, 1986) points out that parties must compete simultaneously in a number of different constituencies and examines the implications of such concurrent competition for the Downsian model. Unfortunately, Austen-Smith generally posits a single-party position that is adopted in all constituencies. Recent work on the causes of divided party rule for the presidency and the Congress suggests that we must be especially attentive to the differences between "national" Democrats (and the issues on which they campaign) and the views espoused by local Democratic congressional and legislative candidates—with the former able to achieve and hold office despite the failure of the national Democratic ticket (Jacobson 1990).

I believe that, in fact, parties adapt to the constituencies in which they compete, but within the constraints set by national differences (party images). In particular, I believe that James Coleman (1970) is correct in ruling out the possibility of the two parties leapfrogging each other so that the candidate of the rightmost party is to the left of the candidate of the leftmost party. Thus, in the United States, we expect to see Democrats to the left of Republicans in *each* constituency, even though a Democrat in a conservative constituency may be far to the right of his or her party's national median, just as a Republican elected in a liberal constituency may be far to the left of his or her party's national median. This is indeed what we find (for the Senate see Poole and Rosenthal 1985; Grofman, Griffin, and Glazer 1990; and for the House Brady and Lynn 1973; Fiorina 1974; and Grofman, Griffin, and Glazer 1991). The metaphor I like to use for party competition is that a party label is like a franchise—it imposes certain constraints on what you can expect to get, but a McDonald's in Tokyo offers a menu that is tilted toward Japanese tastes (e.g., fishburgers).

Single Election with a Single Candidate

Coleman (1970, 1972) and Peter Aranson and Peter C. Ordeshook (1972) look at the implication of a primary competition on candidate strategy. If candidates must win both a primary and a general election, they will locate between the overall median and the median location of the party electorate.

Martin Wattenberg and I (chap. 11) look at voter choice for the tie-in bundle consisting of a president and a vice-president. Several authors (Baron 1984; Fiorina 1989) have suggested that some voters look not just at a single election but at the "balance" across several elections (e.g., preferring a Democratic Congress if there is a Republican president). In light of the 1988 election, this view is now becoming part of the common wisdom (see especially Jacobson 1990). In principle, of course, we could treat such preferences as part of a sophisticated "expectational" model of a multiactor political game.

Also, as Downs himself clearly recognizes (Downs 1957b, chap. 16, proposition 10), voters may look beyond a single election to influence their party by a protest vote to shift its policies in a particular election, or with the hope of creating in the long-run a viable alternative to the existing parties. In the United States, third-party movements have often been the vehicle for introducing new policy ideas, or they have been way stations on the way to realignment (as may have been true for George Wallace voters in 1968: Grofman, Glazer, and Handley 1988).

Single Dimension

Downs (1957b, 54–62) describes how, if there is more than one policy choice to be made, there will not be a policy platform that can be adopted that is invulnerable to defeat, when voters differ in their intensities of preferences across different issues. There is now a vast literature on the absence of an equilibrium outcome when there is more than one policy dimension (see relatively nontechnical reviews of much of this literature in Riker 1982a; Feld and Grofman 1985). However, recent work has suggested that, when voting is probabilistic and not deterministic, even when issues are multidimensional, equilibria are very likely to result (see an excellent review of this work in Coughlin 1990a; cf. Coughlin 1990b). Also, there is a considerable body of recent literature about the near-core properties of the area within four radii of the center of the yolk (McKelvey 1986; Feld et al. 1987).[2]

Downs suggests that parties will use ideology as a shorthand way of communicating issue positions to the voters. As James R. Simmons (1987, 4) rather sarcastically points out, however,

> textbook writers almost invariably ascribe the number of U.S. political parties and their tactics to the distribution of opinion of potential voters along a left-right ideological continuum. Few writers see any contradiction between this view of party motivation and their description of American opinion in other chapters which is portrayed as disorganized, incoherent, inconsistent and dispersed among many dimensions. . . . Nor does there seem to be much reason for parties to organize their public policy offerings according to the left-right scaling if so few voters are informed or view issues in these ways.

One answer to this puzzle is provided by Scott L. Feld and myself (1986, 1988b). We argue that ideological consistency is best viewed as a "collective" phenomenon and thus, even though most voters may not be ideological, the electorate's majority rule decision processes approximate closely, if not perfectly, ideological (single-peaked) choices.[3] One reason that elite perceptions of a right-left continuum are possible is that the meaning of left and right is not fixed. Remarkably, the left-right dimension seems almost infinitely stretchable to contain diverse issues (e.g., ecological issues, feminist issues, race-related issues).

Downs's own views about convergence to the center are actually considerably more complex than the usual modeling that is used to represent them. In particular, Downs allows for parties to have a mix of centrist and extremist positions.

---

2. The relevance of this recent literature on the microstructure of majority rule preferences in multidimensional issue space for models of candidate competition remains largely unexplored.

3. According to Simmons (1987, 4), "The primary textbook explanation for the continuing relevance of Downs is the presence of a small subset of the public (activists, opinion-leaders, elites, etc.) with beliefs that are consistent with the model and whose extensive participation in the political process prevents the differences between the major parties from disappearing altogether." However, Simmons claims that "this interpretation begs the question of why the existing parties concentrate on these 'customers' rather than the demand of the much larger nonideological mass, many of whom don't vote."

> Each party casts some policies into the other's territory in order to convince voters there that its net position is near them. In such maneuvering, there is much room for skill because voters assign different weights to the policies. . . . However, each party will sprinkle these moderate policies with a few extreme stands in order to please far-out voters. . . . Therefore, it is possible to detect on which side of the midpoint each party is actually located by looking at the extremist policies it espouses. (135)[4]

One aspect of Downs's work that has only recently seen development is his emphasis on the possibility of putting together winning coalitions based on minority groups with intense preferences for the outcomes on particular issue dimensions. There has been a spate of recent empirical work on single issue constituencies such as antiabortion activists or strong feminists. Thomas H. Hammond and Brian D. Humes (chap. 9) develop the idea of political competition across multiple issue dimensions of differing interest to different voters.

Well-defined Candidate Positions

Downs (297, proposition 3) argues that, in two-party competition, party policies will be vague, yet this point is not recognized in many neo-Downsian models (see, however, Shepsle 1972; and literature review in chap. 3). In my work, I argued that a ring of uncertainty about candidate location is created when candidates are allowed to "finagle" (i.e., to move ever so slightly from an initial position in order to improve their likelihood of defeating a challenger). In that work (Wuffle et al. 1989), my coauthors and I show that here are positions from which incumbents can, by finagling, stay safe from defeat. Benjamin I. Page (1978) offers perhaps the most extensive empirical discussion of candidate ambiguity, in the context of U.S. presidential politics.

Another limitation of the notion that candidates have well-defined positions known to all the voters is that voter preferences (and voter party loyalties) condition voter perceptions of candidate issue positions (as well as affect voter perceptions of incumbent performance), so that different voters will see candidates in different locations. The most-sophisticated empirical work on such rationalization and reciprocal causation phenomena is found in papers by Page and Calvin C. Jones (1979) and Gregory B. Markus and Philip E. Converse (1979).

I should also note that Downs (1957b, 137–39) provides a brief but intriguing discussion of a potential contradiction in his model: it is in the interests of parties to be ambiguous but of voters to have clear-cut choices.

---

4. Downs goes on to say, "In fact, this may be the only way to tell the two parties apart ideologically, since most of their politics are conglomerated in an overlapping mass in the middle of the scale."

According to Downs (139), "if parties succeed in obscuring their policy decisions in a mist of generalities, and voters are unable to discover what their votes really mean, a *rationality crisis* develops."

Policy-Driven Voters with an Election-Specific Time Frame

There is not a complete model in *An Economic Theory of Democracy* on how voters come to form expectations of which policies each candidate is expected actually to *implement* (see however, Downs 1957b, 41–47, 107–11), although Downs is clear that voters need not simply take the policy positions announced by each candidate as the position that the candidate would actually be *expected* to implement. Thus, Downs clearly recognizes that the candidate's campaign location (what is commonly referred to as the candidate's *platform*) need not coincide with the location that the candidate succeeds in implementing after election (in chap. 3, referred to as the candidate's *issue performance*).[5]

Downs recognizes the possibility that

10. some voters use the party affiliation of the candidate as a cue about the candidate's policy views.

Downs also considers it likely that

11. When it is available, some voters use information about a candidate's past *performance* to develop expectations about the candidate's future behavior (see 298, proposition 8).

Indeed, in our view, Downs should be credited as the grandfather of the theory of retrospective voting, even if Morris P. Fiorina's clear exposition of the thesis entitles him to paternity.

As I have elaborated elsewhere (Grofman 1987), most of the early attempts to test what I called assumption 6 neglect the development of voter expectations about candidate policy *performance*. Instead they assume

---

5. I regard it as useful to make a further distinction, by distinguishing expectations that may be formed about an intermediate state, namely the location that the candidate seeks to implement once in office (what is referred to in chap. 3 as the candidate's *issue effort*), from either platform or issue performance. In particular, even if John Ferejohn (chap. 7), following Downs, is correct that politicians seek to implement their promises, there will often be circumstances in which it is essentially impossible for them to do so. Frequently, I would argue, the likelihood that a politician will be unable to deliver on promises can be anticipated by the voter (see Grofman 1987).

6.' Voters choose the candidate whose (announced) policy stands are closest to their own.

But assumption 6' is explicitly rejected by Downs (See especially Downs 1957b, 39).

Also, voters may care about matters other than the anticipated policy differences between the candidates/parties. Among the factors that may be relevant are demographic attributes of the candidate (the traditional "balanced ticket" in sectional or ethnic terms, and the "friends and neighbors" effects of V. O. Key, Jr.); other generalized attributes of the candidate (e.g., competence, trustworthiness—see e.g., chap 8); party loyalty (Campbell et al. 1960; cf. chap. 1); a "benefit of the doubt" awarded to incumbents on nonpolicy grounds such as risk avoidance (Feld and Grofman 1991); and aspects of the support coalition of the candidate, that is, (southern) whites' unwillingness to vote for the candidate whom blacks support (Glazer, Grofman, and Owen 1991).

As noted, one way in which voters violate the basic Downsian assumption that they are policy maximizing is by giving the benefit of the doubt to a candidate or to a party, for example, by continuing to vote for a given candidate/party as long as the policy positions of the opposing candidate/party is not "significantly" better (closer to the voters' own preferred position). Feld and I (1991) show that, when all voters give their preferred candidate even a very small benefit of the doubt, that candidate, by choosing a location properly (i.e., centrally), can become invulnerable to defeat even though, otherwise, the voting game would lack a core. We also show that a sufficiently large benefit of the doubt from a small, randomly located set of voters (based, for example, on that candidate's constituent service) can also guarantee a "centrist" candidate invulnerability to challenge, or even provide the candidate with a very large margin of victory. In such situations, if the candidate who enjoys the benefit of the doubt is vulnerable at all, it can be shown that the only locations that can defeat him or her are ones that are nonidentical to his or her position. Indeed, the greater the benefit of the doubt, the further away must any location be that can defeat the candidate enjoying the benefit of the doubt.

The difference in voter behavior depending upon which party/candidate holds a given position violates the standard assumption of the simplified Downsian model that office seekers' exchange of locations would simply reverse vote choices, an assumption that we may think of as that of "anonymous competition." However, as suggested earlier, *An Economic Theory of Democracy* anticipates the view that risk-averse voters, in a situation of uncertainty, will give incumbents—whose probable behavior in office can be better estimated—a benefit of the doubt (see also chap. 2).

Still another complication introduced by Downs is the possibility of "extremist" voters choosing not to vote if the party they would otherwise support has become too centrist. This is intended to hold the party to a more ideologically pure position. According to Downs, if the ideological distribution of voters is bimodal and if abstention by extremists is practiced, "a two-party system need not lead to the convergence on moderation that Hotelling and Smithies predicted" (Downs 1957b, 118). There have been several attempts to make this intuition more precise, beginning with Gerald Garvey (1966) and Aranson and Ordeshook (1972).

Other routes to avoid convergence, based largely on voter rather than candidate behavior, revolve around the notion that voters take their cues less from what a candidate says than from other information available about the candidate, such as the nature of the groups that support the candidate and which voters who are expected to vote for him or her.[6] The notion of voter choice as being driven by the nature of the party/candidate support coalition has been developed by several authors, including John H. Aldrich (1983a), Amihai Glazer, myself, and Guillermo Owen (1991),[7] and, Timothy J. Feddersen (1991).

Still another complication to the notion that voters are choosing the candidate/party that lies closest to their preferences is the notion that voters are choosing probabilistically rather than deterministically. There is now a sizable literature on probabilistic voting (see the excellent review in Coughlin 1990b).

Still another wrinkle on voter choice is the view that voter choice is directional rather than positional. The most important model is that of G. Rabinowitz and S. MacDonald (1989). Their work has both theoretical and empirical components. Grofman (1987) develops a neo-Downsian model in which voters discount candidate policy positions by looking only at expected movement relative to the status quo. Thus, as the status quo shifts, voter *choices* can shift even though voter *preferences* for policy outcomes remain the same. I argue this model helps account for moderate voters sometimes choosing "conservative" and sometimes "liberal" candidates—to move a status quo back toward the center, which has shifted too far toward one or the other extreme.

Election-oriented Parties

On the second night of the 1988 Democratic convention, an ABC reporter for the local D.C. affiliate interviewed a delegate who was asked what he wanted

---

6. See review in chapter 3.
7. See also chapter 5.

to see come out of the convention. Without hesitation the delegate said, "We want to win." The reporter then opined, "We've just seen the 'soul' of the Democratic party." We must recognize, however, some important caveats to such a Vince Lombardian portrait of American politics. U.S. politicians do have policy positions to which they are attached (e.g., Dukakis never retreated from his opposition to the death penalty, albeit, in the age of videotape replay, flip-flopping has become more difficult). Moreover, party images tend to be durable, and there are rational incentives for party consistency (Downs 1957b; chap. 7). It helps to recognize that, for parties—absent realignment-like shocks—vote-maximizing occurs (1) at the margin and (2) primarily in the long-run (by replacement of those politicians associated with politically nonviable positions).

Downs asserts (1957b, 300, proposition 24) that "political parties tend to maintain ideological positions that are consistent over time unless they suffer drastic defeats, in which case they change their ideologies to resemble those of the party that defeated them." We believe that Downs is right about this, but the time frame for change may not be a single election. It took a series of massive election defeats before the Republican party reconciled itself to the basic elements of the New Deal. Indeed, we might argue, paralleling Thomas S. Kuhn's (1970) claims about the importance of cohort change for acceptance of "paradigm" shifts in the sciences, that it was only as a new generation of politicians came to power in the Republican party that the Republican party position could shift to reflect the new political realities (for example, Thomas Dewey didn't learn—he just kept losing; Hoover never learned).[8]

In my view, it is difficult to overestimate the importance of inertia and hardened arteries (both metaphorically and literally) in understanding political change (or rather, the lack thereof).[9] Also, short-run constraints on policy movement (e.g., the probability of credibility if a politician attempts to repudiate past positions) mean that even politicians who themselves care for nothing but winning, will often act *as if* they had fixed policy positions.

---

8. If both parties have policy concerns, and if parties are concerned only with winning and not with plurality maximizing, the paradoxical result is that, in the short-run, there may be little or no pressure for convergence to a median position. The majority party need not change its position much because it is virtually assured of election since its policies are already relatively close to those of the median voter. The minority party won't change its position much because, regardless of what it does, until voter preferences change, it will still lose the election—while maintaining its position preserves ideological purity.

9. Compare the discussion of rates of party convergence in chapter 10. The comedian Severn Darden, then with the Second City comedy troupe, had a routine in which he asked whether or not fish could think. He concluded that they could, but given life-threatening changes in their environment, *could not do so fast enough* to avoid death by starvation. In this regard, political parties are a lot like fish.

Furthermore, the model of parties as coalitions of voters, developed by scholars such as Aldrich (1983a, 1983b) and Glazer, myself, and Owen (1991), argues for stability in party positions absent fundamental realignments in voter coalitions. From the perspective of parties as coalitions of voters, the received view in the public choice literature that the legislator is "a placeholder opportunistically building up an *ad hoc majority* for the next election" (Riker and Weingast 1988, 396, emphasis added) misses the key point about the relative underlying durability of party coalitions.

Reinhard Selten (1971), Donald A. Wittman (1973, 1983), Manfred Holler (1978), T. Ingemann Hansen and Charles Stuart (1984), and Henry W. Chappell, Jr., and William R. Keech (1986), among others, have modeled two-party (unidimensional) political party competition as one in which parties (or candidates), rather than merely seeking a vote-maximizing location as in the classical Hotelling-Downs framework, trade off the probability of their winning an election against the achievement of desired policy goals. Wittman (1990) provides a thorough review of the formal modeling work that introduces policy-oriented concerns. He shows that allowing policy motivations permits a much more realistic picture of party divergence.[10]

As Wittman (1983) observes, candidates/parties guaranteed election ought to be more likely to indulge their policy preferences than are candidates/parties in a more competitive situation where the pressure to converge to the median voter location is stronger (cf. Fiorina 1974). Wittman (1983) reviews a considerable body of evidence from U.S. congressional and senatorial elections that supports this conclusion. What Wittman (1983) does not note, but what follows straightforwardly from the logic of his analysis, is that the same is true for parties that are certain to lose; that is, such parties can be free to "indulge" their policy preferences.[11]

Unified Party Team

Once we recognize that there is intraparty competition as well as interparty competition, then we need to modify the assumption that all candidates of a given party can be treated as identical in their goals. Once we add in primaries

---

10. A Wuffle (1985) carries the idea of policy orientation to its reductio ad absurdum by permitting parties to derive utility even if the policy goals they seek are implemented by the opposing party.

11. If both parties have policy concerns, and if parties are concerned only with winning and not with plurality maximizing, the paradoxical result is that, in the short-run, there may be little or no pressure for convergence to a median position. The majority party need not change its position much because it is virtually assured of election since its policies are already relatively close to those of the median voter. The minority party won't change its position much because, regardless of what it does, until voter preferences change, it will still lose the election—while maintaining its position preserves ideological purity.

as a means of resolving intraparty disputes (see discussion of assumption 3), the argument for convergence disappears—although exactly what should replace it is not completely clear.

Aldrich (1983b) shows that party activists, if they have policy preferences, will shift the location of their party's candidates away from the overall median toward those of the party activists. Moreover, the role of party activists, when combined with primaries and with the importance of durable "party images," virtually guarantees that there will be a self-selection and weeding out process in which candidates gravitate to and are chosen by the party whose policy positions most resemble their own.[12] Thus, in recognizing these complicating factors, contra the classic comic book version of *An Economic Theory of Democracy*, we would expect that candidates will in general be closer to the median voter in their own party than to the overall median voter. As noted earlier, this is what the empirical data show (see, e.g., McCrone and Stone 1986; Grofman, Griffin, and Glazer 1990; cf. Shapiro et al. 1990).

Yet another modification of the view that parties can best be viewed as unified actors comes from the work of Edward G. Carmines and James A. Stimson (1989). The standard Downsian model of political competition is a demand side model—a model driven by voter preferences. In that model, vote-maximizing parties *react* to voter preferences by seeking a winning location. The party that best anticipates the views of the electorate by appropriately choosing its platform wins. In contrast, Carmines and Stimson have what I call a *supply side* model of politics, albeit the term is mine not theirs. In their model, competition within the party among party leaders and activists leads to replacement of old internal cadres by new ones—a process that may be accelerated by external events such as a recession. A change in party leadership and elites in turn often triggers a concomitant change in the proposed and perceived policy positions of the party. They emphasize the role of leadership rather than treating political parties as passive respondents to changing currents of public opinion.

Carmines and Stimson illustrate the critical role of leadership in U.S. Party competition by examining the consequences of decisions by national party leaders over a three-year period (1963–65), which led to a complete reversal of the racial stance of the two political parties. The key events included the decision by Johnson to press for the Civil Rights Act of 1964 and the Voting Rights Act of 1965 and the opposition to those pieces of legislation by Barry Goldwater and the party activists who supported his takeover of the

---

12. Glazer (personal communication, 1988), for example, assumes that primary voters will seek a candidate who can win the general election, but that would seem to me to be only one of the concerns influencing voter choice in a primary. Also, expectations of winability are conditioned by preferences; that is, there is a "wishful thinking" effect, frequently one of some magnitude (Granberg and Brent 1983; Uhlaner and Grofman 1985).

party machinery in 1964. The consequences included a dramatic gain for the Democrats among black voters, especially those southern blacks who were newly enfranchised, and an almost equally dramatic decline in southern white support for the Democratic national ticket—triggering a sectional realignment at the presidential level. The choices made by party leaders in the 1960s have largely shaped the nature of national party competition ever since (see, e.g., Edsall and Edsall 1991). As Carmines and Stimson emphasize, the party issue positions define the options open to the voters and thus structure the characteristics of the voter coalitions that support each party.[13]

Discussion

Although the notion of Tweedledum-Tweedledee politics is fundamentally misguided, what is certainly true is that in 1988 (as in 1964 and 1972 and 1980) there has been an attempt to define the political "mainstream" and to argue that one's opponent isn't in it. Success in such an endeavor, for example, making *liberal* a dirty word, suggests that Downs is in some ways fundamentally right in treating two-party competition as a quest for the center, even though we need a more institutionally rich model to capture the complex realities of political competition in the United States. That model must take into account institutional features of U.S. election practices such as the role of multiple (and frequently simultaneous) elections taking place at different levels of government and in overlapping constituencies in shaping both voter perceptions of party differences and voter and party strategies, the modifications to the standard model required by the existence of the electoral college and the president and vice-president package, and barriers to registration that require turnout to be a premeditated act. In addition that model must contain a supply side component that recognizes factors such as the role of party activists in motivating party divergence and defining party images.

---

13. Carole Jean Uhlaner, in chapter 4 and in her earlier work, emphasizes the entrepreneurial role of group leaders in motivating political participation. A similar argument is set forth in Hansen and Rosenstone 1984.

Part 4
Reflections on *An Economic Theory of Democracy*

CHAPTER 13

The Origins of *An Economic Theory of Democracy*

Anthony Downs

When I had finished my written and oral examinations for a Ph.D. in economics at Stanford University in 1955, it was time to choose a dissertation topic. Since my father was head of a real estate research firm, I first turned to urban economics. I proposed to study the effects of a major expressway—the Nimitz Freeway in the San Francisco East Bay—on land values along its route. I even obtained a grant for about $3,500 from the Social Science Research Council for that purpose. But when I began to gather data for this topic, I discovered that almost none existed. Moreover, it would be impossible to disentangle the impact of the highway from the impacts of myriad other factors influencing the area concerned. Therefore, I rejected this topic as not feasible.

What to do? I asked one of my professors, Julius Margolis, for suggestions. He said he has always been intrigued by an idea presented by Joseph A. Schumpeter in *Capitalism, Socialism, and Democracy.* Schumpeter rejects the still-prevailing economic theory that governments behave so as to maximize the welfare of society. That theory implies that elected officials are directly motivated by a desire to carry out their social function: the creation of government policies. Instead, Schumpeter espouses a somewhat more cynical view. He argues that political parties in democracies really behave just like competing private entrepreneurs. They are not directly motivated to pursue their social functions. Rather, their private motives are separate from those functions. Thus, the social function of General Motors is to produce automobiles and trucks, but its leaders and owners are motivated by making profits. A similar division of social function and private motivation exists within democratic political parties. Their social function is to formulate and carry out government policies, but their motivation is different. It is to get elected and to remain in power so as to enjoy the perquisites and privileges of office as long as possible.

The views in this article are solely those of the author, and not necessarily those of the Brookings Institution, its trustees, or its other staff members.

Professor Margolis suggested that I explore the implications of this notion for economic theory. I was intrigued by the idea, and my adviser—Professor Kenneth J. Arrow—also liked it. So I asked the Social Science Research Council to shift its grant to this new topic. The council refused and canceled my grant. But Professor Arrow talked the Office of Naval Research, for which he was a consultant, into providing me with a somewhat smaller grant in support of this topic. Why the navy would be interested I still do not know; I am sure their grant to me was entirely a testimonial to Ken Arrow's powers of persuasion.

Then began one of the most delightful years of my entire life, before or since. This topic could only be explored through reading relevant literature and inventing likely behavior patterns of hypothetical government officials. No statistical or quantitative analysis seemed possible, so I did not pursue any. Every morning for four hours, I would either sit in front of my typewriter or pace up and down in my tiny Stanford Village dormitory room, inventing behavior patterns, or visit the Stanford library. Most afternoons and all evenings I played tennis or otherwise goofed off. The weather in Palo Alto was splendid, and I was also falling in love with my future wife, a fellow graduate student who lived in the next dormitory. I took no more exams and attended no more classes. I had never had a more relaxed year since entering kindergarten, and I have not had another one like it since!

In order to prevent the thesis from being totally unrealistic, I decided to introduce information costs into the analysis. This decision was heavily influenced by my prior experience as the elected president of the student body at Carleton College, where I had done my undergraduate work. When I ran for that office in my junior year, I formulated a campaign platform that contained about ten major goals. Those goals were mainly invented just so I could present the voters with some plausible program, rather than because I had a burning desire to accomplish the policies involved. I was clearly motivated more by the desire to win office than the desire to achieve particular policies—though that is certainly not what I said while running! This behavior fit perfectly into the theory I later developed.

After I was elected, I accomplished almost all ten of my campaign goals. But the vast majority of students, who had enthusiastically participated in the election campaign, were totally indifferent to my achievements in office. Their apathy was almost universal. Why? I obviously could not attribute this indifference to my own boring personality or incompetence. Rather, I reasoned that students were indifferent because the results of my policies did not really affect them much. Moreover, most of those results involved details of campus life of which they were not aware. Why not? Because they were too busy doing more interesting things. Thus, I had already formulated a tentative hypothesis that the voters in at least this form of democracy were *rationally ignorant* of government affairs. It was not reasonable for them to stay well-informed about the details of government, or whether or not the people they elected kept their promises. Doing so could not affect their lives very significantly but would consume a lot of their valuable time and effort.

This insight was transferred to *An Economic Theory of Democracy* and spelled out in a formal manner. I personally believe that the way information costs are treated in that book is perhaps its most important contribution to economic literature. It is more important than the spatial analysis of parties, although the latter has become much more famous.

Two people played especially important roles in the development of *An Economic Theory of Democracy*. Ken Arrow was a fantastic adviser who encouraged me and discouraged me simultaneously. I would work for two weeks developing new ideas, then discuss them with him. In ten minutes, he would either demolish those ideas or show me how to develop them in much more effective ways. He is one of the most brilliant and fastest-thinking persons I have ever encountered, and I owe him an immense debt.

The second key contributor was Professor C. Edward Lindblom of Yale University. When I had finished my thesis—which I had always conceived only as a thesis, not as a publishable book—Ken Arrow showed a copy to Professor Robert Dahl, who was then spending a year at the Behavioral Research Center in Palo Alto near Stanford. Dahl in turn showed it to Lindblom, who was back at Yale. Lindblom was so impressed by this document that he persuaded three major publishers to send me signed contracts for its publication. He also wrote a wonderfully positive statement for the book's cover, calling it "a pile-driver of a book." I had never met Professor Lindblom and did not meet him until ten years later. But without his amazing initiative, my thesis would never have become a published book at all. In fact, such publication never dawned on me as a possibility while I was writing the thesis. (Incidentally, the book contains exactly the same text as the draft thesis; I did not change a word for publication.)

Thus, at every stage in the development and creation of this book, I benefited greatly from the ideas, suggestions, and actions of others. I am grateful to all of them for their contributions to what will undoubtedly be the most well-known work I ever write.

CHAPTER 14

The Early Impact of Downs's *An Economic Theory of Democracy* on American Political Science

Gabriel A. Almond

My first encounter with Anthony Downs's *An Economic Theory of Democracy* took place during my study at the Center for Advanced Study in the Behavioral Sciences at Stanford in August 1956. Kenneth J. Arrow, a fellow that same year, and Downs's principal adviser, gave me a copy of it, then a dissertation, and asked me to tell him what I thought of it. Robert Dahl had been a fellow at the center the preceding year and had served as second reader. Downs was supported during his dissertation year by a contract with the Office of Naval Research (ONR). And the study was first published in the form of a technical report for ONR. The title of the report was *An Economic Theory of Government Decision-making in a Democracy;* the date of the report (technical report no. 32) was May 31, 1956. It circulated as a government document for another year until published by Harper and Row in 1957.

I spent the first month or two at the center unwinding, looking out of my floor-to-ceiling window at a beautiful oak tree, the Stanford hills, and the inevitable Hoover Tower. Ken Arrow occupied one of the studies on the tier just below. He often walked along the path during the course of the day looking somewhat abstracted, flipping a pencil in the air and deftly catching it. My neighbor Allan Wallis used to bring fresh figs as they ripened on his tree from day to day, and he would share a few with me.

The atmosphere of the center—the consequence of the setting and the laid-back administration of Ralph Tyler and Preston Cutler—encouraged this relaxation. While most of the fellows signed up for courses in statistics and mathematics, as well as a host of special seminars on arcane themes, nobody seemed to take this flurry of activity seriously. This year was supposed to be an opportunity to acquire new skills, slough off bad intellectual habits, and work one's way out of ruts. One had to relax in order to open one's mind to all of these creative possibilities. I took this admonition seriously.

The Downs dissertation seemed like a good way to begin my fellowship year. I was an empirically oriented political scientist, a product of the

Merriam-Lasswell-Gosnell political science department at the University of Chicago. I was strongly "inductivist," believing that political reality was far more complicated than anything the human mind could invent, and distrustful of the formal, deductive, mathematical impulses that were then being felt in the discipline. A year before we had had a seminar at the Center of International Studies at Princeton, led by Karl Deutsch, on the applicability of game theory to the study of international relations, and it had not gone very well. But I respected the scholars who respected the dissertation. So in between coffee-drinking encounters with new colleagues in the wonderful sunshine, games of darts, volleyball, Ping-Pong, and simply daydreaming through my picture window, I read it, and it made a lasting impression on me.

One of my special fields of interest had been comparative political parties. In the analysis of the American party system we had come pretty close to using the market metaphor in describing the interaction between party leaders and voters. Continental European political parties were viewed as ideological parties with relatively nonnegotiable programs, while American parties were viewed as pragmatic bargaining parties. The issue positions of party leaders were viewed as heavily influenced by calculations as to the preferences of voters, and voters were viewed as casting their ballots according to their immediate interests. The wholesale adoption of much of the New Deal by the Republican party after its disastrous electoral defeat in 1936 was a dramatic illustration of this fact. Studies of the "Boss" and the "Machine," which abounded in the reformist literature of the late nineteenth and early twentieth centuries, drew attention to the perversion of politics into an actual market in which voters sold their votes to politicians and were responsive to price differentials in money or in kind, and in which legislators and bureaucrats sold their votes and/or decisions to utility companies and other economic enterprises for cash. V. O. Key, Jr., describes some of these operations in his doctoral dissertation, "Techniques of Graft," in which he elaborates on Mr. Dooley's distinction between honest and dishonest graft, the latter being the actual exchange of votes or political-administrative decisions for bribes, and the former, "I seen my opportunities and I took 'em," an early version of insider trading.

Interpreters of American democracy—for example, Joseph A. Schumpeter, Pendleton Herring, Elmer E. Schattschneider, and others—had noted this pragmatic bargaining quality of American politics. The popular argot of politics was indicative. Politicians were viewed as "trimmers" or "fence-sitters." The Algonquin Indian expression *Mogquomp* (great chief) was converted to *mugwump,* translated as one who has his mug on one side of the fence and his wump on the other. This moral cost of lack of principle in politics was balanced against the benefit of rendering politics compromisable, lowering the stakes, and avoiding impasse and violence. The collapse of the Weimar

Republic and the immobilism of the Third Republic of France were the historical experiments that validated this model of pragmatic-bargaining democracy, as one more likely to prove stable and durable.

From the Marxist side Otto Kirchheimer had thrown in the sponge, publishing simultaneously with the Harper and Row issuance of the Downs book, his brilliant "The Waning of Opposition in Parliamentary Regimes" (*Social Research,* Summer, 1957). "The modern party is thus forced to think more and more in terms of profit and loss," he writes, and he writes of a "transition from the ideologically oriented continental party of earlier times to the more limited congeries of interest oriented groups" (reprinted in John Wahlke and Heinz Eulau, *Legislative Behavior* Glencoe, IL: [Free Press, 1959], 91–92).

I experienced a number of internal resistances as I began to read the Downs book. The literature of American political science didn't fully accept "market" politics. It was dishonest: its practitioners were trimmers: there was guilt and ambivalence in according approval to it. From the European side there was a sense of the loss of dignity associated with the decline of ideology. Could one condone dishonesty and the pursuit of power even if it could be shown to be supportive of democratic institutions and processes? The application of Adam Smith's "invisible hand of providence" to the world of politics was being hinted at in the political science of the time, but not explicitly validated. Schumpeter made this ethical logic explicit, and Downs echoed it enthusiastically and fully elaborated it. The bulk of the profession, while perfectly prepared to recognize that producers and sellers of goods pursuing their own interests might be unintentionally colluding to enhance the material welfare, was not quite ready to adopt the view that democratic good could come out of the power hunger of politicians selling their souls to interests in exchange for support and votes. There was a moral cramping and narrowing here, and even the argument that this was a heuristic device was not enough to quiet these moral pangs.

The second resistance I encountered as I read the manuscript was a feeling of confinement, as though, having been accustomed to roam freely among the data of history and in the colorful variety of comparative institutions, I was now being asked to dance in a mincing manner, not inducting anything until I had deducted what I ought to find, if a certain proposition was true.

Despite these qualms Downs's dissertation changed the way I thought about political parties and politics. Since his model enabled me to organize and interpret my data more systematically and parsimoniously than my earlier constructs did, I adopted and used this method, along with others then in use, and not to their exclusion, as some "rational choice" advocates such as John C. Harsanyi (1969) were soon to urge. Returning to Princeton the following year I recall illustrating my lectures on types of party systems with the graphs that appear on pages 159–61 of the ONR report version of the book. Downs himself recognizes the costs as well as the benefits of his deductive modeling approach and, in particular, his assumption of rationality and of "self-interest." Unlike most of the later literature of this genre, Downs places his modeling method in the context of the larger social science literature. More than two-fifths of the books and articles he cites in his *An Economic Theory of Democracy* are sociological, social psychological, psychiatric, psychoanalytical, political philosophical, and political science studies. The later literature on "public choice," with rare exceptions, tends to be almost entirely cut off from the social science disciplines other than economics.

Anthony Downs's own representation of his work, as well as C. Edward Lindblom's presentation of it in the immediate aftermath of its appearance, are of this ecumenical sort. In a prophetic piece written and published even before the Downs book was published (Lindblom was instrumental in interesting Harper and Row in the dissertation) Lindblom describes it as "bold, imaginative, creative, to say the least, and persuasive beyond any expectation with which I approached it. I believe its impact on political science, as well as on economics, will be deeply registered in the next ten years" ("In Praise of Political Science," *World Politics,* January 1957, 242). Much of Lindblom's article shows how Downs's theory simply made explicit theories already to be found in the political science literature. Referring to the work of Pendleton Herring, David Truman, Elmer E. Schattschneider, Herbert A. Simon, Robert Dahl, David Easton, Harold Lasswell, and others, Lindblom asks,

> Do they in fact possess any underlying implicit theoretical system? I would argue that a number of works are beginning to show that they do, and I can now point to Downs's splendid book as clinching evidence. The fact that it is not a professional political scientist who has here integrated a large part of political science into an explicit theoretical system doubly bears out my argument that the profession itself has not appreciated its riches. (242)

In a long and thoughtful review the political theorist, Martin Diamond, in the *Journal of Political Economy* (1959), recognizes, "the merits of the book, its seriousness of purpose and execution, the author's competence, imagination, and rigor. The book makes its contribution by the boldness and clarity of its presentation of a method thought by many to hold promise for a new understanding of politics" (211). Diamond points out that Downs's model restates ideas already made familiar by Hobbes and Locke. He shows that Madison in *Federalist 51* had already anticipated the application of the "invisible hand" to politics. But while these writers were aware of what was lost or left out by this narrow immediate self-interest model of politics, Downs, according to Diamond, minimizes the importance of those aspects of political behavior that do not fit within it, at the cost of both the empirical and normative validity of his theory. Diamond reaches this conclusion about the general import of *An Economic Theory of Democracy*.

> Earlier, prescientific democratic theory depended upon an "idealistic" view of man. Modern thought has taught us what a low fellow man really is. But democracy can be rescued because of new knowledge of the formerly hidden ways whereby man as he really is can yet make democracy work; that is, its success depends upon the expression of the lowest common human denominator. I would argue that the alleged salvation depends not upon new knowledge but rather upon a crude simplification or debasement of older views of democracy and politics. If my view of what those things are is normative, so is the view I have here been criticizing. And upon the right judgment of what those things are depends the utility of logical constructions like Downs's model. (211)

This encounter between Diamond and Downs is an early version of the rational choice polemic, still unresolved, regarding the assumptions of the model as to whether or not they are simply postulates, or whether or not they are taken to be descriptive of reality. Downs appears to have fudged this a bit as did Milton Friedman before him, and William H. Riker afterward. This made him vulnerable to Diamond's criticism while a simple postulative claim would have avoided the onus of seeming to argue from a sordid view of human nature. In a brief comment in the December, 1959 issue of the *American Political Science Review* Downs does offer a purely heuristic defense of his study (Downs 1959). He felt called upon to reply to a rather confused criticism of his book by W. Hayward Rogers, which had appeared in the June issue of the *American Political Science Review* (Rogers 1959). Downs replies that Rogers couldn't tell the difference between an axiom and a hypothesis, didn't understand what models were all about, and didn't understand the relation between theory and research. He then concludes his defense of his work with some diffidence, "If such models aid in guiding empirical research—as they certainly have in the past—or even if they merely provide enlightening insights into politics, I believe they are a methodologically sound way in which to advance our knowledge of political reality" (53, 1097).

Other early reviews are moderately approving or skeptical. The lead reviews in both the *American Economic Review* and the *American Political Science Review* are described as "+ −" in the *Book Review Digest,* Abram Bergson predicts, "if political science is ever to evolve into a more theoretically grounded discipline, it is doubtful that Downs charts the way" (*Ameri-*

can Economic Review 48, 1958, 437). Roland Pennock disagrees with Bergson, venturing to predict that "Downs's volume will give a substantial fillip to democratic theory" but that "many of Downs's conclusions, especially with regard to the party system, fall into the category of the commonplace" (*American Political Science Review,* 52, 1958, 539).

Edward Banfield, in a review published in the then *Western Journal of Political Science,* expresses a mix of disappointment over the obviousness of most of Downs's predictions and strong approval of its formal elegance and its logical explication of aspects of political behavior. He concludes, "Certainly it will provoke much thought and discussion, some of which is likely to have beneficial results for political theory" (1958, 324). It is intriguing here that what Lindblom cites as evidence of the power of the Downs book—its rendering explicit what was already in the literature—is cited by other reviewers to its discredit, as belaboring the obvious.

Among the reviewers only Lindblom fully appreciated the potential impact of the Downs book. It is surely one of the great social science triumphs of our time.

The citation curve of Downs's classic probably starts relatively low in the first ten years or so. The index only begins in 1966, nine years after publication of the Downs study. In the first four years of the Citation Index, 1966 to 1970, the book receives ca. 160 citations.[1] The rate doubles (from ca. 160 citations to ca. 300 citations) in the first five years of the 1970s, rises by 50 percent in the interval 1976 to 1980 (ca. 450 citations), and levels off in the 1980s at the very high steady rate of more than 100 citations per year. In other words citations have more than doubled in annual numbers in the quarter-century lifetime of the Citation Index, from roughly 40 per year in the early 1960s to over 100 in current years.

I would suppose that the shape of this curve is the opposite of the typical citation curve for most contemporary classics where in the first years are many citations with the number declining over time. Here we have a rising curve that reflects the truly classic character of the Downs book: it received low and specialized attention in the first years then gathered momentum as the area of research triggered by this and one or two other exemplary works took off. Perhaps some historian of political science, or better, of the social sciences, will compare the citation curves of major creative works, and check the validity of these impressions.

It is also noteworthy in the first years of *An Economic Theory of Democracy* it stood out as an example of its genre. To be sure, Arrow's *Social Choice* and John von Neumann's and Oskar Morganstern's theory of games

---

1. The figures suggested here are rounded numbers estimated from column inches of citations from appropriate volumes of the Social Science Citation Index.

were already around, knocking on the doors of political science and international relations. Duncan Black's *Theory of Committees and Elections* appeared a year after the Downs book; in 1962 it was joined by Riker's *Theory of Political Coalitions,* and James M. Buchanan and Gordon Tullock's *Calculus of Consent,* and then by a host of studies of the rational choice variety in the 1960s and 1970s as this movement took on momentum. The Downs book had the great virtue, among others, of being exemplary to rational choice virtuosos and neophytes, as well as being accessible to other political and social scientists.

CHAPTER 15

An Economic Theory of Democracy as a Theory of Policy

M. Stephen Weatherford

Two contrasting images of how policies originate coexist uneasily among political scientists. The first is a descriptively rich tradition, animated by a normative conception of politics as infused with the purposive pursuit of "the good for man." This approach emphasizes the role of leaders, ideas, and institutions in shaping vague public grievances into acknowledged policy problems, and in managing the discourse through which responsibility is allocated and solutions designed.[1] It gains verisimilitude by focusing attention on the *process* of policy-making and governmental leadership. The approach is traditional, even old-fashoined, both in the sense that its method is inductive and explanations commonsensical, and in that its era as the discipline's dominant approach is largely past.

A quite different perspective, persuasively expressed in Anthony Downs's *An Economic Theory of Democracy,* gives rise to the second image. Here politics is understood by way of analogy with economic markets, and the intellectual approach is positive, deductive, and theoretically self-conscious. The starting point for explanation is the assumption that individuals have fixed preferences for particular policies, which they register with their votes. Because voters are assumed to punish a party that goes back on its campaign promises (it is "unreliable") or whose policies are not consistent with the actions it took when last in power (it is "irresponsible"), it follows that parties will enact the policies they have promised, to the best of their ability (Downs 1957b, chap. 7). Perhaps the signal contribution of this line of models, and the primary source of the models' gain in parsimony over traditional ones, is Downs's initial achievement in drawing the dynamics of governance out of a model of the political campaign. With policy goals given by election outcomes, governments can be judged by efficiency criteria, leaders are largely

---

1. Examples include Schlesinger 1959; Sundquist 1968; Neustadt 1980; Heclo 1974; Wilson 1973; or DeNeufville and Barton 1987.

fungible, and institutions merely mediate the fundamental relationship between the demand for and supply of policies.

William H. Riker and Peter C. Ordeshook (1973, xi) make a persuasive case for viewing the second image as a natural successor to the first—signaling maturity and progress in a discipline developing as a science. Indeed, it is remarkable that rational choice modeling has so quickly come to dominate theorizing in political science fields as disparate as elections, legislatures, bureaucracy, and international relations. But such transitions are never smooth, and the hasty adoption of a new approach is more likely to connote faddishness than thoughtful acceptance. It would be unfortunate if rational choice models emerged as the only theoretical orientation, not only because in general theoretical pluralism rather than unity provides a better foundation for scientific progress but also because some of the most important insights of the traditional model have been set aside before being carefully evaluated.

This chapter pursues the question of what economic models can learn from the traditional approach, by focusing on the problem of explaining national economic policy. The justification for choosing this policy area is straightforward: accounting for economic policy moves is intrinsically important, and both approaches are well-developed in this area, so that they can be compared on relatively equal footing. The comparison is especially clear in modeling national economic policy, both because of the salience of economic policy as a political issue and because of the relatively centralized character of the economic policy-making process. For rational choice models, it is important that the economy is a high-profile issue and that variations in economic conditions have direct, visible impacts on individual welfare, for this supports the plausibility of the assumption that voters have clear, fixed preferences for economic outcomes and that elections express demands for policies to achieve those outcomes. For traditional models, the significance of the economy as the ideological theme in party realignments and in major historical shifts of party control of government supports an interpretation in terms of the role of ideas or alternative formulations of the public interest. The centralization of the economic policy-making system in the presidency supports the plausibility of the rational model's image of policy outputs as the result of choices by a unitary decision maker attempting to optimize within constraints. For the traditional approach, the predominant role of the president justifies focusing on leadership skills and on the president's economic ideology in explaining policy outputs.

The theme of the argument is that economic models cannot deliver the product they promise—explanation of economic policy outputs[2]—and that to correct their shortfalls it is necessary to look to the traditional model and its emphasis on the policy-making process, striving to integrate previous insights without too severely compromising parsimony. Two resilient insights, crucial to the earlier tradition's explanations of policy, are notably absent from the new one, and this chapter argues for their integration. The first is the role of *ideas*, specifically the lasting commitment of political leaders to particular ideas or ideologies arising out of an image of the good society, ideas that are more than congeries of issue positions packaged together for campaign purposes. The second is the role of *deliberation*, where this entails active, reciprocal attempts at persuasion involving alternative views of the appropriate frame or context of ideas in which a policy is to be understood. This notion of voice points to a conversation both more normative and more thoughtful than the relationships of entry and exit the economic model depicts among politicians or between politicians and voters.

The chapter proceeds in three parts. The first briefly reviews the two predominant versions of rational choice models of economic policy, noting that the incompatibilities between them cannot be resolved without admitting additional information about the dynamics of the policy-making process. The next assumes (for purposes of argument) that one or the other rational choice version must be an adequate explanation of policy goals and then asks what minimal additional specification of the policy-making process would be necessary to ensure that the government had the means to accomplish its aim. The third section considers the implications of the argument in light of the behavioral assumptions of rational choice models.

Economists depict stabilization policy in terms of a relatively well-defined cybernetic system: given a model of the economy's operation, the task of government economic managers is to adjust their instruments of fiscal and monetary policy to minimize fluctuations around the economy's growth path.[3] The image of a unitary policymaker optimizing well-defined goals has been retained as research on political business cycles has enriched this picture, emphasizing that economic policy choice is inevitably influenced by political incentives.[4] The predominant role of the president in economic policy, that is, has fostered models that remain close to their abstract Downsian roots by

---

parsimony can be used as sound ancillary standards for evaluating theories, but in this case each is the natural ally of one of the approaches, and thus not an appropriate candidate for sole criterion.

3. "Outside" lags occasioned by the size and complexity of the economy, and by lags in reporting economic conditions, and "inside" lags in the policy system mean that macroeconomic management will be inevitably imperfect, but the fluctuations that occur should be symmetrical around the equilibrium growth path.

4. Political business cycle research is not the first to call into question the purity of economic stabilization models as technical responses to objectively measurable shortfalls between targets and policy instruments. Various authors have emphasized the critical importance to econometric predictions of empirically unverifiable hunches about plausible values of imprecise indicators or uncertain causal relations (cf. Ascher 1978; McNown 1986).

linking policies directly to election outcomes. In contrast, rational choice models of the regulatory process or of legislative politics have increasingly utilized game-theoretic formulations to capture the complexities of a policy process typified by power sharing.

It is worth noting the drastic limits this imposes on the substantive content of the models. If policy outputs are to be derived directly from the competition for votes, then the implied policy reasoning cannot blatantly contradict the established facts about political reasoning in the mass public.[5] Distinctions among the models result from different assumptions about how voters think about and respond to economic conditions as political issues. The common theme uniting these models holds that politicians are anxious about their prospects in the next election, and that electoral insecurity dictates that short-term popularity maximizing take precedence over economic optimizing (Keech 1980). Two major variants have emerged over the last decade or so, one centered on the median voter and one depicting parties as class coalitions.

Gerald H. Kramer's initial imputation of an evaluative standard to voters, based on a satisficing rule, is generally consistent with what we know about the public's political sophistication:

> if the performance of the incumbent party is "satisfactory" according to some simple standard, the voter votes to retain the incumbent governing party . . . while if the incumbent's performance is not "satisfactory," the voter votes against the incumbent, to give the opposition a chance to govern. (1971, 134)

While this assumption was sufficient to motivate Kramer's analysis of economic voting, it is too vague for modeling the electoral mandate to which policymakers are assumed to respond. In order to model the effect of elections on economic policy outputs, William Nordhaus (1975; cf. MacRae 1977) proposes that politicians timed growth cycles to appeal to voters who were assumed to have short memories and no foresight. Democratic responsiveness to voters like these was pathologically simple: stop-go cycles of preelection stimulus and postelection contraction maximized votes in the short run, and politicians were never electorally punished in the long run. In the economy, however, the result was a succession of wasteful cycles and excessive inflation. Early enthusiasm for this insight into the potential danger of politicizing

---

5. I do not mean to rule out "as if" reasoning, but there are limits to the extent that the replicated findings of political behaviorists can be stretched, even in the interests of theory (cf. Moe 1978). If, for instance, stabilization policy required sticking to deflationary instrument settings while public opinion surveys or election results showed the unpopularity of rising unemployment (cf. Fellner 1976), the Downsian model would imply that the policy should be abandoned.

economic policy-making led not only to praise for the model's parsimony and its counterintuitive results but also to the claim that its story was descriptively accurate (e.g., Tufte 1978; Buchanan and Wagner 1977). This depiction of voters is not entirely implausible, but in fact the model's empirical implications do not fit the data: the postwar American economy has been virtually free of such cycles (McCallum 1989; Golden and Poterba 1980; Gordon 1980).

Perhaps the most obvious way to revise the model is to assume that voters are smarter, and the work of Henry W. Chappell, Jr., and William R. Keech (1985; cf. Kramer 1983) typifies this approach. They surmise that, given the relatively successful history of stabilization policy in the United States, voters must be much better informed and more sophisticated than the initial model supposed:

> assume that the president, through fiscal and monetary policies, controls real output, Q. We then define the variable, Z_t to serve as an indicator of policy stance, where
>
> $$Z_t = Q_t/QN_t - 1,$$
>
> and QN is natural real gross national product. . . . A simple linear feedback rule relating Z_t to the lagged rate of inflation, P_{t-1}, is used to define desirable policies:
>
> $$Z_t^* = dP_{t-1}, d < 0$$
>
> Z_t^* denotes the optimal value of Z_t as perceived by sophisticated voters.
>
> To measure economic performance, then, it is appropriate [for voters] to judge policymakers on the basis of how far they deviate from the optimum policy, Z_t^*. (13)

In this version of the model, presidents respond as if the election results delivered an unambiguous policy mandate, and good economic policy results because the median voter, capable of readily deploying a sophisticated macromodel when choosing between candidates, communicates just such a mandate.

Unfortunately, nothing in the voluminous empirical literature on the political thinking and behavior of ordinary citizens supports an attribution this heroic (Flanigan and Zingale 1987; Kelley 1983). What is known about voters suggests that Chappell and Keech are correct in rejecting the image of the myopic maximizer, continually demanding that government lower taxes and increase spending and growth, but they are not correct in imputing an econometric model guiding the policy evaluations. Indeed, empirical information may not even be necessary to judge the validity of assuming that voters manifest this degree of sophisticated calculation. The logic of information costs and "rational ignorance" imply that the return on a citizen's one vote (out of tens of millions) could never match the cost of using that citizen's time and intellectual resources to employ a decision rule this demanding.

The research evidence contradicts the image of voters as economists, but it reveals respectable levels of information and skill. We know, for instance, that, although voters only infrequently link outcomes with specific policies, they can readily understand, and punish, deteriorating economic conditions (Goodman and Kramer 1975; Bloom and Price 1975)—and negative judgments carry more weight than positive ones (angry voters are more likely to turn out and more likely to vote against the incumbent [Kernell 1977; Lau 1985; Fiorina and Shepsle 1986]). Moreover, voters place great weight on competence and trustworthiness, and thus they value policy coherence and consistency and punish policies that appear to be indecisive, devious, or manipulative (Popkin et al. 1976).[6] Finally, we know that group affiliations, particular with classes and parties, provide valuable cues to voters interpreting policy actions and campaign promises (Hinich and Pollard 1981; Enelow and Hinich 1982a; Weatherford, 1983; Brady and Sniderman 1985; Vanneman and Cannon 1987; Green 1988).

The role of parties and classes in structuring electoral competition, and the persistence of party differences in economic policies, imply a quite different image of the competition in election campaigns. Here the party is a group of politicians united with each other and distinguished from other parties by the politicians' shared commitment to advancing the interests of their core constituency (Hibbs 1982, 1987). Each party would like to amass a large electoral mandate, and this leads it to advocate its class-interested goals by attempting to show that they are consistent with the long-run interests of the whole society, but the fundamental commitment to a distinctive socioeconomic constituency anchors the party against moving to the median (Stokes 1966; Aranson and Ordeshook 1972; Aldrich 1983a; cf. Calvert 1985b). Both for the United States and for other industrialized economies, the empirical support for this formulation is stronger than that for the simple political business cycle version (Eulau and Lewis-Beck 1985; Beck 1982, 1987; Woolley 1988; Havrilesky 1988). It is worth emphasizing that this is not a median

---

6. "Politicians are selected [by winning a cumulative sequence of competitions] not as a result of the consequences of their actions, but as a result of the judgmental qualities that are revealed by their actions. . . . 'In politics you never recover from a single grave mistake in judgment'" (Elster 1979, 136).

voter model: even when it produces compromise policies or coalition governments, they are the result of bargaining or repeated interaction between distinctive class parties, rather than the convergence of malleable party platforms at the median (Przeworski and Wallerstein 1982; Alesina and Sachs 1988). This model lies intermediate between the Downsian economic model and the traditional model. It parts company with the spatial competition literature in abandoning the notion that parties and candidates are motivated solely by the desire to win the next election: policy and ideology are core commitments. But the model is distinguished from the traditional approach in that the dynamics of policy are driven directly by election outcomes, rather than requiring any specification of the policy-making process.

These two versions of the rational choice approach pose a genuine dilemma. Neither theme is obviously wrong. Both begin from intuitively attractive premises about political officials' goals and voters' responses, multiple versions of both models have been estimated and have produced respectable statistical fits to historical data, and at least one especially egregious instance of each pattern can be cited (Nixon's preelection boom in 1972, Eisenhower's electorally costly pursuit of anti-inflationary Republican fundamentals in 1958 and 1960) to breathe historical life into deductive inferences. But the two look incompatible from any angle. From a theoretical perspective, politicians' objective functions are clearly different in the two versions; from the perspective of empirical time series analysis, the two lead to different predictions for the time paths of major economic variables. Close historiographic observation sharpens the distinction even further—presidents and their advisers realize that at a host of decision points the choice is available to strengthen short-run popularity or pursue traditional long-run party goals, and the choice is often made with surprisingly full discussion of the alternatives (Hargrove and Morley 1984; Stein 1969). Moreover, the dilemma is not resolvable in the terms in which these models present it: deductive arguments can offer equally plausible assumptions and logically consistent inferences in either version, and empirical tests all pass through a mesh of time series data with only sparse observations of critical political variables, so that a good conventional model of the economy will produce a comfortable statistical fit for any reasonable model of political interactions.[7]

To complicate matters further, the assumption, common to both versions, that politicians are homogeneous (at least within the same party) is an unjustified abstraction. As Nathaniel Beck (1982) shows, it misses an essential element of variation between administrations, which can be captured only if

---

7. Chappell and Keech (1988) substantiate this point with a (presumably unintended) reductio ad absurdum, deploying a powerful macroeconomic model around an anemic image of the policy process, and concluding that changes in party, president, or congressional majority have almost no impact on economic outcomes.

each presidency is separated out. Beck's analysis serves as a critical corrective to excessive abstraction, not only cautioning against imputing goals to actors without attempting to view the choice situation from the perspective of the decision makers but also emphasizing that—even when the goal is given—administrations vary in their efficacy in translating intentions into policy. Clearly, more information is needed than these models allow us to consider about the process of economic policy-making.

The Puzzle of Policy Consistency

Noting that an adequate explanation of economic policy outputs requires taking more-detailed account of the policy-making process is a sound inference, but it is not a research strategy. Viewing the process from a game-theoretic perspective will help to sharpen the question. Let us assume that one of these versions of the rational choice approach provides a generally correct depiction of the *goal* of economic policy, and then focus on the conditions for accomplishing the goal.

Whether the president is a purely Downsian politician concerned only to ensure that economic policy moves help to maximize his or her vote total in the next election or the president is the representative of a class party aspiring to advance the party's agenda via the pursuit of faster growth or less inflation, his or her central problem is with consistency and credibility. Given an election campaign in which the economy was an issue, voters, the media, and economic notables will naturally view the president as responsible for pursuing a particular economic goal, and inconsistency and frequent policy shifts will worsen aggregate economic performance (Kydland and Prescott 1977; Barro and Gordon 1983; Blanchard 1985; Cagan and Fellner 1984) and undermine the reputation for coherent policy that voters will expect at the next election (Brody 1982). What sorts of problems might confront a president seeking to pursue a consistent policy?

Various economic shocks will surely occur. Some of these will be serious enough to require changing the course of policy to smooth adjustment (e.g., the oil supply shocks of the 1970s); others will be small or localized and clearly fall short of justifying a shift in national economic policy (e.g., the decline of the timber industry in the Northwest during the 1970s). But most will fall in the middle, generating credible claims for redress that, if accepted, would distort the administration's priorities or force unexpected trade-offs. In addition, political pressures from various sectors and interests will demand higher spending, lower interest rates, or some other deviation from the planned policy course. The president knows that acceding to one group's demand (e.g., to subsidize a particular industry) will produce "nine enemies and one ingrate" and will also make it more difficult to resist the demands of others.

Denying all demands for adjustment or amelioration is out of the question, for some will undoubtedly turn out to have been justified. But most will not, and at the time the decision must be made, no economic indicator or political information will be available that would resolve the uncertainty about future consequences. Finally, it is worth calling attention to the fact that demands for the microlevel exceptions that distort macrolevel stability come predominantly from the president's partisan and ideological supporters, not from the opponent's camp, so that denying such a request (if the situation requires it), without undermining the government's support coalition, is a sensitive and subtle challenge.

Such demands pose a series of dilemmas confronting the intention to pursue a global maximum with opportunities (or temptations) to seek local maxima, whose pursuit would compromise the ability to reach the longer-term goal. If the president could perfectly predict the economic and political consequences of each potential exception (by some objective, technical means), then the problem would disappear. But such "perfect rationality" (Elster 1979) is not possible; something more is needed to foster global maximizing by emulating rationality, even if only imperfectly. Two kinds of situations pose problems. The first are crisis situations, when the time for consultation and decision is cut short and the danger is that impulses contrary to prior, more carefully reasoned, intent have to be controlled. The literature on foreign policy decision making is rich in analyses and recommendations for cases like this. Cases in the second category are more puzzling but more likely to occur in economic policy-making. These are foreseeable situations in which "the preferences governing his decision are contrary to his current preferences with regard to that future occasion" (Schelling 1985, 362).[8] A rule is needed here, to restrict or channel behavior around the choice that, if made voluntarily at the time, would violate current preferences.

Precommitment may provide such a guide (Elster 1979, chap. 2; cf. Ainslie 1975; Strotz 1955; Pollack 1968; Taylor 1976). Precommitment involves setting in motion some causal process at t_1 that will make it easier to resist temptation and adhere to one's long-run intentions at t_2—as when the

---

8. Puzzling because the situation appears to violate the conventional rational choice assumption that individual preferences are stable and continuous. The classic case is Ulysses and the Sirens (Elster 1979), but there are analogies to this dilemma in everyday life: the family attempting to save despite a tight budget but faced with an attractive spending opportunity, the business executive intent on holding back a portion of profits for research or investment but faced with employee or shareholder demands, a person trying to break a bad habit (cf. Schelling 1984, chap. 3). In each situation, the individual knows what needs doing; the problem is with staying firmly on the course to carry the intention through to accomplishment. Aristotle, for instance, likens a person in a situation of akrasia to a city with a good legislature but an incompetent executive (1962, 1152a). Recent work by philosophers on "weakness of will" has enriched and deepened the analysis of the concept (Pears 1984; cf. Rorty 1985).

dieter or the smoker trying to quit announces the intention to friends or asks them to monitor and sanction misbehavior. The point is to reinforce the initial resolution by rearranging the context of future decisions so that, even if one's will to resist is weak, the structure of the new situation will make it easier to keep the resolution. Precommitment appears to be on the right track, because it distinguishes global from local maximizing behavior and short-run from long-run optimizing strategies. Moreover, precommitment is the policy rule implied in both median voter and class party models.[9]

This does seem the appropriate rule for "binding oneself" in cases when all deviations are identically impermissable (every cigarette to the recent nonsmoker, every sugary treat to the dieter). But a simple all or nothing rule is inappropriate for the case of economic policy-making, because the problem of maintaining consistency is more subtle than the rule envisions. Precommitment has the advantage of clarity, in the sense of posing a "bright line" between compliance and violation (Schelling 1985), and the success of a practical rule for maintaining consistency will depend on its being simple and unambiguous. But in practical situations of economic policy-making, some exceptions will be warranted, and ruling out all exceptions *ex ante* would turn consistency into compulsiveness. The primary rule needs to be strengthened by anticipating the need for exceptions and setting up a standard procedure for dealing with them. The situation requires a supplementary or ancillary rule that names a referee or states the objective indicators that can be checked to adjudicate whether or not claims for exceptions are justified.

In considering the properties of a good rule for this situation, it is worthwhile to describe the institutional and political context where it will serve. Economic policy-making is a thoroughly political process, and the president, although a primary participant, is charged with motivating others to contribute to a collective action where the president cannot order them to do so. The change in perspective is important, for it shifts the emphasis from the technical economic assessment of what would be the optimal policy for an authoritative unitary actor to choose toward the political aspects of the collective choice process by which policies are set.[10] The hallmarks of that process are

---

9. That is, they postulate an objective function and derive a time path for the economy that would maximize that function. All that remains is for the government to set its aim at the appropriate goal and adjust the relevant instruments at the indicated times. "Thus, a politically maximizing government with a four-year electoral term must choose sixteen quarterly values for government spending, while noting that the constraints implied by the eight equations in the macro model must bind in each of the sixteen quarters. The problem facing the politician is simply a constrained optimization problem, albeit a rather large one" (Chappell and Keech 1983, 76).

10. The interplay between rules and discretion is currently receiving much attention from economists interested in advising the monetary authority (e.g., Rogoff 1987) But the situation in which a president needs to discriminate justified exceptions is not a protected forum of authorita-

familiar: it is publicly open, visible, and politically charged, and the president cannot accomplish policy wishes without voluntary cooperation from other elite actors and representatives of organized interests, whose self-interest seldom coincides perfectly with the president's—even though they (and their constituents) all claim loyalty to the president's ideological coalition (Neustadt 1980). The problems of concerting individual interests toward a collective goal comprise the reasons why presidential power is the power to persuade.

For instance, although each of the interests making up the president's electoral coalition might benefit from adhering to a policy of stable growth,[11] if one industry or group were able to secure a subsidy, or one agency to secure an unusual increase in its budget, aggregate economic conditions would probably not be severely distorted, and that interest could free ride on the actions of others. A typical challenge to policy consistency might occur in an exchange between the president and a member of Congress, with each having a favorite cause for which he or she would like an exception to be made. The member of Congress knows that a particular project in his or her district would contribute to the member's electoral chances more than being seen as loyal to the president, but the member also knows that, if the president's program is derailed by a number of exceptions like his or hers, then the economy's resulting poor performance will be held against all the party's incumbents (Hibbing and Alford 1981). In this situation, the problem of maintaining a coherent economic policy course, like many collective action problems, resembles a Prisoner's Dilemma. Several aspects of the situation undermine collective action: the impact on aggregate economic activity caused by any one exception may seem small and hence not worth fighting over; the cumulative transaction costs of coordinating on separate grounds with each claimant will be high, and the supply of potential side payments usable as selective incentives (e.g., public works projects for farm-state representatives, in exchange for a vote for smaller farm subsidies) is limited by the same economic conditions that required cooperation in the first place.

Let C and D stand for cooperating and defecting (that is, insisting on gaining an exception for one's own favored project), and let numbered sub-

---

tive experts challenged intellectually by imperfections in information and inefficiencies in instruments. It is all these challenges transposed into an open, highly politicized context, in which the president does not decide and order but deliberate with and persuade. Managing policy in a consultative, politicized process increases the complexity by several orders of magnitude, and merely spurious exactitude would be gained by adopting the terminology of that literature here.

11. Since potential supporters are relevant to calculating where and how additional votes might be gained in the next campaign, this might also include the sympathetic-but-unmobilized and weak adherents to the other party's coalition.

scripts stand for different actors. Then the preference orderings (ranked from most favored to least) for politicians 1 and 2 are

$$D_1C_2, C_1C_2, D_1D_2, C_1D_2$$

$$C_1D_2, C_1C_2, D_1D_2, D_1C_2$$

Defecting is the dominant strategy for each. That is, assuming neither can influence the action of the other, and no formal procedure exists for making and enforcing a contract, then—whatever action the other chooses—defecting is the better option. The conflict between individual rationality and collective welfare is clear: D_1D_2 will be the outcome, although both prefer C_1C_2.[12] The problem cannot be finessed by any rule that simply admonishes actors to maximize their own utility.[13] Its resolution depends on tying individual action to the outcome for all.

An established link between individual and collectivity already exists, of course, in the common sense of loyalty to the president's economic goals that unites the members of the president's ideological coalition. The sense of *commitment* to an idea,[14] to what we might call the president's economic ideology, is the critical element in the practical resolution of this dilemma, and hence the key to defining the rule the president needs in order to protect the consistency of his or her economic policy. Defining the rule involves specifying what sort of claims will be made for exceptions, and the standard against which claims will be adjudicated.

The most forceful challenges to the continuity and coherence of the administration's economic policy will come from members of the president's electoral coalition, each claiming that a particular exception is justified by past support. These challenges cannot be credibly denied by way of an appeal

---

12. The optimum (C_1C_2) is individually inaccessible (no one will take the first step toward it) and individually unstable (each player would find it in his or her self-interest to take the first step away from it).

13. This is true even if the substantive content of individual preferences is "altruistic"—that is, if the D's are not expensive projects within each district of a member of Congress but rather alternative, inconsistent conceptions of the public interest.

14. *Commitment* is used here in the sense proposed by Amaryta K. Sen (1977, 1987, 20). Hannah Pitkin notes the essential role such a concept plays: "in fact one of the most important features of representative government is its capacity for resolving the conflicting claims of the parts on the basis of their common interest in the welfare of the whole" (1967, 217). Although I emphasize commitment to the president's economic goals, loyalty may arise, of course, out of a broader loyalty to the president, the party, or the conception of the public interest that motivates the president's economic goals. In general, the coalition will be delineated by party, but commitment to the president's economic ideology is the essential criterion, so that for a Republican president this might include conservative Democrats. The notion of presidential economic ideology is elaborated in Weatherford 1988.

to a universal collective good—one that would be advantageous to all citizens, whether they had been past supporters or not (e.g., "greater productivity," or "maximum employment with stable prices")—for this would undermine future support by implying that members of the president's electoral coalition would not be treated differently from nonsupporters. Instead, the president's rationale for denying members' exception must be formulated in a way that emphasizes their common and distinctive identification with the government's national policy aspirations, while deemphasizing the uniqueness lent by their constituency's particular economic grievance.

In this respect, the role of the president's economic ideology, in the deliberation with a member of Congress claiming (on the basis of a calculation of his or her short-run popularity) that his or her exception is justified, is to frame the decision in terms that raise the salience of (1) loyalty to party and ideology and (2) the medium-term advantage—for the member of Congress as well as the party—of a successful economic program.[15] As with any persuasive attempt, success is not guaranteed the president, but it is important to note that the goal is to reframe the dialogue to focus on the divided loyalties of the member of Congress, rather than allowing the issue to be posed as a question of who wins and who loses. Nor does the president attempt to change the legislator's preferences: they may well both agree that the project in the district will do more for the legislator's short-run popularity than for supporting the president.[16] The goal is to persuade the legislator to forbear from pressing the opportunity to advance selfish interests; the persuasive dialogue is about behavior, not preferences. From the perspective of a legislator explaining to constituents a cooperating (rather than a constituency interest-maximizing defecting) decision, the president's economic ideology lends an attractive rationale: "The President needed our support to help achieve the strong Republican economic policy we elected him for" (Fenno 1978).

If the president can successfully advance an economic ideology as a counterpoise to the claim of a member of Congress, then this produces a small but crucial difference in the game. The member of Congress now reasons that it is worthwhile to cooperate, not unconditionally, but only if everyone (or virtually everyone) else goes along; otherwise, the member will defect and

---

15. That is, the decisional frame is wider (more universalistic) in terms of both social context and time horizon. The experimental evidence on the influence of framing on choice is impressive both for its strength and consensus: compare Tversky and Kahneman 1986; Kahneman, Knetsch, and Thaler 1986.

16. The conversation takes the form of an explicit comparison of different preference orderings for immediate policy moves, in light of a common commitment to (i.e., identical preferences for) longer-run policy goals. The deliberation that takes place here is analogous to Albert O. Hirschman's notion of "reflective change of values" (1982, 1985), or Sen's use of the concept of metapreferences (1973, 1974), and it resembles the inner dialogue that precedes an act of precommitment (Elster 1979; Schelling 1984, 1985; Pears 1984).

hold out for his or her own project. The correspondingly altered payoff matrix would show the following ordering (Sen 1967):

$C_1C_2, D_1C_2, D_1D_2, C_1D_2$

$C_1C_2, C_1D_2, D_1D_2, D_1C_2$

It is immediately apparent that there is no dominant strategy in this game. In the absence of information about the prospective move of the other player, the maximin criterion dictates defection, but the best outcome is not free riding. The optimum in this game (C_1C_2) is individually inaccessible, but individually stable—that is, convergence on the optimum is not impossible to achieve. Unlike a Prisoner's Dilemma, the outcome is sensitive to changes in expectations about the other player's actions. Reframing eases the conditions for cooperation. It does not guarantee that cooperation will emerge.[17]

The appeal to a common commitment to national economic policy goals will not elicit cooperation if the member of Congress supposes that the president will still make an exception for another claimant with no stronger justification than the member's own. To elicit cooperation, the rule also must involve an essential element of *assurance* that no exceptions will be granted for claims that are equal to or weaker than this one. Although the president may lack the material resources to offer side payments, the president is in a position to offer such an assurance, because in general the White House is the ultimate arbiter of claims to budgetary exceptions.[18]

This is obviously an abstract and stylized depiction of the process of economic policy-making: it assumes that the goals of the program are given and seeks a parsimonious specification of the conditions for policy coherence. Yet it highlights the danger of economic policy models that move directly from electoral competition to policy outputs. The problem of maintaining economic policy consistency is a problem of concerting collective action in the absence of hierarchy or material incentives. The rule the president needs for this situation must directly address the most plausible threats to consistency—from the members of the president's electoral coalition—by striving

---

17. Note that cooperation is not a dominant strategy (it is one among several Nash equilibria), and that even once established it remains unstable. One can think of the sense of commitment and loyalty as providing the foundation for the exercise of tentative trust or conditional altruism that yields the initial cooperative move (Taylor 1976; Hardin 1982; Axelrod 1984).

18. The sense of satisfaction that results from contributing to a goal articulated in terms of commitment may, moreover, lend the process the potential for going from success to success, rather than quickly exhausting resources, as would a strategy that relied on selective distribution of material incentives. The likelihood of achieving such a goal is subject to bandwagon effects, in which a few early victories promise to weaken the opposition's cohesion, so that the good is nonrival and the significance of individual contributions will decline only slowly with increasing group size (cf. Chamberlain 1974).

to frame the issue as the ongoing pursuit of a shared goal. The existence of a common identity, based on shared loyalty to the president's economic aspirations, helps to resolve the collective action problem because it frames the choice in a context that encourages the recognition of others' goals and that facilitates behavior that moderates the aggressiveness with which individualistic goals are pursued. Reframing does not accomplish cooperation, but by easing the conditions for cooperation, it makes the next step easier. That step is then one that the president is in a position to supply, by assuring potential cooperators that they can count on the similar forbearance of others.

Implications: The Self-interest Assumption and the Conditions for Credibility

We can see the implications of this argument more clearly if we step back from the problem of modeling policy outputs to view from a wider perspective the concept of a policy rule grounded in the president's economic ideology. This section briefly surveys the operation of the rule from a theoretical perspective, by considering the behavioral assumptions of rational choice models, and from a political perspective, by considering the problem of credibility in relation to the traits of the president.

A number of different routes have been proposed for explaining how Prisoner's Dilemmas are resolved, each relaxing one of the critical assumptions that structures the dilemma. It may be useful to compare the way the rule proposed here would work for other solutions. Amaryta K. Sen's (1985, 342–43) enumeration of the conventional behavioral assumptions of game theory provides an apt organizing device:

> Goal-completeness: Every player's goal takes the form of maximizing according to a complete order of the resulting states, and—given uneliminated uncertainty—a complete order of lotteries over the states.
> Mutual knowledge: Each player is well-informed on the other players' goals, values, and knowledge.
> Goal-self-regardingness: Each player's goal takes the form of maximizing his or her own welfare, and in particular the individual orderings can be used to assess Pareto optimality and related welfare-based achievements.
> Goal-priority: Each player pursues his or her goal subject to feasibility considerations, without being restrained by any other values.

The assumption of *goal-completeness* focuses on the capacities of decision makers as careful, sophisticated calculators of trade-offs. It makes stringent demands on the information that choosers have about the alternatives and on actors' cognitive capacities, especially in practical political situations—and good arguments can be advanced against its appropriateness (cf. Simon 1985). But it cannot be relaxed without changing the game, so that weakening this assumption is not an admissible program for resolving the dilemma. The assumption of *mutual knowledge* focuses on the information actors have about each other's preferences and payoffs. Game-theoretical approaches usually attempt to resolve the dilemma in ways that weaken this assumption, relying on uncertainty on the part of at least one player about the other (Kreps et al. 1982; cf. Levi 1982; Axelrod 1984). This scheme has a certain charming perversity about it, in that rational cooperation turns out to be founded in "socially helpful *ignorance*" (Sen 1985, 344), but for explaining outcomes of a well-established elite policy-making circle, placing much weight on ignorance about others' behavior seems most unrealistic.

The remaining two assumptions embody the supposition that rational actors are self-interested. If *rationality* is defined strictly in terms of consistency, then these assumptions are not needed. But such a thin theory of rationality is not adequate to motivate substantively interesting explanations or predictions (Elster 1983; Simon 1985), and the use of the concept of rationality conventionally goes beyond mere consistency to imply self-interest (cf. Gibson 1977; Sen 1987). The assumption of *goal–self-regardingness* focuses on the content of preferences. Most approaches by empirical political scientists to explaining how collective action problems might be resolved have focused on weakening this assumption (e.g., the literature on sociotropic versus self-interested attitudes as antecedents of political behavior).[19] A change in the content of preferences, that elevated actors' perspectives beyond their narrow selfish interests, probably would diminish the likelihood of Prisoner's Dilemmas, but there is no guarantee that everyone's image of what is good for society would be the same, so that even if preferences were entirely unselfish, the dilemma would still occur.

The assumption of *goal-priority* relates to behavior rather than preferences, focusing on the question of how aggressively or single-mindedly a given preference is pursued in a particular situation.[20] Goal-priority postulates

---

19. For example, Kinder and Kiewiet 1981; Weatherford 1983; compare Wildavsky 1987. This route has also been pursued by sociologists (e.g., Granovetter 1985; DiMaggio and Powell 1983), and anthropologists (e.g., Douglas 1986; Meyer and Rowan 1977; Sahlins 1976). Compare Hirsch, 1978; Parfit 1984.

20. The assumption of goal-priority thus operates in the territory between preferences and behavior. In one version of the "revealed preference" approach, in which the only admissible source of information about preferences is defined to be observed behavior, this territory is arbitrarily ruled out of existence. This assumption is radically inconsistent with a large body of empirical research (cf. Schuman and Presser 1981); Sen (1971, 1973) has argued cogently against the tactic, not only as an unnecessarily limiting empirical operation but more importantly as a disguised (or ill-understood) conceptual move; and Hirschman (1982, 1985) and others (cf. Schelling 1984) have made good progress in scouting the boundaries of the territory.

a single, highly restrictive image of how individuals act on their preferences. This assumption does a great deal of work in game-theoretic models, and on that ground alone it deserves better than an unconsidered acceptance. The assumption of goal-priority seems especially questionable when we think of the process of deliberation through which policy choices are made, for two sorts of reasons. First, the relatively small group of participants involved in national economic policy discussions comes close to constituting an ideal typical community, in the sense of shared background, beliefs, and knowledge of each other. To some extent, each of the participants derives his or her own political identity from the participants' joint efforts, and thus the context contributes to recognizing and taking account of others' interests, and of the potential for conflict in the individualistic pursuit of goals (Sandel 1984; Rawls 1985; Guttman 1985). Second, historical and traditional political science research on the deliberations that occur over claimed exceptions to the president's economic plan suggests that the deliberations typically concentrate not on persuading preference change but on advocating forbearance from pressing claims that would undermine the administration's game plan, frequently by appealing to larger loyalties and common party membership or ideological beliefs.[21]

These arguments fall short of showing that rationality (defined as the consistent pursuit of electoral self-interest) will lead to policy consistency,[22] but they do suggest that the appeal to communal loyalties and to the shared

---

21. Herbert McClosky's (1964) depiction of the role of ideology among the American elite, for example, seems to have in mind compromise via forbearing from aggressively pressing one's claim, rather than changing long-held beliefs or simply invoking hierarchy to resolve disputes (cf. Neustadt 1980). On presidential economic policy decision making, see Weatherford and McDonnell 1990).

The president essentially attempts to avoid arguing about the precise quantitative impact of the exception on his or her economic game plan. By focusing on the value of the overarching goal, the implication is that any deviation would be unjustifiably costly. Michael D. Cohen (1984), in an article on organizational search effectiveness, shows that errors in making choices from the feasible set increase as it becomes harder for decision makers to tell how sizable a loss they risk in adopting a proposed policy change (443–46). In the terms of Cohen's discussion, the effect of the president's economic ideology is to depress the estimated gains and exaggerate the estimated losses from short-run policy shifts. This leads to the rejection of stabilization interventions that might be judged acceptable on econometric calculations from a short-run stabilization model. Experimental evidence consistent with this interpretation is presented in Einhorn and Hogarth 1986.

22. Sen (1985, 346) notes that the ambiguity is intrinsic:

The fact that each person could have done *even better* by departing from that common behavior pattern, provided others did not do anything like that on similar reasoning, does of course introduce a conflict between the communal and individualistic principles. But it does not make nonsense of the communal principle, especially since that principle achieves better for everyone than the individualistic principle does. The point is not that rationality must take us to the communal principle, rejecting the individualistic one, but that there is a genuine ambiguity here about what rationality might require.

commitment to common economic goals will frequently be a workable scheme for resolving the Prisoner's Dilemmas that undermine the president's attempt to hold to a policy course.[23]

If the appeal to a common economic ideology could work this well, why doesn't every president use it? The answer is that every president does attempt such appeals, but most of the time presidents fail. To see why, consider the conditions for successfully offering a credible assurance.

The president's copartisans and ideological sympathizers are disposed to cooperate with his or her request, if the president can assure them that relevant others will not be allowed exceptions. The problem of establishing the president's credibility shares some features with the problem of making credible threats (particularly the absence of a structure of contract law to specify and enforce agreements), which game theorists and economists have considered at some length (Schelling 1960), but the difference is fundamental—broadly, between "reciprocal acts designed to safeguard a relationship [versus] unilateral efforts to pre-empt an advantage" (Williamson 1983, 519). Even this distinction, however, does not fully capture the sense in which the president's power really does rely on persuasion. The context in which the president's credibility is put to the test, in relatively egalitarian interactions with interdependent elites who have their own separate bases of political power, is one in which *sanctioning* defection (as the credible threat literature suggests) is virtually impossible, and in which the notion of exchanging *hostages* (Williamson 1983) can be invoked only in a metaphorical or literary sense. The political reality is that the president has few, if any, material resources to barter with the other elites who could undermine his or her economic plan; the president must rely on solidary and purposive incentives. The rule that protects the consistency of the president's economic plan must motivate largely by moral authority or psychological force (cf. Pears 1984; Schelling 1984, 1985). Establishing the credibility of the president's assurance that no unjustified exceptions will be allowed to his or her economic plan depends, then,

---

23. It is worthwhile noting the distinction between the appeal to group loyalty in this argument and similar appeals in the literature. John C. Harsanyi's (1955) classic article, for instance, counterposes self-interest to a universalistic concern for "the public interest." This formulation seems implausible on empirical grounds, for there is little evidence that, outside of wartime, individuals feel a sense of loyalty to the society as a whole that is anywhere near strong enough to counterbalance the pursuit of self-interest. My reliance in this argument on party and ideological loyalty concentrates on the primary group affiliation for elite political actors and on an essential defining source of personal political identity for politicians. It is a group affiliation about which political science has a good deal of understanding, based on verifiable observational data, and it is related in a theoretically clear way to party alignments and social cleavages, and thence to elections and party competition. Finally, the sense of loyalty to the president's economic ideology is not called on to do the heavy work of altruism but only the lighter task of facilitating conditional cooperation.

on the properties of the president's economic goal as a convincing idea and on the personal characteristics that make the president a credible advocate:

> The economic goal itself is more convincing and credible the simpler it is, and the brighter the line it draws between policy actions consistent and inconsistent with it.
> The president's assurance is the more credible the more the president appears to be committed to sacrificing other goals, if necessary, to achieve this one.
> The assurance carries more weight the more other politicians view the president as reliable or strong willed, in the sense of being capable of reliably binding his or her own future actions.

For instance, Reagan's commitment to cutting taxes and cutting domestic social spending illustrates all three of these properties. The goal was phrased in a simple and unambiguous way, his use of the theme in the campaign and especially in prioritizing his legislative agenda underlined the salience of his economic plan, and the widespread knowledge among elite actors of his stubborn single-mindedness and even his penchant for ignoring conflicting information substantiated the impression that his resolve would not be swayed (Weatherford and McDonnell 1990). Carter's performance as an economic policy leader was virtually the opposite. Although he claimed a strong resolve to halt inflation, he simply could not say no to insistent interest groups, agency heads, and members of Congress, with the result that his requests for party discipline, although initially successful (the presidential-congressional honeymoon succeeds on conditional cooperation), were soon met with skepticism and defection.[24]

The discussion to this point has focused on the importance of formulating the rule in an unambiguous way, but the contribution of credibility to persuasiveness makes clear that personal traits, or reputation, are also essential. Specifically, the president must be seen to have the personal commitment to promote the plan over other attractive goals, and to have the toughness of character to stick with the initial resolve even under pressure. As George A. Akerlof (1983) points out, there are many situations in which the efficient accomplishment of collective projects would be enhanced by the ability to give credible assurances, and to an economist, this suggests that the incentive

---

24. Michael D. Cohen's (1984) discussion of organizational search effectiveness is helpful in depicting the difference. From the perspective of the president with unclear or less salient economic goals, decisions about exceptions to the administration's long-run policy direction appear like the top two panels of Cohen's figure 6 (445), while a president with a firm and clearly formed long-run economic policy goal would view demands for exceptions as depicted in the bottom panel.

structure should consistently evoke sham assurances in which the identical rhetoric is used for selfish ends. The reason this works so seldom is that the credibility of assurances rests on the hearers' assessment of the trustworthiness and reliability of the speaker, and these assessments are grounded in biography and personal interaction. Unlike threat situations, where fairly fine predictions of credibility and strategy can be made on the basis of observable resource endowments, the outside evidence needed to support promises resides in observers' evaluations of the quality of the promiser's character. But for the elite political actors, such information is readily available from other politicians and indeed is frequently known to the media and the public. The irony at the heart of Akerlof's formulation of the economics of loyalty also works to undermine merely rhetorical appeals to party or ideological commitment: the personal characteristics that would be needed to take others in with a false promise are the same ones that make the promiser the sort of person who would never do something like that.

Of course, the process of formulating and advancing the myriad components of a national economic policy is much more complicated than this stylized analysis implies, but its essential element is the problem of dealing with conflicts of interest and goals among the policy's potential supporters. How individual politicians think about their own objectives and obligations, in light of their common membership in the governing coalition, is critical to resolving this collective action problem. A coherent economic ideology, advanced forcefully and convincingly by the president, brings the electoral coalition together in the presence of a common commitment to a long-range goal, and it makes possible the emergence of the solidary ties needed to support the conditional altruism that transforms a Prisoner's Dilemma into an assurance game.

Conclusion

Economic policy has appeared especially amenable to models that trace policy outputs directly to electoral competition—the policy process is unusually centralized (justifying the assumption of a unitary decision maker), and voters' demands seem unambiguous (justifying the assumption that there exists an informative incentive to which officials can respond). This chapter argues that, even if we assume that elections deliver mandates interpretable in terms of specific policy demands, and assume that economic policy-making is dominated to an unusual extent by the president, spatial theory–based models of economic policy outputs still do not provide the logical apparatus needed to explain why some presidents perform well and others poorly as economic managers. The criticism points to the need for more information about the policy process itself and, at a more fundamental level, carries an implication for the behavioral assumptions of the economic approach as a model of political interactions.

To summarize, I began by supposing that the spatial competition approach is correct in inferring the government's economic policy goals from election outcomes. Given that, what assumptions about the policy-making process would be needed to produce the implied policy outputs? The problem facing the president, as the head of the party in power, is to maintain the consistency and coherence of the administration's policy trajectory, once the election dictates its direction. Given the predictable occurrence of exogenous economic shocks as well as requests for budgetary or other exceptions from members of the president's own political coalition, the problem is with persisting on a globally maximizing course in the face of attractive opportunities for digressions toward local maxima.

Some rule is needed to keep the policy on course, a rule that is simple enough to be credible but applied with enough legitimate flexibility to meet unforeseen circumstances that justify exceptions. Jon Elster's notion of precommitment is considered and rejected, for its uniformity assumes too simple challenges to consistency. Moreover, precommitment pays insufficient attention to policy-making as a deliberative process that functions to tie the individual actions of potential defectors to the collective outcome for the government as a whole. The contrast between two formulations of the policy game, the Prisoner's Dilemma and the assurance game, highlights the importance of the expectations each potential defector forms about the actions of all the other members of the president's coalition. The role of the president as a persuasive advocate, and of the president's economic ideology as the "bright line" that demarcates consistency, can then be seen as key to the president's ability to offer credible assurances that enable individuals to take the collectivity into account. The concept of an economic ideology is an unambiguously political one: it focuses policy on an economic goal by appealing to that goal's political implications, it requires no great macroeconomic sophistication on the president's part, and it performs an essentially political function in addressing problems of mobilizing and concerting collective action. The credibility of the president's persuasive attempts also depends on the president's own ability to demonstrate the salience of the economy among his or her policy priorities and the strength of will that supports his or her own commitment to consistency.

What of the contrast between the economic and historical approaches to explaining policy outputs? What are the implications, for economic or game theory models of policy-making, of the notion of common commitment to the president's economic goals as the foundation for resolving the conflicts of interest that threaten economic policy consistency? The economic policy process clearly illuminates a Prisoner's Dilemma typical in representative government, between advancing the short-run interests of the individual constituency or joining with others to promote the collective interest. Clearly, such Prisoner's Dilemmas are, at least occasionally, resolved in favor of the collectivity, and understanding how this is accomplished might lead to useful advice to policymakers.

The rational choice model, as it is conventionally formulated, suggests two routes by which this resolution can be accomplished—by changing the goals actors are assumed to pursue, or by assuming a peculiarly favorable distribution of ignorance on the part of each player about the characteristics of other players—but both of these appear to make assumptions that, particularly when applied to experienced members of the national political elite, are highly unrealistic. The notion of commitment, in suggesting that actors depart systematically from the pursuit of individual goals because they are motivated by the sense of what they should do, as members of the president's coalition, attacks the problem from a Burkean or communitarian perspective. The effect of the resulting behavioral norm, to reframe individual action in terms of collective welfare, derives its motivating force from the sense of communal identification with the economic goals of the president and thus emphasizes the way in which behavior can be both instrumental and social.

CHAPTER 16

Downsian Logic and the Comparative Study of Party Systems

Arend Lijphart

Anthony Downs has had a strong influence on modern political science, especially the analysis of electoral competition under plurality voting rules in basically two-party systems like the United States and Great Britain. In this chapter, I call attention to the much less well-known but equally important insights that *An Economic Theory of Democracy* (1957b) offers for the *comparative* study of voting and parties, including proportional representation (PR) and multiparty systems. I shall argue that Downs refines and improves the traditionally posited causal link between electoral systems, party systems, and the stability and quality of democracy in a number of crucial respects: he adds an important variable (the distribution of voters' opinions), new directions of causality, and significant nuances to the usual claims about the effects of party systems on the operation of democracy. Most of these refinements are explicitly stated in *An Economic Theory of Democracy,* but others are only implicit. Part of my task is to make the latter explicit.

Electoral Systems, Party Systems, and the Distribution of Voters

The conventional wisdom in comparative politics in the 1940s and 1950s concerning the causes and consequences of party competition and Downs's refinements of the traditional model are depicted in figure 1. The traditional model sees the electoral system—especially the difference between plurality systems and PR—as the main explanation of whether the party system will have a two-party or a multiparty format. The party system in turn is linked to two aspects of the performance of democracy: political stability and democratic quality. The term *stability* is variously defined, but its essence is the democratic system's capacity to survive intact, which depends on its capacity to deal effectively with the problems confronting it and to adjust flexibly to changing circumstances. Similarly, there are very many different aspects to

Traditional model:

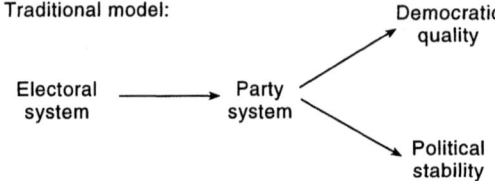

Downs's refinements:

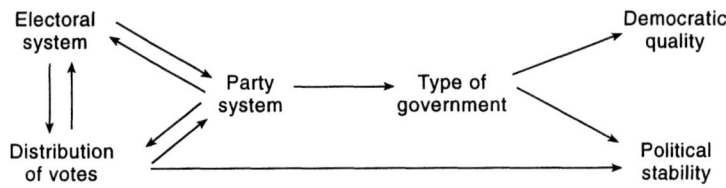

Fig. 1. Models of the causes and consequences of party systems

the quality of democracy, but the main concerns have tended to be the voter's ability to make an effective and meaningful choice and the government's accountability.

In this section, I focus on the first part of the causal chain, that is, on the causes of party systems. As indicated in figure 1, Downs introduces the distribution of voters (along a one-dimensional, basically socioeconomic or left-right, scale) as a new explanatory variable: "Whether the political system contains two or many parties . . . depends upon (1) the nature of the limit upon the introduction of new parties [that is, the electoral system] and (2) the shape of the distribution of voters" (123). Moreover, he clearly believes that the second variable is more important than the first. He concedes that, all other factors being equal, "a multiparty system is encouraged" by PR (124), but these other factors, especially the distribution of voters, are usually not equal and "the distribution is a crucial political parameter" (140).

Downs states the paramount influence of the distribution of the voters' opinions even more emphatically by paying special attention to the two combinations of contradictory tendencies: a unimodal distribution combined with PR, and a polymodal distribution in combination with plurality elections. In the latter case, he repeatedly states that a multiparty system will be the most probable result without even mentioning the countervailing effects of plurality: if a nation's voters are distributed polymodally—he specifically refers to a figure showing a distribution with four small modes—"a multiparty system will almost inevitably result" (122). And a few pages later, he repeats that "multiparty systems—those with three or more major parties—are likely to occur whenever the distribution of voters is polymodal"—again without mentioning any opposite influence that the electoral system might exert (125).

In the former case, that of a unimodal distribution with the use of PR, a two-party system is still likely to result, although he adds the qualification that not only the number of modes but also the spread of opinions is part of the explanation:

> If a proportional representation system is established in a society where the distribution of voters has a single mode and a small variance, it is possible that only two parties will exist in equilibrium because there is not enough political room on the scale for more than two significantly different positions to gain measurable support. (125)

The same logic leads him to the conclusion that there is no tendency toward uncontrolled multiplication in PR systems, contrary to what is often asserted about PR: "a given distribution of voters can support only a limited number of parties even under proportional representation" (124).

Another important insight in Downs's treatment of party systems is that the relationships among the three variables at the left in figure 1 are all two-way causal links. First, let me simply quote the two paragraphs in which Downs lays out the bidirectional connection between the distribution of voters and the electoral system in a superbly lucid fashion:

> The type of electoral structure extant in a political system may be either a cause or a result of the original distribution of voters along the scale. Thus if the distribution has a single mode around which nearly all voters are clustered, the framers of the electoral structure may believe that plurality rule will not cause any large group to be ignored politically. Or if the distribution has many small modes, the law-makers may choose proportional representation in order to allow sizeable extremist groups to have a voice in government.
>
> Causality can also be reversed because the number of parties in existence molds the political views of rising generations, thereby influencing their positions on the scale. In a plurality structure, since a two-party system is encouraged and the two parties usually converge, voters' tastes may become relatively homogeneous in the long run; whereas the opposite effect may occur in a proportional representation structure. (124–25)

The second of these paragraphs provokes two further comments. First, the two-way causation between voters' distribution and the electoral system weakens the thesis of the paramount importance of the distribution at least slightly, since, in addition to the direct influence of the electoral system on the party system, the electoral system now also influences the party system via its effect on the distribution of opinions. Second, and probably more important, the relationship between the distribution of voters and the party system is now also logically shown to be a bidirectional one: while the distribution is of primary significance for the number of parties that a democracy is likely to have—with the number of parties roughly equaling the number of modes in the distribution of voters—the number of parties in the long run also affects and reinforces the number of modes.

The two-way character of the third side of the triangle is not explicitly stated by Downs; the electoral system is his independent variable and the party system the dependent variable. However, it seems to me to be correct to attribute the reverse effect to him, too, since he sees such a close connection between the distribution of voters and the party system. This proposition is now widely accepted in comparative politics, and the usual example is that of Britain: its two-party system is clearly maintained by the plurality system of elections, and the plurality system is maintained by the two big parties whose interests are so well served by this electoral arrangement. Similarly, PR encourages multipartyism, but in addition, in multiparty systems there are too many parties that would be hurt by the abolition of PR to make it likely that PR will in fact be maintained.

Party Systems and Democratic Performance

Let us now turn to the second part of Downs's model. On the surface, there appears to be considerable similarity between the traditional model and Downs's refinements. Downs adds the type of government—one-party versus coalition governments—as an intervening variable, but it is fair to say that this variable is also implied in the traditional version: single-party government is associated with two-party systems and coalitions with multipartyism. Moreover, Downs's explicitly stated conclusions are very close to those of the traditional model. On the question of democratic quality, he argues that "rational voting in a multiparty system is . . . more difficult . . . than in a two-party system" (148), and as far as stability and effectiveness are concerned, he maintains that "in a multiparty system governed by a coalition, the government takes less effective action to solve basic social problems, and its policies are less integrated and consistent, than in a two-party system" (297). However, a careful reading of Downs's own arguments does not support these unequivocal conclusions.

The reasons why Downs finds great problems for rational voting in a multiparty system are that (1) he assumes that rational voting means that "voters look upon elections purely as means of selecting governments" (145)

Downsian Logic and the Comparative Study of Party Systems   235

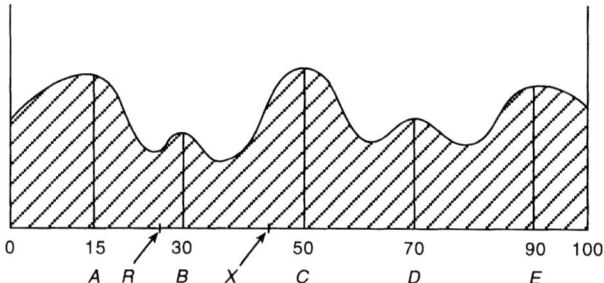

Fig. 2. Hypothetical distribution of voters along a left-right scale. The horizontal scale represents political orientation; the vertical scale represents number of voters (Downs 1957b, 130).

and (2) that, although voters can vote for the party that is closest to them, they do not know in advance with which other parties their preferred party will form a coalition. He uses a figure, reproduced here as figure 2, as an illustration. Consider the problems for voter X, and assume that BCD has been the governing coalition. X will probably cast his or her vote for party C both because it is the closest party and because the center of gravity of the BCD coalition is also close to his or her position. But C may well enter a coalition with D and E. If this happens, X would be better off voting for party B, since B is closer to his or her position than D, which is the position of coalition CDE, and since a vote for B, by strengthening B, would make it more likely that C would choose to enter a BCD instead of a CDE coalition. Hence, "it may not be clear to a voter just what his [or her] ballot is supporting when he [or she] casts it" (148).

Four important qualifications must be added to this line of reasoning. First, as Downs points out himself, the difference between multiparty and two-party systems is not all that great. Downs shows at great length that, in two-party systems, the two parties will tend to take positions close to the center of the political spectrum and will tend to adopt "ambiguous policies and similar ideologies." This makes voting "less than perfectly rational as a mechanism for selecting governments." In multiparty systems, on the contrary, parties tend to "narrow the spread of their policies, differentiate their platforms more sharply, and reduce ambiguity" (138). But, Downs feels, the coalition problems noted in the previous paragraph outweigh the advantage of greater clarity and differentiation. It is important, however, to note the moderate tone of Downs's conclusion: "it is *doubtful* whether the change [from a two-party to a multiparty system] would improve prospects for rational voting; they *might* get worse" (138–39, emphasis added).

Second, the problem of how to vote rationally in a multiparty system is not equally great for all voters. Consider the voters to the left of *A* and to the right of *E* in figure 2, and assume, as Downs does, that three parties are needed to form a majority coalition. For these voters (about 25 percent of the total), the optimal coalitions are *ABC* and *CDE* respectively. To get this optimal result, a vote for *A* and *E* respectively can be safely recommended. In other words, for these voters rational voting does not pose a problem at all.

Third, voters in a two-party system may be able to vote more rationally, but they have a much more-restricted choice than voters in a multiparty system. Voter *X* in figure 2 would be better off in a two-party system because his or her position coincides with the likely position that the party to the left of *X* would have in such a system. But the story is different for voter *R*. In a multiparty system, *R* has problems similar to those of voter *X*. For *R*, the *ABC* coalition is optimal, but voting for party *B* may also result in that party joining a *BCD* coalition, and hence a vote for *A* might be more advisable. On the other hand, if voting for *B* makes coalitions *ABC* and *BCD* equally likely, *R* has at least an even chance of contributing to the formation of a government with a position close to himself or herself (approximately position *B*), whereas in a two-party system the best he or she can hope for would be a government at about the position of *X*.

Fourth, Downs logically concludes that, given the uncertainty of the various coalition possibilities, the safest choice for voters is to simply vote for the party closest to them. Elections become expressions of preference instead of direct methods to select governments: "In systems usually governed by coalitions, most citizens do not vote as though elections were government-selection mechanisms" (300). But why should this be regarded as irrational behavior? If rational voting, as Downs defines it, is not possible for many voters (especially the voters in the middle of the spectrum), it makes more sense to say that the next logical and rational step is to vote for one's closest party. Downs can only argue that "the complexity of behaving rationally has led them to behave irrationally" (153) on the basis of his very narrow definition of rationality.

In short, when we look more closely at Downs's own arguments and assumptions and when we relax his restrictive definition of rationality, the difference in the degree to which two-party and multiparty systems permit the voter a rational and meaningful choice largely disappears. And since, for Downs, this is the crucial consideration for democratic quality, the difference between the two in the quality of democracy also becomes insignificant.

Downs's refinement of the traditional model with regard to the link between the party system, the type of government, and political stability can be stated much more succinctly. His main reason why a multiparty coalition is less likely to adopt effective government policies is that "the coalition must adopt a wider spread of policies to get the support of a majority of voters than must the government in a two-party system" (156). This argument is similar to the assumptions of the traditional model. However, the traditional model further assumes that coalitions, simply because they consist of more than one party, are prone to internal disunity. On this point, Downs argues very convincingly that coalitions will be affected by both centrifugal and centripetal forces. An example of a centripetal force is that "the electorate appreciates efficient action by the coalition. To be efficient, the parties in the coalition must act in unison. . . . This desire causes them to adopt similar policies; it sets up a centripetal force like that in most two-party systems" (157).

Downs's model differs from the traditional model not only in attributing decisive importance to the explanation in terms of the spread of voters' opinions but further in arguing that this distribution of opinions is of direct importance. I have therefore also drawn a direct arrow between the distribution of voters and political stability in figure 1. For Downs, the reason why multiparty systems and coalitions lead to less effective government is that they are associated with a wider and polymodal distribution of voters' opinions. This logically means that it is not multipartyism and coalitions per se that cause ineffectiveness but the distribution of voters that gives rise to all three outcomes: multipartyism, coalitions, and ineffectiveness. Downs states this conclusion explicitly: "the distribution of voters along the political scale is what determines how well integrated a government's policies are. . . . In the last analysis, neither the number of parties nor their platforms are as important as the shape of this distribution in influencing government ideology and policy in a democracy" (156).

Conclusion

This chapter focuses on a series of refinements in the analysis of party systems suggested by Downs. There is no need for a general conclusion since all of the main points are summarized in figure 1. I would like to close with three brief comments, however. The first is that, while I have frequently spoken in terms of "conclusions," these are merely *hypotheses* based on logical derivations from clearly stated assumptions; they are tentative conclusions only. This is also obviously how Downs himself views his endeavors: at the end of the book, he summarizes his arguments as a series of "testable propositions" (295–300).

Second, I take the argument in this essay from the rather simple, and deliberately simplified, traditional model to Downs's alternative model in a step-by-step fashion, emphasizing individual and small elements of the two models. When we take an overall look at figure 1, however, these individual improvements add up to a new model of much greater richness and complexity. Finally, I think that it is worth emphasizing the central role played in Downs's model by the variable of the distribution of voters—an element completely missing from the traditional model. Thus the model has become both more complex and simpler at the same time.

CHAPTER 17

On the Gentle Art of Rational Choice Bashing

Bernard Grofman

Rational choice models of both the hard and the soft variety fill the political science journals. In part as a reaction to the increasing importance of both formal models and rational choice ideas, there has been a recent wave of "rational choice bashing."[1] While much of this is an appropriate reaction to the exaggerated claims, confusion of technical elegance with theoretical significance, and limited empirical performance of the literature inspired by rational choice ideas, still I see the usual critiques of rational choice models as often resting on one or more of the following errors.

The most common and perhaps most important error made about rational choice modeling is the belief that there is such a thing as, for example, *the* rational choice model of party competition, *the* rational choice model of voter participation, or *the* rational choice model of voter choice. There are only models—some simple, some complex; some that work (at least sometimes), and some that don't. Most rejections of rational choice models are premature in that they attack a particular model as inaccurate and claim that its predictive failure disqualifies the approach as a whole.[2] Even the notion that there is such a thing as the Downsian model of voter choice or the Downsian model of

---

I am indebted to Ziggy Bates for manuscript typing and to Dorothy Gormick for bibliographic assistance. This research was partially funded by the University of California, Irvine, Interdisciplinary Focused Research Program in Public Choice.

1. In the space of two years there have been three major edited collections dealing with the limitations of rational choice models: Mansbridge 1990; Cook and Levi 1990; and Monroe 1991. Moreover, within the public policy field there have also been major recent attacks on the public choice perspective, for example, Rhoads 1985; and Reich 1988. Political theorists have been bemoaning rational choice's effects on the narrowing of public discourse and the legitimating of self-interest as the mainspring of political choice (Petracca 1991). Interchanges between critics and defenders of rational choice also are frequent in journals such as *Rationality and Society*.

2. For example, it is premature to reject a rational choice approach to coalition formation because the minimal winning coalition implication of William H. Riker's (1962) model of coalition formations as a zero sum game is falsified by data on European cabinet formation—especially since newer models have had a considerably better (although still far from perfect) fit (see Laver and Schofield 1991).

party competition is wrong. For example, as I show in a review essay (Grofman 1987), Anthony Downs can be credited with a number of different models of voter choice (e.g., pocketbook voting, retrospective voting, prospective voting, incumbency-oriented voting, party-based voting) in addition to the platform comparison–based policy distance–minimizing model that is the (simplistic) notion most commonly associated with Downs.[3]

A second common error is the belief that, because rational choice models cannot account for why people salute the flag when no one is looking or cry when they hear "God Bless America," rational choice modeling is inherently flawed in its ability to explain human behavior. Only an idiot (or an economist) would claim that rational choice models can explain all of human behavior.[4] And even most economists are not so foolish (Gary S. Becker's oft-quoted silly assertion to the contrary notwithstanding).[5] But identifying areas where human behavior is neither calculated nor even a conscious choice does not demonstrate that rational choice modeling is fundamentally misguided. Also, you can't beat something with nothing, and so it is not enough to show that some given rational choice model does not fit the data, it is necessary to show that some other perspective leads to a model with better fit and predictive power. Moreover, the faults of the rational choice approach are often exaggerated by failure to give credit to the accuracy of its more commonsensical predictions.[6]

As a "reasonable" choice modeler, I do not have any trouble accepting that sometimes it may be more useful to model behavior as operantly conditioned or otherwise socialized rather than as "choice" behavior, or even that, as sociobiologists claim, some types of behavior may be largely "hard wired." But where a particular rational choice model works and where it must give way to some other approach (rational choice or otherwise) that demonstrates superior explanatory power is a matter for empirical investigation, not a matter that can be resolved by introspective reflections on human nature or impressionistic counterexamples. Indeed, I find most of the ongoing debate

---

3. See also chapter 12.

4. The original meaning of *idiot* was "noncitizen." And, in Greek philosophy, citizenship was bound up with an idea of republican virtue that recognized a public interest that transcended claims based on private interests (Stockton 1990).

5. According to Becker: "human behavior is not compartmentalized, sometimes based on maximizing, sometimes not, sometimes motivated by stable preferences, sometimes by volatile ones, sometimes resulting in an optimal accumulation of information, sometimes not. Rather, *all* human behavior can be viewed as involving participants who *maximize* their utility from a *stable* set of preferences and accumulate an *optimal* amount of information and other inputs in a variety of markets" (Becker 1976, 14, emphasis mine).

6. See chapter 6.

about the limitations of rational choice modeling a waste of time because it does not involve an attempt to test competing models of human behavior.[7] Let a thousand models bloom, and let the data decide among them! For example, the fact that parties in the United States do not converge does not invalidate rational choice theory; what it does is require us to provide better and more institutionally rich models.[8]

Third, the fact that most rational choice models posit self-interested behavior does not mean either that self-interest must be narrowly defined or that reasonable rational choice modelers would see self-interest as all there is.[9]

Fourth, while it is true that rational choice modelers generally take basic preferences as given, it is a mistake to think that there is anything in the rational choice approach that requires preferences to be fixed and exogenously determined,[10] although the simplicity of this assumption has much to recommend it—especially for models designed to predict short-run changes in behavior. Indeed Downs himself (1957b, 83–88) outlines the beginnings of a rational choice model of persuasion, and some further development of ideas related to rational persuasion is found in chapters 9 and 15 of this volume.

Fifth, while it is certainly true that almost all of the most famous exponents of rational choice modeling are ideologically conservative, there is nothing inherent in the nature of rational choice modeling that makes it a tool of either the left or the right. On the one hand, rational choice modelers seek to understand (changes in) choices as a function of the nature of institutional rules and incentive structures and of constraints on resources, and on the other hand, they seek to explain how preferences for outcomes condition preferences for candidates and preferences for institutions.[11]

Finally, let me note that I take the almost certainly heretical view that, despite the importance of concepts like party convergence, public goods dilemmas, and rational ignorance, the principal contributions of rational

---

7. Here my Popperian predispositions are showing.

8. In like manner, the fact that incumbents are almost invariably reelected and that policies do not cycle, while incompatible with expectations fueled by early social choice models, is completely reconcilable with more complex models based on rational choice premises. See, for example, references cited in chapter 12; and Feld and Grofman 1991.

9. It is often in one's interest to take into account the interests and/or needs of others, or to temper instant gratification with a concern for long-run consequences. See my earlier comment about Becker's view. Even Gordon Tullock does not believe that behavior is never altruistic. He merely believes that altruistic behavior is rare. But how rare is an empirical question!

10. For example, Carole Jean Uhlaner (1989a; and chap. 4) outlines a theory of group-based choice where political leaders play a role in shaping the preferences of members of their groups.

11. Here I paraphrase John Ferejohn's well-known characterization of rational choice theory.

choice theory to date have been in the questions it asks rather than the answers it has given. For example by showing that citizens motivated only by instrumental rationality would, in general, not vote, Downs created an important puzzle to be solved, where before there was merely a habit to be taken for granted. But rational choice approaches to the understanding of political phenomena are still in their infancy, and the future is, I believe, a very bright one![12]

---

12. Moreover, the payoff from rational choice ideas has already been considerable, even in areas where rational choice bashers have been most skeptical of their utility. For example, to name but one instance, rational choice models of turnout do give rise to nontrivial predictions that are confirmed by the evidence once we recognize that short-run instrumental rationality is only one factor affecting the decision to vote, and once we focus our attention on factors that affect *changes* in turnout (chap. 6).

References

Ainslie, G. 1975. "Specious Reward." *Psychological Bulletin* 82:463–96.
Akerlof, George A. 1970. "The Market for 'Lemons': Quality Uncertainty and the Market Mechanism." *Quarterly Journal of Economics* 84:488–500.
———. 1983. "Loyalty Filters." *American Economic Review* 73:54–63.
Aldrich, John H. 1983a. "A Downsian Spatial Model with Party Activism." *American Political Science Review* 77:974–90.
———. 1983b. "A Spatial Model with Party Activists: Implications for Electoral Dynamics." *Public Choice* 41:63–100.
Alesina, Alberto. 1987. "Macroeconomic Policy in a Two-Party System as a Repeated Game." *Quarterly Journal of Economics* 102 (1987): 651–78.
———. 1988. "Credibility and Policy Convergence in a Two Party System with Rational Voters." *American Economic Review* 78:796–805.
Alesina, Alberto, and Alex Cukierman. 1989. "The Politics of Ambiguity." Hoover Institution working paper in political science, January.
Alesina, Alberto, and Jeffrey Sachs. 1988. "Political Parties and the Business Cycle in the United States, 1948–1984." *Journal of Money, Credit, and Banking* 20:63–82.
Alt, James E. 1985. "Political Parties, World Demand, and Unemployment: Domestic and International Sources of Economic Activity." *American Political Science Review* 79:1016–40.
———. 1994, forthcoming. "Race and Voter Registration in the South." In *Quiet Revolution: The Impact of the Voting Rights Act in the South, 1965–1990*, ed. Chandler Davidson and Bernard Grofman. Princeton: Princeton University Press.
Aranson, Peter, and Peter C. Ordeshook. 1972. "Spatial Strategy for Sequential Elections." In *Probability Models of Collective Decision Making*, ed. Richard G. Niemi and Herbert F. Weisberg. Columbus, OH: Merrill.
Aristotle. 1962. *Nichomachean Ethics*. Trans. Martin Ostwald. Indianapolis: Bobbs-Merrill.
———. 1984. *The Rhetoric and Poetics of Aristotle*. Ed. Rhyf Roberts and Ingram Bywaters. New York: McGraw Hill.
Arrow, Kenneth J. [1951] 1962. *Social Choice and Individual Values*. Reprint. New York: John Wiley and Sons.
Ascher, William. 1978. *Forecasting: An Appraisal for Policy-Makers and Planners*. Baltimore: Johns Hopkins University Press.
Austen-Smith, David. 1984. "Two-Party Competition with Many Constituencies." *Mathematical Social Sciences* 7:177–98.

———. 1986. "Legislation Coalitions and Electoral Equilibrium." *Public Choice* 50:185–210.
Axelrod, Robert. 1984. *The Emergence of Cooperation*. New York: Basic Books.
———. 1986. "An Evolutionary Approach to Norms." *American Political Science Review* 80:1096–11.
———. 1987. "The Evolution of Strategies in the Iterated Prisoner's Dilemma." In *Genetic Algorithms and Simulated Annealing*, ed. L. Davis. London: Pittman.
Badger, Wade. 1983. "Political Individuals, Positional Preferences, and Optimal Decision Rules." In *Probability Models of Collective Decision Making*, ed. Richard G. Niemi and Herbert F. Weisberg. Columbus, OH: Merrill.
Banfield, Edward. 1958. Review of *An Economic Theory of Democracy*. *Western Journal of Political Science* 11(2): 324–25.
Banks, Jeffrey. 1990. "A Model of Electoral Competition with Incomplete Information." *Journal of Economic Theory* 50(2): 309–25.
Banks, Jeffrey, and David Austen-Smith. 1989. "Electoral Accountability and Incumbency." In *Models of Strategic Choice in Politics*, ed. Peter C. Ordeshook. Ann Arbor: University of Michigan Press.
Barber, Benjamin R. 1984. *Strong Democracy: Participatory Politics for a New Age*. Berkeley and Los Angeles: University of California Press.
Baron, Alan. 1984. *Baron Report* 218 (November 19): 2.
Barro, Robert. 1973. "The Control of Politicians: An Economic Model." *Public Choice* 14:19–42.
Barro, Robert, and David Gordon. 1983. "Rules, Discretion, and Reputation in a Model of Monetary Policy." *Journal of Monetary Economics* 12:101–22.
Barry, Brian. 1964. "The Public Interest." *Proceedings of the Aristotelian Society* 38:9–14.
———. [1970] 1978. *Sociologists, Economists, and Democracy*. New York: Collier Macmillan. Reprint. Chicago: University of Chicago Press.
Bartels, Larry M. 1988. *Presidential Primaries and the Dynamics of Public Opinion*. Princeton, NJ: Princeton University Press.
Barzel, Yoram, and Eugene Silberberg. 1973. "Is the Act of Voting Rational?" *Public Choice* 16:51–58.
Beck, Nathaniel. 1982. "Parties, Administrations, and American Macroeconomic Outcomes." *American Political Science Review* 76:83–94.
———. 1987. "Elections and the Fed: Is There a Political Monetary Cycle?" *American Journal of Political Science* 31: 194–216.
Becker, Gary S. 1976. *The Economic Approach to Human Behavior*. Chicago: University of Chicago Press.
Becker, Gary, and George Stigler. 1974. "Law Enforcement, Malfeasance, and the Compensation of Enforcers." *Journal of Legal Studies* 3:1–18.
Berelson, Bernard, Paul Lazarsfeld, and William McPhee. 1954. *Voting: A Study of Opinion Formation in a Presidential Campaign*. Chicago: University of Chicago Press.
Bergson, Abram. 1958. Review of *An Economic Theory of Democracy*. *American Political Science Review* 48(2): 437–40.

Bernstein, Robert A. 1988. "Do Senators Moderate Strategically?" *American Political Science Review* 82(1988): 237–41.
———. 1991. "Appeals to the Non-Median Voter." Paper presented at the annual meeting of the American Political Science Association, Washington, DC, September.
Black, Duncan. 1958. *The Theory of Committees and Elections.* Cambridge: Cambridge University Press.
Black, Duncan, and R. A. Newing. 1951. *Committee Decisions with Complementary Valuation.* Edinburgh: William Hodge and Co.
Black, Jerome H. 1980. "The Probability-Choice Perspective in Voter Decision Making Models." *Public Choice* 35: 565–74.
Blanchard, Olivier. 1985. "Credibility, Disinflation, and Gradualism." *Economic Letters* 17:211–17.
Bloom, Howard S., and Douglas H. Price. 1975. "Voter Response to Short-run Economic Conditions: The Asymmetric Effect of Prosperity and Recession." *American Political Science Review* 69: 1240–54.
Brady, David W., and Naomi B. Lynn. 1973. "Switched-Seat Congressional Districts: Their Effects on Party Voting and Public Policy." *American Journal of Political Science* 17:523–43.
Brady, Henry E., and Paul M. Sniderman. 1985. "Attitude Attribution: A Group Basis for Political Reasoning." *American Political Science Review* 79:1061–78.
Brams, Steven J. 1980. "Spatial Models of Election Competition." University Modules in Applied Mathematics. COMAC, Lexington, MA.
Brams, Steven J., and Philip Straffin. 1982. "The Entry Problem in a Political Race." In *Political Equilibrium,* ed. Peter C. Ordeshook and Kenneth A. Shepsle, 181–95. Holland: Kluwer-Nijhoff.
Brennan, Geoffrey, and Loren F. Lomasky. 1985. "The Impartial Spectator Goes to Washington: Toward a Smithian Theory of Electoral Behavior." *Economics and Philosophy* 1:189–211.
———. 1987. "The Logic of Electoral Preference." *Economics and Philosophy* 3:131–38.
Brody, Richard A. 1982. "Public Evaluations and Expectations and the Future of the Presidency." Paper presented at the Conference on the Future of the Presidency. Charlottesville, VA.
———. N.d. "Change and Stability in Partisan Identification: A Note of Caution." Unpublished manuscript, Stanford University.
Brody, Richard A., and Benjamin I. Page. 1972. "The Assessment of Policy Voting," *American Political Science Review* 66:450–58.
Brody, Richard A., and C. R. Shapiro. 1989. "A Reconsideration of the Rally Phenomenon in Public Opinion." In *Political Behavior Annual,* ed. Samuel Long, vol. 2. Denver: Westview Press.
Bruner, Jerome, and Sheldon Korchin. 1946. "The Boss and the Vote: A Case Study in City Politics." *Public Opinion Quarterly* 10:1–23.
Brunk, Gregory C. 1980. "The Impact of Rational Participation Models on Voting Attitudes." *Public Choice* 35:549–64.

Buchanan, James M. 1974. "Hegel on the Calculus of Voting." *Public Choice* 17:99–101.

Buchanan, James M., and Gordon Tullock. 1962. *The Calculus of Consent: Logical Foundations of Constitutional Democracy.* Ann Arbor: University of Michigan Press.

Buchanan, James M., and Richard E. Wagner. 1977. *Democracy in Deficit: The Political Legacy of Lord Keynes.* New York: Academic Press.

Budge, Ian, David Robertson, and Derek Hearl (eds.). 1987. *Ideology, Strategy, and Party Change: Spatial Analyses of Post-War Election Programmes in 19 Democracies.* Cambridge: Cambridge University Press.

Builder, Carl H. 1989. *The Masks of War: American Military Styles in Strategy and Analysis.* Baltimore: Johns Hopkins University Press.

Bullock, Charles, and David W. Brady. 1983. "Party, Constituency, and Roll-Call Voting in the U.S. Senate." *Legislative Studies Quarterly* 8:29–43.

Cagan, Philip, and William Fellner. 1984. "The Cost of Disinflation, Credibility, and the Deceleration of Wages, 1982–83." In *Essays in Contemporary Economic Problems,* ed. William Fellner, 7–19. Washington DC.: American Enterprise Institute.

Calvert, Randall. 1985a. "The Value of Biased Information: A Rational Choice Model of Political Advice." *Journal of Politics* 47:530–55.

———. 1985b. "Robustness of the Multidimensional Voting Model: Candidate Motivations, Uncertainty, and Convergency." *American Journal of Political Science* 29:69–95.

———. 1986. *Models of Imperfect Information in Politics.* New York: Harwood.

Campbell, Angus, Gerald Gurin, and Warren E. Miller. 1954. *The Voter Decides.* Evanston, IL: Row, Peterson.

Campbell, Angus, and Robert L. Kahn. 1952. *The People Elect a President.* Ann Arbor: University of Michigan.

Campbell, Angus, and the University of Michigan Survey Center. 1960. *The American Voter.* New York: Wiley.

Carmines, Edward G., and James A. Stimson. 1989. *Issue Evolution: Race and the Transformation of American Politics.* Princeton, NJ: Princeton University Press.

Carter, John R. 1984. "Early Projections and Voter Turnout in the 1980 Presidential Election." *Public Choice* 43:195–202.

Cebula, Richard J., and Dennis R. Murphy. 1980. "The Electoral College and Voter Participation Votes: An Exploratory Note." *Public Choice* 35:185–90.

Chamberlain, Gary, and Michael Rothschild. 1981. "A Note on the Probability of Casting a Decisive Vote." *Journal of Economic Theory* 25:152–62.

Chamberlain, John. 1974. "Provision of Collective Goods as a Function of Group Size." *American Political Science Review* 68:707–16.

Chapman, Randall G., and Kristian S. Palda. 1983. "Electoral Turnout in Rational Voting and Consumption Perspectives." *Journal of Consumer Research* 9:337–46.

Chappell, Henry W., Jr., and William R. Keech. 1983. "Welfare Consequences of the Six-Year Presidential Term Evaluated in the Context of a Model of the U.S. Economy." *American Political Science Review* 77:75–91.

———. 1985. "A New View of Political Accountability for Economic Performance." *American Political Science Review* 79:10–27.

———. 1986. "Policy Motivation and Party Differences in a Dynamic Spatial Model of Party Competition." *American Political Science Review* 80:881–99.

———. 1988. "Choice and Circumstance: The Consequences of Partisan Macroeconomic Policies." Paper presented at the annual meeting of the American Political Science Association, Washington, DC, August 29 to September 2.

Cohen, Linda R., and Steven A. Mathews. 1980. "Constrained Plott Equilibria, Directional Equilibria, and Global Cycling Sets." *Review of Economic Studies* 47:975–86.

Cohen, Michael D. 1984. "Conflict and Complexity: Goal Diversity and Organization Search Effectiveness." *American Political Science Review* 78:435–51.

Coleman, James. 1970. "The Benefits of Coalition." *Public Choice* 8:45–62.

———. 1972. "The Positions of Political Parties in Elections." In *Probability Models of Collective Decision Making*, ed. Richard G. Niemi and Herbert F. Weisberg. Columbus, OH: Merrill.

Collins, William P. 1981. "Political Participation under the Unit Rule: A Research Note." *Public Choice* 36:165–69.

Condorcet, Marquis de. 1785. Essai sur l'Application de l'Analyse à la Probabilité des Decisions Rendues a le Pluralité des Voix. Paris.

Cook, Karen S., and Margaret Levi (eds.). 1990. *The Limits of Rationality.* Chicago: University of Chicago Press.

Coughlin, Peter J. 1982. "Pareto Optimality of Policy Proposals with Probabilistic Voting." *Public Choice* 39:427–33.

———. 1990a. "Candidate Uncertainty and Electoral Equilibria." In *Advances in the Spatial Theory of Voting*, ed. James M. Enelow and Melvin J. Hinich, 145–66. New York: Cambridge University Press.

———. 1990b. "Majority Rule and Election Models." *Journal of Economic Surveys* 3:157–88.

Coughlin, Peter J., and Melvin J. Hinich. 1984. "Necessary and Sufficient Conditions for Single-Peakedness in Public Economic Models." *Journal of Public Economics* 25:161–79.

Coughlin, Peter J., Dennis Mueller, and P. Murrell. 1988. "Electoral Politics, Interest Groups, and the Size of Government." Unpublished paper, University of Maryland at College Park.

Coughlin, Peter J., and Schmuel Nitzan. 1981. "Electoral Outcomes with Probabilistic Voting and Nash Social Welfare Maxima." *Journal of Public Economics* 15:113–22.

Cox, Gary. 1987. "Electoral Equilibrium under Alternative Voting Institutions." *American Journal of Political Science* 3:82–108.

———. 1988. "Closeness and Turnout: A Methodological Note." *Journal of Politics* 50:768–75.

———. 1990. "Multicandidate Spatial Competition." In *Advances in the Spatial Theory of Voting*, ed. James M. Enelow and Melvin J. Hinich, 179–98. New York: Cambridge University Press.

Crain, W. Mark, and Thomas H. Deaton. 1977. "A Note on Political Participation as Consumption Behavior." *Public Choice* 32:131–35.

Dalkey, Norman C. 1986. "Information Pooling as the Composition of Inquiry Systems." In *Information Pooling and Group Decision Making*, ed. Bernard Grofman and Guillermo Owen, 73–90. Westport, CT: JAI Press.

Dalton, Russell. 1988. *Citizen Politics in Western Democracies*. Chatham, NJ: Chatham House Publishers.

Davis, Otto A., Melvin J. Hinich, and Peter C. Ordeshook. 1970. "An Expository Development of a Mathematical Model of the Electoral Process." *American Political Science Review* 64:426–48.

De Groot, Morris H. 1974. "Reaching a Consensus." *Journal of American Statistical Association* 69 (March): 118–21.

De Nardo, J. 1980. "Turnout and the Vote—The Joke's on the Democrats." *American Political Science Review* 74:406–20.

DeNeufville, Judith I., and Stephen E. Barton. 1987. "Myths and the Definition of Policy Problems." *Policy Sciences* 20:181–206.

Diamond, Martin. 1959. Book Review of A. Downs's "An Economic Theory of Democracy." *Journal of Political Economy*. 67:208–12.

DiMaggio, Paul J., and Walter W. Powell. 1983. "The Iron Cage Revisited: Institutional Isomorphism and Collective Rationality in Organizational Fields." *American Sociological Review*. 48:47–60.

Douglas, Mary. 1986. *Risk Acceptability according to the Social Sciences*. New York: Russell Sage.

Downs, Anthony. 1956. *An Economic Theory of Government Decision-making in a Democracy*. Office of Naval Research technical report no. 32.

———. 1957a. "An Economic Theory of Political Action in a Democracy." *Journal of Political Economy* 64:135–52.

———. 1957b. *An Economic Theory of Democracy*. New York: Harper and Row.

———. 1959. "Dr. Roger's Methodological Difficulties—A Reply to His Critical Work." *American Political Science Review* 53 (4):1094–97.

———. 1967. *Inside Bureaucracy*. Boston: Little Brown.

Durden, Garey C., and Patricia Gaynor. 1987. "The Rational Behavior Theory of Voting Participation: Evidence from the 1970 and 1982 Elections." *Public Choice* 53:231–42.

Duverger, Maurice. 1951. "The Influence of Electoral Systems on Political Life." *International Social Science Bulletin* 3 (Summer):314–52.

———. 1954. *L'Influence des Systemes Electoraux sur la Vie Politique*. Paris: Armand Colin.

———. 1984. "Which is the Best Electoral System?" In *Choosing an Electoral System: Issues and Alternatives*, ed. Arend Lijphart and Bernard Grofman, 44–58. New York: Praeger.

Easton, David. 1965. *A Framework for Political Analysis*. Englewood Cliffs, NJ: Prentice Hall.

Eaton, B. C., and Richard Lipsey. 1975. "The Principle of Minimum Differentiation Reconsidered: Some New Developments in the Theory of Spatial Competition." *Review of Economic Studies* 42:27–50.

Edelman, Murray. 1964. *The Symbolic Uses of Politics*. Urbana: University of Illinois Press.

Edsall, Thomas, and Mary Edsall. 1991. *Chain Reaction.* New York: Norton.

Einhorn, Hillel J., and Robin M. Hogarth. 1986. "Decision Making under Ambiguity." In *Rational Choice,* ed. Robin M. Hogarth and Melvin W. Reder, 41–66. Chicago: University of Chicago Press.

Elster, Jon. 1979. *Ulysses and the Sirens.* Cambridge: Cambridge University Press.

———. 1983. *Sour Grapes: Studies in the Subversion of Rationality.* Cambridge: Cambridge University Press.

Enelow, James M., and Melvin J. Hinich. 1982a. "Nonspatial Candidate Characteristics and Electoral Competition." *Journal of Politics* 44:115–30.

———. 1982b. "Ideology, Issues, and the Spatial Theory of Elections." *American Political Science Review* 76:493–501.

———. 1984. *The Spatial Theory of Political Competition: An Introduction.* New York: Cambridge University Press.

———. 1989. "A General Probabilistic Spatial Theory of Elections." *Public Choice* 61:101–13.

———. (eds.). 1990a. *Advances in the Spatial Theory of Voting.* New York: Cambridge University Press.

———. 1990b. "The Theory of Predictive Mappings." In *Advances in the Spatial Theory of Voting,* ed. James M. Enelow and Melvin J. Hinich, 167–78. New York: Cambridge University Press.

Enelow, James M., Melvin J. Hinich, and N. Mendell. 1986. "An Empirical Evaluation of Alternative Spatial Models of Elections." *Journal of Politics* 48:675–93.

Epstein, Laurily K., and Gerald S. Strom. 1981. "Election Night Projections and West Coast Turnout." *American Politics Quarterly* 9 (4): 479–91.

Erikson, Robert S. 1981. "Why Do People Vote? Because They Are Registered." *American Politics Quarterly* 9 (3): 259–76.

Erikson, Robert S., and D. Romero. 1990. "Candidate Equilibrium and the Behavioral Model of the Vote." *American Political Science Review* 84:1103–26.

Etzioni, Amitai. 1988. *The Moral Dimension—Toward a New Economics.* New York: Free Press.

Eulau, Heinz, and Michael S. Lewis-Beck, eds. 1985. *Economic Conditions and Electoral Outcomes.* New York: Agathon Press.

Farber, Daniel A., and Philip P. Frickey. 1991. *Law and Public Choice: A Critical Introduction.* Chicago: University of Chicago Press.

Farquharson, Robin. 1969. *Theory of Voting.* New Haven: Yale University Press.

Feddersen, Timothy J. 1991. "A Voting Model Implying Duverger's Law and Positive Turnout." Paper presented at the annual meeting of the American Political Science Association, Washington, DC, September.

Feigenbaum, Susan, Lynn Kardy, and David Levy. 1988. "When Votes Are Words Not Deeds: Some Evidence from the Nuclear Freeze Referendum." *Public Choice* 58:201–16.

Feld, Scott L., and Bernard Grofman. 1985. "Necessary and Sufficient Conditions for a Majority Winner in N-Dimensional Spatial Voting Games: An Intuitive Geometric Approach." *American Journal of Political Science* 32:709–28.

———. 1986. "Competence of Groups with Added Members." *Public Choice* 80:863–79.

———. 1988a. "Majority Rule Outcomes and the Structure of Debate in One-Issue-at-a-Time Decision-making." *Public Choice* 59:239–52.

———. 1988b. "Ideological Consistency as a Collective Phenomenon." *American Political Science Review* 82:64–75.

———. 1991. "Incumbency Advantage, Voter Loyalty, and the Benefit of the Doubt." *Journal of Theoretical Politics* 3 (2): 115–37.

Feld, Scott L., Bernard Grofman, Richard Hartley, Mark O. Kilgour, and Nicholas R. Miller. 1987. "The Uncovered Set in Spatial Voting Games." *Theory and Decision* 22:129–56.

Fellner, William. 1976. Toward a Reconstruction of Macroeconomics. Washington DC: American Enterprise Institute.

Fenno, Richard F. 1978. *Home Style: House Members in Their Districts*. Boston: Little, Brown.

Ferejohn, John. 1977. "On the Decline of Competition in Congressional Elections." *American Political Science Review* 71:177–81.

———. John. 1986. "Incumbent Performance and Electoral Control." *Public Choice* 50:5–25.

Ferejohn, John, and Morris P. Fiorina. 1974. "The Paradox of Not Voting: A Decision Theoretic Analysis." *American Political Science Review.* 68:525–36.

———. 1975. "Closeness Counts Only in Horseshoes and Dancing." *American Political Science Review* 69:920–25.

Ferejohn, John, and James Kuklinski (eds.). 1990. *Information and Democratic Processes*. Urbana: University of Illinois Press.

Ferejohn, John, Richard D. McKelvey, and Edward W. Packel. 1984. "Limiting Distributions for Continuous State Markov Models." *Social Choice and Welfare* 1:45–67.

Ferejohn, John, and Roger G. Noll. 1978. "Uncertainty and the Formal Theory of Campaigns." *American Political Science Review* 72:492–505.

Filer, John E., and Lawrence W. Kenny. 1980. "Voter Turnout and the Benefits of Voting." *Public Choice* 35:575–85.

Fink, Evelyn. 1987. "Political Argument and Strategy Choice." In "The Ratification Conventions on the U.S. Constitution." Unpublished Ph.D. dissertation, Rochester University, Rochester, NY.

Fiorina, Morris P. 1974. *Representatives, Roll Calls, and Constituencies*. Lexington, MA: Lexington Books.

———. 1976. "The Voting Decision: Instrumental and Expressive Aspects." *Journal of Politics* 38:390–413.

———. 1977. *Congress: Keystone of the Washington Establishment*. New Haven: Yale University Press.

———. 1979, 1981, 1989. *Retrospective Voting in American National Elections*. New Haven: Yale University Press.

Fiorina, Morris P., and Roger G. Noll. 1978. "Voters, Bureaucrats, and Legislators." *Journal of Public Economics,* 9 (3): 239–54.

Fiorina, Morris P., and Kenneth A. Shepsle. 1986. "Negative Voting: An Explanation Based on Principal-Agent Theory." Political economy working paper, Washington University.

---. 1989. "Is Negative Voting an Artifact?" *American Journal of Political Science.* 33:423-39.
Fireman, B., and W. A. Gamson. 1979. "Utilitarian Logic in the Resource Mobilization Perspective." In *The Dynamics of Social Movements,* ed. M. N. Zald and J. D. McCarthy, 8-44. Cambridge, MA: Winthrop Publishers.
Fishel, Jeff. 1985. *Platforms and Promises.* Washington, DC: Congressional Quarterly Press.
Flanigan, William H., and Nancy H. Zingale. 1987. *Political Behavior of the American Electorate.* 6th ed. Boston: Allyn and Bacon.
Foster, Carroll B. 1984. "The Performance of Rational Voter Models in Recent Presidential Elections." *American Political Science Review* 78:678-90.
Frank, Robert H. 1985. *Choosing the Right Pond: Human Behavior and the Quest for Status.* Oxford: Oxford University Press.
Frazer, Russell. 1972. "Political Participation and Income Level: An Exchange." *Public Choice* 13:113-18.
Frey, Bruno S. 1971. "Why Do High Income People Participate More in Politics?" *Public Choice* 11:101-5.
---. 1972. "Political Participation and Income Level." *Public Choice* 13:119-22.
Friedman, Milton. 1953. *Essays in Positive Economics.* Chicago: University of Chicago Press.
Frohlich, Norman, Joe Oppenheimer, Jeffrey Smith, and Oran Young. 1978. "A Test of Downsian Voter Rationality: 1964 Presidential Voting." *American Political Science Review* 72:178-97.
Frohlich, Norman, Joe Oppenheimer, and Oran Young. 1971. *Political Leadership and Collective Goods.* Princeton, NJ: Princeton University Press.
Garvey, Gerald. 1966. "The Theory of Party Equilibrium." *American Political Science Review* 60:29-38.
Geertz, Clifford. 1964. "Ideology as a Cultural System." In *Ideology and Discontent,* ed. David Apter, 47-76. Glencoe, IL: Free Press.
Gibson, Mary. 1977. "Rationality." *Philosophy and Public Affairs* 6 (3): 193-225.
Glazer, Amihai. 1987. "A New Theory of Voting: Why Vote When Millions of Others Do?" *Theory and Decision* 22:257-70.
Glazer, Amihai, and Bernard Grofman. 1989. "Why Representatives Are Ideologists Though Voters Are Not." *Public Choice* 61:29-39.
---. 1992. "A Positive Correlation between Turnout and Plurality Does Not Refute the Rational Choice Model." *Quality and Quantity.* 26:85-93.
Glazer, Amihai, Bernard Grofman, and Guillermo Owen. 1991. "A Formal Model of Group-oriented Voting." Paper presented at the annual meeting of the Public Choice Society, New Orleans, March 19-21.
Goffman, Erving. 1959. *The Presentation of Self in Everyday Life.* New York: Doubleday.
---. 1974. *Frame Analysis.* New York: Harper and Row.
Golden, D., and James Poterba. 1980. "The Price of Popularity: The Political Business Cycle Reexamined." *American Journal of Political Science* 24:696-714.
Goodman, S., and Gerald Kramer. 1975. "Comment on Arcelus and Meltzer: The

Effect of Aggregate Economic Conditions on Congressional Elections." *American Political Science Review* 69:1255–65.
Gordon, Robert J., 1980. "Postwar Macroeconomics: The Evolution of Events and Ideas." In *The American Economy in Transition,* ed. Martin Feldstein. Chicago: University of Chicago Press. 101–62.
Granberg, Donald, and Edward Brent. 1983. "When Prophecy Bends: The Preference-Expectation Link in U.S. Presidential Elections, 1952–1980." *Journal of Personality and Social Psychology* 45:477–91.
Granovetter, Mark. 1985. "Economic Action and Social Structure: The Problem of Embeddedness." *American Journal of Sociology* 91:481–510.
Gray, Virginia. 1976. "A Note on Competition and Turnout in the American States." *Journal of Politics* 38:153–58.
Green, Donald Philip. 1988. "On the Dimensionality of Public Sentiment toward Partisan and Ideological Groups." *American Journal of Political Science* 32:758–80.
Greenberg, Joseph, and Kenneth A. Shepsle. 1987. "The Effect of Electoral Rewards in Multiparty Competition with Entry." *American Political Science Review* 81:525–37.
Grofman, Bernard. 1975. "A Comment on Democratic Theory: A Preliminary Mathematical Model. *Public Choice* 21:99–104.
———. 1978. "Judgmental Competence of Individuals and Groups in a Dichotomous Choice Situation: Is a Majority of Heads Better than One?" *Journal of Mathematical Sociology* 6:47–60.
———. 1980. "A Preliminary Model of Jury Decision-making." In *Frontiers of Economics,* ed. Gordon Tullock, vol. 3, 98–110. Blacksburg, VA: Center for the Study of Public Choice.
———. 1982. "A Dynamic Model of Protocoalition Formation in Ideological *N*-Space." *Behavioral Science* 27:77–90.
———. 1983. "Models of Voter Turnout: An Idiosyncratic Review." *Public Choice* 41:55–61.
———. 1985a. "Criteria for Districting: A Social Science Perspective." *UCLA Law Review* 33 (1): 77–184.
———. 1985b. "The Neglected Role of the Status Quo in Models of Issue Voting." *Journal of Politics* 47:230–37.
———. 1987. "Models of Voting." In *Micropolitics Annual,* ed. Samuel Long, 31–61. Greenwich, CT: JAI Press.
Grofman, Bernard, and Scott L. Feld. 1984. "Group Size and the Performance of a Composite Group in Multi-Item Decision Tasks." *Organizational Behavior and Human Performance* 33:350–59.
———. 1986. "Determining Optimal Weights for Expert Judgment." In *Information Pooling and Group Decision Making,* ed. Bernard Grofman and Guillermo Owen, 167–72. Westport, CT: JAI Press.
Grofman, Bernard, Amihai Glazer, and Lisa Handley. 1988. "In the Footsteps of George Wallace: Race and Politics—or the Republican Majority Has Already Emerged: Color it White." Paper presented at the annual meeting of the American Political Science Association, Washington, DC, August 31–September 3.

Grofman, Bernard, Robert Griffin, and Amihai Glazer. 1990. "Identical Geography, Different Constituencies, See What a Difference Party Makes." In *Developments in Electoral Geography*, ed. R. J. Johnston, F. Shelley, and P. Taylor, 207–17. London: Croom Helm.

———. 1991. "Partisan Ideological Polarization in State Delegations in the House of Representatives." Unpublished manuscript, School of Social Sciences, University of California, Irvine.

Grofman, Bernard, and Barbara Norrander. 1987. "Efficient Use of Information in an Information Rich Environment." Unpublished manuscript, School of Social Sciences, University of California, Irvine.

———. 1990. "Efficient Use of Reference Group Cues in a Single Dimension." *Public Choice* 64:213–27.

Grofman, Bernard, Guillermo Owen, and Scott L. Feld. 1983. "Thirteen Theorems in Search of the Truth." *Theory and Decision.* 15:213–24.

Groves, T., and John O. Ledyard. 1977. "Optimal Allocation of Public Goods: A Solution to the 'Free Rider' Problem." *Econometrica* 45:783–809.

Gurin, Patricia, Shirley Hatchett, and James S. Jackson. 1990. *Hope and Independence: Blacks' Response to Electoral and Party Politics.* New York: Russell Sage Foundation.

Guttman, Amy. 1985. "Communitarian Critics of Liberalism." *Philosophy and Public Affairs* 14:308–22.

Halperin, Morton H. 1974. *Bureaucratic Politics and Foreign Policy.* Washington, DC: Brookings.

Hammond, Thomas H. 1979. "Jurisdictional Preferences and the Choice of Tasks: Political Adaptation by Two State Fish and Game Departments." Unpublished Ph.D. dissertation, Department of Political Science, University of California, Berkeley.

Hammond, Thomas H., and Gary J. Miller. 1987. "The Core of the Constitution." *American Political Science Review* 81:1155–74.

Hansen, John Mark, and Steven J. Rosenstone. 1984. "Context, Mobilization, and Political Participation." Unpublished manuscript, Yale University, February.

Hansen, T. Ingemann, and Charles Stuart. 1984. "Voting Competitions with Interested Politicians: Platforms Do Not Converge to the Preference of the Median Voter." *Public Choice.* 44 (3): 431–42.

Hardin, Russell. 1982. *Collective Action.* Baltimore: Johns Hopkins University Press.

Hargrove, Erwin C., and Samuel A. Morley. 1984. *The President and the Council of Economic Advisers.* Boulder, CO: Westview.

Harrington, Joseph. 1988. "The Revelation of Information through the Electoral Process." Johns Hopkins working paper.

Harsanyi, John C. 1955. "Cardinal Welfare, Individualistic Ethics, and Interpersonal Comparisons of Utility." *Journal of Political Economy* 63:309–21.

———. 1969. "Rational Choice Models of Political Behavior versus Functionalist and Conformist Theories." *World Politics,* June: 513–38.

Hastie, Reid. 1986. "Review Essay: Experimental Evidence on Group Accuracy." In

Information Pooling and Group Decision Making, ed. Bernard Grofman and Guillermo Owen, 129–57. Westport, CT: JAI Press.

Havrilesky, Thomas M. 1987. "A Partisanship Theory of Fiscal and Monetary Regimes." *Journal of Money, Credit, and Banking* 19:308–25.

———. 1988. "Two Monetary and Fiscal Policy Myths." In *Political Business Cycles,* ed. Thomas D. Willett. Durham, NC: Duke University Press, 320–36.

Heclo, Hugh. 1974. *Studying the Presidency.* New York: The Ford Foundation.

Hegel, Georg Wilhelm Friedrich. 1957. *Philosophy of Right.* Oxford: Clarendon Press.

Hibbing, John R., and John A. Alford. 1981. "The Electoral Impact of Economic Conditions: Who is Held Responsible?" *American Journal of Political Science* 25:423–39.

Hibbs, Douglas A., Jr. 1977. "Political Parties and Macroeconomic Policies." *American Political Science Review* 71:1467–87.

———. 1982. "The Dynamics of Support for American Presidents among Occupational and Partisan Groups." *American Journal of Political Science* 26:312–32.

———. 1987. *The American Political Economy.* Cambridge: Harvard University Press.

Hinich, Melvin J. 1978a. "Some Evidence on Non-Voting Models in the Spatial Theory of Electoral Competition." *Public Choice* 33:83–102.

———. 1978b. "The Mean versus the Median in Spatial Voting Games." In *Game Theory and Political Science,* ed. Peter C. Ordeshook, 357–74. New York: New York University Press.

———. 1981. "Voting as an Act of Contribution." *Public Choice* 36:135–40.

Hinich, Melvin J., John O. Ledyard, and Peter C. Ordeshook. 1972. "Nonvoting and the Existence of Equilibrium under Majority Rule." *Journal of Economic Theory* 14:144–53.

Hinich, Melvin J., and Peter C. Ordeshook. 1969. "Abstentions and Equilibrium in the Electoral Process." *Public Choice* 8:81–100.

———. 1970. "Plurality Maximization vs. Vote Maximization: A Spatial Analysis with Variable Participation." *American Political Science Review* 64:772–91.

Hinich, Melvin J., and Walker Pollard. 1981. "A New Approach to the Spatial Theory of Electoral Competition." *American Journal of Political Science* 18:501–23.

Hirsch, Fred. 1976. *The Social Limits to Growth.* Cambridge: Harvard University Press.

Hirschman, Albert O. 1982. *Shifting Involvements: Private Interest and Public Action.* Princeton, NJ: Princeton University Press.

———. 1985. "Against Parsimony: Three Easy Ways to Complicate Some Categories of Economic Discourse." *Economics and Philosophy* 1:7–21.

Holland, John. 1975. *Adaptation in Natural and Artificial Systems.* Ann Arbor: University of Michigan Press.

Holland, John, Keith Holyoak, Richard Nisbett, and Paul Thagard. 1986. *Induction— Processes of Inference, Learning, and Discovery.* Cambridge: MIT Press.

Holland, John, and John Miller. 1990. "Artificial Adaptive Agents in Economic Theory." Paper presented at the annual meeting of the American Economic Association. Washington DC. December 28–30.

Holler, Manfred. 1978. "Public Choice: Competition and Co-operation in a Two-Party Spatial Model." *Munich Social Science Review.*
Hotelling, Harold. 1929. "Stability in Competition." *Economic Journal* 39:41–57.
"How Bush Won: The Inside Story of Campaign '88." 1988. *Newsweek,* special election issue, November 21, 100.
Huckfeldt, Robert, and Carol Kohfeld. 1989. *Race and the Decline of Class in American Politics.* Champaign: University of Illinois Press.
Humes, Brian D. 1993. "Majority Rule Outcomes and the Choice of Germaneness Rules." *Public Choice.* 75:301–16.
Iyengar, Shanto, and Donald R. Kinder. 1988. *News That Matters.* Chicago: University of Chicago Press.
Jackson, John E. 1973. "Intensities, Preferences, and Electoral Politics." *Social Choice Research* 2:231–46.
Jacobson, Gary C. 1983. *The Politics of Congressional Elections.* Boston: Little, Brown.
———. 1990. *The Electoral Origins of Divided Government: Competition in U.S. House Elections, 1946–1988.* Boulder, CO: Westview Press.
Kadane, Joseph B. 1972. "On Division of the Question." *Public Choice* 13:47–54.
Kahneman, Daniel, Jack L. Knetsch, and Richard Thaler. 1986. *Fairness and the Assumptions of Economics.* In *Rational Choice,* ed. Robin M. Hogarth and Melvin W. Reder, 101–16. Chicago: University of Chicago Press.
Kahneman, Daniel, Paul Slovic, and Amos Tversky (eds.). 1982. *Judgment under Uncertainty: Heuristics and Biases.* New York: Cambridge University Press.
Kalt, Joseph, and Mark Zupan. 1984. "Capture and Ideology in the Economic Theory of Politics," *American Economic Review* 74:279–300.
Katz, Elihu. 1957. "The Two-Step Flow of Communications." *Public Opinion Quarterly* 21:61–78.
Katz, Elihu, and Paul Lazarsfeld. 1955. *Personal Influence.* Glencoe, IL: Free Press.
Katz, Richard S. 1978. *A Theory of Parties and Electoral Systems.* Baltimore: Johns Hopkins University Press.
Kau, James B., and Paul H. Rubin. 1976. "The Electoral College and the Rational Vote." *Public Choice* 27:101–7.
———. 1977. "The Electoral College and the Rational Vote: A Correction." *Public Choice* 29:155–56.
Keech, William R. 1980. "Elections and Macroeconomic Policy Optimization." *American Journal of Political Science* 24:345–67.
Kelley, Stanley. 1983. *Predicting Elections.* Princeton, NJ: Princeton University Press.
Kelley, Stanley, and Thad Mirer. 1974."The Simple Act of Voting." *American Political Science Review.* 68 (2):572–91.
Kernell, Samuel. 1977. "Presidential Popularity and Negative Voting." *American Political Science Review* 71:44.
Key, V. O., Jr. 1949. *Southern Politics.* New York: Alfred A. Knopf.
———. 1966. *The Responsible Electorate.* New York: Vintage.
Keynes, John M. 1936. *General Theory of Employment, Interest, and Money.* New York: Harcourt Brace Jovanovich.

Kiewiet, D. Roderick, and Mathew D. McCubbins. 1989. "The Spending Power: Congress, the President, and Appropriations." Unpublished book manuscript.

Kinder, Donald R., and Robert P. Abelson. 1981. "Appraising Presidential Candidates: Personality and Affect in the 1980 Campaign. Paper presented at the annual meeting of the American Political Science Association, New York, September 3–6.

Kinder, Donald R., and D. Roderick Kiewiet. 1981. "Sociotropic Politics." *British Journal of Political Science* 11:129–61.

Kirchheimer, Otto. 1957. "The Waning of Opposition in Parliamentary Regimes." *Social Research,* Summer. Reprinted in John Wahlke and Heinz Eulau. 1959. *Legislative Behavior,* 91–92. Glencoe, IL: Free Press.

Kleppner, Paul. 1985. *Chicago Divided: The Making of a Black Mayor.* Dekalb: Northern Illinois University Press.

Kramer, Gerald H. 1971. "Short-term Fluctuations in U.S. Voting Behavior, 1896–1964." *American Political Science Review* 55:131–43.

———. 1973. "Sophisticated Voting over Multidimensional Choice Spaces." *Journal of Mathematical Sociology* 2:165–81.

———. 1977. "A Dynamical Model of Political Equilibrium." *Journal of Economic Theory* 15:310–34.

———. 1978. "Existence of Electoral Equilibrium." In *Game Theory and Political Science,* ed. Peter C. Ordeshook, 375–91. New York: New York University Press.

———. 1983. "The Ecological Fallacy Revisited." *American Political Science Review* 77:92–111.

Krause, Elliott. 1968. "Functions of a Bureaucratic Ideology: Citizen Participation." *Social Problems* 16:129–43.

Krehbiel, Keith. 1990. *Information and Legislative Organization.* Ann Arbor: University of Michigan Press.

Kreps, David M. 1988. "Corporate Cultures and Economic Theory." Graduate School of Business working paper. Stanford University.

Kreps, David M., Paul Milgrom, John Roberts, and Robert Wilson. 1982. "Rational Cooperation in the Finitely Repeated Prisoner's Dilemma." *Journal of Economic Theory* 27:245–52.

Krosnick, Jon, and Matthew K. Berent. 1990. "The Impact of Verbal Labeling of Response Alternatives and Branching on Attitude Measurement Reliability in Surveys." Unpublished paper.

Kuhn, Thomas S. 1970. *The Structure of Scientific Revolutions.* 2d ed. Chicago: University of Chicago Press.

Kuran, Timur. 1990. "Private and Public Preferences." *Economics and Philosophy* 6:1–26.

Kydland, F., and E. Prescott. 1977. "Rules Rather Than Discretion: The Inconsistency of Optimal Plans." *Journal of Political Economy* 85:473–92.

Lau, Richard R. 1985. "Two Explanations for Negativity Effects in Political Behavior." *American Journal of Political Science* 29:119–38.

———. 1978. "Existence of Electoral Equilibrium." In *Game Theory and Political*

Science, ed. Peter C. Ordeshook, 375–91. New York: New York University Press.
Laver, Michael, and Norman Schofield. 1991. *Multi-Party Government.* Oxford: Oxford University Press.
Lazarsfeld, Paul, Bernard Berelson, and Helen Gaudet. 1948. *The People's Choice: How the Voter Makes Up His Mind in a Presidential Campaign.* 2d ed. New York: Columbia University Press.
Ledyard, John O. 1981. "The Paradox of Voting and Candidate Competition: A General Equilibrium Analysis." In *Essays in Contemporary Fields of Economics,* ed. G. Horwich and J. P. Quirk, 54–80. West Lafayette, IN: Purdue Research Foundation.
———. 1984. "The Pure Theory of Large Two Candidate Elections." *Public Choice* 44:7–41.
Levi, Isaac. 1982. "Liberty and Welfare." In *Utilitarianism and Beyond,* eds. Amar Sen and Bernard Williams. Cambridge: Cambridge University Press.
Lindblom, Charles E. 1957. "In Praise of Political Science." *World Politics,* January: 240–53.
Lodge, Milton, David Moskowitz, Michael Pfau, and Subha Ramachandran. 1985. "Discriminating Tweedledum from Tweedledee: Perceived Party Preferences as a Function of Social Class and Racial Differences." Paper presented at the annual meeting of the American Political Science Association, New Orleans, August.
Lodge, Milton, David Moskowitz, Michael Pfau, and John Wahlke. 1986. "Race and Class Components of Party Differences: An Experiment in Political Information Processing." Unpublished manuscript, Laboratory for Behavioral Research, State University of New York at Stony Brook.
Lott, John. 1987. "Political Cheating." *Public Choice* 52:169–87.
Lott, John, and W. Robert Reed. 1987. "Shirking and Sorting in a Political Market with Finite Lived Politicians." Hoover Institution working paper in political science, July.
"Louisiana Gubernatorial Primary Result Triggers Unprecedented Registration Activity." 1991. *Election Administration Reports,* November 11, 6.
Lubell, Samuel. 1952. *The Future of American Politics.* New York: Harper.
Luce, R. Duncan. 1992. "Where Does Subjective Expected Utility Fail Descriptively?" *Journal of Risk and Uncertainty* 5:5–27.
Luce, R. Duncan, and Howard Raiffa. 1957. *Games and Decisions.* New York: Wiley.
Lupia, Arthur. 1990. "Direct Democracy, Political Information, and the 'Will of the Majority.'" Paper presented at the annual meeting of the American Political Science Association, San Francisco, September.
———. 1991a. "Voter Information, Endorsements, and Electoral Outcomes: Insurance Reform in California." Paper presented at the eighth annual Political Methodology Meeting, Durham, NC, July 19.
———. 1991b. "The Effect of Majority Preferences, Information, and Credibility on Policy Selection: The Case of Direct Legislation." Paper presented at the annual meeting of the American Political Science Association, Washington, DC, September.

McCallum, Bennett. 1989. *Monetary Economics: Theory and Policy.* New York: Macmillan.

McClosky, Herbert. 1964. "Consensus and Ideology in American Politics." *American Political Science Review* 58:361–82.

McConahay, John B. 1982. "Self-interest versus Racial Attitudes as Correlates of Anti-Busing Attitudes in Louisville: Is It the Buses or the Blacks?" *Journal of Politics* 44:692–720.

McCrone, Donald J., and Walter J. Stone. 1986. "The Structure of Constituency Representation: On Theory and Method." *Journal of Politics* 48:956–75.

MacDonald, S., and G. Rabinowitz. 1990. "Direction and Uncertainty in a Model of Issue Voting." Delivered at the annual meeting of the American Political Science Association, San Francisco, August 30–September 2.

Mackelprang, A. J., Bernard Grofman, and N. Keith Thomas. 1975. "Electoral Change and Stability: Some New Perspectives." *American Politics Quarterly* 3 (3): 315–39.

McKelvey, Richard D. 1976. "Intransitivities in Multidimensional Voting Models and Some Implications for Agenda Control." *Journal of Economic Theory* 12:472–82.

———. 1979. "General Conditions for Global Intransitivities in Formal Voting Models." *Econometrica* 47:1085–1111.

———. 1980. "Ambiguity in Spatial Models of Policy Formation." *Public Choice* 35:385–402.

———. 1986. "Covering, Dominance, and Institution Free Properties of Social Choice." *American Journal of Political Science* 30:283–315.

McKelvey, Richard D., and Peter C. Ordeshook. 1972. "A General Theory of Calculus Voting." In *Mathematical Applications in Political Science*, ed. James F. Herndon and Joseph L. Bernd, Vol. 6, 32–78. Charlottesville: University Press of Virginia.

———. 1976. "Symmetric Spatial Games without Majority Rule Equilibrium." *American Political Science Review* 70:1171–84.

———. 1984. "Rational Expectations in Elections: Some Experimental Results Based on a Multidimensional Model." *Public Choice* 44:61–102.

———. 1985a. "Elections with Limited Information: A Fulfilled Expectations Model Using Contemporaneous and Poll and Endorsement Data as Information Sources." *Journal of Economic Theory* 36:55–85.

———. 1985b. "Sequential Elections with Limited Information." *American Journal of Political Science* 29:480–512.

———. 1986. "Information, Electoral Equilibria, and the Democratic Ideal." *Journal of Politics* 48:909–37.

———. 1987. "Elections with Limited Information: A Multidimensional Model." *Mathematical Social Sciences* 14:77–99.

———. 1990. "A Decade of Experimental Research on Spatial Models of Elections and Committees." In *Advances in the Spatial Theory of Voting*, ed. James M. Enelow and Melvin J. Hinich, 99–144. New York: Cambridge University Press.

McNown, Robert. 1986. "On the Uses of Econometric Models: A Guide for Policymakers." *Policy Sciences* 19:359–80.

MacRae, C. Duncan. 1977. "A Political Model of the Business Cycle." *Journal of Political Economy* 85:239–63.
Mansbridge, Jane. 1990. *Beyond Self Interest*. Chicago: University of Chicago Press.
Margolis, H. [1982] 1984. *Selfishness, Altruism, and Rationality: A Theory of Social Choice*. Cambridge: Cambridge University Press. Reprint. Chicago: University of Chicago Press.
Markus, Gregory B., and Philip E. Converse. 1979. "A Dynamic Simultaneous Equation Model of Electoral Choice." *American Political Science Review* 73:1055–70.
Meyer, John, and Brian Rowan. 1977. "Institutionalized Organizations: Formal Structure as Myth and Ceremony." *American Journal of Sociology* 83:66–94.
Miller, Arthur H., Patricia Gurin, Gerald Gurin, and Oksana Malunchuk. 1981. "Group Consciousness and Political Participation." *American Journal of Political Science* 25:494–511.
Miller, John H. 1987. "The Evolution of Automata in the Repeated Prisoner's Dilemma." Mimeo, University of Michigan.
Miller, Nicholas R. 1983. "Pluralism and Social Choice." *American Political Science Review* 77:734–47.
———. 1986. "Information, Electorates, and Democracy: Some Extensions and Interpretations of the Condorcet Jury Theorem." In *Information Pooling and Group Decision Making*, ed. Bernard Grofman and Guillermo Owen, 175–94. Westport, CT: JAI Press.
Miller, Warren E., and the National Election Studies. 1982, 1986, 1989. *American National Election Studies, 1980, 1984, 1988* (computer file). Ann Arbor: Interuniversity Consortium for Political and Social Research (producer and distributor).
Moe, Terry M. 1978. "On the Scientific Status of Rational Models." *American Journal of Political Science* 23:215–43.
Mohr, Lawrence B. 1973. "The Concept of Organizational Goal." *American Political Science Review* 67:470–81.
Monroe, Kristen (ed.). 1991. *The Economic Approach to Politics: A Critical Reassessment of the Theory of Rational Action*. New York: Harper Collins.
Munro, William Bennett. 1928. *Invisible Government*. New York: Macmillan.
Neumann, Russell. 1989. "Public's Knowledge of Civics Rises Only a Bit." *New York Times*, May 28, 31.
Neustadt, Richard. 1980. *Presidential Power*. New York: Wiley.
Nie, Norman, and Sidney Verba. 1976. *The Changing American Voter*. Cambridge: Harvard University Press.
Niemi, Richard G. 1976. "Costs of Voting and Nonvoting." *Public Choice* 27:115–19.
Niemi, Richard G., Guy Whitten, and Mark N. Franklin. 1991. "Constituency Characteristics, Individual Characteristics, and Tactical Voting in the 1987 British General Election." Paper presented at the annual meeting of the American Political Science Association, Washington, DC, August 29 to September 1.
Nitzan, Schmuel, and Jacob Paroush. 1981. "The Characterization of Decisive Weighted Majority Rules." *Economics Letters* 7:119–24.
———. 1982. "Optimal Decision Rules in Uncertain Dichotomous Choice Situations." *International Economic Review* 23 (2): 289–97.

———. 1983. "Small Panels of Experts in Dichotomous Choice Situations." *Decision Sciences* 14:314–25.

———. 1984a. "Are Qualified Majority Rules Special?" *Public Choice* 42:257–72.

———. 1984b. "The Significance of Independent Voting under Uncertain Dichotomous Choice Situations." *Theory and Decision* 17:47–60.

———. 1985. *Collective Decision Making: An Economic Outlook.* London: Cambridge University Press.

Nordhaus, William. 1975. "The Political Business Cycle." *Review of Economic Studies* 42:169–90.

Olson, Mancur, Jr. [1965] 1971. *The Logic of Collective Action.* Rev. ed. New York: Schocken. Books by arrangement with Harvard University Press.

Opp, Karl-Dieter. 1986. "Soft Incentives and Collective Action: Participation in the Anti-Nuclear Movement." *British Journal of Political Science* 16:87–112.

Ordeshook, Peter C., and William H. Riker. 1968. "A Theory of the Calculus of Voting." *American Political Science Review* 52:25–42.

Owen, Guillermo, and Bernard Grofman. 1984. "To Vote or Not to Vote: The Paradox of Nonvoting." *Public Choice* 42:311–25.

Page, Benjamin I. 1976. "The Theory of Political Ambiguity." *American Political Science Review* 70:742–52.

———. 1978. *Choices and Echoes in Presidential Elections: Rational Man in Electoral Democracy.* Chicago: University of Chicago Press.

Page, Benjamin I., and Calvin C. Jones. 1979. "Reciprocal Effects of Policy Preferences of Two Quebec Elections." *American Political Science Review* 73:1071–89.

Page, Scott E., Ken Kollman, and John H. Miller. 1992a. "Political Parties and Electoral Landscapes." CMSEMS Working Paper #997, Northwestern University.

———. 1992b. "Adaptive Parties in Spatial Elections." *American Political Science Review* 86(4):929–37.

Paine, Scott C. 1989. "Persuasion, Manipulation, and Dimension." *Journal of Politics* 51:36–49.

Palfrey, Thomas R., and Howard Rosenthal. 1984. "A Strategic Calculus of Voting." *Public Choice* 41:7–53.

———. 1985. "Voter Participation and Strategic Uncertainty." *American Political Science Review* 79:62–78.

Parfit, Derek. 1984. *Reasons and Persons.* Oxford: Clarendon Press.

Patterson, Samuel C., and Gregory A. Caldeira. 1983. "Getting out the Vote: Participation in Gubernatorial Elections." *American Political Science Review* 77:675–89.

Pears, David. 1984. *Motivated Irrationality.* Oxford: Clarendon Press.

Peltzman, Samuel. 1984. "Constituent Interest and Congressional Voting." *Journal of Law and Economics* 27:181–210.

Pennock, Roland. 1958. Review of *An Economic Theory of Democracy. American Political Science Review* 52(2):539–41.

Petracca, Mark. 1991. *The Politics of Interests: Interest Groups Transformed.* Boulder, CO: Westview Press.
Pitkin, Hannah. 1967. *The Concept of Representation.* Berkeley and Los Angeles: University of California Press.
Plott, Charles R. 1967. "A Notion of Equilibrium and Its Possibility under Majority Rule." *American Economic Review* 57:787–806.
Plott, Charles R., and Michael E. Levine. 1978. "A Model of Agenda Influence on Committee Decisions." *American Economic Review* 68:146–60.
Poisson, S. D. 1837. *Recherches sur la Probabilité des Judgments on Matiere Civile: Procedées des Regles Generales du Cakul des Probabilitiés.* Paris: Bachelier, Imprimateu Libraire.
Pollack, R. A. 1968. "Consistent Planning." *Review of Economic Studies* 35:201–8.
Pomper, Gerald M. 1969. *Elections in America: Control and Influence in Democratic Politics.* New York: Dodd Mead.
Poole, Keith T., and Howard Rosenthal. 1985. "A Spatial Model for Legislative Roll Call Analysis." *American Journal of Political Science* 29:357–84.
Popkin, Samuel L. 1991. *The Reasoning Voter.* Chicago: University of Chicago Press.
Popkin, Samuel L., John W. Gorman, Charles Phillips, and Jeffrey A. Smith. 1976. "What Have You Done for Me Lately? Toward an Investment Theory of Voting." *American Political Science Review* 70:779–805.
Przeworski, Adam, and Michael Wallerstein. 1982. "The Structure of Class Conflict in Democratic Capitalist Societies." *American Political Science Review* 76:215–39.
Rabinowitz, G., and S. MacDonald. 1989. "A Directional Theory of Issue Voting." *American Political Science Review* 83:93–121.
Radner, Roy. 1986. "Review Essay: Information Pooling and Decentralized Decision Making." In *Information Pooling and Group Decision Making,* ed. Bernard Grofman and Guillermo Owen, 197–219. Westport, CT: JAI Press.
Rae, Douglas W. 1969. "Decision Rules and Individual Values in Constitutional Choice." *American Political Science Review* 63:40–56.
Rahn, Wendy M. 1989. "The Role of Partisan Stereotypes in Information Processing about Political Candidates." Paper presented at the annual meeting of the American Political Science Association, Atlanta GA, August 31–September 3.
Rapoport, Amnon, Dan Felsenthal, and Zeev Maoz. 1988. "Proportional Representation: An Empirical Evaluation of Single-Stage Non-ranked Voting Procedures." *Public Choice* 59:161–65.
Rawls, John. 1985. "Justice as Fairness: Political, Not Metaphysical." *Philosophy and Public Affairs* 14:223–51.
Reich, Robert D. (ed.). 1988. *The Power of Public Ideas.* Cambridge, MA: Ballinger.
Rhoads, Steven E. 1985. *The Economist's View of the World: Government Markets and Public Policy.* Cambridge: Cambridge University Press.
Riker, William H. 1958. "The Paradox of Voting and Congressional Rules for Voting on Amendments." *American Political Science* 52 (June): 349–66.
———. 1961. "Voting and the Summation of Preferences: An Interpretive Bibliographic Essay of Selected Developments during the Last Decade." *American Political Science Review* 55:909–11.

———. 1962. *The Theory of Political Coalitions*. New Haven: Yale University Press.

———. 1982a. *Liberalism against Populism: A Confrontation between the Theory of Democracy and the Theory of Social Choice*. San Francisco: W. H. Freeman.

———. 1982b. "The Two-Party System and Duverger's Law: An Essay on the History of Political Science." *American Political Science Review* 76:753–66.

———. 1983. "Political Theory and the Art of Heresthetics." In *Political Science: The State of the Discipline*, ed. Ada W. Finifter 47–67. Washington, DC: American Political Science Association.

———. 1984. "The Heresthetics of Constitution-making: The Presidency in 1787, with Comments on Determinism and Rational Choice." *American Political Science Review* 78:1–16.

———. 1986. *The Art of Political Manipulation*. New Haven: Yale University Press.

———. 1988. *Liberalism against Populism*. 2d ed. Prospect Heights, IL: Waveland Press.

———. 1990. "Heresthetic and Rhetoric in the Spatial Model." In *Advances in the Spatial Theory of Voting*, ed. James M. Enelow and Melvin J. Hinich 46–65. New York: Cambridge University Press.

Riker, William H., and Peter C. Ordeshook. 1968. "A Theory of the Calculus of Voting." *American Political Science Review* 62:25–42.

———. 1972. "A Theory of the Calculus of Voting." *American Political Science Review* 62:25–42.

———. 1973. *An Introduction to Positive Political Theory*. Prentice-Hall Contemporary Political Theory Series. Englewood Cliffs, NJ: Prentice Hall.

Riker, William H., and Barry Weingast. 1988. "Constitutional Regulation of Legislative Choice: The Political Consequences of Judicial Deference to Legislators." *Virginia Law Review* 74:373–402.

Rogers, W. Hayward. 1959. "Some Methodological Difficulties in Anthony Downs's *An Economic Theory of Democracy*" *American Political Science Review* 53(2):483–85.

Rogoff, Kenneth. 1987. "Reputational Constraint on Monetary Policy." *Carnegie-Rochester Conference Series on Public Policy* 26:141–81.

Rorty, Amelie Oksenberg. 1985. "Self-deception, *Akrasia* and Irrationality." In *The Multiple Self*, ed. Jon Elster. 115–31. Cambridge: Cambridge University Press.

Rothschild, Michael. 1974. "Searching for the Lowest Price When the Distribution of Prices Is Unknown." *Journal of Political Economy* 82:689–711.

Rourke, Francis E. 1969. *Bureaucracy, Politics, and Public Policy*. Boston: Little, Brown.

Russell, K. P. 1972. "Political Participation and Income Level: An Exchange." *Public Choice* 13:113–14.

Russell, Thomas, and Richard Thaler. 1985. "The Relevance of Quasi Rationality in Competitive Markets." *American Economic Review* 75:1071–82.

Sahlins, Marshall. 1976. *Culture and Practical Reason*. Chicago: University of Chicago Press.

Sandel, Michael (ed.). 1984. *Liberalism and Its Critics*. Oxford: Blackwell.

Sartori, Giovanni. 1986. *The Theory of Democracy Revisited Part II: The Classical Issues*. Chatham, NJ: Chatham House Publishers.

Schattschneider, Elmer E. 1960. *The Semi-Sovereign People: A Realist's View of Democracy in America.* New York: Holt, Rinehart and Winston.
Schelling, Thomas C. 1960. *The Strategy of Conflict.* Cambridge: Harvard University.
———. 1984. *Choice and Consequence: Perspectives of an Errant Economist.* Cambridge: Harvard University Press.
———. 1985. "Enforcing Rules on Oneself." *Journal of Law, Economics, and Organization* 1:357–74.
Schlesinger, Arthur M. 1959. *The Coming of the New Deal.* Boston: Houghton-Mifflin.
Schofield, Norman. 1972. "Is Majority Rule Special?" In *Probability Models of Collective Decision Making,* ed. Richard G Niemi and Herbert F. Weisberg, 60–82. Columbus, OH: Merrill.
Schuman, Howard, and Stanley Presser. 1981. *Questions and Answers in Attitude Surveys.* New York: Academic Press.
Schumpeter, Joseph A. 1950. *Capitalism, Socialism, and Democracy,* 3d ed. New York: Harper and Row.
Schwartz, Thomas. 1987. "Your Vote Counts on Account of the Way It Is Counted: An Institutional Solution to the Paradox of Not Voting." *Public Choice* 54:101–21.
Sears, David O., Carl P. Hensler, and Leslie K. Speer. 1979. "White's Opposition to Busing: Self-interest or Symbolic Politics?" *American Political Science Review* 73:369–84.
Sears, David O., and Donald R. Kinder. 1971. "Racial Tensions and Voting in Los Angeles." In *Los Angeles: Viability and Prospects for Metropolitan Leadership,* ed. Werner Z. Hirsch, 51–88. New York: Praeger.
Selten, Reinhard. 1971. "Anwendungen der Spieltheorie auf die Politische Wissenschaft." In *Politik und Wissenschaft,* ed. H. Maier, Hrsg. V. Hans Maier, Klaus Ritter, and Ulrich Matz. Munich: Verlag C. H. Beck.
Selznick, Philip. 1949. *TVA and the Grass Roots.* Berkeley and Los Angeles: University of California Press.
Sen, Amaryta K. 1967. "Isolation, Assurance, and the Social Rate of Discount." *Quarterly Journal of Economics* 80:112–24.
———. 1971. "Choice Functions and Revealed Preference." *Review of Economic Studies* 38: 307–17.
———. 1973. "Behaviour and the Concept of Preference." *Economica* 40:241–59.
———. 1974. "Choice, Orderings, and Morality." In *Practical Reason,* ed. S. Korner, 54–67. Oxford: Blackwell.
———. 1977. "Rational Fools: A Critique of the Behavioral Foundations of Economic Theory." *Philosophy and Public Affairs* 6:317–44.
———. 1980. "Description as Choice." *Oxford Economic Papers* 32:353–69.
———. 1985. "Goals, Commitment, and Identity." *Journal of Law, Economics, and Organization* 1:341–55.
———. 1987. *On Ethics and Economics.* Oxford: Blackwell.
Settle, Russell F., and Burton A. Abrams. 1976. "The Determinants of Voter Participation: A More General Model." *Public Choice* 27:81–89.
Shapiro, Catherine R., David W. Brady, Richard A. Brody, and John Ferejohn. 1990.

"Linking Constituency Opinion and Senate Voting Scores: A Hybrid Explanation." *Legislative Studies Quarterly* 15:599–623.

Shapley, Lloyd S., and Bernard Grofman. 1984. "Optimizing Group Judgmental Accuracy in the Presence of Interdependencies." *Public Choice* 43:329–43.

Shepsle, Kenneth A. 1972. "The Strategy of Ambiguity: Uncertainty and Electoral Competition." *American Political Science Review* 66:415–70.

———. 1979a. "The Role of Institutional Structure in the Creation of Policy Equilibrium." In *Public Policy and Public Choice,* ed. Douglas W. Rae and Theodore J. Eismeier, vol. 6, Sage Yearbooks in *Politics and Public Policy* 249–82. Beverly Hills: Sage.

———. 1979b. "Institutional Arrangements and Equilibrium in Multidimensional Voting Models." *American Journal of Political Science* 23:27–59.

Shepsle, Kenneth A., and Ronald N. Cohen. 1990. "Multiparty Competition, Entry, and Entry Deterrence in Spatial Models of Elections." In *Advances in the Spatial Theory of Voting,* ed. James M. Enelow and Melvin J. Hinich, 12–45. New York: Cambridge University Press.

Silberman, Jonathan, and Garey C. Durden. 1975. "The Rational Behavior Theory of Voter Participation: The Evidence from Congressional Elections." *Public Choice* 23:101–8.

Silver, Morris. 1973. "A Demand Analysis of Voting Costs and Voting Participation." *Social Science Research* 2:111–24.

Simmons, James R. 1987. "Economic Theory of Democracy Revisited." Paper presented at the annual meeting of the Midwest Political Science Association, Chicago, April.

Simon, Herbert A. 1985. "Human Nature in Politics: The Dialogue of Psychology with Political Science." *American Political Science Review* 79:293–304.

Simon, Herbert A., Donald W. Smithburg, and Victor A. Thompson. 1950. *Public Administration.* New York: Knopf.

Slovic, Paul, and S. Lichtenstein. 1983. "Preference Reversals: A Broader Perspective." *American Economic Review* 73:590–605.

Smithies, A. 1941. "Optimum Location in Spatial Competition." *Journal of Political Economics* 49:423–39.

Sniderman, Paul M., and Michael Gray Hagen. 1984. *Race and Inequality: A Study in American Values.* Chatham, NJ: Chatham House Publishers.

Stanley, Harold. 1987. *Voter Mobilization and the Politics of Race: The South and Universal Suffrages, 1952–1982.* New York: Praeger.

Stein, Herbert. 1969. *The Fiscal Revolution in America.* Chicago: University of Chicago Press.

Stephens, Stephen V. 1975. "The Paradox of Not Voting: Comment." *American Political Science Review* 69:914–15.

Stockton, David. 1990. *The Classical Athenian Democracy.* New York: Oxford.

Stokes, Donald E. 1965. "Some Dynamic Elements of Contest for the Presidency." *American Political Science Review* 60:19–28.

———. 1966. "Spatial Models of Party Competition." In *Elections and the Political Order,* ed. Angus Campbell, Philip E. Converse, Warren E. Miller, and Donald E. Stokes, 161–79. New York: Wiley.

Stokes, Donald E., Angus Campbell, and Warren E. Miller. 1958. "Components of the Electoral Decision." *American Political Science Review* 52:367–87.

Strom, Gerald S. 1975. "On the Apparent Paradox of Participation: A New Proposal." *American Political Science Review* 69:908–13.

Strotz, R. H. 1955. "Myopia and Inconsistency in Dynamic Utility Maximization." *Review of Economic Studies* 23:165–80.

Sullivan, John L., and Robert E. O'Connor. 1972. "Electoral Choice and Popular Control of Public Policy: The Cases of the 1966 House Elections." *American Political Science Review* 66:1256–68.

Sullivan, John L., and Eric M. Uslaner. 1978. "Congressional Behavior and Electoral Marginality." *American Journal of Political Science* 22:536–53.

Sundquist, James L. 1968. *Politics and Policy: The Eisenhower, Kennedy, and Johnson Years*. Washington, DC: Brookings.

———. 1973. *Dynamics of the Party System*. Washington, DC: Brookings.

Taagepera, Rein, and Bernard Grofman. 1987. "Rethinking Duverger's Law. Predicting the Effective Number of Parties in Plurality and PR Systems—Parties Minus Issues Equals One." *European Journal of Political Research* 13:341–52.

Taylor, Michael. 1969. "Proof of a Theorem on Majority Rule." *Behavioral Science* 14:228–31.

———. 1976. *Anarchy and Cooperation*. New York: Wiley.

Tideman, Nicolaus T. 1985. "Remorse, Elation, and the Paradox of Voting." *Public Choice* 46:103–6.

Tilly, Charles. 1969. "Collective Violence in European Perspective." In *History of Violence in America*, ed. Hugh D. Graham and Ted R. Gurr, 4–45. New York: Signet Books.

———. 1975. "Revolutions and Collective Violence." In *Handbook of Political Science*, ed. F. I. Greenstein and Nelson W. Polsby, vol. 3, 483–555. Reading, MA: Addison-Wesley.

Tollison, Robert D., W. Mark Crain, and Paul Paulter. 1975. "Information and Voting: An Empirical Note." *Public Choice* 24:43–49.

Tollison, Robert D., and T. D. Willett. 1973. "Some Simple Economics of Voting and Not Voting." *Public Choice* 16:59–71.

Trilling, Richard. 1976. *Party Image and Electoral Behavior*. New York: John Wiley.

Tucker, H. J., A. Vedlitz, and J. De Nardo. 1986. "Does Heavy Turnout Help Democrats in Presidential Elections?" *American Political Science Review* 80:1291–1304.

Tufte, Edward. 1978. *Political Control of the Economy*. Princeton: Princeton University Press.

Tullock, Gordon. 1967. *Toward a Mathematics of Politics*. Ann Arbor: University of Michigan Press.

Tversky, Amos, and Daniel Kahneman. 1986. "Rational Choice and the Framing of Decisions." In *Rational Choice*, ed. Robin M. Hogarth and Melvin W. Reder, 67–94. Chicago: University of Chicago Press.

Tversky, Amos, Paul Slovic, and Daniel Kahneman. 1990. "The Causes of Preference Reversal." *American Economic Review* 80:204–17.

Uhlaner, Carole Jean. 1986. "Political Participation, Rational Actors, and Rationality: A New Approach." *Political Psychology* 7:551–73.

———. 1989a. "Rational Turnout: The Neglected Role of Groups." *American Journal of Political Science* 33:390–422.

———. 1989b. "'Relational Goods' and Participation: Incorporating Sociability into a Theory of Rational Action." *Public Choice* 62:253–85.

———. 1989c. "Turnout in Recent Presidential Elections." *Political Behavior* 11:57–79.

Uhlaner, Carole Jean, and Bernard Grofman. 1985. "The Race May Be Close but Our Horse Is Going to Win: Wish Fulfillment in the 1980 Presidential Election." *Political Behavior* 8:101–29.

Urken, Arnold B. 1980. "Competence and the Choice of a Voting System." Paper presented at the American Political Science Association Meeting, Washington, DC, September.

Vanneman, Reeve, and Lynn Weber Cannon. 1987. *The American Perception of Class*. Philadelphia: Temple University Press.

Wattenberg, Martin. 1984. *The Decline of American Political Parties*. Cambridge: Harvard University Press.

———. 1991. *The Rise of Candidate Centered Politics: Presidential Elections of the 1980s*. Cambridge: Harvard University Press.

Weatherford, M. Stephen. 1983. "Economic Voting and the 'Symbolic Politics' Argument: A Reinterpretation and Synthesis." *American Political Science Review* 77:158–74.

———. 1988. "The Interplay of Ideology and Advice in Economic Policymaking: The Case of Political Business Cycles." *Journal of Politics* 49:925–52.

Weatherford, M. Stephen, and Lorraine M. McDonnell. 1990. "The Economic Policy Legacy of the Reagan Administration." In *Looking Back on the Reagan Presidency* ed. Larry Berman, 122–55. Baltimore: Johns Hopkins University Press.

Weisberg, Herbert F., and Bernard Grofman. 1981. "Candidate Evaluations and Turnout." *American Political Quarterly* 9:197–219.

Wildavsky, Aaron. 1987. "Choosing Preferences by Constructing Institutions: A Cultural Theory of Preference Formation." *American Political Science Review* 81:3–22.

Williamson, Oliver E. 1983. "Credible Commitments: Using Hostages to Support Exchange." *American Economic Review* 73:519–40.

Wilson, James Q. 1973. *Political Organizations*. New York: Basic.

Witcover, Jules. 1977. *Marathon: The Pursuit of the Presidency, 1972–1976*. New York: Viking.

Wittman, Donald A. 1973. "Parties as Utility Maximizers." *American Political Science Review* 18:490–98.

———. 1977. "Candidates with Policy Preferences: A Dynamic Model." *Journal of Economic Theory* 14:180–89.

———. 1983. "Candidate Motivation: A Synthesis of Alternative Theories." *American Political Science Review* 72:78–90.

———. 1990."Spatial Strategies When Candidates Have Policy Preferences." In *Ad-*

vances in the Spatial Theory of Voting, ed. James M. Enelow and Melvin J. Hinich. New York: Cambridge University Press.

Wolfinger, Raymond E. 1993, forthcoming. "The Rational Citizen Faces Election Day or What Rational Choice Theorists Don't Tell You about American Elections." In *Elections at Home and Abroad: Essays in Honor of Warren E. Miller,* ed. Thomas Mann and Kent Jennings. Ann Arbor: University of Michigan Press.

Wolfinger, Raymond E., and Steven J. Rosenstone. 1980. *Who Votes?* New Haven: Yale University Press.

Wolfram, Gary L., and Carroll B. Foster. 1981. "The Electoral College and Voter Participation Rates: Reexamination of the Cebula-Murphy Hypothesis." Paper presented at the Public Choice Society meetings, New Orleans.

Woolley, John T. 1988. "Partisan Manipulation of the Economy: Another Look at Monetary Policy with Moving Regression." *Journal of Politics* 50:335–60.

Wright, Gerald C. 1977. "Contextual Models of Electoral Behavior: The Southern Wallace Vote." *American Political Science Review* 71:497–508.

———. 1988. "Policy Positions in the U.S. Senate: Who's Represented?" Paper presented at the Hendricks Symposium on the United States Senate, Lincoln, NE.

Wuffle, A. 1984. "Should You Brush Your Teeth on November 6, 1984?" *PS,* Summer, 577–80.

———. 1985. "Winning by Losing: Policy vs. Vote-maximizing Goals in Two-Party Spatial Competition." Unpublished manuscript.

Wuffle, A, Scott L. Feld, Guillermo Owen, and Bernard Grofman. 1989. "Finagle's Law and the Finagle Point." *American Journal of Political Science* 33:348–75.

Young, H. P. 1986. "Optimal Ranking and Choice from Pairwise Comparisons." In *Information Pooling and Group Decision Making,* ed. Bernard Grofman and Guillermo Owen, 113–22. Westport, CT: JAI Press.

Contributors

About the Editor

Bernard Grofman is Professor of Political Science and Social Psychology at the University of California, Irvine. His major fields of interest are in American politics, comparative election systems, and social choice theory. He is the author of over 100 articles and research notes on topics in public choice, comparative electoral systems, jury decision making, research methodology, Congress, and race and politics. He has edited eight other books of which the most recent are: *Political Gerrymandering and the Courts* (1990); *Controversies in Minority Voting: The Voting Rights Act in Perspective* (coedited with Chandler Davidson, 1992); and *Quiet Revolution: The Impact of the Voting Rights Act in the South, 1965–1990* (coedited with Chandler Davidson, 1994 forthcoming). He is a coauthor with Lisa Handley and Richard G. Niemi of *Minority Representation and the Quest for Voting Equality* (1992).

About the Authors

Gabriel A. Almond has taught at Brooklyn College, Yale University, Princeton University, and Stanford University, where he served as Department Chair 1964–69 and became emeritus in 1976. He served as President of the American Political Science Association in 1965–66. He is a Fellow of the American Academy of Arts and Sciences and the American Association for the Advancement of Science and a member of the American Philosophical Society and of the National Academy of Science. Among his books are *A Discipline Divided* (1990); *Comparative Politics: System, Process, and Policy* (1978); *Crisis, Choice, and Change (1973); The Civic Culture* (1963); *The Politics of the Developing Areas* (1960); *The Appeals of Communism* 1954), and *The American People and Foreign Policy* (1950).

Anthony Downs is a Senior Fellow in the Economic Studies Program at the Brookings Institution. He is the author of *An Economic Theory of Democracy* (1957), *Inside Bureaucracy* (1967), *Urban Problems and Prospects* (1970), *Neighborhoods and Urban Development* (1981), *The Revolution in Real Estate Finance* (1985), *Stuck in Traffic* (1992), and seven other books on housing, urban affairs and real estate, plus over 390 articles on urban economics or political science.

James W. Endersby is Assistant Professor of Political Science at the University of Missouri-Columbia. His research and teaching interests include American government, formal theory, methodology, political organizations, and political behavior. He has written articles for a number of publications including the *Journal of Politics, Mathematical and Computer Modelling, Journal of Labor Research,* and *Social Science Quarterly.*

James M. Enelow is Professor of Government, University of Texas at Austin. He has written extensively on the spatial theory of voting and elections, including coauthorship, with Melvin J. Hinich, of *The Spatial Theory of Voting* (1984) and coeditorship, also with Hinich, of *Advances in the Spatial Theory of Voting* (1990). He has served twice on the editorial board of the *American Journal of Political Science* and is currently a member of the editorial board of *Public Choice.*

John Ferejohn is the Carolyn S. G. Munro Professor of Political Science and Senior Fellow of the Hoover Institution at Stanford University. He has written in the areas of American politics, positive political theory, and most recently in political and legal theory; and he has published his work in books and articles in various disciplinary journals. He is a member of the National Academy of Sciences and the American Academy of Arts and Sciences.

Amihai Glazer is Professor of Economics at the University of California, Irvine. His current work focuses on how governments deal with commitment problems. His work in public choice has appeared both in economics journals (such as *American Economic Review* and *Quarterly Journal of Economics*) and in political science journals (such as the *American Political Science Review* and *American Journal of Political Science*).

Thomas H. Hammond is Associate Professor of Political Science at Michigan State University. His research interests primarily involve the development of models of political institutions. Recent projects include the development of models of organizational hierarchies, models of equilibrium outcomes in bicameral legislative institutions, and models of the relationships between bureaucracies and legislatures. His most recent article is "Toward a General Theory of Hierarchy: Books, Bureaucrats, Basketball Tournaments, and the Administrative Structure of the Nation-State" (1993) in the *Journal of Public Administration Research and Theory.*

Brian D. Humes is Assistant Professor of Political Science, University of Nebraska-Lincoln. His work, which has been published in the *American Political Science Review, Legislative Studies Quarterly,* and *Public Choice,* has considered many aspects of politics from a game theoretic perspective. One of his primary interests is the development of legislative institutions. He has recently coauthored a paper with Kenneth Shepsle on the development of the committee system in the United States House of Representatives.

Ken Kollman is Assistant Professor of Political Science at the University of Michigan. His major research interests are in political parties, electoral systems, and interest groups. He is the coauthor of a recent article in the *American Political Science Review.*

Arend Lijphart is Professor of Political Science at the University of California, San Diego. His field of specialization is comparative politics, and his current research entails the comparative study of democratic regimes and of electoral systems. He is a member of the American Academy of Arts and Sciences. His most recent books are

Democracies: Patterns of Majoritarian and Consensus Government in Twenty-One Countries (1984), *Power-Sharing in South Africa* (1985), *Parliamentary versus Presidential Government* (1992), and, coedited with Bernard Grofman, *Choosing an Electoral System: Issues and Alternatives* (1984) and *Electoral Laws and Their Political Consequences* (1986).

John H. Miller is Assistant Professor of Economics and Decision Sciences, Department of Social and Decision Sciences, Carnegie Mellon University and External Faculty, Sante Fe Institute. His research focuses on understanding the complex adaptive behavior that emerges in social systems, through the use of mathematical and computational methods. He is coauthor of a recent article in the *American Political Science Review*.

Michael C. Munger is Pearsall Chair of State and Local Government, and Director of the MPA program, in the Department of Political Science at the University of North Carolina at Chapel Hill. He specializes in research on public policy and decision making, including radioactive waste disposal and campaign finance. His publications include over twenty articles in professional journals, and he is coauthor with Melvin J. Hinich of *Ideology and the Theory of Political Choice* (1994 forthcoming).

Roger G. Noll is the Morris M. Doyle Professor of Public Policy in the Department of Economics at Stanford University. His primary areas of research are the economics of regulation and the politics of microeconomic policy. Noll is the author or coauthor of seven books and more than one hundred scholarly articles dealing with such topics as television regulation, methods of statutory interpretation by the judiciary, professional sports, medical care delivery systems, air pollution controls, federal research policies, and the political causes and economic consequences of administrative procedures. He is currently undertaking research on public-private research consortia, comparative telecommunications policy in OECD countries, and nineteenth-century economic policies in the United States.

Scott E. Page is Assistant Professor of Economics at the California Institute of Technology. His research interests include public economics, political economy, and the role of complexity in the performance and design of political and economic systems. He is the coauthor of a recent article in the *American Political Science Review*.

Samuel L. Popkin is Professor of Political Science at the University of California, San Diego. His fields of specialization are American politics and comparative politics. He is author of *The Reasoning Voter: Communication and Persuasion in Presidential Campaigns* (1991) and *The Rational Peasant: The Political Economy of Peasant Society in Vietnam* (1979). He is coeditor with Samuel Kernell of *Chief of Staff: Twenty-five Years of Managing the Presidency* (1986), and coauthor with Ithiel deSola Pool and Robert Abelson, of *Candidates, Issues, and Strategies* (1964). Professor Popkin has served as a consultant on polling and strategy with the McGovern, Carter, and Clinton presidential campaigns, and as a consultant to CBS News on polling and election coverage.

Carole Jean Uhlaner is Associate Professor of Political Science at the University of California, Irvine. Her research has centered on the study of mass political activity, especially political participation. She has published a series of articles developing a rational choice model of political participation. She has also published widely on the political behavior of ethnic minorities, public choice analyses of electoral behavior, and women and politics.

Martin P. Wattenberg is Professor of Political Science at the University of California, Irvine. He is author of *The Decline of American Political Parties 1952–1988*, currently in its third edition (1990). Most recently, he has written *The Rise of Candidate-Centered Politics: Presidential Elections of the 1980s* (1991). In addition, he has contributed many professional articles to such journals as the *American Political Science Review, American Journal of Political Science, American Politics Quarterly, Public Opinion Quarterly*, and *Public Opinion*.

M. Stephen Weatherford is Professor of Political Science at the University of California, Santa Barbara. His interests center on the interplay between economics and politics in the United States, including research on how public opinion and election outcomes are shaped by economic conditions, as well as on how governments select among policy options, in the context of economic trends, public opinion, and international concerns. His recent publications have included articles on the role of ideas in economic policy-making, on political alienation, and on the similarities and differences between economic policy-making in Japan and the United States.

Julie Withers teaches economics at the University of Southern California's School of Business Administration. Her research focuses on the role of information in spatial competition, both in political and in economic contexts.

Index

AAA (artifical adaptive agent), 162, 163
Abrams, Burton A., 101–2
Abstention, 3, 38, 39, 67, 189. *See also* Threshold models; Turnout
Action threshold, definition of, 39
ACU (American Constitutional Union), 180
ADA (Americans for Democratic Action), 9n.17, 90, 180
Adaptive party models: basis of need for, 161, 163–64; conclusions resulting from, 168–72; description of, 11, 161–62, 164–68
Additive models, of platforms: in additive/competence-adjusted hybrid model, 10, 130, 138–40; description of, 129; empirical analysis of, 130–38, 140
Adverse selection models (signaling models), 120–21
Advertising, negative, 48, 156
AFL-CIO, 74–75
Agencies, government, issue-framing applied to, 157–59
Agitators (Downsian voter category), 39
Akerlof, George A., 227–28
Aldrich, John H., 85, 189, 192
Alesina, Alberto, 119, 120–21
Almond, Gabriel A., 12, 201–7
Alt, James E., 115
Ambiguity, in platforms, 58–59, 186–87
Ambitiousness (election-orientation; office-seeking), 9, 162, 166, 168–72, 189–91, 198

American Constitutional Union (ACU), 180
Americans for Democratic Action (ADA), 9n.17, 90, 180
Anonymous competition, 188
Anti-nuclear protests, 70
Aranson, Peter, 184
Aristotle, 32
Arrow, Kenneth J.: Arrow's paradox, 84; importance of works of, 1, 2n.4, 5n.15, 206; influence on Downs, 2n.6, 12, 198, 199, 201; on unstable outcomes problem, 6, 41
Artificial intelligence, 11, 162, 163
Austen-Smith, David, 119, 121, 183
Axelrod, Robert, 163

Banfield, Edward, 206
Banks, Jeffrey, 119, 120, 121
Bargaining, political, 202–3, 209
Barry, Brian, 70, 72
Bay of Pigs invasion, 21
Beck, Nathaniel, 215–16
Becker, Gary S., 240
Behavioral science: and adaptive party model, 163; cited in Downs's work, 204; platform models in, 135
Benefits, of voting: in citizen duty, 67, 69, 71, 74–75, 83; in expressive voting, 85–86; and group affiliation, 70, 73–76, 85–86; party differential in, 69–70; pleasure, 86; in solutions to turnout paradox, 7, 69–70, 73–78, 83, 85–86, 94–95
Berelson, Bernard, 2n.5
Berent, Matthew K., 26n.18

273

274   Index

Bergson, Abram, 205–6
Bernstein, Robert A., 116–17
Bias, in information sources, 64. *See also* Status quo bias
Black, Duncan, 1, 2n.4, 108, 207
Black voter turnout: effect on turnout/closeness link, 98; effect on white turnout, 8, 90–92, 188, 193; motivation for, 84, 103
Bounded rationality, 11, 162, 165, 166, 172
Bradley, Tom, 28
Brams, Steven J., 183
Brand name metaphor, for platforms, 123
Brennan, Geoffrey, 84
Brody, Richard A., 21, 114
Bruner, Jerome, 29–30
Buchanan, James M., 1, 5n.15, 207
Builder, Carl H., 158
Bureaucracy, issue-framing applied to, 157–59
Bush, George, 21n.4, 28, 33, 133, 138, 141, 174

Caldeira, Gregory A., 82, 98
Calvert, Randall, 6–7, 64
Campaign advertising, negative, 48, 156
Campaign behavior, as an information source, 19
Campbell, Angus, 2n.5, 25, 27, 27nn.19 and 20
Candidates: in adaptive party model, 165; demographic traits of, 19, 27–28, 188; in disputes with parties, 191–92; group affiliation of, 85–90; morality of, 32–33, 188, 202–3; in turnout paradox solutions, 73–74, 85–90; two-candidate vs. multicandidate theory, 182–83; vice-presidential candidates in presidential elections, 11, 173–77, 184. *See also* Platforms (issue positions); Presidential candidates
Carmines, Edward G., 90, 192

Carter, Jimmy, 18, 22, 33, 114–15, 126, 133, 227
CBS/*New York Times* poll, 91
Cebula, Richard J., 99
Centrifugal and centripetal incentives, 12
Centrism. *See* Issue convergence; Party convergence
Certainty condition, definition of, 56n.1
Chamberlain, John, 81
Chappell, Henry W., Jr., 191, 213–14, 215n.7
Citizen duty, 67, 69, 71, 74–75, 83
Civil Rights Act of 1964, 192
Climbing adaptive parties (CAP), 166–70
Closeness, electoral: probability of ties, 81, 96; and turnout, 8, 76, 93, 94–103
Cohen, Linda R., 6
Cohen, Michael D., 225n.21, 227n.24
Coleman, James, 183, 184
Columbia University presidential campaign studies, 22–23, 23n.8
Commitment, in economic policy models, 220, 230
Comparative study, of party systems, 12–13, 231–38
Competence, information sources on, 29–32
Competence-adjusted model: in additive/competence-adjusted hybrid model, 10, 130, 138–40; described, 10, 126–30; empirical analysis of, 130–38, 140
Competition: anonymous, 188; electoral closeness in, 8, 76, 81, 93, 94–102. *See also* Party competition; Platforms (issue positions); Spatial models
Computers for modeling, 163
Condorcet Jury Theorem, 61–62
Congress, United States, 20n.3, 33n.30, 115, 117, 180, 183, 219–22
Constituency, in single constituency theory, 183–84
Constitution of the United States, Twelfth Amendment, 11

Convergence, of issues, 109, 144. *See also* Party convergence
Converse, Philip E., 186
Costs, of information. *See* Information costs
Costs, of voting: Downs on, 81, 198; and economic policy, 214; and platform models, 142; and turnout paradox, 7, 67, 70–71, 77, 82, 83–84, 95, 96–97. *See also* Information costs, of aquisition
Coughlin, Peter J., 10, 126–27
Crain, W. Mark, 98
Crime problems, as an information source, 18, 18n.1
Crosscutting issues, 143
Cukierman, Alex, 120–21
Curley, "Boss," James Michael, 29–30
Cutler, Preston, 201
Cycle effects, electoral, 116, 117
Cycles: political business cycles, 211; of preference, 5n.15

Dahl, Robert, 199, 201, 204
Darden, Severn, 190n.9
Davis, Otto A., 109
Deliberation, in policy-making, 211
Democracy: preservation of, as voting motivation, 67, 69, 71, 74–75, 83; textbook model of, 2
Democratic quality, definition of, 231–32
Demographic traits, of candidates, 19, 27–28, 188
Deutsch, Karl, 202
Dewey, Thomas, 32, 190
Diamond, Martin, 204–5
Dictatorships, 157
Differential, between parties. *See* Party differential
Dimensions. *See* Issue dimensions; Issue-framing model
Divergence in platforms, 10, 127, 140. *See also* Party differential
Divided government, 103n.6, 183
Dooley, Mr., 202

Downs, Anthony: defense of *An Economic Theory of Democracy* by, 205; misconceptions on theories of, 239–40; on origins of *An Economic Theory of Democracy*, 12, 197–99; personal life of, 198. *See also Economic Theory of Democracy, An* (Downs)
Drift in parties' issue positions, 41
Drug problems, as an information source, 18n.1
Dukakis, Michael, 21n.4, 28, 31–32, 33, 91, 190
Duke, David, 103
Dunne, Finley Peter ("Mr. Dooley"), 202
Durden, Gary C., 98
Duverger, Maurice, 182–83

Eagleton, Thomas, 31
Easton, David, 157, 204
Economic conditions, as an information source, 6, 17–18, 27, 27n.19
Economic models of voting, definition of, 7
Economic policy models: argument for modifications to, 216–23; conclusions on, 228–30; costs of voting in, 214; Downs on, 212n.5; implications of argument on, 223–28; rational choice models, described, 211–16; traditional models, 210–11
Economic stabilization models, 211, 211n.4
Economic Theory of Democracy, An (Downs): citation curve of, 2n.5, 206; critical reviews of, early, 12, 204–6; critiques of, Grofman's overview of errors in, 13, 239–42; Downs on origins of, 197–99; Downs's defense of, 205; early impact of, 201–7; negative reactions to, summarized, 3–4; postulative vs. reality-based claims in, 205; publication of, 199, 201; reasons for importance of, 1–3, 2n.5, 3n.9, 4n.12, 12, 206, 242; scholarly neglect of, 4;

276 Index

Economic Theory of Democracy, An (Downs) (*continued*)
Schumpeter's influence on, 2, 2n.6; spatial modeling in, in general, 3, 107, 141, 142, 199. *See also* Spatial models, suggested modifications to
—applications of: to information-pooling models, 55–56, 57n.3, 58, 58n.6, 59; to information shortcuts, 5, 6, 17, 19, 19n.2, 23–25, 24nn.9–11, 29; to issue-framing models, 158; model for vice-presidential candidates in presidential elections, 11, 173–77; to platform models, 3, 9, 11, 108–9, 110–11, 112–14, 141, 142, 161; to threshold theory, 37–41, 39n.3, 42, 43, 44–45, 46, 47, 52; to turnout models, 7–8, 67, 68, 69, 81, 82, 83, 85, 94–95, 97
—on specific topics: on bureaucratic ideologies, 158; on costs of voting, 81, 198; on economic policy, 212n.5; on government action, 2–3; on ideology, 23–24, 24nn.9–11, 55, 57n.4, 112, 113, 117, 122, 123, 158, 185, 190; on information acquisition, 5, 19, 19n.2, 23–25, 42, 43; on information costs, 17, 44–45, 56, 81, 198; on information distribution, 6; on information types, 44; on issue performance, 57n.3; on median voter model, 87, 89–90; on minority group coalitions, 186; on party competition, 2, 2n.5, 3, 11, 231–32; on party convergence, 3, 11, 108–9, 161, 179–80, 182, 185–86, 189, 193; on party labels, 23–25, 56; on party systems, 12–13, 231, 232–37; on party unity, 192; on past performance, 56; on persuasion, 38, 55, 241; on platforms, 9, 85, 110–11, 112–14, 141, 142, 184, 186–87; on policy outcomes, 46; on proximity voting, 29; on rational ignorance, 3, 56, 198–99; on self-interest, 179; on status-quo bias, 56; on thresholds, 6, 37–41, 52; on turnout, 2n.5, 67, 68, 83, 94–95; on uncertainty, 5, 37, 39n.3, 40, 56, 112, 113, 236

Edelman, Murray, 84, 157
Education level, in information acquisition, 6, 34, 35
Eisenhower, Dwight David, 30, 215
Election-orientation (ambitiousness; office-seeking), 9, 162, 166, 168–72, 189–91, 198
Election outcomes: in adaptive party model, 161, 168, 169; relation to policy goals, 12, 209–10, 212, 228–29; stability of, 6, 41, 161; turnout and knowledge of, 90
Elections, single vs. multiple, 184
Electoral closeness. *See* Closeness, electoral
Electoral cycle effects, 116, 117
Endersby, James W., 10, 10n.19, 57, 125–40
Enelow, James M., 10, 10n.19, 57, 125–40; Enelow & Hinich's spatial model, 10, 109, 125–26, 127, 128, 129, 130, 132, 133, 135, 142, 143n.1
Entrepreneurs, political, 45n.15, 74, 193n.13, 197
Epton, Bernard, 85
Equilibrium: in adaptive party model, 163, 168; in economic policy models, 222; in spatial models on platforms, 108–10, 123, 124, 156, 161, 184–85; in turnout paradox solutions, 71, 81–82, 86–87, 95 [need reverse]
Erikson, Robert S., 82, 126–27
Ethnicity. *See* Black voter turnout
Etzioni, Amitai, 72
Expected utility model, and turnout paradox, 67, 72, 77–78
Expressive voting, in turnout paradox solutions, 7–8, 84–92
Extremist voters, 189

Fedderson, Timothy J., 189
Federalist Papers, 2, 204
Feigenbaum, Susan, 84

Feld, Scott L., 61n.9, 143, 185, 188
Fenno, Richard F., 85
Ferejohn, John, 9, 57, 72, 107–24
Finagling, in platforms, 186
Fink, Evelyn, 143
Fiorina, Morris P., 26, 46n.18, 69, 72, 93, 187
Fireman, B., 75
Fischel, Jeff, 114
Ford, Gerald, 26, 33
Foster, Carroll B., 98, 99, 101–2
Framing effects. *See* Issue-framing model
Franchise metaphor, for party label, 9n.17, 184
Frank, Robert H., 85
Free information, 5, 17–18, 56. *See also* Information-pooling models; Information shortcuts
Free-rider behavior, 68, 81–82, 99
Frey, Bruno S., 82
Friedman, Milton, 205
Frohlich, Norman, 67n.1, 74, 76n.6

Gallup Poll, 22n.6
Game theory: applied to adaptive party models, 163; applied to economic policy models, 212, 216, 219, 223–26; applied to platform models, 108, 122; applied to turnout/closeness relationship, 99; origin of economics' use of, 1n.2; Prisoner's Dilemma game, 163, 219, 223–26, 229–30
Gamson, W. A., 75
Garvey, Gerald, 189
Geertz, Clifford, 24
Genetic adaptive parties (GAP), 166–71
Genetic algorithms, 11, 163, 167
Glazer, Amihai: on closeness/turnout relationship, 95–96, 100n.4; on group affiliations in turnout, 7–8, 8n.16, 70, 84–92, 189; on primary elections, 192n.12
Glenn, John, 21n.4
Goal-completeness/-priority/-self-regardingness, in economic policy models, 223–25

Goffman, Erving, 159
Goldwater, Barry, 162, 192–93
Government agencies, issue-framing applied to, 157–59
Governmental action, Downs on, 2–3
Graft, 202
Gray, Virginia, 101
Grofman, Bernard: on closeness/turnout relationship, 93, 94–102; on competence, 127; on Condorcet Jury Theorem, 61n.9; influence on Enelow & Endersby, 10; on information-pooling models, 6–7, 55–64, 61n.9, 62n.11; overview of errors in critiques of rational choice, 13, 239–42; on probability of tied elections, 81; on structure of debate, 143; suggested modification to current models, 179–93; summaries of chapters by, 6–7, 8, 11–12, 13; on vice-presidents in presidential elections, 11, 173–77
Group affiliation: and benefits of voting, 70, 73–76, 85–86; of candidates, 85–90; and economic policy, 214; and turnout, 7–8, 8n.16, 70, 71, 73–76, 84–92, 189. *See also* Black voter turnout; Reference groups, as an information source
Group leaders, in turnout, 68, 73–74, 76
Gubernatorial elections, turnout/closeness relationships in, 98, 99
Gurin, Patricia, 75

Halperin, Morton H., 158
Hammond, Thomas H., 10, 141–59
Hanson, Ingeman, 191
Harrington, Joseph, 120
Harsanyi, John C., 203, 226n.23
Health care conditions, as an information source, 18, 18n.1
Heresthetics, 143, 159
Herring, Pendleton, 202, 204
Heterogeneity of voters, and information distribution, 6, 34
Heuristics, for information acquisition, 3, 7. *See also* Information-pooling models; Information shortcuts

Hibbs, Douglas A., Jr., 114
Hinich, Melvin J.: applied to turnout, 69, 83; Enelow & Hinich's spatial model, 10, 109, 125–26, 127, 128, 129, 130, 132, 133, 135, 142, 143n.1
Hirschman, Albert O., 221n.16, 224n.20
Holland, John, 163
Holler, Manfred, 191
Hoover, Herbert, 190
Horton, Willie, 141
Hotelling, Harold, 2, 108, 141, 179n.1, 189
House of Representatives, 33n.30
Huckfeldt, Robert, 90, 92
Humes, Brian D., 10, 141–59, 143
Humphrey, Hubert, 91, 174

Ideas, in policy-making, 211
Identity. *See* Group affiliation; Party identification
Ideological shirking, 115–17, 119, 123
Ideology: in adaptive party model, 162, 166, 168–72; bureaucratic, 158–59; definition of, 24; Downs on, 23–24, 24nn.9–11, 55, 57n.4, 112, 113, 117, 122, 123, 158, 185, 190; and economic policy, 220n.14, 220–21, 225; vs. election orientation, 162, 166, 168, 169, 189–91, 198; ideological shirking, 115–17, 119, 123; as an information source, 3, 6, 23–24, 55, 56–57, 185; and platforms, 57, 112, 113, 117–18, 122–23
Ignorance, rational. *See* Rational ignorance
Incentives: for information acquisition, 18; to keep campaign promises, 111, 118; to party competition, 12. *See also* Benefits, of voting
Income, personal, effect on turnout, 71, 82, 88, 96
Incumbency: in adaptive party model, 165, 167; effect on voting in general, 30n.23, 180, 181, 188; and group affiliation, 88; in information shortcuts, 31, 33, 34–35; and platforms, 110–11, 113, 116, 118, 119, 138–39; and thresholds, 46. *See also* Status-quo bias
Inductivism, 202
Inertia, 6, 41, 43–44, 52, 54, 190–91
Inflation rate, as an information source, 17–18
Information, for candidate/party positioning, 162, 165
Information, for voting decisions: Downsian types of, 44; Downs on, 5, 19, 19n.2, 23–25, 42, 43; evaluation of effects of, methods for, 20; free, 5, 17–18, 56; incentives for seeking, 18; and spatial models of platform effects, 142; uneven distribution of, 6. *See also* Information costs; Information-pooling models; Information shortcuts; Information sources
Information costs: of acquisition, Downs on, 17, 44–45, 56, 81, 198; of delivery, 38–41, 39n.3; and economic policy, 214; in information-pooling models, 56; and information shortcuts, 17; and thresholds, 38–54, 56; in turnout paradox solutions, 71, 82
Information delivery: campaign advertising, 48, 156; costs of, 38–41, 39n.3; targeted, 47–48
Information heuristics, 3, 7. *See also* Information-pooling models; Information shortcuts
Information-pooling models: descriptions of, 60–64; Downs's work applied to, 55–56, 57n.3, 58, 58n.6, 59; issues affecting need for, 55–59; summary of chapter on, 6–7
Information shortcuts: consequences of use of, summarized, 33–35; and costs of information, 17; demographic traits of candidates as, 19, 27–28, 188; Downs's work applied to, 5, 6, 17, 19, 19n.2, 23–25,

24nn.9–11, 29; factors in choice of, 19; and incumbency, 31, 33, 34–35; for inferring competence, 29–32; interpersonal influence as, 19n.2, 19–22; in limiting voter manipulation, 33, 35; morality of candidates as, 32–33, 188, 202–3; overview of, 6, 18–19, 33–35; party identification in, 19, 22–27. *See also* Information sources

Information sources: bias in, 64; on competence, 29–32; demographic traits of candidates as, 19, 27–28, 188; Downs on, 19, 19n.2, 23–25, 42, 43; economic conditions as, 6, 17–18, 27, 27n.19; ideology as, 3, 6, 23–24, 55, 56–57, 185; issue performance as, 57, 57n.3, 187; media as, 6, 20–22, 23, 28, 31–32; morality of candidates as, 32–33, 188, 202–3; neutral, 64; party identification as, 19, 22–27, 33–34, 187; past performance as, 31, 33, 34–35, 56, 187; social conditions as, 18; war and peace as, 21, 27n.19. *See also* Information-pooling models; Information shortcuts

Institution-rich theory, 181
Intensity of voter preference, 102–3, 162
Interest groups, 45, 46–47, 68. *See also* Group affiliation
Interpersonal influence, as an information source, 19n.2, 19–22
Intraparty disputes, 192
Issue-based voting, 26–27, 29, 33–34
Issue competition. *See* Issue dimensions
Issue convergence, 109, 144. *See also* Party convergence
Issue dimensions: in adaptive party model, 161, 164; in competence-adjusted model, 127–28; in issue-framing model, 10, 141–42, 144–45, 156, 157; and platform models in general, 10n.19, 109, 110, 111, 112–14, 115, 119, 121, 122, 123, 124, 184–85. *See also* Issue-framing model
Issue effort, 57
Issue-framing model: description of, 10, 144–56; Downs's work applied to, 158; modifications of, 156–57; nonelectoral applications of, 157–59; previous research on, 142–43
Issue performance, as an information source, 57, 57n.3, 187. *See also* Policy outcomes
Issue positions: of candidates, *see* Platforms (issue positions); of officeholders (issue effort), 57; outcome of (issue performance), 57, 57n.3, 187, *see also* Policy outcomes; of voters, party knowledge of, 11
Issue strength, 102–3, 162

Jackson, Jesse, 8, 22, 84, 91, 103
Johnson, Lyndon Baines, 21, 192
Jones, Calvin C., 186

Kalt, Joseph, 115, 123
Kardy, Lynn, 84
Keech, William R., 191, 213–14, 215n.7
Kennedy, John Fitzgerald, 21
Key, V. O., Jr., 61, 91, 202
Kiewiet, Roderick, 116
Kinder, Donald R., 90
King, Coretta Scott, 22n.5
King, Martin Luther, Sr., 22n.5
Kirchheimer, Otto, 203
Kohfeld, Carol, 90, 92
Kollman, Ken, 10–11, 161–72
Korean War, 29n.22, 30
Kramer, Gerald H., 163, 212
Krause, Elliott, 158–59
Kreps, David, 123
Krosnick, Jon, 26n.18
Kuhn, Thomas S., 190
Kuran, Timur, 84

Lasswell, Harold, 204
Lazarsfeld, Paul, 2n.5

Leaders: of groups, in voter turnout, 68, 73–74, 76; of parties, 192–93
Ledyard, John O., 95, 125
Levy, David, 84
Lijphart, Arend, 12–13, 231–38
Lindblom, C. Edward, 199, 204, 206
Lodge, Milton, 90
Logit model, 63
Logrolling, 5n.15
Lomasky, Loren F., 84
Lott, John, 117
Lotteries, candidates as, 58–59
Lubell, Samuel, 180
Luce, R. Duncan, 56n.1, 77
Lupia, Arthur, 63–64

McCloskey, Herbert, 225n.21
McCubbins, Mathew D., 116
MacDonald, S., 189
McGovern, George, 21, 31
Mackelprang, A. J., 62n.11
McKelvey, Richard D., 6–7, 59, 60, 62n.10, 109–10, 161
McPhee, William, 2n.5
Madison, James, *Federalist Papers*, 2, 204
Manifesto Project, 114
Manipulation of voters, 33, 35, 143
Margolis, Howard, 70
Margolis, Julius, 2, 12, 197–98
Market metaphor for politics, 202–3, 209
Markus, Gregory B., 186
Marxism, 203
Mathematical models: Downsian, overview of, 3; in threshold theory, 49–54. *See also* Spatial models
Mathews, Steven A., 6
Media, as an information source, 6, 20–22, 23, 28, 31–32. *See also* Negative campaigning
Median voter model, 87, 89–90
Mendell, N., 10, 133
Metzenbaum, Howard, 21n.4
Microeconomics, 1n.2
Miller, Gary J., 147n.3

Miller, John H., 10–11, 161–72
Miller, Nicholas R., 6–7, 61–62, 143
Miller, Warren E., 27n.19
Minimax regret rule, 72, 84
Minority group coalitions, 186
Mondale, Walter, 133, 174
Moral hazard models, 118–20, 121, 122
Morality of candidates, 32–33, 188, 202–3
Morganstern, Oskar, 206–7
Mueller, Dennis, 126–27
Mugwump, 202
Multicandidate competition theory, 182–83
Multiconstituency theory, 183–84
Multiple election vs. single election theory, 184
Munger, Michael C., 10, 125–40
Murphy, Dennis R., 99
Murrell, P., 126–27
Mutual knowledge, in economic policy models, 223, 224

Nash equilibrium, 82, 86–87, 222n.17
National Election Survey (NES), 10, 127, 130–38, 140
National interest, in policy motivation, 197, 209–11, 220n.14
Negative campaigning, 48, 156
NES (National Election Survey), 10, 127, 130–38, 140
Neumann, Russell, 19–20
Neutrality of voters, and information, 39
New Deal, 190, 202
Newsweek, 33
Nie, Norman, 2n.5
Nitzan, Schmuel, 10, 63, 126–27
Nixon, George, 91
Nixon, Richard Milhous, 21, 26, 59, 115, 174, 215
Noll, Roger G., 6, 37–54, 56
Nordhaus, William, 116, 212
Normative theory of democracy, 5n.15
Norrander, Barbara, 6–7, 63–64

Nuclear power, protests against, 70
Nunn, Sam, 21n.4

Office of Naval Research (ONR), 198, 201
Office seeking (ambitiousness; election-orientation), 9, 162, 166, 168–72, 189–91, 198
Olson, Mancur, Jr., 1, 68
One-party governments, 157, 234
Opinons of others, as an information source, 19n.2, 19–22
Opp, Karl-Dieter, 70, 71
Oppenheimer, Joe, 67n.1, 74
Ordeshook, Peter C.: information-pooling model by, 60, 62n.10; on platforms, 110; on primary competition, 184; on probabilistic models, 125; on rational choice models in general, 210; on turnout, 68, 69, 73, 83; on voter ignorance, 6–7
Oscillation in party control of government, 180
Outcomes. *See* Election outcomes; Policy outcomes
Owen, Guillermno, 61n.9, 81, 189

Packel, Edward, 110
Page, Benjamin I., 114, 143, 186
Page, Scott E., 10–11, 161–72
Paine, Scott C., 143
Palfrey, Thomas R., 82, 95, 95n.2
Paroush, Jacob, 63
Participation threshold, definition of, 39
Parties: as coalitions of voters, 191; disputes within, 191–92; and economic policy, 214; ideological vs. office seeking, 9, 162, 166, 168–72, 189–91; information for positioning of, 162, 165; in information supply and demand, 39, 39n.3, 40, 192; leadership of, 192–93; unity of, 191–93. *See also* Adaptive party models; *headings beginning with* Party
Party competition: in comparative study of party systems, 231–32; Downs on,

2, 2n.5, 3, 11, 231–32; Grofman's thought on, summarized, 11–12, 184; intraparty vs. interparty, 191; in threshold mathematical model, 49–54. *See also* Closeness, electoral
Party convergence: in adaptive party model, 161, 164, 168, 169, 170–71, 172; Downs on, 3, 11, 108–9, 161, 179–80, 182, 185–86, 189, 193; and election orientation, 190; history of research on, 179–80; and inertia, 190n.9; lack of, and need for modification of current models, 11, 179–80, 181–83, 185–86, 189, 191, 193. *See also* Issue convergence
Party differential: in benefits of voting, 69–70; and economic policy, 214; and multiple constituencies, 183–84; and platforms in spatial models, 114; and thresholds, 37–38, 40, 41, 43–44, 45; in turnout paradox solutions, 69–70, 71. *See also* Platforms (issue positions), divergence in
Party identification: changes in, short-term, 25–26; as an information source, 19, 22–27, 33–34, 187; and issue- vs. performance-based voting, 26–27, 33–34; lack of, in current voters, 34; in rational choice model in general, 6
Party labels: Downs on, 23–25, 56; in information-pooling models, 56; as information sources, 3, 6, 9, 19, 22–27, 30; metaphors for, 9, 9n.17, 184
Party leadership, 192–93
Party loyalty, 223, 225–26
Party platforms. *See* Platforms (issue positions)
Party systems, comparative study of, 12–13, 231–38
Party unity, 191–93
Past performance, 31, 33, 34–35, 56, 187
Patterson, Samuel C., 82, 98
Paulter, Paul, 98
Pennock, Roland, 206

Pepper, Claude, 20
Perception thresholds, 39, 41
Performance. *See* Issue performance; Policy outcomes
Persuasion, 4n.13, 38, 55, 56, 241
Pitkin, Hannah, 220n.14
Platforms (issue positions): ambiguity in, 58–59, 186–87; in behavioral models, 135; divergence in, 10, 127, 140 (*see also* Party differential); Downs on, 9, 85, 110–11, 112–14, 141, 142, 184, 186–87; drift in, and thresholds, 41; and information-pooling models, 57–59, 60; vs. issue dimensions, 10n.19; predictive value of, empirical research on, 114–18; summaries of chapters on, 9, 10, 11; in turnout paradox solutions, 74, 84; and uncertainty, 57–58, 112, 113; vagueness in, 58–59, 186–87
—spatial models on: adverse selection models, 120–21; vs. behavioral models, 135; and cost of voting, 142; Downsian paradox of, 110–14, 123–24; Downs's work applied to, 3, 9, 11, 108–9, 110–11, 112–14, 141, 142, 161; Enelow & Hinich model, 10, 109, 125–26, 127, 128, 129, 130, 132, 133, 135, 142, 143n.1; moral hazard models, 118–20, 121, 122; overview of models, 108–10, 125–27, 141–42. *See also* Adaptive party models; Additive models, of platforms; Competence-adjusted model; Economic policy models; Issue-framing model
Pleasure, as a voting benefit, 86
Plott, Charles R., 109, 161
Policy, economic. *See* Economic policy models
Policy, social function of, 197
Policy goals, election outcomes in, 12, 209–10, 212, 228–29
Policy-making process, 211, 216–23
Policy outcomes: Downs on, 46; in information-pooling models, 57; as an information source, 57, 57n.3, 187; interest groups in, 46–47; vs. policy rule, 223; rational ignorance of, 198–99; and threshold model, 6, 41, 46–48. *See also* Economic policy models
Political business cycles, 211
Political parties. *See* Adaptive party models; Parties; *headings beginning with* Party
Political persuasion, 4n.13, 38, 55, 56, 241
Polling agencies: CBS/*New York Times*, 91; Gallup, 22n.6; National Election Survey (NES), 10, 127, 130–38, 140; University of Michigan Survey Research Center, 25–26, 26n.16, 27n.19
Poole, Keith, 117, 123
Popkin, Samuel L., 5–6, 17–35
Popper, Sir Karl Raimund, 241n.7
Postulative vs. reality-based claims, 205
Pragmatic-bargaining democracy, 202–3
Precommmitment, 118, 217–18, 221n.16
Preference cycles, 5n.15
Preference intensities, 102–3, 162
President, in economic policy. *See* Economic policy models
Presidential candidates: Columbia University studies on, 22–23, 23n.8; information sources on competency of, 30
Presidential elections: turnout/closeness relationships in, 99, 101–2; vice-presidential candidates in, 11, 173–77, 184. *See also* names of specific candidates
Primary elections, 8, 103, 184, 191–92
Prisoner's Dilemma game, 163, 219, 223–26, 229–30
Probabilistic voting models, in general, 125–26, 161, 162, 185, 189. *See also* Platforms (issue positions), spatial models on

Probabilities, in turnout paradox solutions, 71
Proximity voting, 29
Public choice movement, founding of, 1
Public good, in policy motivation, 197, 209–11, 220n.14

Rabinowitz, G., 189
Racial voting, 84, 90–92, 98, 103. *See also* Black voter turnout
Raiffa, Howard, 56n.1
Random adaptive parties (RAP), 166–70
Rational choice models, in general: Downs on, 3; Grofman on errors in critiques of, 13, 239–42; inspiration for, 1; and pluralism, 210; postulative vs. reality-based claims in, 205; turnout in, 8, 75, 93–94, 103
Rational ignorance: Downs on, 3, 56, 198–99; and economic policy, 214; information-pooling for avoidance of, 59; in threshold model, 41–46, 49–54, 56
Rationality, bounded, 11, 162, 165, 166, 172
Rationality crisis, 187
Reagan, Ronald, 21, 114, 126, 133, 227
Reed, W. Robert, 117
Reference groups, as an information source, 7, 63, 189. *See also* Group affiliation
Referendum endorsements, 63
Regret (minimax regret rule), 72, 84
Relational goods, 75–76
Reputational effects, 113, 118, 120. *See also* Past performance
Retrospective voting: past performance in, 31, 33, 34–35, 56, 187; reputational effects in, 113, 118, 120
Riker, William H., 1n.1, 207; on coalition formation, 239n.2; on Duverger's hypothesis, 183; on heresthetics, 143, 159; influence on Arrow and Black, 2n.4; postulative vs. reality-based claims in, 205; on rational choice models in general, 210; on turnout, 68, 69, 73, 83
Risk aversion, 33, 56, 84, 188. *See also* Status quo bias
Risk condition, definition of, 56n.1
Rogers, W. Hayward, 205
Romero, D., 126–27
Rosenstone, Steven J., 82
Rosenthal, Howard, 82, 95, 95n.2, 117, 123
Rothschild, Michael, 81
Rourke, Francis E., 158

Schattschneider, Elmer E., 142–43, 202, 204
Schumpeter, Joseph A., 2, 2n.6, 12, 197, 202, 203
Schwartz, Thomas, 70, 71, 83
Sears, David O., 90
Selective exposure, 23
Selten, Richard, 191
Selznick, Philip, 158
Sen, Amaryta K., 220n.14, 221n.16, 223, 224n.20, 225n.22
Senate, 33n.30, 180
Settle, Russell F., 101–2
Shapiro, C. R., 21
Shapley, Lloyd S., 63
Shepsle, Kenneth A., 58–69, 143
Shirking, ideological, 115–17, 119, 123
Signaling models (adverse selection models), 120–21
Silberman, Jonathan, 98
Silver, Morris, 69
Simmons, James R., 185, 185n.3
Simon, Herbert A., 158, 204
Single constituency theory, 183–84
Single election vs. multiple election theory, 184
Single-issue voting blocs, 3
Smith, Adam, 203
Smith, Jeffrey, 67n.1
Smithburg, Donald W., 158
Smithies, A., 179n.1, 189

Social conditions, as an information source, 18
Social function vs. private motivation in policy, 197, 209–11, 220n.14
Social Science Citation Index, 206
Spatial models: probabilistic, empirical justification for, 125–26; summary of chapters on, 9–12; on vice-president in presidential elections, 11, 173–77. *See also* Platforms (issue positions), spatial models on
—suggested modifications to: convergence vs. divergence in basis for, 11, 179–80, 181–83, 185–86, 189, 191, 193; empirical evidence in need for, 180–81; incumbency effect in basis for, 180, 181; specific theoretical strategies for, 182–93; summary of basis for, 179–80
Stability, definition of, 231
Status-quo bias, 56, 189. *See also* Risk aversion
Stephens, Stephen V., 83
Stimson, James A., 90, 192
Stokes, Donald E., 27n.19
Straffin, Philip, 183
Stuart, Charles, 191
Success-orientation (ambitiousnesss; election-orientation; office-seeking), 9, 162, 166, 168–72, 189–91, 198

Taagepera, Rein, 183
Targeted information, 47–48
Technological innovations in information delivery, and thresholds, 47
Television, as an information source, 20–21, 28, 31–32
Thomas, N. Keith, 62n.11
Thompson, Victor A., 158
Threshold models: Downs on, 6, 37–41, 52; Downs's work applied to, 37–41, 39n.3, 42, 43, 44–45, 46, 47, 52; and information costs, 38–54, 56; and information technology, 47–48; mathematical model, 49–54; neglect of Downs's contributions in, 4n.13; participation threshold in, definition of, 39; party differential in, 37–38, 40, 41, 43–44, 45; perception thresholds in, 39, 41; and persuasion, 38; and policy outcomes, 6, 41, 46–48; and rational ignorance, 41–46, 49–54, 56
Tideman, Nicholas T., 83
Tilly, Charles, 71
Tollison, Robert D., 98
Trilling, Richard, 27n.19
Truman, David, 204
Tufte, Edward, 116
Tullock, Gordon, 1, 5n.15, 70, 95, 207, 241n.9
Turnout: citizen duty in, 67, 69, 71, 74–75, 83; Downs on, 2n.5, 67, 68, 83, 94–95; and free-rider problem, 68, 81–82, 99; group leaders in, 68, 73–74, 76; in high-interest elections, 102–3, 162; income as predictor of, 71, 82, 88, 96; and knowledge of election outcome, 90; in rational choice models, in general, 8, 75, 93–94, 103; summary of chapters on, 7–8. *See also* Black voter turnout; Turnout paradoxes
Turnout paradoxes: and benefits of voting, 7, 69–70, 73–78, 83, 85–86, 94–95; in closeness/turnout relationship, 8, 76, 93, 94–103; competition in solutions to, 94–102; and costs of voting, 7, 67, 70–71, 77, 82, 83–84, 95, 96–97; criticism related to, overview of, 93; descriptions of, 67–68, 93; Downs's work applied to solutions to, 7–8, 67, 68, 69, 81, 82, 83, 85, 94–95, 97
—minimal turnout prediction: and adaptive party model, 161; and expected utility model, 67, 72, 77–78; expressive voting in solutions to, 7–8, 84–92; Glazer's solution to, 70, 84–92; group affiliations in solutions to, 7–8, 8n.16, 70, 71, 73–76, 84–92, 189; standard solutions to, described, 68–

72; Uhlaner's solution to, 70, 71, 72–78
Twelfth Amendment, 11
Two-candidate competition theory, 182–83
Tyler, Ralph, 201

Uhlaner, Carole Jean, 7, 67–79, 84, 193n.13
Uncertainty: Downs on, 5, 37, 39n.3, 40, 56, 112, 113, 236; and information, 5, 24, 35, 39n.3, 40, 57; and party systems, 236; and platforms, 57–58, 112, 113; in status-quo bias, 55–56; and thresholds, 37, 39n.3
Uncertainty condition, definition of, 56n.1
Unemployment rate, as an information source, 17–18
United States Congress, 20n.3, 33n.30, 115, 117, 180, 183, 219–22. *See also* Divided government
United States House of Representatives, 33n.30
United States Senate, 33n.30, 180
Unity, of parties, 191–93
University of Michigan Survey Research Center survey, 25–26, 26n.16, 27n.19
Utility differential. *See* Party differential

Verba, Sidney, 2n.5
Vice-presidents, and presidential elections, 11, 173–77, 184
Vietnam War, 21, 59
Von Neumann, John, 206
Voter coalitions, parties as, 191

Voter heterogeneity, and information distribution, 6, 34
Voter issue positions, party knowledge of, 11
Voter participation. *See* Threshold models; Turnout
Voter preference intensities, 102–3, 162
Voter registration, and turnout, 8, 94, 96–97, 102n.5
Voters, Downs's categories of, 39
Voter turnout. *See* Turnout
Voting: competence-based, 29–32; issue- vs. performance-based, 26–27, 29, 33–34. *See also* Costs, of voting
Voting blocs, single-issue, 3
Voting Rights Act of 1965, 192

Wallace, George, 84–85, 91–92, 184
Wallis, Allan, 201
War and peace, as an information source, 21, 27n.19
Washington, Harold, 85, 102
Watergate affair, 29n.22
Wattenberg, Martin, 2n.5, 5n.14, 11, 173–77, 184
Weatherford, M. Stephen, 12, 209–30
Withers, Julie, 6–7, 55–64, 96
Wittman, Donald A., 191
Wolfinger, Raymond E., 82, 102n.5
Wolfram, Gary L., 101–2
Wright, Gerald C., 91, 116–17
Wuffle, A, 3n.9, 5n.14, 94, 98, 191n.10

Young, Andrew, 22n.5
Young, Oran, 67n.1, 74

Zupan, Mark, 115, 123